INDIAN CITIZENSHIP AND IMMIGRATION LAW

Amish Tandon

NIYOGI BOOKS

Published by
NIYOGI BOOKS
Block D, Building No. 77,
Okhla Industrial Area, Phase-I,
New Delhi-110 020, INDIA
Tel: 91-11-26816301, 26818960
Email: niyogibooks@gmail.com
Website: www.niyogibooksindia.com

Design: Shaju K Anthony

ISBN: 978-93-91125-68-4
Publication: 2022

Printed at: Niyogi Offset Pvt. Ltd., New Delhi, India

Jayant Nath
Judge

HIGH COURT OF DELHI, SHER SHAH ROAD
NEW DELHI 110 503 TEL. : +91-11-23383175
RESIDENCE : 62, LODHI ESTATE
NEW DELHI-110003 TEL. : +91-11-21421130

Dated 29.10.2021

FOREWORD

India is home to diverse cultures, beliefs and communities. The Indian subcontinent has always witnessed migration (both legal and illegal migration). The concept of citizenship is somewhat intertwined with concept of migration in as much, in incoming migrant often seeks to make the host country his permanent home.

In his latest authorship, Mr.Amish Tandon takes us through the development of Indian law in the field of citizenship and immigration, right from the inception till date. While the first half of the book covers almost every .area, aspect and feature of the Indian citizenship and immigration law regime including the Citizenship law, Foreigners Law, Passports Law and Emigration Law; the second half deals with all contemporary issues on the subject, including the Citizenship Amendment Act of 2019, the National Register of Citizens, migration in Assam *et al.*

The author writes with simplicity and attempts to provide a holistic coverage of every nuance of the Indian Citizenship and Immigration law. This book contains a comprehensive database of case law which will be useful for every legal practitioner working in this area of law. This book should serve as a useful research tool for lawyers and academics practicing in this niche area of law. Separately, for a lay reader, this book provides a detailed insight into all recent and contemporary issues pertaining to citizenship law.

This is book is perhaps the first of its kind and will serve as a comprehensive guide for every person who wishes to gain a greater understanding of this evergreen area of law. I congratulate Mr.Tandon for this excellent work and wish him all successes going forward.

(Jayant Nath)

HIGH COURT OF DELHI
सत्यमेव जयते

VIBHU BAKHRU
JUDGE
HIGH COURT OF DELHI

18, TUGHLAK CRESCENT, NEW DELHI-110011
OFF. : 011-23383319 Fax : 23383375, 23381240 E-mail : vibhulegal@gmail.com
RES. : 011-21410822

MESSAGE

The law relating to citizenship has been a subject matter of much debate in recent times. Some of the amendments introduced by the Citizenship (Amendment) Act, 2019 have sparked protests as well.

In the aforesaid context, the present book is of significance as it seeks to comprehensively look at the current laws relating to citizenship and immigration. In addition, it also covers the relevant law relating to issuance, impounding and cancellation of passports.

A large number of Indian citizens and persons from Indian origin, are now resident overseas. A majority of them have travelled overseas for gainful employment. The need to afford minimal level of protection to such immigrants, is a matter of some importance. There are a number of persons of Indian origin, who now wish to return to India and reclaim their citizenship. Some Indian citizens have married citizens of other countries, who seek citizenship of this country. Paradoxically, whilst there are a large number of Indian citizens who aspire citizenship of developed countries, this country also has a large influx of immigrants who wish to settle here. The present book is also relevant in this regard as it examines the procedure for acquiring Indian citizenship.

VIBHU BAKHRU
JUDGE
HIGH COURT OF DELHI
18, TUGHLAK CRESCENT, NEW DELHI-110011
OFF. : 011-23383319 Fax : 23383375, 23381240 E-mail : vibhulegal@gmail.com
RES. : 011-21410822

Mr. Amish Tandon has made a commendable effort to comprehensively offer the commentary on the laws relating to or connected to citizenship. In his endeavor to provide a compressive text, he has also covered other enactments such as the Foreigners Act, 1946; the Passports Act, 1967 and; the Emigration Act, 1983.

The simplicity of the language and structure of the book makes it easy to use. Considering that there are limited number of texts that offer such comprehensive commentary on these laws, I expect that this book would serve as a valuable reference to the general public as well as legal practitioners.

I wish Amish Tandon all the success with this book !

(Vibhu Bakhru)

Contents

Chapter 8
The Assam History

Chapter 10
The CAA Debate

Chapter 11
The Amendments to the Citizenship Act: Position in Assam

Chapter 12
CAA & NRC: The Road Ahead

Preface

Like any other modern state, India has two kinds of people: citizens and aliens/foreigners (non-citizens). An Indian citizen is one who is a legally recognised subject or national of India and owes his allegiance to India. He enjoys civil, economic and political rights in India. Every person who is not an Indian citizen is a foreigner. While foreigners may enjoy some civil rights (such as right to life, equality etc.) and some economic rights (such as right to work, wages etc.), they do not enjoy any political rights (such as right to vote, contest elections etc.).

A person need not remain a citizen of 1 (one) country all his life. Subject to applicable law, he may migrate to, settle down in, and obtain citizenship of another country. Migration, in simple terms, refers to a situation where a citizen of one country moves to another country, whether temporarily or permanently; or whether legally or illegally. Migration is broadly of various types: (i) Economic migration: movement for business or employment; (ii) Social migration: movement for better quality of life or to be with persons of similar community; and (iii) Political migration: to escape persecution and war.

Over the last several decades, India has experienced migration from various neighbouring countries including Bangladesh, Pakistan, Nepal, Sri Lanka, Myanmar and Afghanistan. These migrants move for a variety of reasons - including economic, social and political. The intensity of migration in India has been high from neighbouring countries especially on account of the fragmentation of the Indian subcontinent into 3 (three) parts (i.e. India, Pakistan and Bangladesh) and India being bound on 2 (two) sides with these countries. A significant amount of migration into India is also through illegal modes i.e. entering illegally, or initially entering on valid visa but staying back despite expiry of visa.

It is crucial that every country with a history of migration has in place a robust statutory and regulatory mechanism to deal with such issues - of foreigners, immigration, passport etc.

India has an entire gamut of statutes and executive policies for this purpose. These legislations have been amended from time to time to keep pace with the changing landscape of immigration. In this book, an attempt has been made to extensively deal with all facets of the Indian citizenship and immigration laws.

The book is broadly classified into the following 4 (four) parts:

1. The Indian citizenship and immigration law framework. This part is further divided into the following: (i) The constitutional provisions relating to citizenship; (ii) The various features of the Citizenship Law regime, which regulates all aspects of (Indian) citizenship, including its grant, withdrawal and termination; (iii) The Foreigner Law regime, which regulates the entry, movement and exit of foreigners ; (iv) The Passport Law regime which regulates all elements relating to passports and international travel/ movement; (v) The Emigration Law regime which seeks to protect and regulate Indian workers who seek employment in a foreign country. .

2. The historical background and importance of Assam in India's immigration discourse, the Assam Accord of 1985, Assam's National Register of Citizens (NRC) exercise; and the progress made thereon till date.
3. The Citizenship Amendment Act of 2019 (CAA), the National Register of Citizens (NRC) generally; and the entire range of controversies surrounding the CAA and NRC.
4. The future and road-ahead for the CAA and the NRC, including the potential challenges emanating therefrom.

An earnest effort has been made to discuss all existing elements of the (Indian) citizenship and immigration law regime. All relevant judgements are discussed. The objective is to give to the readers a ready reference and instructional material on the subject. This book should aid students, academics as well as practitioners in the field of law.

CHAPTER 1

Citizenship and the Indian Constitution

INTRODUCTION

Citizenship, in common parlance, may be described as the legal right to belong to a particular country. Citizenship bestows upon individuals, membership in a national political community. Citizenship in a democracy is an extremely important feature of modern life.

The notion of citizenship, so far as the Republic of India is concerned, gained significance only with Independence and the coming into force of the Constitution. During the British rule, Indians virtually had no right of citizenship.

Previously, India did not have any specific law of citizenship to deal with aspects such as acquisition and termination of citizenship and other ancillary/related matters. This issue came to the fore at the time of adoption and enactment of the Indian Constitution. At the time of drafting of the Constitution, while certain necessary 'of the moment' or 'interim' provisions were engrafted in the Constitution itself, all other aspects, including the legal and regulatory framework of this area was left open to be subsequently evolved by the legislature (which ultimately enacted the Citizenship Act for dealing with and regulating citizenship rights). This chapter summarises the provisions of the Indian Constitution which govern the issue of citizenship.

CITIZENSHIP: CONSTITUTION OF INDIA

In 1947, India was divided primarily on the basis of religion. After Partition, India became a religion neutral (and later secular) state but the other nations namely Pakistan (subsequently Bangladesh as well), chose to become theocratic or religion centric states.

The Constitution of India was approved on 26.11.1949 and came into force on 26.01.1950. On the aspect of citizenship, the Constitution restricted itself primarily to determination of 'Indian citizenship' at the time of its enforcement (i.e. in the year 1950). These provisions are discussed below.

Citizenship Law: Commencement of the Constitution

Articles 5 to 8 of the Constitution delineated the classes of persons who were to be recognised as citizens of India at the time of commencement of the Constitution. These provisions dealt with the citizenship of (a) persons domiciled in India; (b) persons who migrated from Pakistan; (c) persons who migrated to Pakistan but later returned; and (d) persons of Indian origin residing outside India. Hence, a classification was made on the following basis: (i) domicile; (ii) migration; and (iii) registration.

Domicile

The word 'domicile' is not defined in the Constitution or the Citizenship Act, 1955. In ordinary parlance, the expression 'domicile' can be described as the intention to reside in a particular territory which is not transient or for a limited period or purpose only.[1] Domicile denotes connection with the territorial system of law.[2]

1 Kirandeep Kaur v. Regional Passport Office, AIR 2006 Del 2.

2 D.P.Joshi v. State of Madhya Bharat, (1955) 1 SCR 1215; Abdus Samad v. State of West Bengal, 1973 CriLJ 1.

Domicile is different from residence. Domicile refers to a 'permanent home'.[3] The jural concept of 'permanent home' in any country necessarily encompasses these 2 (two) elements which must coexist: permanent residence and an intention to reside permanently or for an indefinite period in that country.[4] In other words, for establishing domicile, 2 (two) conditions are necessarily to be satisfied: (i) fact of residence; (ii) intention to make the country his permanent home. Domicile cannot be inferred from the mere fact of long residence. For establishing domicile, it is imperative that long residence is coupled with an absolute and positive present intention to make the country a permanent home.[5]

The 4 (four) general principles governing domicile are as follows: (i) no person can be without a domicile; (ii) no person can have simultaneously 2 (two) or more domiciles; (iii) domicile denotes the connection of a person with a territory system of law; (iv) the presumption is in favour of continuance of an existing domicile.[6]

Every independent person must have a domicile, either of origin or of choice.[7] Essentially, there are 3 (three) types of domicile: (i) domicile of origin; (ii) domicile of choice; (iii) domicile of dependence.[8]

The original domicile is acquired by birth, but the domicile so acquired may subsequently be changed by some voluntary act, involving a change of residence and an intention to reside

---

3 Mere residence or following a particular profession in India by a person is not conclusive evidence for the purposes of determining his domicile. Mst. Rihena Maryam v. The State, 1969 RLW 322.

4 *See* Shabbir Hussain, *infra*

5 State v. Ghoraishi (Qureshi) Sayed, AIR 1964 Bom 235.

6 Moosa v. Union of India, 2000 (1) KLJ 417; Yogesh Bhardwaj v. State of U.P., (1990) 3 SCC 355; Dr. Pradeep Jain v. Union of India, (1984) II LLJ 481 SC.

7 Moosa v. Union of India, 2000 (1) KLJ 417.

8 Sham Roj v. Additional Superintendent of Police, AIR 1978 Cal 252.

in another country permanently or for an indefinite period. The domicile of origin is retained until the domicile of choice is acquired.[9] A domicile of choice is retained until it is abandoned, whereupon either (i) a new domicile of choice is acquired; or (ii) the domicile of origin is resumed.[10]

The burden of proving a change in domicile is on those who allege that a change has occurred.[11] A minor's domicile is that of the father.[12] Typically, upon marriage, a woman acquires the domicile of her husband, if she had not the same domicile before.[13]

Domicile & Migration

There exists a clear and fine line of distinction between the concepts of 'change of domicile' and 'migration'. In the case of migration, a person leaves the country of his permanent home, but, at the back of his mind, there is always an intention to return to the country of his domicile; whereas, in the case of a change of domicile, the person not only leaves the country of his home but he does so with the intention of never returning to the country of his domicile. In the latter case, the intention is to change his

---

9 The concept of 'domicile of origin' serves 2 (two) purposes: (i) to ensure that every person at birth has a domicile; (ii) to ensure that there is no legal gap in the adherence of domicile. Sham Roj v. Additional Superintendent of Police, AIR 1978 Cal 252.

10 Shabbir Hussain, *infra*

11 Abdus Samad v. State of West Bengal, Criminal Appeal No. 216/1969 (12.09.1972, Supreme Court of India). Generally, strong and positive evidence would be required to substantiate a change of domicile, particularly when the change is from domicile of origin to domicile of choice. State v. Ghoraishi (Qureshi) Sayed, AIR 1964 Bombay 235.

12 Ismail v. State of Rajasthan, 1959 RLW 299. A child acquires at birth, a domicile of religion, by operation of law, namely, if legitimate and born in his father's lifetime, the domicile of his father; if legitimate or born after his father's death, the domicile of his mother. *See generally* Private International Law by G.C. Cheshire (IV Edn) reproduced in Shamim Bano v. Union of India, 1979 RLW 444.

13 *See* Section 15 of the Indian Succession Act, 1925. *See also* Moosa v. Union of India, 2000 (1) KLJ 417.

civil status, but not so in the former case. In the first case, he does not severe his ties with the country of his domicile but intends to retain it. He leaves the country of his permanent home for some such purpose as following a profession, or for earning a fortune, or for pursuing an employment, and it does not make any difference even though he may have to stay away for a long or indefinite period from his home to achieve this object.[14]

Citizenship based on Domicile

As per Article 5 of the Constitution, every person having domicile in India at the time of commencement of the Constitution, and fulfilling any of the following conditions, was considered a citizen of India: (i) he was born in India; (ii) either parent was born in India; (iii) he was ordinarily resident in India for not less than 5 (five) years immediately preceding the commencement of the Constitution.[15] The Indian Constitution recognises only one domicile namely, domicile in India.[16]

Migration

The partition resulted in mass exodus of people from Pakistan into India. These migrants were not entitled to Indian citizenship under Article 5. Therefore, special provisions were enacted in the Constitution to accommodate them. Articles 6 and 7 of the Constitution cover this aspect. Articles 6 & 7 of the Constitution lay down certain special criteria envisaging 'deemed citizenship' of India for this class of persons.

---

14 Habatullah Haji Fazale Hussain v. The State, AIR 1964 Guj 128.

15 Article 5 of the Constitution confers the right of citizenship on every person who, at the commencement of the Constitution, had his domicile in the territory of India and who or whose parents were born in the territory of India or who had been ordinarily residing in the territory of India for not less than 5 (five) years immediately preceding the commencement of the Constitution. *See* Noor Mohammad v. The State, Civil Misc. Case No. 17/1956 (07.05.1956, Madhya Pradesh High Court).

16 Dr. Pradeep Jain & Ors. v. Union of India, (1984) 3 SCC 654.

For the purposes of the Constitution (specifically Article 6 and 7), the expression 'migration' refers to voluntary movement from one place to another (may or may not be for a specific purpose), for a reasonably long period of time.[17] Migration is a question of fact and intention; and the immediate requirement of intention in migration, is that the person intended to change his abode from one place to another.[18]

In the context of the Constitution, the expression 'migrate' has the notion of transference of allegiance from the country of departure to the country of adoption. The movement from one country to another must be voluntary. Further, the purpose of movement is also relevant.[19]

Migration from Pakistan

Under Article 6 of the Constitution, an immigrant from Pakistan became a citizen of India if he, or either of his parents, or any of his grandparents, were born in pre-independent India, and in addition, fulfilled either of the following 2 (two) conditions: (i) in case he migrated to India before 19.07.1948 and had been a resident of India since; or (ii) in case he migrated to India on or after 19.07.1948 and had been registered as a citizen of India.[20]

---

17 Kulathil Mammu v. The State of Kerala, AIR 1966 SC 1614. Previously, the Supreme Court, in Shanno Devi v. Mangal Sain, AIR 1961 SC 58, had observed that the expression 'migration', in the context of Articles 6 and 7 of the Constitution, ought to be described in its narrower connotation (explained above). Shanno Devi was overruled by Kulathil Mammu, *supra*

18 *Per* M. Hidayatullah, J in Kulathil Mammu, *supra*. The question of intention has to be determined with reference to the point of time when the person removed to the territory of the other Dominion. Golam Rasul v. Superintendent of Police, AIR 1965 Cal 302.

19 State (Delhi Administration) v. Master Tameej, ILR (1985) II Delhi; Golam Rasul v. Superintendent of Police, AIR 1965 Cal 302

20 A pre-requisite for registration was residence of the applicant in India for at least 6 (six) months preceding the application for registration. It is further pertinent to note that Article 6 of the Constitution does not apply to a migration which took place post commencement of the Constitution.

Article 6 deals with the movement of population from Pakistan to India while Article 7 deals with movement from India to Pakistan. Both these articles begin with a non-obstante clause, which indicates that these provisions were meant to deal with an exigent situation (resulting from movement of persons), on account of the Partition.[21]

While Article 6 indicates as to who are deemed to be citizens of India at the commencement of the Constitution, Article 7 indicates as to who are deemed 'not to be citizens of India' in spite of their fulfilling qualifications specified in Articles 5 and 6.

In short, persons who migrate to Pakistan from India with an intention to settle in Pakistan would not be considered Indian citizens. This includes persons who have migrated from the territory of India to the territory now included in Pakistan after 01.03.1947. There are some exceptions to this rule which are described in Article 7 of the Constitution.

Migration to Pakistan

As discussed above, the word 'migration' under Articles 6 and 7 of the Constitution refers to movement between the two countries which is voluntary, is not for a specific purpose and not for a short or limited period.[22] It is reiterated that both Articles 6 and 7 refer to 'migration' made before the date of the Constitution coming into force.

Article 7 of the Constitution explains when a person (who otherwise qualifies to be an Indian citizen as per Articles 5 and 6 above) would not be considered a citizen of India. As per Article

21 Kulathil Mammu v. The State of Kerala, AIR 1966 SC 1614. Both Articles 6 and 7 of the Constitution are silent on the question of domicile and the presence of a non-obstante clause in the beginning of both these Articles clearly shows that the concept of domicile was required to be overlooked while determining 'deemed citizenship'envisaged therein.

22 Mahammad Nazaharul Haque v. B. Bagchi, A.F.O.O No. 479/2961 (29.11.1972, Calcutta High Court).

7, a citizen of India, by domicile or by migration, would cease to be a citizen if he migrated to Pakistan after 01.03.1947.[23] This legal position is, however, reversible, subject to the following condition: If, post migration to Pakistan, he returned to India by the date of commencement of the Constitution under a permit of resettlement, or permanent return, he could register himself in the same manner as a person migrating from Pakistan after 19.07.1948.[24] This provision would be applicable where the movement was voluntary and only for a short time.[25]

Movement to Pakistan for 'employment purposes' would qualify to be a 'migration' within the meaning of Article 7.[26] For the purposes of Article 7, circumstances such as 'parents continue to remain in India' would be of little or no relevance. In other words, for the purpose of 'migration' under Article 7 it is not essential that one must also remove one's parent(s) from India.[27]

---

23 Where the father migrates to Pakistan, his minor son loses Indian citizenship along with his father. Mohd. Umar v. State, AIR 1961 Orissa 150.

24 Article 7 overrides Article 5. The effect of Article 7 is that even if a person is a citizen of India by virtue of Article 5, he cannot be deemed to be a citizen of India if he has migrated to Pakistan after 01.03.1947 unless his case falls under the *proviso* to Article 7. *See* State of Bihar v. Amar Singh, AIR 1955 SC 282. Article 7 begins with a non-obstante clause and is in the nature of a *proviso* to Articles 5 and 6. Firoz Meharuddin v. Sub-Divisional Officer, *infra*

25 Article 7 applies only to persons who migrated to Pakistan between 01.03.1947 and 26.01.1950. An important clue to the interpretation of the expression 'migrated from the territory of India to the territory now included in Pakistan' occurring in Article 7 of the Constitution, is provided by the *proviso* to that Article. If a person has so migrated to Pakistan and wants to return to India, he can do so only under a permit for resettlement or a permanent return. The expression 'resettlement or permanent return' clearly implies that the person concerned was once settled in India and had gone over to Pakistan and settled there, and he wants to return to India for resettlement or permanent stay. *See generally* Shabbir Hussain v. The State of Uttar Pradesh, AIR 1952 All 257.

26 Aslam Khan v. Fazal Haque Khan, AIR 1959 All 79. In this case, the court held that where a government servant employed under the Government of India, exercises his option for transferring a service to Pakistan and crosses over to Pakistan for that purpose, his removal cannot be construed as merely temporary in nature.

27 Golam Rasul, *supra*

According to international law, a child acquires the nationality of the father. Where a minor migrated to Pakistan along with his father, since the father did not have Indian nationality under Article 7 of the Constitution, the minor too must be taken to have acquired the nationality of the father.[28] The provisions of the Citizenship Act prevail over the preferential right of custody of the minor children (available with the mother) under Mohamadan Law. Despite the fact that the mother (an Indian citizen) had a right of preferential custody over the minor children (born in Macca) under the Mohammedan Law, the children were held to acquire the nationality of their father (a Pakistani citizen).[29]

The Cut-off Date in Articles 6 & 7 of the Constitution

There exists a cut-off date in Articles 6 and 7 of the Constitution i.e. 19.07.1948. The genesis of this cut-off date merits some discussion.

On 15.08.1947, India was partitioned into 2 (two) dominions pursuant to the Indian Independence Act, 1947. This resulted in mass migration of the population from one dominion to the other, along with unfortunate incidents such as riots, arson etc. Uncontrolled and unregulated entry/exit of persons was considered antithetical to the economy and security of the country. It is in these attending circumstances that a law was enacted to control and regulate influx of persons from Pakistan into India.

Between 15.08.1947 and 19.07.1948, there was no restriction on the movement of people between the two nations. Finally, the Influx from The West Pakistan (Control) Ordinance, 1948 was promulgated and brought into force on 19.07.1948, for the purpose of regulating the movement of persons between India and Pakistan. This ordinance prospectively prohibited entry of

28 State v. Abdul Hamid, AIR 1957 Punj 86.

29 Shamin Bano v. Union of India, 1979 RLW 444.

any person from West Pakistan into India without a valid permit. Through this ordinance, the central government was empowered to remove persons who entered India without a valid permit. This ordinance was subsequently replaced by the Influx from Pakistan (Control) Ordinance, 1948 (issued on 10.11.1948). This subsequent ordinance applied to persons entering into India from both West Pakistan and East Pakistan.[30]

The above-mentioned second ordinance was finally succeeded by the passing of the Influx From Pakistan (Control) Act, 1949 (on similar lines as the second ordinance). The primary objective of this legislation was to regulate the admission and movement of persons from Pakistan into India through a system of permits.[31] Eventually, the Constitution of India formalised this date (i.e. 19.07.1948) as the cut-off date for determining citizenship of persons who had travelled to and fro between India and Pakistan, for the purposes of Articles 6 and 7 of the Constitution.

Citizenship by Registration

Article 8 of the Constitution made provision for grant of citizenship to persons of Indian origin residing overseas who wished to acquire Indian citizenship. There was no cut-off date in Article 8 of the Constitution. A person who, or either of whose parents, or any of whose grandparents, was born in pre-Independence India and who was ordinarily residing in any country outside India and Pakistan, could register himself as a

---

30 *See generally* Ebrahim Vazir Mavat v. The State of Bombay, AIR 1954 SC 229.

31 Finally, the Indian government arrived at a mutual understanding with the Pakistan government that this permit system should be replaced by a system of passports. Accordingly, the Influx from Pakistan (Control) Repealing Ordinance, 1952 was promulgated to repeal the influx from Pakistan (Control) Act, 1949 (made effective from 15.10.1952) pursuant to which traffic between the two countries came to be regulated by a passport system. With effect from 26.12.1952, the Influx from Pakistan (Control) Repealing Ordinance, 1952 became the Influx from Pakistan (Control) Repealing Act, 1952.

citizen of India with the diplomatic or consular representative of India in the country of residence, on an application made by him, in the prescribed form and manner.

Loss of Indian Citizenship

Article 9 of the Constitution provided for certain situations by which Indian citizenship would be considered to be lost (prior to coming into force of the Constitution). As per Article 9, upon coming into force of the Constitution (i.e. on 26.01.1950), a person would not be considered an Indian citizen in case he had voluntarily acquired the citizenship of any foreign state at any prior point in time. This Article sets out the policy basis of India's disinclination to accept the concept of dual or plural citizenship. Simply put, no Indian citizen can hold citizenship of any other country. Acquisition of a foreign citizenship by an Indian citizen results in termination of his Indian citizenship.[32]

Article 9 was framed in relation to acquisition of any foreign citizenship prior to the commencement of the Constitution.[33] In other words, it did not apply to a case of acquisition of foreign citizenship after the Constitution come into force, but only applied to cases where foreign citizenship was acquired before the commencement of the Constitution.[34] So far as any subsequent acquisition of foreign citizenship was concerned, the same was left to the wisdom of the Parliament. Consequently, the Parliament framed the Citizenship Act, 1955, which followed a similar premise and principle.[35]

---

32 Article 9 does not use the word 'migration' and deals only with voluntary acquisition of foreign citizenship before the Constitution came into force. Mahammad Nazaharul Haque v. B. Bagchi, A.F.O.O No. 479/2961 (29.11.1972, Calcutta High Court).

33 State of Madhya Pradesh v. Peer Mohd., AIR 1963 SC 645.

34 Peer Mohd, *supra*

35 *See* State of Uttar Pradesh v. Shah Mohammed, 1969 (1) SCC 771; State of Madhya Pradesh v. Peer Mohd., AIR 1963 SC 645. *See also* S. 10 of the Citizenship Act.

Continuation of Citizenship

Article 10 of the Constitution provided for continuation of Indian citizenship subject to the laws made by the Indian Parliament. Article 10 explains that citizenship once acquired in terms of the Constitution was not to be divested, except in accordance with any law that Parliament may make on that behalf.[36]

Article 10 laid down the framework for Article 11 (discussed below) which left the aspects of acquisition and termination of citizenship (and other related matters) in the hands of the Indian Parliament.

Citizenship Law: Gap in the Constitution

The Constitution of India did not lay down any comprehensive law on the issue of citizenship but left it to the wisdom of the Parliament to formulate an appropriate legislation on the subject. The constitutional provisions supplied the parameters for determining citizenship at the time of enforcement of the Constitution. This becomes evident from a bare reading of Article 11 of the Constitution, which is reproduced below:[37]

> 11. Nothing in the foregoing provisions of this Part shall derogate from the power of Parliament to make any provision with respect to the acquisition and termination of citizenship and all other matters relating to citizenship.

Clearly, the Constitution expressly left the entire regulatory framework of citizenship, including acquisition and termination

36 Firoz Meharuddin v. Sub-Divisional Officer, AIR 1961 MP 110.

37 Article 10 of the Constitution states that the continuation of citizenship of a person so acquired (under Articles 5 to 8 of the Constitution) is subject to any law made by the Parliament, thereby suggesting that it should be the Parliament which should have the final word on these matters.

of citizenship to the Parliament.[38] This aspect was well explained by Dr B.R. Ambedkar, the Chairman of the Drafting Committee of the Constitution, in the following words:[39]

> this Article refers to, citizenship not in any general sense but to citizenship on the date of commencement of this Constitution. It is not the object of this particular Article to lay down a permanent law of citizenship for the country. The business of laying down permanent law of citizenship has been left to the Parliament, and as members will see from the wording of Article 6 (present day Article 11) as I have moved, the entire matter regarding citizenship has been left to Parliament to determine by any law it may deem fit...... but the Parliament may make altogether a new law embodying new principles. That is the first proposition that has to be borne in mind...' and also that '...they must not understand that the provisions that we are making for citizenship on the date of commencement of this constitution are going to be permanent or unalterable. All that we are doing is to decide ad hoc for the time being...... It is not possible to cover every kind of case for a limited purpose, namely, the purpose of conferring citizenship on the date of commencement of the constitution. If there is any category of people India who are left out by the provisions contained in this amendment, we have given power to Parliament subsequently to make provision for them.

38 It can be inferred from the above that the scope of Article 5 of the Constitution was meant to be very limited and was required to work as an interim measure until the Parliament enacted a legislation which comprehensively and holistically dealt with the subject of citizenship.

39 It may also be noted that the Parliament, as per Entry 17 of List I, has the exclusive power to legislate with respect to matters pertaining to citizenship.

THE CITIZENSHIP ACT

In exercise of its power under Article 11 & Entry 17 of List I of the Constitution, the Indian Parliament enacted the Citizenship Act, 1955 which came in force on 30.12.1955 (hereinafter '**Citizenship Act**'). The Citizenship Act essentially provides for the acquisition and termination of the Indian citizenship.[40] The broad structure of the Citizenship Act is as follows: (i) Acquisition of Indian citizenship by birth, descent, registration, naturalisation and incorporation of territory[41]; (ii) Renunciation of Indian citizenship[42]; (iii) Termination of Indian citizenship by an order of the central government[43]; (iv) Deprivation of Indian citizenship.[44]

It is important to highlight at the outset that the provisions of the Citizenship Act apply to the period after the commencement of the Constitution. The Citizenship Act does not impinge upon the rights of those persons who were citizens or deemed to be citizens at the time of the commencement of the Citizenship Act, except in the context of the termination of such citizenship. Hence, the provisions in the Constitution and the Citizenship Act supplement each other and have to be read together. The next chapter comprehensively deals with the provisions of the Citizenship Act.

---

40 The Indian Constitution and the Citizenship Act exhaustively deal with the issue of citizenship, confined only to a natural person. *See generally* State Trading Corporation of India Ltd. v. Commercial Tax Officer, AIR 1963 SC 1811.

41 Ss. 3 to 7 of the Citizenship Act.

42 S. 8 of the Citizenship Act.

43 S. 9 of the Citizenship Act.

44 S. 10 of the Citizenship Act.

CHAPTER 2

The Citizenship Act

INTRODUCTION

As discussed in the previous chapter, the Constitution of India laid down the initial criteria for determination of citizenship (as on the date of its commencement) and did not make any further provisions on the subject.[1] All else was left to the wisdom of the Indian Parliament. Article 11 of the Constitution granted power to the Indian Parliament to fill this gap and make laws with respect to aspects of acquisition and termination of citizenship as also all related matters.[2] This was done by means of the Citizenship Act, 1955.[3] The Citizenship Act came into force on 30.12.1955. Post its enactment, this legislation has been amended on numerous occasions in keeping with changing times and demography.

Under Indian law, the Citizenship Act is the principal legislation on this subject. Generally speaking, the Citizenship Act provides for aspects such as acquisition of citizenship by birth, descent, registration, naturalisation and incorporation

1 The State of Assam v. Moslem Mondal, Review Petition No. 22/2010 (03.01.2013, Guwahati High Court). *See also* Articles 5 to 10 of the Constitution.

2 This power of the Parliament is not fettered by any provision of the Constitution. *See* R. Venkateshwara Rao v. Union of India, W.P. No. 12998/1998 (23.04.1999, Andhra Pradesh High Court).

3 Pursuant to Article 11 (read with Item 17, List I, Schedule VII) of the Constitution.

of territory. It also contains provisions for the termination and deprivation of citizenship.[4]

This chapter summarises the (Indian) law of 'citizenship'. The reader will find in this chapter all key aspects of the Citizenship Act and Citizenship Rules (CAA excepting, which is discussed in a separate chapter).

INDIAN CITIZENSHIP FOR NATURAL PERSONS

At the outset, it is important to point out that the Citizenship Act does not include within its scope artificial entities or juristic persons. In other words, only natural persons can be recognised as citizens of India. Companies or corporations may qualify to be nationals of countries for the purpose of international laws but they will not be considered as citizens of India for the purposes of Indian law.[5]

SCOPE OF THE CITIZENSHIP ACT

Generally speaking, the Citizenship Act provides for the mode and manner of acquisition (and loss) of Indian citizenship. Under Indian law, citizenship can be acquired by birth, descent, registration, incorporation of territory and naturalisation; whereas loss of Indian citizenship can be by renunciation, termination or deprivation.

Broadly speaking, under the Citizenship Act, there are 2 (two) categories of citizenship in India: (i) citizenship as a matter of right or entitlement, i.e. citizenship acquired by a person by birth or by descent; and (ii) conferred citizenship i.e. citizenship

---

4 *See* Statement of Objects and Reasons to the Citizenship Act. The Citizenship Act does not apply to cases of persons migrating to Pakistan prior to its enactment. Citizens of India, who by virtue of Article 7 of the Constitution, would be deemed to be 'no longer citizens of India', can only regain citizenship by returning to India under a valid permit, and if they did not regain Indian citizenship prior to enactment of the Citizenship Act, then in such cases the provisions of the Citizenship Act would not apply to them. Mohammed Naseeruddin v. State of Andhra Pradesh, AIR 1960 AP 106.

5 S. 2 (1) (f) of the Citizenship Act. *See generally* State Trading Corporation of India Limited v. The Commercial Tax Officer, Vishakapatnam, AIR 1963 SC 1811.

acquired by preferring an application to the central government post fulfilment of certain prescribed eligibility criteria. The central government has the discretion to decide as to whether the applicant should be granted citizenship or not. Conferred citizenship may further be classified into 2 (two) types: (i) citizenship by registration; and (ii) citizenship by naturalisation.[6]

Though the Indian Constitution envisages a federal character for the Indian Republic, it however, propagates the concept of single citizenship.[7] Indian laws do not permit dual or plural citizenship.[8] Under Indian law, an Indian citizen, who obtains foreign citizenship will no longer be considered a citizen of India. Similarly, a foreigner seeking Indian citizenship, will, amongst other things, be required to give up his foreign citizenship.

ACQUISITION OF CITIZENSHIP

There exist various modes of acquisition of Indian citizenship. These modes are discussed in detail below, along with the legislative background of each aspect. At the outset, it is apt to remark that acquisition of Indian citizenship has become more stringent over the decades. The Citizenship Act prescribes the following ways of acquiring Indian citizenship, i.e. by birth, descent, registration, naturalisation and incorporation of territory.

CITIZENSHIP BY BIRTH

'Citizenship by birth' is the most common way of obtaining citizenship of any country, including India. Most Indians have acquired citizenship through this mode. Section 3 of the Citizenship Act contains provisions relating to acquisition of Indian citizenship

6 Under Indian law, the expression 'central government' includes the President. *See* Article 77 (1) of the Constitution and the General Clauses Act, 1897. *See generally* Rahmat Ullah v. State, AIR 1969 All 165.

7 The concept of single citizenship has been borrowed from the British Constitution.

8 Indian law however, does recognise the concept of 'overseas citizenship of India' which has some trappings of 'citizenship' and may be described as is the middle ground in this context. This concept is discussed later in this chapter.

by birth. It is important to take note of the evolution of the legal position with respect to acquisition of citizenship by birth, by dividing it into 3 (three) timelines or phases.

Phase I: The Initial Position

Initially (at the time of the enactment of the Citizenship Act) the legal position was that all persons born in India 01.01.1950 onwards would be considered as Indian citizens. In other words, the procurement of Indian citizenship was automatic upon taking birth in India. There were no other conditions or factors involved. Even the parenthood or ancestory of the new-born was irrelevant.[9] This position continued until 31.06.1987 after which the provisions started to become tighter.

Phase II: The Amendment of 1987

In the year 1987, the Citizenship Act underwent an amendment wherein a condition for obtaining citizenship by birth was imposed for persons born on or after 01.07.1987, i.e. at least one of the parents of the new-born must be an Indian citizen.[10]

This amendment is one of the earliest measures taken by the legislature to ensure that children of illegal migrants or refugees do not become automatically entitled to Indian citizenship. The 1980s was a period of turmoil for India in the context of illegal migration (especially from Bangladesh, Sri Lanka etc.). This amendment appears to be the first curb on illegal immigration.[11]

Phase III: The Amendment of 2003

Thereafter, in the year 2003,[12] an additional condition was imposed for persons born on or after 03.12.2003 i.e. either parent

9 S. 3 (1) (a) of the Citizenship Act.

10 S. 3 (1) (b) of the Citizenship Act.

11 *See generally* Rashtriya Mukti Morcha v. Union of India, 137 (2007) DLT 195.

12 Under Indian law, an 'illegal migrant' is who one enters India illegally or who enters 'legally' but overstays without sanction. S. 2 (1) (b) of the Citizenship Act.

must not be an 'illegal migrant'.[13] Through this amendment, the expression 'illegal migrant' was formally introduced to the statute book. In the considered view of the author, it is at this point that the government became fully alive to the issue of illegal migration into India and declared that the offspring(s) of illegal migrants would not be entitled to Indian citizenship.

The present position with regard to 'acquisition of Indian citizenship by birth' is summarised as follows:

S. No.	Period of Birth/ Timeline	Legal Requirements for obtaining citizenship by birth
1.	Persons born in India from 01.01.1950 until 31.06.1987	• Person should be born in India
2.	Persons born on or after 01.07.1987 until 02.12.2003	• Person should be born in India; and • One of the parents of the new-born must be an Indian citizen
3.	Persons born on or after 03.12.2003*	• Person should be born in India; and • One of the parents of the new born must be an Indian citizen; and • The other parent must not be an 'illegal migrant'

13 In 2003, sweeping changes were made to the Citizenship Act. These included the following: (i) the process of acquisition of citizenship by registration and naturalisation was made more stringent (discussed later in this chapter); (ii) 'illegal migrants' were made ineligible for grant of Indian citizenship; (iii) induction of the concept of 'national identity cards' and 'national register of citizens' (discussed later in the book); (iv) introduction of the concept of 'overseas citizenship of India' (discussed later in this chapter); and (v) removal of the concept of 'commonwealth citizenship'.

* S. 3 (1) (c) of the Citizenship Act. A child born in India to a surrogate mother (an Indian citizen) whose biological father is a foreign citizen, would be entitled to Indian citizenship by birth, in terms of Section 3 (1) (c) (ii) of the Citizenship Act. The gestational surrogate who has given birth to the child, would be recognised as the natural mother for the purposes of the Citizenship Act. The wife of the biological father, who has neither donated the ova, nor conceived or delivered the babies, cannot, in the absence of legislation, be treated as a legal mother or a natural mother. See Jan Balaz v. Anand Munipality, LPA No. 2151/2009 (11.11.2009, Gujarat High Court).

Automatic Citizenship

Grant of citizenship by birth is automatic in nature. There are no procedural formalities involved. Unlike other categories of citizenship (by registration and naturalisation) which require an application to be made for grant or recognition of citizenship, no such application process is envisaged under Section 3 of the Citizenship Act.[14]

Government Circulars

The provisions of the Citizenship Act, especially on the core aspects of 'acquisition of citizenship' cannot be altered, overridden or defeated by means of government circulars, notifications etc.[15] By a mere correspondence or an inter-ministerial meeting, the statutory provisions of the Citizenship Act cannot be defeated. No decision taken in an inter-ministerial meeting can override a statutory provision.[16]

Waiver of Citizenship

Under Indian law, Indian citizenship cannot be waived by conduct of the citizen. Further, there cannot be waiver of the right to be recognized as an Indian citizen by birth.[17] Simply because a person (of Tibetan origin) has stated that she is a Tibetan national, she cannot be said to have 'renounced' or 'waived' her Indian citizenship which has been acquired by birth in accordance with the provisions of the Citizenship Act.

---

14 Namgyal Dolkar v. Government of India, Ministry of External Affairs, W.P. (C) No. 12179/2009 (22.12.2010, Delhi High Court).

15 Karma Gyaltsen Neyratsang v. Union of India, W.P. (C) No. 6074/2014 (29.08.2017, Delhi High Court).

16 Phuntsok Wangyal v. Ministry of External Affairs, W.P. (C) No. 3539, 4275 & 7983/2016 (22.09.2016, Delhi High Court).

17 Phuntsok Wangyal, *supra*

A renunciation of citizenship can be made only in the manner prescribed under the Citizenship Act.[18]

CITIZENSHIP BY DESCENT

Persons born outside India may, subject to fulfilment of certain conditions, be considered to be Indian citizens, by descent.

The expression 'descent' refers to the origins or background of a person through his family or nationality. Simply put, citizenship by descent can be granted under Indian law, to persons (even if born outside India) who have a connection with India through lineage, subject to the conditions discussed below.

There are 2 (two) timelines, which are discussed in turn:

(i) Persons born between 26.01.1950 and 09.12.1992 (both dates included) ('**Timeline I**'); and
(ii) Persons born 10.12.1992 onwards ('**Timeline II**'). Both timelines are discussed in turn.

<u>Timeline I</u>

The eligibility of a child (during Timeline I) to become an Indian citizen was contingent upon the below mentioned factors:

a) At the time of his birth, his father was an Indian citizen.
b) In case the father was an Indian citizen by descent, then in such case, the following additional conditions were required to be qualified: (i) The child's birth was registered at an Indian consulate within a period of 1 (one) year of birth or after expiry of the said 1 (one) year period, with the permission of the central government; (ii) The father was in government service at the time of his birth.

---

18 Namgyal Dolkar, *supra*

Timeline II

The eligibility of a child (during Timeline II) to become an Indian citizen is contingent upon the below mentioned factors:

a) At the time of his birth, either or both his parents are Indian citizen(s).
b) In case the Indian citizen parent has acquired his/her citizenship by descent, then in such case, the following additional conditions are required to be qualified: (i) The person's birth is registered at an Indian consulate within a period of 1 (one) year of birth or with the permission of the central government after expiry of the said 1 (one) year period; (ii) The father is in government service at the time of his birth.

The Background to Introduction of Timeline II

Prior to 1992, the only means of acquiring 'citizenship by descent' was on the basis of the 'Indian citizenship' of the child's father (i.e. Timeline I). The concept of Timeline II was introduced to the Citizenship Act in the year 1992 with the objective of aligning its provisions with the provisions of the Convention on Elimination of all Forms of Discrimination against Women (CEDAW) to which India is a signatory. Timeline II introduced some gender parity.[19]

Timeline II essentially provides a new born with an option of obtaining Indian citizenship by descent on the basis of the 'Indian citizenship' of his mother.

Registration of Birth: Additional Requirement

With effect from 03.12.2004, certain further mandatory requirement(s) (regarding registration of birth) were added to the statute. The following conditions have been added:

19 Article 9 (2) of CEDAW requires its signatories to create parity between men and women in the context of the nationality of their children.

a) The child's birth is required to be registered at an Indian consulate within 1 (one) year of birth or with the permission of the central government, after expiry of the said 1 (one) year period.
b) A pre-requisite of the registration is a declaration from the parents that the child does not hold the passport of any other country.
c) The application for registration is to be made in the prescribed form, to the Indian consulate in the country where the child was born along with the declaration (specified in point (b) above).[20]

GRANT OF CITIZENSHIP

This section lists out the various modes by which an alien (foreigner) can obtain Indian citizenship. At the outset, it is important to note that the aspect of 'grant of citizenship' is the domain of the central government and is regulated by the provisions of the Citizenship Act and Citizenship Rules.

Acceptance of an application for citizenship is akin to grant of a privilege by the central government in exercise of its sovereign power. No alien has an inherent right to be accepted as a citizen of India. The decision (whether a person should be granted Indian citizenship) vests entirely and exclusively with the central government. The merits of such a decision cannot be normally questioned unless the same are capricious, *mala fide*, whimsical or in violation of applicable law.[21]

CITIZENSHIP BY REGISTRATION

One of the ways by which a foreigner can become a citizen of India is through registration. As mentioned above, a foreigner does not have a right to acquire citizenship of India; it is only a privilege that may be conferred by the central government. No

20 R. 3 of the Citizenship Rules.

21 *See* Stadtmuller Gabriele v. Union of India, 254 (2018) DLT 384.

foreigner can have a fundamental right or much less a right to register himself as an Indian citizen.[22]

The central government has a statutorily recognised discretion to grant or refuse an application for registration without assigning any reason for such grant or refusal.[23] Once a certificate of registration is issued to an applicant, such person continues to be an Indian citizen until the said registration is cancelled, annulled or withdrawn by the government.[24]

Eligibility for Citizenship by Registration

The below mentioned categories of persons are eligible to obtain citizenship by registration. At the outset, it is pertinent to note that 'illegal migrants' are debarred from seeking Indian citizenship, under any circumstances.[25]

Category I: Persons of Indian Origin

As the term suggests, a 'Person of Indian Origin' is one who was born or whose parents were born in undivided India. The following persons are eligible to apply:

a) A person of Indian origin who has been 'ordinarily a resident in India' for a period of 7 (seven) years before making an application for registration.

22 David John Hopkins v. Union of India, W.P. No. 11063/1995 (31.08.1995, Madras High Court).

23 S. 14 of the Citizenship Act. *But See* Soumen Paul v. Union of India, W.P. No. 19153 (W)/2001 (06.02.2002, Calcutta High Court) which observes that non-assignment of reasons while rejecting an application for registration of citizenship is violative of the principles of natural justice, in as much as, the applicant is deprived of an effective opportunity of contesting the reasons for rejection of citizenship.

24 Hari Shanker Jain v. Sonia Gandhi, AIR 2001 SC 3689.

25 S. 5 (1) of the Citizenship Act. Section 5 (1) (b) does not make statelessness or potential statelessness as a condition precedent for registration. *See* Azimusshan Haider v. Union of India, W.P. (C) No. 3087/1996 (04.07.2008, Delhi High Court).

b) A person of Indian origin who is ordinarily a resident of any country or place outside undivided India.

A person shall be considered as 'ordinarily resident in India' in case: (i) he has resided in India for the period of 12 (twelve) months immediately preceding the date of application for registration, and (ii) he has resided in India for at least 6 (six) years out of 8 (eight) years immediately preceding the above mentioned 12 (twelve) month period.[26] The central government is empowered to relax the above said '12 (twelve) month stay' requirement, in exceptional circumstances, for reasons recorded in writing, for up to 30 (thirty) days which may be in different tranches. In other words, from this 12 (twelve) month period, the central government may condone a collective absence of 30 (thirty) days which may be spread across several visits.

A person shall be considered to be of 'Indian origin' if he or either of his parents, were born in undivided India or in any other territory which became a part of India post 15.08.1947.

Category II: Marriage to Indian Citizen

A person who is married to a citizen of India and is 'ordinarily resident in India' for a period of 7 (seven) years before making an application for registration.[27]

26 The expression 'ordinarily resident in India' does not mean continuous uninterrupted residence but refers to residence without any serious break(s).

27 A foreigner who is otherwise eligible to apply for Indian citizenship registration in terms of Section 5 of the Citizenship Act (especially if he is married to an Indian citizen and is also an ordinary resident of India) may, in appropriate circumstances, be permitted time to apply for citizenship, with interim protection from deportation during the pendency of such application with the authorities. *See* Md. Ishaque v. The Under Secretary to the Government of India, Const. Writ Appellate Side (17.12.1990, Calcutta High Court). *See also* Khair Mohd. Reas Mohd. v. State of Maharashtra, First Appeal No. 541/1978 (27.06.1994, Bombay High Court). Marriage of a foreigner to an Indian citizen does not, *per se*, make her entitled to Indian citizenship. She only becomes eligible to apply for Indian citizenship by registration in terms of and in the manner prescribed under Section 5 of the Citizenship Act. Raj Kumari v. State of U.P, Civil Misc.W.P. No. 2098/2017 (17.01.2017, Allahabad High Court).

The central government is empowered to exempt any person (applying for registration under this category) from the residence requirement, in special situations, for reasons to be recorded in writing.[28]

<u>Category III: Minor Children of Citizens</u>
Minor children of persons who are citizens of India.

<u>Category IV: Parent's Citizenship by Registration or Naturalisation</u>
A person of full age and capacity whose parents have obtained Indian citizenship by the process of registration or naturalisation (discussed below).

<u>Category V: Parents Past Citizenship</u>
A person of full age and capacity, whose at least 1 (one) parent was an erstwhile citizen of India and who is ordinarily resident in India for a period of 12 (twelve) months immediately before making an application for registration. The central government may, in special circumstances, by an order in writing, reduce this period of 12 (twelve) months up to 30 (thirty) days which may be in different breaks.

<u>Category VI: Overseas Citizen</u>
A person of full age and capacity who has been a duly registered 'overseas citizen of India' (explained later in this chapter) for a period of 5 (five) years and has been 'ordinarily resident in India' for 12 (twelve) months before making an application for registration. The central government, may, in special circumstances, by an order in writing, reduce this period of 12 (twelve) months to a maximum of 30 (thirty) days which may be in different tranches.

28 S. 5 (6) of the Citizenship Act.

Category VII: Minor Children

The central government may, in special circumstances, register any minor as a citizen of India.[29]

Central Government: The Adjudicating Authority

Section 14 of the Citizenship Act mandates that the central government is permitted to grant or reject an application for registration. Assigning reasons for rejection of the application is not mandatory. Normally, if the government chooses not to disclose the reasons behind the grant or refusal of citizenship, then the court may not insist upon disclosure of reasons.[30] The position, however, may not be the same in case the government, has, on its own, disclosed the reasons for rejection and the said disclosed reason is patently irrelevant to a proper consideration of the matter. The central government cannot pass an order for a reason that is wholly extraneous to the scheme of the law or factors not relevant for proper consideration of the matter. Put pithily, an order of the central government can be set aside by courts in case it comes to their notice that the reasons assigned (in the order) for rejection of an application are untenable.[31]

Oath of Allegiance

No person shall be registered as a citizen of India until he takes an oath of allegiance in the form and manner prescribed in the Citizenship Act.[32] An oath of allegiance is an oath whereby a person acknowledges his allegiance towards the Indian

29 S. 5(4) of the Citizenship Act.

30 It may uphold the order on the settled legal position that a foreigner does not have a fundamental right to reside and settle in India and the government has an unrestricted right to expel him.

31 Asimusshan Haider v. Union of India, W.P. (C) No. 3087/1996 (04.07.2008, Delhi High Court).

32 *See* Second Schedule of the Citizenship Act.

Constitution and India in general. The Second Schedule of the Citizenship Act sets out the oath of allegiance which a person obtaining Indian citizenship is required to take.

Restriction on Re-obtaining Indian Citizenship

A person who has renounced Indian citizenship once shall not be permitted to re-obtain Indian citizenship by registration without an order of the central government.[33] Similarly, an order of the central government is also required for a person who wishes to re-obtain Indian citizenship after it is terminated in accordance with the provisions of the Citizenship Act.[34]

Prospective Effect of Registration

Grant of citizenship by registration has a prospective effect. Hence, a person registered under the Citizenship Act shall be considered to be an Indian citizen only from the date of registration.[35]

Grant of Citizenship by Registration: Procedure

The Citizenship Rules provide the procedure for obtaining Indian citizenship by the process of registration.[36] The said procedure is summarised below.

Application to Collector

An application for registration can be made by an eligible applicant, in the prescribed form to the jurisdictional collector (on

33 *See generally* A.K. Mukherji v. Prodip Ranjan, A.F.A.D 51/1985 (19.08.1987, Calcutta High Court).

34 S. 5 (3) of the Citizenship Act.

35 S. 5 (5) of the Citizenship Act.

36 Relinquishment of original citizenship, per se, may not be indicative of an intention to obtain Indian citizenship. The Citizenship Act does not provide for a scenario where a person residing in India, upon relinquishing his original citizenship is automatically considered to be a citizen of India. The processes and procedures prescribed under the Citizenship law must be followed. *See* Kiran Gupta v. The State Election Commission, 2020 (6) BLJ 539.

the basis of the residence of the applicant).[37] The said application is required to be accompanied with the appropriate declarations, undertakings, affidavits and documents as mentioned in the Citizenship Rules.[38] The collector shall issue an acknowledgement of receipt to the applicant in the prescribed form.[39] An oath of allegiance shall be administered by the collector to the applicant whose application is found to be satisfactory and in order.

The application shall then be forwarded to the state government or the union territory administration, as the case may be, within a period of 60 (sixty) days from the date of its receipt, along with a report certifying the following:[40]

a) The application satisfies all conditions laid down under the applicable provisions of the Citizenship Act.
b) The applicant has an intention of making India his permanent home.
c) The applicant has signed the oath of allegiance.
d) The applicant is of good character and fit and proper to be registered as a citizen of India.

Role of the Collector

The collector does not possess any adjudicatory function in the matter. The collector is required to forward all applications (along with his report) to the central government so that they can decide whether or not to register a person as a citizen of

37 R. 11 of the Citizenship Rules.

38 *See* R. 4 to 10 of the Citizenship Rules. Possession of a foreign passport is not mandatory for preferring an application for registration of citizenship under S. 5 (1) (3) of the Citizenship Act. However, the concerned authorities need to be provided with a cogent explanation as to its unavailability. *See* Bismillah Khan v. Union of India, W.P. No. 928/2020 (24.02.2020, Calcutta High Court).

39 Form IX.

40 R. 12(1) of the Citizenship Rules.

India.[41] In other words, the collector is only a forwarding authority and he cannot allow or reject an application for registration.[42] The only authority empowered by law to adjudicate an application for registration is the central government.[43] The collector is only required to carry out an inquiry to check the antecedents of the applicant and make a report thereon.

Application to the Central Government

The state government or the union territory administration, as the case may be, shall forward the application along with the collector's report, with its recommendations to the central government, within a period of 30 (thirty) days from receipt of the application, such period being extendable to a maximum of 90 (ninety) days.[44]

The applicant is permitted to make a representation to the central government in case his application is not forwarded by the collector or the state government within a period of 90 (ninety) days from the date of receipt of the application. The central government, upon receipt of such representation, may take up the matter with the state government to expedite the process.[45]

Scrutiny of Application

The central government, upon receipt of the application, shall scrutinize the same, along with the collector's report and the recommendations of the state government. It may also carry out

41 National Human Rights Commission v. State of Arunachal Pradesh, [1996] 1 SCR 278.

42 Devan Parameswaran v. The Union of India, W.P. No. 4617/1997 (19.04.2004, Madras High Court).

43 R. 13 of the Citizenship Rules. *See also* Ghaurul Hasan v. The State of Rajasthan, W.P. (C) No. 26/1957 (08.04.1958, Rajasthan High Court).

44 R. 12 (2) of the Citizenship Rules.

45 R. 12 (4) & (5) of the Citizenship Rules.

necessary inquiry to ascertain the suitability of the applicant. In case the central government is satisfied, then it shall grant Indian citizenship to the applicant.[46] The certificate of registration shall be issued to the applicant in the prescribed form.[47]

Maintenance of Records

The central government shall maintain a register containing the details of persons who have been issued a certificate of registration.[48]

CITIZENSHIP BY NATURALISATION

Naturalisation is another method of granting citizenship to an alien/foreigner. Typically, the process of naturalisation involves residence in India for a certain period of time, apart from satisfaction of other conditions imposed by the concerned authorities.

Under Indian law, a person of full age and capacity, who is not an 'illegal migrant' and who qualifies the conditions mentioned below is entitled to make an application to the central government for grant of certificate of citizenship 'by naturalisation'.[49]

Qualifications for Naturalisation

The Third Schedule of the Citizenship Act contains eligibility requirements for grant of citizenship by naturalisation. An applicant must qualify the following conditions:

a) He should not be a citizen of a country which prevents Indian citizens from becoming citizens/subjects of that country by naturalisation.

46 R. 13 of the Citizenship Rules.

47 R. 14 of the Citizenship Rules.

48 R. 17 & 18 of the Citizenship Rules.

49 S. 6 of the Citizenship Act.

b) He should undertake to renounce his existing foreign citizenship in case his application for Indian citizenship is accepted. Renunciation of existing foreign citizenship is an imperative requirement. The central government has the discretion to reject the request for Indian citizenship in case the certificate of renunciation issued by the foreign nation is not produced by the applicant.[50]
c) He should have resided in India or been in service of a government in India, or both, for a period of 12 (twelve) months immediately preceding the date of filing of the application. The said period of 12 (twelve) months may be relaxed/reduced by the central government, for reasons recorded in writing, to 30 (thirty) days. The central government may, in special cases, grant further relaxations/reductions in this regard.
d) The minimum aggregate period of stay in India and/or service in a government in India, during the period of 14 (fourteen) years immediately preceding the above mentioned 12 (twelve) month period, should be 11 (eleven) years. The central government may, in special cases, grant further relaxations/reductions in this regard.
e) He should be of good character.[51]
f) He should have adequate knowledge of a language specified in the Eighth Schedule of the Constitution. The Eighth Schedule

---

50 Indian law does not recognize dual citizenship. Even if the concerned foreign country recognises dual citizenship, the Indian government can still insist on a certificate of renunciation of foreign citizenship from the applicant. *See generally* Sahar Gharachorloo v. Union of India, C.W.P. No. 16577/2014 (30.06.2016, Punjab & Haryana High Court).

51 The onus to establish that the applicant qualifies the test of 'good character' rests with the applicant himself and not with the central government. The expression 'good character' is not defined in the Citizenship Act. The central government has wide discretion in setting the standards for its satisfaction as to the good character requirement. However, the standards to qualify the good character requirement must be reasonable and as expected of a good and responsible citizen espousing the values engrafted in the Indian Constitution. *See generally* Stadtmuller Gabriele v. Union of India, 254 (2018) DLT 384.

of the Constitution recognises the following languages: (i) Assamese; (ii) Bengali; (iii) Bodo; (iv) Dogri; (v) Gujarati; (vi) Hindi; (vii) Kannada; (viii) Kashmiri; (ix) Konkani; (x) Maithili; (xi) Malayalam; (xii) Manipuri; (xiii) Marathi; (xiv) Nepali; (xv) Odia; (xvi) Punjabi; (xvii) Sanskrit; (xviii) Santali; (xix) Sindhi; (xx) Tamil; (xxi) Telugu; and (xxii) Urdu.

g) In the event of his application for naturalisation being allowed, he should have an intention to reside in India, or to enter into or continue in service under a government in India or under an international organisation of which India is a member, or under a society, company or body of persons established in India.

The central government is empowered to waive off any or all of the above-mentioned conditions, if it is of the opinion that the applicant is a person who has rendered distinguished service to the cause of science, philosophy, art, literature, world peace or human progress generally.[52]

Procedure for Naturalisation

The procedure for naturalisation is largely similar to the procedure for registration. The same set of procedural rules apply to applications for registration as well as for naturalisation. A summary of the said procedure is mentioned below.

The application for naturalisation is required to made by the applicant in the prescribed form along with necessary particulars to the concerned collector.[53] The collector conducts a background and antecedent check and makes a report thereon.[54] The application (along with the report) is forwarded to the state government, which in turn forwards the same to the central

52 S. 6 (1) *proviso* of the Citizenship Act.

53 R. 10 & 11 of the Citizenship Rules.

54 R. 12 (1) of the Citizenship Rules.

government along with its recommendation.[55] A scrutiny and inquiry is carried out by the central government which ultimately grants citizenship by naturalisation to the applicant upon being satisfied with the application.[56] An oath of allegiance is mandatory for grant of citizenship.[57]

The central government maintains a record of persons who are granted citizenship by naturalisation.[58]

There exists no straight jacket formula or codified parameters for adjudication of an application for naturalisation. Wide discretion is invested in the central government in this regard. The decision cannot be subjected to judicial review of courts except where the order is ridden with capriciousness, arbitrariness or whimsicality.[59]

OVERSEAS CITIZEN OF INDIA

In the year 2000, the government set up a committee for the purpose of studying the global Indian diaspora and for suggesting ways to develop a constructive relationship with them. Through this report, the said committee laid the ground work for introduction of the concept of 'overseas citizenship'. The Citizenship Act was subsequently amended in the year 2003 to, amongst other things, introduce the concept of 'overseas citizen of India' to the statute book. The scope of 'overseas citizenship' was expanded in the subsequent amendments. Recently, in fact, the government also appears to have taken two steps back and placed some restrictions on 'overseas citizenship'. This section elaborately deals with the concept of 'overseas citizenship'.

55 R. 12 (2) of the Citizenship Rules.

56 R. 13 & 15 of the Citizenship Rules.

57 R. 16 of the Citizenship Rules.

58 R. 17 (e) & 18 of the Citizenship Rules.

59 *See* Stadtmuller Gabriele, *supra*

As discussed previously, Indian law does not recognize the concept of 'dual or plural citizenship' (under which citizens are permitted to simultaneously hold and enjoy citizenship of 2 (two) or more countries). Foreign nationals of Indian origin had, for long, sought from the Indian government, some form of 'recognition' and 'privilege' owing to their Indian roots. This recognition came in the form of 'overseas citizenship'.

The decision to introduce the concept of 'overseas citizenship' appears to be based on considerations of expediency since persons of Indian origin contribute significantly to the economic prosperity of the nation in the form of foreign exchange and thus it would be fair to afford to them some special incentives otherwise not available to foreigners. The concept of 'overseas citizenship' was promulgated and brought into the Indian legal landscape with an amendment to the Citizenship Act (i.e. by introduction of Sections 7A to 7D of the Citizenship Act).[60] The provisions pertaining to overseas citizenship have been amended several times in the past in order to give effect to the government's policy on such matters.[61]

Scope & Extent of OCI Rights

Before proceeding to discuss the various aspects of 'overseas citizenship', it is important to bear in mind the following features thereof:

a) Overseas citizenship is not actually 'dual citizenship' as the Indian Constitution forbids dual citizenship.
b) An overseas citizen does not hold rights akin to that of an Indian citizen.[62]

---

60 *See generally* https://www.mea.gov.in/overseas-citizenship-of-india-scheme.htm

61 *See generally* Rajat Gangwar v. State of U.P., PIL No. 2497/2019 (27.12.2019, Allahabad High Court).

62 An OCI Cardholder does not enjoy rights akin to Non Resident Indians (who are citizens). The Notifications only provide parity to OCI cardholders (with NRIs) on certain limited aspects. Otherwise, OCI cardholders are to be considered as foreigners.

c) Overseas citizenship is registration based i.e. the scheme requires eligible persons to apply for and obtain registration as an Overseas Citizen of India (OCI).
d) Rights of OCI are statutory right(s) and not fundamental or constitutional rights.[63] OCI registration does not confer any political rights.[64]
e) An OCI can carry out only such activities which are permitted by the government from time to time.[65] For instance, OCI card holders may not represent India in international sporting events.[66] Further, they cannot seek election to the Lok Sabha, Rajya Sabha, Legislative Assembly or Legislative Council; or hold constitutional positions such as President, Vice President, Judgeship of High Court(s) or the Supreme Court of India; or be appointed to any public services or posts in connection with the affairs of the central or state government(s).[67]

Benefits of OCI Registration

Although, an OCI is not an Indian citizen, yet he enjoys certain privileges in India such as multiple entry visa, exemption from foreigners registration, parity on some aspects with NRIs etc. Specifically speaking, a person registered as an OCI has the following benefits:[68]

---

63 Karm Kumar v. Union of India, (2010) 172 DLT 521.

64 G. Venkatesh v. Bridge Federation of India, W.P. (C) No. 2559/2011 (24.06.2015, Madras High Court).

65 G. Venkatesh, *supra. See also* Karm Kumar v. Union of India, (2010) 172 DLT 521. Whatever limited rights are conferred on OCI are primarily based on the policy of the government. Such rights can be extended, withdrawn, qualified or amended on the basis of government policy.

66 G. Venkatesh *supra. But see* Sorab Singh Gill v. Union of India, C.W.P. No. 18093/2009 (18.03.2010, Punjab and Haryana High Court).

67 S. 7B (2) of the Citizenship Act.

68 *See generally* Notification No. S.O. 1050 (E), dated 04.03.2021 issued by the Ministry of Home Affairs, Government of India which supersedes Notification No. S.O. 12 (E), dated 05.01.2007, Notification No. S.O. 542 (E), dated 11.04.2005

a) Grant of multiple entry, multi-purpose, lifelong visa for visiting India.[69]
b) Exemption from registration with Foreign Regional Registration Officer or Foreign Registration Officer (FRRO) for any length of stay in India.[70]
c) Entitlement to parity with Indian citizens and Non-Resident Indians in respect of matters explained below.[71]

The Ministry of Home Affairs, Government of India, has, by means of notifications, granted the following benefits to OCI cardholders:[72]

a) Parity with Non-Resident Indians in the matter of inter-country adoption of Indian children in compliance of the procedures laid down for such adoption.
b) Parity with resident Indians in matters of tariffs in domestic

---

& Notification No. S.O. 36 (E) dated 05.01.2009 issued by the Ministry of Home Affairs, Government of India *See also* Christo Thomas Philip v. Union of India, W.P (C) No. 1775/2018 (08.01.2019, Delhi High Court) & Raghuram v. Union of India, W.P. (C) No. 7524/2018 (13.04.2018. Madras High Court). It is pertinent to point out that recently, a challenge to the Notification No. S.O. 1050 (E) dated 04.03.2021 was rejected by the Karnataka High Court in Alekhya Ponnekanti v. Union of India, W.P. Nos. 11504/2021 et al (08.11.2021, Karnataka High Court).

69 Note that OCI cardholders require a special permission for undertaking the following activities: (i) to undertake research; (ii) to undertake any missionary or tabligh or mountaineering or journalistic activity; (iii) to undertake internship in any foreign diplomatic mission or foreign government organisation in India or to take up employment in any foreign diplomatic mission in India; (iv) to visit any place which falls within the protected/restricted/prohibited areas.

70 OCI cardholders who are normally resident in India are required to intimate the jurisdictional foreigners office, by email, in case of change in permanent residential address or occupation.

71 Previously there existed several entitlements for OCI cardholders, including a general parity with Non-Resident Indians in respect of all facilities available to them in economic, financial and educational life. These entitlements have been significantly curtailed through Notification No. S.O. 1050(E), dated 04.03.2021, issued by the Ministry of Home Affairs, Government of India.

72 *See* Notification No. S.O. 1050 (E), dated 04.03.2021, Ministry of Home Affairs, Government of India.

air fares and for visiting national monuments, historical sites and museums in India.

c) Parity with domestic Indian visitors in respect of entry fee for visiting national parks and wildlife sanctuaries in India.

d) Parity with Non-Resident Indians in respect of practicing the following professions in India: (i) Doctors, dentists, nurses and pharmacists; (ii) Advocates; (iii) Architects; (iv) Chartered Accountants.

e) Parity with Non-Resident Indians in respect of entitlement to appear for the All India entrance tests to make them eligible for admission only against any non-resident Indian seat or any supernumerary seat.[73]

f) Parity with Non-Resident Indians in respect of sale or purchase of immovable property, other than agricultural land or farmhouse or plantation property.[74]

An OCI cardholder shall be considered akin to a foreigner for all other purposes which are not covered in the notifications of the Ministry of Home Affairs or the Reserve Bank of India.[75]

The above-mentioned special privileges available to an OCI can be withdrawn upon occurrence of any of the events

---

73 Note that an OCI is not eligible for admission against any seat reserved exclusively for Indian citizens.

74 Notification No. FEMA 21 (R)/2018-RB, dated 26.03.2018 issued by the Reserve Bank of India titled 'Foreign Exchange Management (Acquisition and Transfer of Immovable Property in India) Regulations, 2018, regulates the sale and purchase of immovable property in India by NRI and OCI. Regulation 3, *inter alia,* provides that an NRI or OCI can acquire immovable property in India, through sale, gift, inheritance etc., subject to certain conditions. Regulation 8 further permits repatriation of the sale proceeds outside India, subject to compliance of certain conditions.

75 Prior to the aforesaid notification, the Delhi High Court appeared to take a *prima facie* view that fundamental rights which are available to citizens of India may also be applicable to OCI Cardholders. *See* Christo Thomas Philip v. Union of India and Ors., W.P. (C) No. 1775/2018 (30.07.2018, Delhi High Court).

mentioned in Section 7D of the Citizenship Act (discussed in detail below).[76]

Government Permission for Certain Activities

Government Permission for Specified Activities

Indian law requires an OCI to obtain special permission from the government for the following activities:

a) Research work in India.[77]
b) Missionary work.[78]
c) Mountaineering activities.[79]
d) Tabligh activities.[80]
e) Journalism.[81]

Government Permission for Visiting Specified Areas

Travel of OCI to certain specified regions of India is regulated by the government.[82] A special permission is required by an OCI for visiting the 'protected and restricted areas' which have been notified by the government under the Foreigners (Protected Areas) Order, 1958 and Foreigners (Restricted Areas) Order,

---

76 *See generally* Lee Anne Arunoday Singh v. Ministry of Home Affairs, W.P. (L) No. 3443/2020 (27.10.2020, Bombay High Court).

77 Application to be made to the Indian Mission/Post/concerned Foreign Registration Officer.

78 Permission required from the Indian Mission/Post/concerned Foreign Registration Officer. Indian law does not proscribe missionary work or missionary activities. Indulging in any missionary activity, *per se*, is neither against Indian law nor can it be construed as being contrary to the sovereignty and integrity of India or in the interest of the general public. *See generally* Christo Thomas Philip v. Union of India, 2019 (256) DLT 671.

79 *supra*

80 *supra*

81 Permission is required from the External Publicity Division, Ministry of External Affairs, Government of India.

82 *See generally* https://www.mha.gov.in/PDF_Other/AnnexVII_01022018.pdf

1963. Generally speaking, all areas falling between the 'Inner Line' as declared under the said order and the international border of the state have been declared as 'protected areas'. The protected areas are located in the following states:

a) Whole of Arunachal Pradesh.
b) Whole of Manipur.
c) Whole of Mizoram.
d) Whole of Nagaland.
e) Whole of Sikkim (partly a 'protected area' and partly a 'restricted' area).
f) Parts of Himachal Pradesh.
g) Parts of Uttarakhand.
h) Parts of Jammu and Kashmir.
i) Parts of Rajasthan.

Restricted areas are located in the following states:

a) Andaman and Nicobar Islands (the entire union territory).
b) Parts of Sikkim.

Passport Requirement for OCI

As discussed above, an OCI is entitled to the benefit of a lifelong visa to India. To enjoy the said benefit, it is imperative for the OCI to maintain a valid passport (of his home country) at all times of his stay in India. Stay of an OCI in India without a valid passport is illegal.

Eligibility Requirements for OCI

Section 7A of the Citizenship Act provides the eligibility criteria for obtaining registration as an OCI. Status of OCI can only be given to a person who is not an Indian citizen but is a 'citizen of a foreign country'.[83]

---

83 Syeda Afshan Rahman v. Union of India, W.P (Civil) No. 12520/2009 (02.07.2010, Delhi High Court).

General Eligibility

(a) A person of full age and capacity:
   (i) who is a citizen of another country, but was a citizen of India at the time of or any time after the commencement of the Constitution of India;
   (ii) a person who is a citizen of another country but was eligible to become a citizen of India at the time of commencement of the Constitution of India.
   (iii) who is a citizen of another country, but belonged to a territory that became part of India after 15 August 1947.
   (iv) who is a child or a grandchild or a great grandchild of such a citizen.

(b) A minor child of a person mentioned in (i) to (iv) above.

(c) A minor child whose either (or both) parent(s) are citizen(s) of India.

(d) A spouse (of foreign origin) of an Indian citizen or spouse (of foreign origin) of an OCI can also apply, with a precondition that their marriage has been registered and subsisted for a continuous period of at least two years immediately prior to filing of the application.[84]

Disqualification

A person belonging to or having ancestry[85] from Pakistan or Bangladesh is not eligible for registration as an OCI, under any circumstances.[86]

For this disqualification, it is sufficient to show that the applicant has been a citizen of Pakistan (or Bangladesh). A good

84 *See* Alibhiya Das v. Union of India, W.P. (C) No. 11865/2018 (11.02.2019, Delhi High Court). Please further note that such persons shall be subject to a prior security clearance from the competent authorities.

85 Person whose either parent, grandparent or great grand-parent is from Pakistan or Bangladesh.

86 S. 7 A (1) *second proviso* of the Citizenship Act.

proof in this regard would be 'issuance of a passport' to the applicant by the foreign country.[87]

Government Policy

The privileges enjoyed by OCI are purely a matter of government policy. Also, the central government enjoys certain overriding power(s) on the aspect of grant of OCI. The central government may, in special circumstances, for reasons to be recorded in writing, register a person as an OCI, even if he does not qualify the criteria described above.[88]

Procedure for Registration

A person eligible to be an OCI will be required to obtain registration with the competent authorities to avail the benefits.[89] Briefly described below is the procedure for such registration.[90]

a) An application for registration shall be made in the prescribed form and manner to the relevant authorities. The application for registration shall be accompanied with documents as prescribed.
b) In case the application is being made in India, then it shall be filed with the appropriate Foreigner Regional Registration Officer or with the Foreigners Division, Ministry of Home Affairs.

87 *See generally* Syeda Afshan Rahman v. Union of India, W.P. (C) No. 12520/2009 (02.07.2010, Delhi High Court).

88 S. 7 A (3) of the Citizenship Act.

89 Registration as an OCI is a pre-requirement for receiving benefits conferred under Section 7A of the Citizenship Act and its notifications. Viraaj Pratap Singh Pannu v. Chandigarh Administration, C.W.P. No. 15667/2012 (29.09.2012, Punjab & Haryana High Court).

90 *See generally* https://ociservices.gov.in/

c) In case the application is being made outside India, then it shall be filed with the appropriate Indian Mission or Post which has jurisdiction over the country of which the applicant is a citizen or an 'ordinary resident'.
d) Upon receipt of the application, the central government shall conduct a preliminary inquiry. Upon being satisfied, the central government shall register the applicant and place the case for a verification of antecedents, which shall be done within a period of 30 (thirty) days.
e) The central government is required to decide the application within a period of 4 (four) months from the date of receipt of the application.
f) Grant of registration to spouses (of foreign origin) or Indian Citizens or OCI cardholders shall be subject to a prior security clearance by the competent authority.

Every person registered as an OCI receives a registration booklet from the government. This registration booklet serves as an identification proof.[91] India has registered OCIs in almost 150 (one hundred and fifty) nations globally.

Renunciation of Overseas Citizenship

An OCI can renounce his 'overseas citizenship' by making a written declaration to the said effect, in the prescribed form and manner. Such declaration shall take effect upon its registration with the central government.[92] Where a person ceases to be an OCI pursuant to a renunciation, his spouse of foreign origin and his minor children shall also automatically lose their OCI registration.[93] Record of every

91 *See* Notification No. S.O. 585 (E), dated 23.03.2012, Ministry of Home Affairs, Government of India.

92 S. 7 C (1) of the Citizenship Act.

93 S. 7 C (2) of the Citizenship Act.

such cancellation/renunciation of registration shall be maintained by the concerned authorities.[94]

Cancellation of Overseas Citizenship

The central government is empowered to cancel registration of an OCI in any of the specific following situations:[95]

a) If the registration as OCI had been obtained by fraud, false representation or concealment of material facts.
b) If the OCI shows disaffection towards the Indian Constitution.
c) If the OCI has, at times of war in which India is engaged, unlawfully traded or communicated with the enemy, or has associated himself with the enemy in a manner so as to assist it in the war.
d) If the OCI has, within 5 (five) years of registration, been sentenced to imprisonment for a minimum term of 2 (two) years.
e) If it is considered necessary to cancel registration in the interests of the sovereignty and integrity of India, security of India, friendly relations of India with a foreign country, or in the interest of the general public.
f) If the marriage of the OCI (who is of foreign origin and who had obtained registration on the basis of marriage to an Indian citizen or to an OCI) is dissolved by legitimate means.[96]

---

94 R. 34 of the Citizenship Rules.

95 S. 7 D of the Citizenship Act. A cancellation of OCI should typically be preceded by a show cause notice and an opportunity of hearing to the concerned person. An intimation of cancellation should also be issued. *See generally* Ligy Abraham v. Union of India W.P. (C) No. 10499/2016 (11.09.2017, Delhi High Court). *But see* Union of India v. Savitha Kumar, LPA 219/2019 (28.08.2019, Delhi High Court) which indicates that where the issue relates to integrity, sovereignty and safety of India, no prior intimation is required to be given to the OCI Cardholder in case of his blacklisting or before passing any order under Section 7 D of the Citizenship Act. *See also* Craig Maxwell Sterry v. Ministry of Home Affairs, Union of India & Ors., W.P. No. 513/2009 (11.09.2009, Bombay High Court at Goa).

96 *See generally* Lee Anne Arunoday Singh, *supra*

Principles of natural justice must be followed when deciding the issue of 'cancellation'. This includes providing a proper show cause notice to the proceedee and an opportunity to the proceedee to meet the contents of the show cause notice.[97]

Once a cancellation order is passed, the certificate of registration of the proceedee shall be returned and cancelled by the central government. Record of every cancellation of registration shall be maintained by the concerned authorities.[98] A person whose OCI registration is cancelled in the manner mentioned above shall also be blacklisted for preventing his future entry into India.[99]

Non-Resident Indian

The concept of OCI must be distinguished from that of an NRI. In common parlance, a Non-Resident Indian is a person who is an Indian citizen but ordinarily resides outside India and holds an Indian passport. Therefore, such a person enjoys a full citizenship rights in India, does not require a visa to travel to India and does not require any registration with the foreigners office(s). The central government has, by means of notifications, handed out various privileges and benefits to NRIs.

Person of Indian Origin

The concept of OCI was introduced in the year 2004. Previously, there existed a scheme under which Persons of Indian Origin (PIO) were issued cards and granted various privileges.[100] Generally speaking, a PIO is a foreigner who was previously an Indian national or whose ancestors were Indian nationals.

97 Ramesh Ganeriwal v. Union of India, W.P. (C) No. 3652/2017 (18.08.2017, Delhi High Court).

98 R. 35 of the Citizenship Rules.

99 *See* https://ociservices.gov.in/

100 Person of Indian Origin Card (PIO Card) Scheme, 2002.

The primary purpose of a PIO card was to make it easier for foreign nationals of Indian origin to enter India by granting them exemption from obtaining Indian visa.

Benefits to PIO Cardholders

Originally, the following benefits, were available to PIO cardholders:[101]

a) Exemption from obtaining a visa for visit to India.
b) Exemption from the requirement of registration with the appropriate registration office even if their stay exceeded 180 (one hundred and eighty days) in a given year.
c) Permission to acquire and dispose immovable property in India, except agricultural property.
d) Parity with Non-Resident Indians in respect to facilities made available to them by the government.

Merger of PIO and OCI Schemes

The PIO scheme was introduced in 2002 and the OCI scheme was introduced in 2005. For some time, both schemes ran concurrently which became a counterproductive exercise since it was only leading to confusion amongst the applicants. To settle this issue, the government decided to devise a single scheme by merging PIO and OCI.[102]

In 2015, the central government issued a notification for merger of these schemes.[103] As per the said notification, all existing PIO cardholders would be deemed to be OCI

101 Please note that persons from the following countries were ineligible to obtain a PIO Card: (i) Pakistan (ii) Bangladesh; (iii) Nepal; (iv) Sri Lanka; (v) Bhutan; (vi) Afghanistan; and (vii) China.

102 A PIO card was considered as a valid document by Indian authorities only till 31.03.2019.

103 Notification F. No. 26011/01/2014-IC, dated 09.01.2015.

cardholders.[104] The PIO Scheme was withdrawn by the government and the PIO cardholders were directed to make an application for conversion/registration to OCI.[105]

CITIZENSHIP BY INCORPORATION OF TERRITORY

If any outside territory becomes a part of India, then the central government, by order issues guidelines for absorbing and granting Indian citizenship to all persons of such territory. In the past, various foreign territories have become a part of India through the process of accession or incorporation.

In the year 1962, Pondicherry became a part of India pursuant to a treaty of accession between France and India (which entered into force on 16.08.1962). As a consequence, the government promulgated the Citizenship (Pondicherry) Order, 1962, for the purpose of specifying the persons who would be considered Indian citizens pursuant to the above-mentioned treaty of accession.[106]

On 16.05.1975, Sikkim (then a monarchy) became a state of India pursuant to a referendum. Dadra & Nagar Haveli became a part of India in 11.08.1961

On 19.12.1961, Goa, Daman and Diu (then Portuguese colonies) were seized by the Indian Armed Forces by force of arms. It came under the Indian administration from 20.12.1961. Eventually, by virtue of the Goa, Daman and Diu (Administration) Act, 1962 and the Constitution (Twelfth Amendment) Act, 1962, Goa, Daman and Diu were included in the union territories.[107]

---

104 *See also* S. 7A (2) of the Citizenship Act.

105 *See* Letter No. 26011/06/2015-OCI (Vol II) dated 26.12.2016 issued by the Foreigners Division-OCI Cell, Ministry of Home Affairs, Government of India.

106 *See* https://www.refworld.org/docid/3ae6b52dc.html#:~:text=Provided%20that%20where%20the%20choice,the%20provisions%20of%20this%20Order%3B

107 *See generally* Rev. Mons Sebastiao Fransisco Xaviar Dos Remedios Monterio v. State of Goa, AIR 1970 SC 329 for the history of annexation of Goa.

As a consequence of all of the above accessions, citizens of such foreign states became Indian citizens.

CESSATION OF CITIZENSHIP

As per the Citizenship Act, Indian citizenship can be determined by various ways, namely, renunciation, termination and deprivation. This section deals with each of the said modes of cessation.

RENUNCIATION OF CITIZENSHIP

The term 'renunciation' in common parlance, means 'to give up'. The Citizenship Act explains the mode and manner in which an Indian citizen can give up his Indian citizenship.

Procedure for Renunciation

An Indian citizen of full age and capacity may renounce his citizenship by making a written declaration in the prescribed form and manner. In the declaration, the person is required to state how he qualifies to be an Indian citizen and the circumstances in which he intends to acquire foreign citizenship.[108] The renunciation takes effect once the declaration is registered by the appropriate authority in the Ministry of Home Affairs, Government of India.[109]

When a person ceases to be an Indian citizen, then every minor child of that person shall automatically cease to be an Indian citizen. However, such child shall, on attaining majority, have an option of resuming Indian citizenship by making an appropriate declaration in the manner stated below.

---

108 R. 23 (1) of the Citizenship Rules.

109 R. 23 (3) of the Citizenship Rules. Recently, the Ministry of Home Affairs, Government of India has simplified the process for renunciation of Indian citizenship by introducing an online process for the applicants to upload their documents and an outer limit of 60 (sixty) days for completion of the renunciation process.

Resumption of Citizenship

Indian citizenship can be resumed by making of a declaration by the person in the prescribed form, within a period of one year from attaining majority along with the oath of allegiance. Such declaration shall be registered at the Ministry of Home Affairs, Government of India. Every person making such a declaration shall be issued a certificate of resumption of Indian citizenship in the prescribed form by the appropriate authorities. The Ministry of Home Affairs, Government of India maintains a record of persons who make declarations for renunciation or resumption of Indian citizenship.[110]

Waiver of Indian Citizenship

There cannot be waiver (express or implied) of the right to be recognized as an Indian citizen by birth. Mere statement of a person (of Tibetan origin) that she is a Tibetan national cannot amount to a waiver of her Indian citizenship (obtained by virtue of her birth in India). The only way to give up Indian citizenship is by way of a renunciation (made in the manner prescribed under the Citizenship Act).[111] Similarly, inter-ministerial correspondences and letters which unilaterally decide to not recognize 'Indian citizenship' of Tibetans (who otherwise qualify to be Indian citizens by virtue of the Citizenship Act) are to be considered inconsequential in as much as inter-ministerial decisions cannot defeat statutory provisions.[112]

TERMINATION OF CITIZENSHIP

Generally speaking, voluntary acquisition of foreign citizenship by an Indian citizen results in cessation of his Indian citizenship.

---

110 R. 23 (4) & 24 (5) of the Citizenship Rules.

111 Namgyal Dolkar v. Government of India, Ministry of External Affairs, W.P. (C) No. 12179/2009 (22.12.2010, Delhi High Court).

112 Tenzin Tselha v. Union of India, W.P. (C) No. 7035/2016 (23.11.2016, Delhi High Court).

The Citizenship Act provides for termination of citizenship of an Indian citizen, if he has voluntarily acquired citizenship of another country.[113] The scope of 'termination' is limited to situations where the question relates to acquisition of foreign citizenship by an Indian citizen. There is no automatic loss of Indian citizenship on acquisition of a foreign passport. The central government is required to adjudicate the issue before taking any steps in this regard. The question of 'acquisition of foreign citizenship by an Indian citizen' is a question of fact requiring careful scrutiny of evidence.

Section 9 of the Citizenship Act is a complete code as regards the termination of Indian citizenship.[114] This provision only applies to Indian citizens and not to foreigners.

Acquisition of Foreign Citizenship

The question as to whether, when or how an Indian citizen has acquired foreign citizenship is to be determined by the relevant authority in the prescribed manner, with due regard to the prescribed rules of evidence.[115] The only authority permitted to make a determination on such issues is the central government.[116]

113 S. 9 of the Citizenship Act. The provisions of Section 9 (1) of the Citizenship Act are prospective in nature. This part of the Citizenship Act further manifests the intention of the legislature to discourage, as far as possible, dual nationality or double allegiance. The genesis of section 9 of the Citizenship Act is traceable to the UK Naturalisation Act, 1870. It is noteworthy that provisions similar to Section 9 of the Citizenship Act can be found in the citizenship laws of many other nations, such as Canada, Australia, to name a few. *See* T.A. Mahomed Usman v. State of Madras, AIR 1961 Madras 29.

114 Bhagwati Prasad Dixit v. Rajeev Gandhi, AIR 1986 SC 1534.

115 S. 9 (2) of the Citizenship Act & R. 40 of the Citizenship Rules.

116 The policy underlying Section 9 of the Citizenship Act appears to be that the 'right of citizenship' of an Indian citizen should not be exposed to attack in all forums in the country, but should be decided by one authority in accordance with the prescribed rules and that every other court or authority would have to act only on the basis of such decision. Prabhat Vikram Sah v. The State of Bihar, MANU/BH/0064/2010 (18.01.2010, Patna High Court). Any action by the state government in this regard without obtaining the decision of the

Even a court does not have jurisdiction to entertain and decide such issues.[117]

In this context, the central government may be considered akin to a special body empowered by law to determine whether, when or how a person has acquired citizenship of another country.[118]

Till the status of citizenship is determined by the central government, the person will not cease to be considered an Indian citizen. In other words, a person found to be a citizen of India cannot be treated as a foreigner as long as the central government does not record a decision to that effect.[119] It is the order passed by the central government which operates as cession of the citizenship of a person and not his acquisition of the passport of a foreign country.[120]

---

central government would be unauthorised and unjustified. Hasan Khan v. State AIR 1961 Raj 182. *See also* Bhagwati Prasad Dixit v. Rajeev Gandhi, AIR 1986 SC 1534. The only question, however, which the civil court is prevented from determining (under Section 9 (2) of the Citizenship Act) is whether an Indian citizen has acquired citizenship of another country or when or how he acquired it. Civil courts are not prevented by this provision from determining other questions concerning the nationality of a person. Hence, in case a suit filed before a civil court raises various issues pertaining to the nationality of a person, including the issues to be determined by the central government under Section 9 (2) of the Citizenship Act, then in such case, the proper course should be to stay the suit until the central government takes a decision on the issues within its jurisdiction and then to dispose of the rest of the suit once the central government has made its determination, on the basis of such determination. Akbar Khan Alam Khan v. Union of India, AIR 1962 SC 70.

117 Saeeda Mohammad Kayum v. State of Rajasthan, AIR 2006 Raj 284. *See also* State of U.P. v. Shah Mohammad (1969) 3 SCR 1006; State of U.P. v. Mohammad Din AIR 1984 SC1714. It is not possible for the High Court, in a writ petition, to express views on such matters. Migration or adoption of nationality of another country are questions of facts which, to a certain extent, also relate to the intention of the party concerned. *See* Nasir Ahmed v. The Chief Commissioner, Delhi, AIR 1959 PH 261.

118 Hasan Khan v. State, AIR 1961 Raj 182.

119 S. Nalini Srikaran v. Union of India, Writ Appeal No. 1599/2006 (07.03.2007, Madras High Court).

120 Nalini Srikaran v. Union of India, Writ Appeal No. 1599/2006 (07.03.2007, Madras High Court).

Where the person concerned is a foreigner, there is no obligation for the central government to conduct an enquiry and/or a determination in the manner prescribed under Section 9 of the Citizenship Act. The case of a foreigner is required to be dealt with in terms of the appropriate foreigner laws (discussed in the next chapter).[121]

The Representation of the People Act

No other court or authority (except the central government) has the power to decide the question as to whether, when or how an Indian citizen has acquired the citizenship of another country. Even where the question of whether a person is qualified to be chosen as a member of the Lok Sabha arises in an election petition filed under the provisions of the Representation of the People Act, 1951, the High Court cannot proceed to decide the question of loss of citizenship of the candidate concerned. It cannot be held that the Citizenship Act, 1955 should yield in favour of the Representation of the People Act, 1951 only because the latter Act is enacted pursuant to Article 327 of the Constitution. When the matter falls within Section 9 (2) of the Citizenship Act, 1955 all other provisions of law are excluded.[122]

The Rules of Procedure

The central government, while making the above determination, shall have due regard to the rules of procedure specified under Schedule III of the Citizenship Rules, which are summarised below:[123]

---

121 *See* Syed Safiullah Qadri v. State of Andhra Pradesh, W.P. No. 11922/1996 (04.09.1996, Andhra Pradesh High Court).

122 Bhagwati Prasad Dixit v. Rajiv Gandhi, Civil Appeal No. 3003 (NCE)/1985 (25.04.1986, Supreme Court of India).

123 Schedule III of the (extant) Citizenship Rules, 2009 is identical to Schedule III of the (erstwhile) Citizenship Rules, 1956. Most of the judgments discussed in this section are in the context of Schedule III of the Citizenship Rules, 1956 but would

a) Burden of Proof: The burden of proof lies on the concerned person to show that he has not 'voluntarily acquired' foreign citizenship. Put differently, when it appears to the central government that an Indian citizen has acquired foreign citizenship, it can cast the burden of proof upon him to prove otherwise.[124] Such person shall have an opportunity to show that he had not voluntarily acquired foreign citizenship.[125]

b) Reference to Embassy or Government: For the purpose of determining the issue of acquisition of foreign citizenship by an Indian citizen, the central government may make a reference to the embassy or government of such foreign country and act upon the information or report received in connection with such reference.[126] The central government should arrive at a considered decision that the concerned Indian citizen has voluntarily acquired foreign citizenship before any action can be taken against him on the footing that his citizenship is terminated.[127]

---

be equally applicable to the Citizenship Rules, 2009. The expression 'shall have due regard to the rules of evidence' appearing in the statute indicates that the rules of evidence contained therein are not mandatory and the concerned authority, though it normally would take them into account, is not strictly bound to do so. *See generally* T.A. Mahomed Usman v. State of Madras, AIR 1961 Madras 29.

124 Abubacker *infra*

125 Abubacker v. Union of India, 2000 (2) ILR 732 (Kerala). If a plea is raised by the Indian citizen that he had not voluntarily obtained passport of another country, then he must be afforded an opportunity to prove that fact. Salim Khan v. Union of India, O.J.C. No. 17236/1998 (24.06.1999, Orrisa High Court).

126 The question whether an Indian citizen has or has not acquired citizenship of another country is a matter dependent upon the municipal law of that other country. If the authorities of that country, who are vested with the power to decide whether a person has or has not acquired the country's citizenship, hold that he has so acquired it under the relevant law and have so declared in a formal document and clothed him with the protection which that government offers to its nationals, then in such case it may not be necessary for the Indian authorities to embark upon an enquiry as to whether the procedural or other requirements of the concerned foreign law have or have not been satisfied. *See generally* T.A. Mahomed Usman *supra*

127 Abubacker v. Union of India, 2000 (2) ILR 732 (Kerala).

c) Presumption on Procurement of a Foreign Passport: The act of obtaining a foreign passport shall be considered as conclusive proof of an Indian citizen having voluntarily acquired foreign citizenship.[128]

d) Consideration(s) for determining voluntary acquisition of foreign citizenship: While determining the issue of 'voluntary acquisition of foreign citizenship' by an Indian citizen, the following aspects may be taken into account by the central government: (i) whether the Indian citizen has migrated to the foreign country with the intention of making it his permanent home; (ii) whether the Indian citizen has taken up permanent residence in that country; (iii) any other relevant circumstances.[129]

e) Deemed acquisition of foreign citizenship: An Indian citizen who leaves India without a proper legal document and resides abroad for a period exceeding 3 (three) years shall be deemed to have voluntarily acquired citizenship of the country of his residence.

f) Special Provisions for Pakistan: An Indian citizen shall be deemed to have voluntarily acquired citizenship of Pakistan

---

128 The expression 'obtained a passport' appearing in Rule 3 of Schedule III does not include the physical or mechanical act of receiving a passport by a person but postulates the securing of a passport willfully and consciously, knowing full well the consequences of the same. *See* S. Mosin Shah v. Union Govt. of India, AIR 1974 J&K 48. Incidents like making of an unconditional representation/application by an Indian citizen to a foreign state for grant of a passport and obtaining a visa under any category typically issued to a national of the said foreign state would be indicative of 'obtaining a passport' under this provision. *See generally* State v. Sharifbhai Jamalbhai, AIR 1959 Bom 192. If a person enters India on the basis and strength of a foreign passport, then this raises a presumption against him that he has acquired citizenship of that foreign country. Such a presumption is rebuttable. The burden of proof in that event shifts on the person to explain that the declaration contained in the passport (that he is a national of the foreign country) is not true. *See* Bhaktiarkhan v. Union of India, AIR 1961 Guj 109.

129 If the document under examination indisputably shows on its face that the concerned person had acquired foreign nationality, then in such case no further enquiry may be necessary in this regard. *See* T.A. Mahomed Usman v. State of Madras, AIR 1961 Mad 29.

in the following situations: (i) if he has migrated to Pakistan with the intention of making it his permanent home; (ii) if he has obtained any certificate of domicile of Pakistan, or declared himself to be a Pakistani citizen or a domicile of Pakistan; (iii) if he has obtained evacuee property in Pakistan;[130] (iv) if he has obtained a temporary permit into India from Pakistan.

Principles of Natural Justice

The power of determination of citizenship (of the central government) is a quasi-judicial power and each case must be considered in accordance with the principles of natural justice.[131] An inquiry should normally be conducted by the central government before making a determination.[132] Whether or not a personal hearing should be given, would depend upon the facts and circumstances of each case.[133]

130 This refers to the person acquiring an evacuee or abandoned property in Pakistan, under any law of Pakistan after 14.08.1947, by a process other than purchase or exchange. *See generally* Administration of Evacuee Property Act, 1950.

131 K. Mohammed Ahmed v. State of Kerala, 1983 KLT 1009. The principles of natural justice have twin ingredients. Firstly, the person likely to be adversely effected by the action of the authorities should be given notice to show cause or granted reasonable opportunity of being heard in consonance with the maxim *audi alteram partem*. Secondly, the order so passed by the authorities should give reasons for arriving at any conclusion showing proper application of mind. Violation of either of these principles normally would render an order, particularly quasi-judicial in nature, invalid. Violation of principles of natural justice is violation of basic rule of law and would invite judicial chasticism. However, this rule is not without exceptions. Of course, the exception to such a rule are rare. Where the legislative scheme of provisions of a statute suggest that intent of the legislature is to take emergent action, in that event and subject to fulfillment of ingredients of the provisions, an order could be passed without affording pre-decisional hearing and an expeditious post-decisional hearing may amount to substantial compliance with the basic rule of law. *See generally* International Cargo Services v. Union of India, 2006 (193) ELT 546 (Del).

132 *See* K. Mohammed Ahmed, *supra*

133 S. Mosin Shah v. Union Govt. of India, AIR 1974 J&K 48. *See also* Mohammad Abdul Moyeed v. Union of India W.P. (C) No. 10587/2016 (20.07.2018, Delhi High Court) which suggests that even if a statute does not provide for a personal hearing, the said right may be read into the statute.

If a plea is raised by a citizen that the obtaining of the foreign passport by him was not voluntary, the central government should consider the desirability of giving him a personal hearing and afford him a reasonable opportunity of proving the fact by adducing evidence.[134]

Inquiry on Complaint

The issue as to whether an Indian citizen has acquired foreign citizenship can be taken up by the government even on the basis of a complaint made to it by a third party. However, not every complaint needs to be investigated. The complaint should be worthy of investigation i.e. it must have some substance and be based on documents that are *prima facie* reliable. When the documents which form the basis of the complaint are of inherently doubtful validity, the central government would not be obligated to act upon such complaint.[135]

Automatic Cessation of Indian Citizenship

A question arises as to whether possession of a foreign passport by an Indian citizen should operate as an automatic cessation of his Indian citizenship and result in a deportation order straightaway. This question was answered in the negative by the Supreme Court in **Government of A.P. v. Mohd. Khan.**[136] The Supreme Court held as follows: (i) Any action proposed against an Indian citizen on the contention that he has acquired a foreign passport or voluntarily acquired foreign citizenship must be preceded by a determination by the central government; (ii) The central government shall make a determination as per applicable rules, including the provisions of Schedule

---

134 S. Mohsfii Shah, *infra*

135 Padam Prasad Sharma v. Union of India, W.P. (C) No. 8077/2009 (15.03.2011, Delhi High Court).

136 AIR 1962 SC1778.

III of the Citizenship Rules; (iii) The determination by the central government about the status of the person shall form the basis on which any further action (including deportation) can be taken against him. Simply put, a determination by the central government is a must (where there exists a dispute as to citizenship) before an order of deportation can be passed against the concerned person.[137]

The mere fact that a passport is given to a person who is an Indian national, whether the passport is legal evidence or not, cannot lead to any irresistible inference that the said person had voluntarily acquired the citizenship of a foreign state, for such a passport could also be issued to a citizen by birth or descent.[138]

Voluntary Acquisition of Foreign Citizenship

As noted above, the central government must arrive at a decision that an Indian citizen has 'voluntarily acquired' foreign citizenship before action can be taken against him resulting in his citizenship being terminated.[139] The objective behind the conduct of a proper determination by the central government is that there should exist a 'satisfaction' that the acquisition of foreign citizenship by the Indian citizen is a voluntary act. The expression 'voluntary' used in Section 9 (1) of the Citizenship Act would mean an act done without compulsion, with explicit consent or volition of the individual.[140]

Generally speaking, there should exist some evidence to show that the concerned Indian citizen, on his own volition,

---

137 *See* Nazir Ahmedkhan v. The Superintendent of Police and Registration Officer 1989 CriLJ 2044; Mumtaz Parveen v. State, (Crl.) Revision Petition No. 367/2006 (28.01.2013, Delhi High Court).

138 Inder Lall v. Lal Singh, AIR 1961 Raj 122; S. Mohsfii Shah v. The Union Govt. of India, W.P. No. 31/1971 (31.10.1973, Jammu & Kashmir High Court).

139 Salim Khan v. Union of India, *supra*

140 *See generally* T.A. Mahomed Usman v. State of Madras, AIR 1961 Madras 29.

acquired foreign citizenship.[141] Mere issuance of a foreign passport by a foreign country should not, by itself, result in termination of Indian citizenship.[142] There can be a situation where a person is compelled or forced to obtain citizenship or a passport of a foreign country[143], or that he alleges force, fear, undue influence, fraud etc. on this issue.[144] It is pertinent that such issues are examined in detail by the authorities before deciding whether the person has acquired foreign citizenship voluntarily or not.[145]

Judicial Review

Ordinarily a court will not sit in judgment over the decision taken by the central government (under Section 9 of the Citizenship Act), unless there is clear evidence that such decision was made *mala fide* or in violation of principles of natural justice.[146]

---

141 The constitutional validity of Section 9 (2) of the Citizenship Act and Schedule III of the Citizenship Rules, 1956 (akin to Schedule III of the extant Citizenship Rules, 2009) has been upheld by the Supreme Court in Izhar Ahmed v. Union of India, AIR 1962 SC 1052. *See also* S. Nalini Srikaran v. Union of India, Writ Appeal No. 1599/2006 (07.03.2007, Madras High Court).

142 Mahammad Nazaharul Haque v. B. Bagchi, A.F.O.O No. 479/2961 (29.11.1972, Calcutta High Court). *See also* Izhar Ahmed v. Union of India, AIR 1962 SC 1052 & State of A.P. v. Abdulkhader, AIR 1961 SC 1467 which suggest that merely obtaining foreign passport does not result in automatic cessation of Indian citizenship. A determination by the central government is important.

143 *See for example* Luingam Luithui v. Union of India, W.P. (C) No. 1546/2014 (23.08.2017, Delhi High Court) where the concerned persons were compelled to obtain Canadian passports when the Indian authorities refused to issue passports to them and further refused to allow them entry into India, despite follow ups.

144 *See* Abubacker v. Union of India, 2000 (2) ILR 732 (Ker) where the Kerala High Court took note of the fact that the applicant, post obtaining a foreign passport, visited India on several occasions on the said passport. Such conduct, in the view of the court, leaned towards 'voluntary acquisition of a foreign passport'. *See also* S. Mosin Shah v. Union Govt. of India, AIR 1974 J&K 48.

145 Mohd. Ayub Khan v. Commissioner of Police, AIR 1965 SC 1623.

146 Abubacker v. Union of India, 2000 (2) ILR 732 (Kerala). It may be open to the person against whom an order is made under Section 9 of the Citizenship Act to seek its quashing in certain circumstances under Article 226 of the Constitution

Courts have emphasised that a determination of citizenship by the central government under Section 9 of the Citizenship Act, being a quasi-judicial proceeding,[147] should be made by giving a notice as well as providing a reasonable opportunity of hearing to the proceedee.[148]

DEPRIVATION OF CITIZENSHIP

Another mode of cessation of citizenship is by 'deprivation'. Under Indian law, 'deprivation' is essentially in the nature of a punishment inflicted by the central government. The concept of 'deprivation' has limited applicability, in the sense that, only naturalised or registered citizens can, subject to satisfaction of the below mentioned conditions, be deprived of their Indian citizenship. A citizen by birth is impervious to 'deprivation'.

Globally, the rationale is that only in cases of grave misdemeanour should a citizen be subjected to the punishment of deprivation, since this could result in statelessness. In countries like Canada and United States of America, a rigorous procedure is prescribed before depriving a person of citizenship. Indian law also provides for a detailed procedure for deprivation of citizenship.

Conditions for Deprivation

Indian Citizenship obtained by the process of naturalisation or registration can be taken away by the central government on the happening of any of the below mentioned 'general

---

and a remand of the matter to the central government, however, it is not open to any third party (i.e. one other than that person) to impugn the order. Brijlal Zumbarlal Sarda v. Amrulla Asadulla Irani, W.P. No. 2788/1986 (11.09.1986, Bombay High Court).

147 *See* Mohd. Ilyas v. Union of India, 1970 (3) SCC 61.

148 Union of India v. Chand Putli, Second Appeal No. 2575/1968 (12.10.1972, Allahabad High Court).

conditions' coupled with the satisfaction of the government that the continuation of citizenship is not conducive to 'public interest'.[149]

General Conditions

a) The registration or certificate of naturalisation was obtained by means of fraud, false representation or concealment of material facts.
b) The citizen has shown himself by act or speech to be disloyal or disaffected towards the Indian Constitution.
c) The citizen has, during any war in which India may be engaged in, unlawfully traded or communicated with the enemy, or has engaged or associated with the enemy in such manner so as to assist it in the war.
d) The citizen has, within 5 (five) years post registration or naturalisation, been sentenced in any country to imprisonment for a term of at least 2 (two) years.
e) The citizen has been ordinarily residing outside India for a continuous period of 7 (seven) years and during such period has: (i) not been a student of any educational institution situated outside India; (ii) not been in the service of a government in India or of an international organisation of which India is a member; or (iii) not registered annually with an Indian consulate his intention to retain Indian citizenship.

Deprivation of Citizenship: The Public Interest Element

The 'public interest' element, as explained above, is the most important element when it comes to the issue of deprivation of citizenship. Despite the existence of any of the situations mentioned above, a person's Indian citizenship shall not be

149 S. 10 (2) of the Citizenship Act. *See also* Subramanian Swamy v. Union of India, W.P. (C) No. 7529/2001 (21.04.2005, Delhi High Court).

taken away unless the central government is satisfied that it is not conducive to public good that such person should continue to be a citizen of India.[150]

Meaning of Public Interest

The expression 'public interest' may be described as something in which the public, the community at large, has some pecuniary interest, or some interest by which their legal rights or liabilities are affected. It does not mean anything so narrow as mere curiosity, or as the interests of the particular localities, which may be affected by the matters in question. The 'interest' should be such which is shared by citizens generally in affairs of local, state or national government. The expression 'public interest' has multidimensional facets having ramifications over the social, economical interests etc. of the nation as a whole.[151]

In **Ramesh Chennamaneni v. Union of India**[152] a question which arose before the court was whether making of false statements or representations would amount to breach of 'public interest'. The court examined the legal position in the United Kingdom (since the Citizenship Act is largely based on the British Act, 1948) and observed as follows:

a) In the United Kingdom, for deprivation of citizenship, in case the competent authority arrives at a conclusion that the person obtained citizenship by fraud, false representation or concealment of material facts, then as a next step, the following twin aspects need to be satisfied before deprivation can be ordered: (i) the continuation of citizenship is considered to

150 Ramesh Chennamaneni v. Union of India, 2019 (5) ALD 118.

151 Craig Maxwell Sterry v. Ministry of Home Affairs, Union of India, W.P. No. 513/2009 (11.09.2009, Bombay High Court at Goa).

152 2019 (5) ALD 118.

be non-conducive to public interest; and (ii) the authority should be satisfied that the deprivation would not make the person 'stateless'.

b) In the United Kingdom, any misdemeanour would not qualify the 'public interest' requirement. This would be attracted in case the concerned citizen is found to be involved in activities of terrorism, espionage, serious organised crime, war crime or unacceptable behaviour.
c) Therefore, a mere false statement or representation on the part of the citizen would not make his citizenship detrimental to public interest.
d) Taking a cue from United Kingdom law, the court observed that though the Citizenship Act is silent on the aspect of 'statelessness', however, this aspect should also be taken into account while determining the 'public interest' element in the matter.

Deprivation of Citizenship: The Procedure

This section summarises the procedure required to be followed by the central government while deciding an issue of 'deprivation of citizenship'.

<u>The Committee of Inquiry</u>

In some specific situations, law provides for constitution of a committee of inquiry (**Committee**) for determining the factual aspects of the matter. No order for deprivation of citizenship should be passed by the government without giving the concerned person an advance written notice (in the prescribed form and manner)[153] and giving the person an opportunity to have his case referred to a Committee if he has been ordinarily resident outside India for a period of 7 (seven) years and his case falls under serial no. (e) of the 'General Conditions' (above)

153 *See* R. 25 of the Citizenship Rules.

(i.e. The citizen has been ordinarily residing outside India for a continuous period of 7 (seven) years and during such period has: (i) not been a student of any educational institution situated outside India; (ii) not been in the service of a government in India or of an international organisation of which India is a member; or (iii) not registered annually with an Indian consulate his intention to retain Indian citizenship.[154]

The Procedure

Once the Committee is appointed, the government need not undertake an inquiry on its own. The Committee shall undertake the inquiry and aid the government in arriving at a decision.[155]

The Citizenship Rules prescribe the mode and manner in which an inquiry is required to be held and conducted by the Committee. Generally speaking, the Committee is permitted to evolve its own procedure for the purpose of conducting an inquiry. However, the below mentioned aspects are to be kept in mind by the Committee while making the inquiry:[156]

a) Before holding the inquiry, the Committee shall cause an advance notice to be given to the person stating the time, place and nature of the inquiry. The person shall be given an opportunity to be represented by an advocate.
b) The notice shall be given at the address of the person personally or by post, at least 30 (thirty) days ahead of the date of inquiry.
c) The notice may require the person to answer it in writing or to furnish any information which the Committee considers material for the purpose of the inquiry.
d) For the purpose of the inquiry, the Committee shall have the

154 *See* R. 26 & 28 of the Citizenship Rules.

155 Ramesh Chennamaneni v. Union of India, 2019 (5) ALD 118.

156 Schedule II of the Citizenship Rules.

powers of a civil court in respect of the following matters: (i) summoning and enforcing the attendance of any person and examining him on oath; (ii) discovery and production of any document; (iii) receiving evidence on affidavit; and (iv) issuing a commission for the examination of witnesses or documents.

e) The Committee is empowered to act on available information regardless of whether such information qualifies to be 'admissible' in a court of law or not.
f) The Committee is permitted to require a participation/ representation from a ministry (which appears to it to be an interested party in the matter).
g) The quorum of the Committee shall be 2 (two) members.

The Report of the Committee

Upon conclusion of the enquiry, a report shall be made and submitted by the Committee to the central government. The central government is to be guided by the report, but is not bound by the report. Further, when the report is adverse to the citizen (and the acceptance of the report can have the effect of deprivation of citizenship) then in such case, the citizen should be put to notice and be given an opportunity to explain his position to the central government before a final decision is taken in the matter.[157]

Effect of a Deprivation Order

Every order of deprivation of citizenship shall be published in the Official Gazette.[158] Upon an order of deprivation of citizenship, the certificate of registration or naturalisation of the Indian citizen shall be delivered to and cancelled by the government.[159]

157 Ramesh Chennamaneni v. Union of India, 2019 (5) ALD 118.

158 R. 27 of the Citizenship Rules.

159 R. 28 of the Citizenship Rules.

The collector does not have the power to cancel citizenship in such matters.[160]

Principles of Natural Justice

A pre-decisional hearing or a highly reasoned order may not be mandatory where an order of cancellation/deprivation of citizenship is being made 'in the interests of the general public' and is based upon adverse remarks from the security agencies.[161]

THE APPELLATE MECHANISM

This section describes the appellate mechanism available to an Indian citizen in the event of an order of cessation of his citizenship. This includes 'revision' and 'review' of orders.

Revision

A person aggrieved by an order passed by any authority (other than the central government) under the Citizenship Act may, within a period of 30 (thirty) days from the date of the order, assail the same before the central government by making an application for revision. Delay in proferring the application beyond the above said period of 30 (thirty) days may be condoned by the central government in case sufficient cause for delay is shown by the aggrieved person. The central government shall make a decision post examination of the application of the aggrieved and of the report thereon which the concerned authority (which passed the order) may submit. The decision of the central government shall be final but shall be subject to a review (discussed below).[162]

160 Ghaurul Hasan v. The State of Rajasthan, AIR 1967 SC 107.

161 Satish Nambiar v. Union of India, 2007 (5) Bom. C.R. 247.

162 S. 15 of the Citizenship Act.

Review

The central government has the power to review its order(s). A person aggrieved by an order of the central government may, within a period of 30 (thirty) days from the date of the order, seek a review of the said order. Delay in preferring the application beyond the above said period of 30 (thirty) days may be condoned by the central government in case sufficient cause for delay is shown by the aggrieved person.[163]

The power of review under the Citizenship Act is wider than what is usually understood by the term 'review' in legal parlance.[164] For instance, under this mechanism, the central government is permitted to modify its previous order even on a fresh evaluation of the material before it.[165]

NATIONAL IDENTITY CARD

The Citizenship Act provides the basis for establishment of a National Register of Citizens. (**NRC**). Under the Citizenship Act, the central government is empowered to compulsorily register every Indian citizen and issue a national identity card to him. The Citizenship Act also postulates the establishment of a National Registration Authority for the said purpose and appoints the Registrar General under the Registration of Births and Deaths Act, 1969 as the National Registration Authority and the Registrar General of Citizen Registration.[166]

---

163 S. 15A of the Citizenship Act.

164 This power of review is not subject to any limitations as such (note that the powers of review under various other statutes like the Civil Procedure Code, 1908, the Consumer Protection Act, 1986 etc. are circumscribed to specific conditions).

165 Satish Nambiar v. Union of India, *supra*

166 S. 14A of the Citizenship Act.

The Citizenship (Registration of Citizens and Issue of National Identity Cards) Rules, 2003

The Citizenship (Registration of Citizens and Issue of National Identity Cards) Rules, 2003 (**NIC Rules**) were promulgated in aid to the NRC. Section 14A and the NIC Rules (which collectively form the basis of the NRC) are discussed in more detail in the subsequent chapters.

PROOF OF INDIAN CITIZENSHIP

Typically, under Indian law, proof of citizenship (by birth) is relatable to the following 3 (three) aspects: (i) Date of birth; (ii) Place of birth; (iii) citizenship status of parents. For persons born before 2003, documents establishing points (i) and (ii) above will suffice. For persons born 2003 onwards, point (iii) will also have to be examined.

At present, there appears to be little or no clarity on the vexing issue of which documents would qualify to be adequate proof of Indian citizenship.[167] This issue has been deliberated by courts in the past and the following documents have been held to be 'insufficient' to prove Indian citizenship:

a) <u>Certificate of Gram Panchayat:</u> A certificate issued by the Gram Panchayat Secretary not to be adequate proof of Citizenship.[168]
b) <u>Voters List:</u> Long stay in India and enrolment in the voters' list would not, by itself, confer any right on an alien to continue to stay in the country.[169]

---

167 Recently, the centre has prepared a 60 (sixty) point action plan which focuses on leveraging IT and technology for governance, improving business climate and upgrading the civil services. The said action plan also contemplates linking birth certificates to citizenship. The said action plan document, while conceding that at present, there exists no proof of citizenship in India, contemplates linking birth certificates through technology.

168 *See* Rupjan Begum v. Union of India, (2018) 1 SCC 579.

169 *See* Bhanwaroo Khan v. Union of India, (2002) 4 SCC 346. *But see* Lal Babu Hussain v. Electoral Registration Officer, (1995) 3 SCC 100.

c) Voter ID: Voter ID is not sufficient and conclusive evidence of citizenship.[170]

d) Permanent Account Number: Permanent Account Number (PAN) is a ten-digit alphanumeric identifier, issued by Income Tax Department. Each assessee (e.g. individual, firm, company etc.) is issued a unique PAN. All taxpayers must have a PAN. PAN can also be issued to foreigners. Possession of a PAN would not confer citizenship.[171]

e) Aadhaar Card: Aadhaar Card is not proof of citizenship.[172]

f) Bank Account: Under Indian law, citizenship is not a criterion for opening a bank account in India. Consequently, possession of a bank account may not serve as adequate proof of citizenship.

g) Revenue and Title records: Records relating to ownership or title of property, once again, may not qualify to be adequate proof of Indian citizenship.

---

170 Enrolment in a voter roll is based on the applicant filing a declaration with authority via Form 6 under Rules 13(1) and 26 of Registration of Electors Rules, 1960, stating that they are a citizen of India. The legal status of the applicant's citizenship precedes her enrolment on the electoral rolls. If such a declaration of Citizenship is found to be false, the applicant is liable for punishment. *See* Vijoy Kumar Chaudhary v. The State Election Commissioner, LPA No. 510 of 2008 (11.04.2008, Patna High Court).

171 *See generally* Kiran Gupta v. The State Election Commission, 2020 (6) BLJ 539.

172 S. 9 of The Aadhaar (Targeted Delivery OF Financial and other Subsidies, Benefits and Services) Act, 2016 states that an Aadhaar number shall not, by itself, confer any right of, or be proof of, citizenship or domicile in respect of an Aadhaar number holder.

CHAPTER 3

Laws Relating to Foreigners

INTRODUCTION

The previous chapter explains in detail the provisions of the Citizenship Act which is the primary legislation governing citizenship in India. This chapter deals with the laws which deal with and regulate various aspects relating to the entry, stay and exit of foreigners in India. For the sake of convenience this chapter is divided into 2 (two) sections: (i) (Indian) Foreigners Laws; (ii) (Indian) Registration of Foreigners Laws.

There exists yet another critical element of Indian Citizenship and Immigration Law regime i.e. Passport Law, which is discussed in detail in the succeeding chapter.

THE (INDIAN) FOREIGNERS LAWS

Every country has two kinds of people citizens and aliens/ foreigners. A foreigner may be described as a person who is not a citizen of India. Entry of foreigners into India is regulated by the central government. The power of the central government in India to expel foreigners is absolute, unlimited and unfettered.[1] Law relating to detection and deportation of foreigners is essentially covered by the following enactments: (i) The

1 Hans Muller of Nurenburg v. Superintendent, Presidency Jail, Calcutta AIR 1955 SC 367; Louis De Raedt v. Union of India (1991) 3 SCC 554.

Foreigners Act, 1946; (ii) The Foreigners Order, 1964; and (iii) The Foreigners Order, 1948.

THE FOREIGNERS ACT

The Foreigners Act, 1946 (**Foreigners Act**), a pre-independence legislation, was enacted with a view to regulate the entry and exit of foreigners in the then British India. Under the said statute, the central government has been granted various powers in respect of entry of foreigners in India, their presence therein and their departure therefrom.[2]

As already mentioned, the Foreigners Act, 1946 regulates the movement of foreigners in India.[3] For the purpose of this law, every person who is not an Indian citizen is considered to be a foreigner.[4] Thus, the provisions of the Foreigners Act, 1946 are inapplicable to citizens of India.[5]

Under the Foreigners Act, the power to deal with foreigners (including the decision to remove a foreigner from India) vests in the central government.[6] The central government is empowered to make orders for matters of detention and deportation of foreigners who violate any provisions of applicable law.[7] Pending a deportation, further orders can be passed by the

2 Post-Independence, this law was made applicable to India. *See* Muslem Mondal v. State of Assam, 2013 (1) GLT 809.

3 *See generally* The State v. G. Karunairaj, Writ Appeal No. 651/2012 (26.11.2013, Madras High Court).

4 S. 2 (a) of the Foreigners Act.

5 *See generally* Sasikumar v. State of Tamil Nadu, W.P. (MD) No. 10080/2008 (25.08.2011, Madras High Court, Madurai Bench).

6 Citizenship, naturalization and aliens; admission into, immigration and expulsion from India; passports and visas are subjects being entries in List-I, i.e. Union List under the 7th Schedule to the Constitution. Therefore, for all intent and purpose, it is the central government which is the authority to deal with illegal migrants and issues relating to them, such as detection and deportation. *See* State of Assam v. Jamait-E-Ulema-E-Hind, Review Pet. No. 5/2017 (13.07.2018, Guwahati High Court).

7 *See generally* Rajesh P. Mankad v. State of Gujarat, Civil Application No. 497 of 2010 (22.04.2011, Gujarat High Court).

government restricting the foreigner's movements or assigning him to a detention/special camp.[8] Some relevant provisions of the Foreigners Act are enumerated below.

Power of Central Government

The Foreigners Act empowers the central government to make orders (either specific or general) with respect to foreigners, in respect of their entry, presence and departure from India.[9]

8 Jeyachandran v. State of Tamil Nadu. H.C.P. No. 2460/2019 (04.06.2020, Madras High Court). An order of the government assigning a detenu to a detention centre or a special camp (pending his deportation) is not violative of law. *See* Momin v. State of Tamil Nadu, W.P. No. 1141/2019 (28.03.2019, Madras High Court). Such orders ought not to be construed as 'preventive detention' or 'absolute prohibition', even if definitive time periods of confinement are not given in the order. Kalavathy v. State of Tamil Nadu, 1995 (2) LW (Crl.) 690. Such orders are only to regulate the presence and movement of foreigners (detenus) under the Foreigners Act and hence should not be equated with 'preventive detention'. Such orders can be passed by the competent authority even without there being any specific case pending against a foreigner. If in the opinion of the government, based on information received through intelligence sources, the presence of a foreigner or the movement of a foreigner should be regulated, then an order under the Foreigners Act could be sustained. The intention of the foreigner to return to his native country is an irrelevant consideration while passing an order of detention. Such aspects may be taken into account by the competent authority while considering deportation. *See* Sasikala v. The State of Tamil Nadu, H.C.P. No. 157/2008 (30.04.2008, Madras High Court).

9 S. 3 of the Foreigners Act. This is a general power conferred on the central government to make provisions by way of orders. It is an enabling provision empowering the central government to make orders. Such orders can be made either generally or with respect to all foreigners or even with respect to any particular foreigner or any prescribed class or description of foreigner. Such orders can contain provisions prohibiting, regulating or restricting the entry of foreigners into India or their departure therefrom or their presence or continued presence therein. *See* Sree Latha v. Secretary to Government, Public Department, Government of Tamil Nadu, (2007) 2 MLJ (Crl.) 1320 where the scope of Sections 3 (1) & (2) of the Foreigners Act was discussed. What appears to have been intended is to confer power on the executive authority to prescribe and specify conditions for continuance of a foreigner in India. Extremely wide kind of or unlimited restrictions and prohibitions and regulations can be validly prescribed and specified. A foreigner can be dangerous to the security of India. A foreigner's presence may be undesirable for any reason and it appears to have been intended by the legislature to leave the whole matter of the foreigner's presence in India to the executive discretion of the government. Bawalkhan v. B.C. Shah, AIR 1960 Bom 27; Ananda Bhavanani and Ors. v. Union of India, 1991 LW (Crl.) 393 Mad.

These powers are plenary in nature and amongst other things, regulate the following aspects regarding the stay of foreigners in India:[10]

a) The time, route, specific point/place of entry and other conditions of entry, as may be prescribed.
b) The time, route, specific point/place of exit and other conditions of departure, as may be prescribed.
c) The places or areas of the foreigner's residence in India.
d) Restriction of movement of the foreigner.
e) Prohibition from associating with persons of specific description.
f) Prohibition from engaging in specific activities.
g) Prohibition from using or possessing specific articles.
h) Arrest, detention or confinement.

The central government has, through notification, authorised/ permitted the state governments of Andhra Pradesh, Assam, Bihar, Jammu and Kashmir, Kerala, Gujarat, Maharashtra, Madhya Pradesh, Madras, Mysore, Odisha, Punjab, Rajasthan,

---

10 S. 3 (2) of the Foreigners Act. The provisions of Section 3 (2) of the Foreigners Act require that the person concerned should qualify to be a 'foreigner' as on date of passing of an order by the competent authority under this provision. The date of his entry into India is not relevant. Abdul Aleem v. State of Andhra Pradesh, AIR 1963 AP 441. The government has, through notifications dated 19.04.1958 and 17.02.1976, entrusted several state governments (and specifically Superintendents of Police and Deputy Police Commissioners of the states), to make orders of the nature specified in Sections 3 (2) (a), (b), (c) and (cc), (e) and (f) of the Foreigners Act after obtaining an opinion from the Foreigners Tribunals by making reference under paragraph 2 (1) of the Foreigners (Tribunals) Order, 1964. These notifications are also applicable to the state of Assam. *See generally* State of Assam v. Jamait-E-Ulema-E-Hind 2018 (4) GLT 264; State of Madhya Pradesh v. Mumtaz Ali Faiz Ali, AIR 1959 MP 387. The power to issue such notifications is traceable to Article 258 of the Constitution. Passing of orders under these provisions by a wrong authority would be invalid. The Central Government issued S. R. O. 1072 and 1073 published in the Government of India Gazette dated 13.05.1955, authorising the state governments to exercise the functions of the central government in making orders of the nature specified in Section 3 (2) (c) of the Foreigners Act. Firoz Meharuddin v. Sub-Divisional Officer and Ors., AIR 1961 MP 110.

Uttar Pradesh, West Bengal and Nagaland to also exercise some of its powers under Sections 3 and 4 of the Foreigners Act.[11]

Arrest Detention & Deportation

The Foreigners Act was amended in the year 1962 pursuant to which powers were also conferred to arrest, detain and confine the foreigners who violate the applicable law. Under Indian law, every foreigner who enters India illegally or who enters India legally but whose stay subsequently becomes illegal, shall be arrested and detained; and deported to his home country.[12] A foreigner does not have a fundamental right to stay in India and/or get Indian citizenship.[13]

The power of the government to expel foreigners is absolute and unlimited; and there is no provision in the Constitution of

---

11 *See* Notification No. F1/45/63, dated 31.12.1964 which authorises/permits the above state governments to also exercise the functions of the central government under Section 3 (2) (g), 4 (1) & 4 (4) of the Foreigners Act, subject to the following conditions: (i) The functions so entrusted shall be exercised in respect of persons to whom Chapter II of the Foreigners (Internment) Order, 1962 applies; (ii) The state government(s) shall comply with any general or special directions issued by the central government from time to time; (iii) the central government may itself, also exercise any of the functions which have been entrusted above. The above notification is traceable to Article 258 of the Constitution which states that the President of India, with the consent of a state government, may entrust to it, either conditionally or unconditionally, functions in relation to any matter to which the executive powers of the union extends. *See generally* Sakeena v. State of Rajasthan, 1968 RLW Raj 143.

12 S. 2 (g) of the Foreigners Act. A foreigner proposed to be ousted from the country is entitled to know the reasons for his proposed expulsion and is also entitled to an opportunity to represent his case before the competent authority. However, in case of compelling reasons involving national security etc., the said procedure need not be followed by the government. Hasan Ali v. Union of India, Writ Petition (Criminal) No. 17/2006 (09.03.2006, Supreme Court of India); R.I. Jebaraj v. Union of India, W.P No. 25613/2008 (19.01.2009, Madras High Court). *But see* Dongh Lian Kham v. Union of India, WP (Crl.) No. 1884/2015 (21.12.2015, Delhi High Court) where the court interfered in the order of deportation issued against a refugee by the government, (citing danger to national security), and ordered re-examination of the matter, including an option to explore third party deportation for the refugee.

13 Thamarai v. Union of India and Ors., H.C.P. No. 1456/2020 & W.P. No. 11754/2021 (23.06.2021, Madras High Court).

India fettering this discretion. While the legal position on this aspect is not uniform in all countries but so far as Indian law is concerned, the executive government has unrestricted right to expel a foreigner.[14]

An appropriate court may, in exceptional circumstances, alter the time lines for deportation or grant extensions to the deportee. In **Rebecca Ann Malstead v. Union of India**,[15] the Madras High Court (exercising writ jurisdiction) extended the deportation date of certain foreigner minors in view of the fact that they were studying in school and a deportation in the middle of the academic year would result in a loss to them.

Detention Centres

Detention centres are set up to house illegal migrants or foreigners (illegally residing in India) prior to their imminent deportation. According to the Ministry of Home Affairs, Government of India, these holding camps are also 'to restrict the movement of foreigners staying back illegally and thereby ensure that they are physically available at all times for expeditious repatriation or deportation'.

The Ministry of Home Affairs has prepared 'Model Detention Centre/Holding Centre/Camp Manual', which was circulated to all States and Union Territories on 09.01.2019. This manual specifies the amenities to be provided in such detention centres/ holding centres/camps. The guidelines, *inter-alia*, provide that such centres should be designed to provide all necessary facilities for the inmates to maintain a standard of living in consonance with human dignity. It mandates provision of basic amenities like electricity, drinking water, hygiene, accommodation with beds, sufficient toilets with running water, communication facilities,

14 Hans Muller of Nurenburg v. Superintendent, Presidency Jail, Calcutta, AIR 1955 SC 367; Louis De Raedt v. Union of India, (1991) 3 SCC 554.

15 2017 (4) CTC 167.

provision for kitchen etc. It further requires special attention for women/nursing mothers, children etc., and educational facilities for children lodged in detention centres among other facilities. The model manual stipulates establishment of detention centres in every state in India. At present, various states in India have detention camps including Delhi, Assam, Karnataka, Goa, Maharashtra, Punjab and Rajasthan.

The government attaches high importance to providing timely consular access to foreign missions for their nationals detained in India. State governments are required to give immediate intimation of the arrest/detention of the foreigner in any part of the country to Ministry of External Affairs, Government of India, which in turn notifies the foreign embassy concerned. Likewise, upon request from any foreign mission for consular access to any of their nationals detained/imprisoned in India, Ministry of External Affairs notifies the relevant authorities who are required to provide consular access thus sought. The Ministry of Home Affairs, Government of India has, from time to time, issued advisories to the states and union territories on various aspects of prison administration, provision of legal aid and video conference facility to prisoners etc.

Determination of Foreigners' Nationality

The Foreigners Act provides guidance on the manner of determining the true/actual nationality of a foreigner. When a foreigner is recognised as a national of more than 1 (one) foreign country, then such person may be treated as a national of the country to which he appears to be most closely connected for the time being. In case a foreigner's nationality is uncertain, then he may be treated as a national of the country to which he was last connected.[16]

---

16 S. 8 of the Foreigners Act. Aspects such as 'mother tongue' and 'local dialect' may be of consideration in appropriate cases. *See* Indira Newar and Ors. v. Union of India, W.P. (C) Nos. 8490/2018 (29.11.2019, Guwahati High Court).

Burden of Proof

The Foreigners Act provides that in case any question arises as to whether a person is a foreigner or not, or is a foreigner of a particular class or description, then the onus of proving that such person is not a foreigner (or a foreigner of a particular class) lies upon the person himself.[17] To put it simply, a person in India, claiming to be an Indian citizen, is responsible for proving the same.[18] This is because all necessary facts and documents would be within his personal knowledge and hence would be in the best position for proving the same.[19]

The general rule of evidence is that when any fact is especially within the special knowledge of a person, then the burden of proving that fact lies on him.[20] It is therefore, the concerned person's obligation to provide enough evidence to establish that he is not a foreigner.[21] This position makes the proceedings before the Foreigners Tribunal a special one.[22] The

17 S. 9 of the Foreigners Act.

18 The provisions of Section 9 of the Foreigners Act is in accordance with the underlying policy of Section 106 of the Evidence Act, which provides that when any fact is especially within the knowledge of any person, the burden of proving that fact is upon him. *See generally* Moslem Mondal, *supra*

19 Even in the case of an an ex-parte proceeding before the Foreigners Tribunal the said position would not change as the burden of proving that the proceedee is not a foreigner continues to be upon the proceedee, which cannot shift, and when the proceedee does not adduce any evidence to discharge such burden, the tribunal has no alternative but to declare the proceedee to be a foreigner. *See* Muslim Mondal, *supra*

20 S. 106 of the Evidence Act.

21 Section 9 of the Foreigners Act starts with a non-obstante clause. A non-obstante clause is a legislative device which is usually employed to give overriding effect to certain provisions over some contrary provisions that may be found either in the same enactment or some other enactment, that is to say, to avoid the operation and effect of all contrary provisions. *See generally* Moslem Mondal, *supra*

22 The 'burden of proof' means the duty of a litigant to prove a disputed assertion or charge. The 'burden of proof' includes both 'burden of persuasion' and the 'burden of production'. The 'burden of persuasion' means the duty imposed on a person to convince the fact finder to view the facts in a way that favours that

said concept of 'burden of proof' contained in the Foreigners Act is also prevalent in the United Kingdom and as well as various other western countries. This concept of 'burden of proof' has attained the imprimatur of the Supreme Court of India in various decisions including the Sarbananda Sonowal judgements which have been discussed in greater detail later.[23]

Establishing Indian Citizenship

Ordinarily, for proving citizenship, evidence would be required of the following: (i) date of birth; (ii) place of birth; and (iii) citizenship status of parents.

The proceedee is entitled to bring out all facts which, either by themselves, or in combination with other facts, establish citizenship. Typically, the proceedee has a wide choice of evidence which can be used to prove citizenship.[24] All material facts specifically within the knowledge of the procedee having a bearing on his claim of citizenship should be disclosed at

---

person. The 'burden of production' is the duty imposed on the person to introduce enough evidence on an issue to have the issue decided in his favour. The party having the 'burden of proof' must introduce some evidence if he wishes to get a certain issue decided in his favour. The 'burden of proof', therefore, denotes the duty of establishing by a fair preponderance of the evidence the truth of the operative facts upon which the issue at hand is made to turn by substantive law. *See generally* Moslem Mondal, *supra*

23 *See also* State of Assam and Others v. Muslem Mondal and Others, 2013 (1) GLT 809; Union of India and Others v. Ghaus Mohammad, AIR 1961 SC 1526; Fateh Mohd. v. Delhi Administration, AIR 1963 SC 1035; Masud Khan v. State of Uttar Pradesh, (1974)3 SCC 469.

24 It is not necessary that all the above-mentioned aspects ought to be proved only by way of documents. A person may prove his citizenship through oral evidence (such as witnesses et cetera). Additionally, one may prove his citizenship without referring accurately to all the aspects mentioned above. For instance, if the date of birth or place of birth is not conclusively proved, but if it is conclusively proved that the father of the concerned person is an Indian citizen, then the claim of the proceedee (as to his Indian citizenship) would not normally be rejected. While revenue records, *per se*, do not evidence title, the same however can be used along with other documents to establish descendants or legacy from persons who have resided in Assam during the relevant time period. *See generally* Haider Ali v. Union of India, W.P (C) No. 1818/2019 (30.03.2021, Guwahati High Court).

the first instance (in his written statement[25]).[26] The Foreigners Tribunal is bound to consider all evidence brought out and decide its relevancy and admissibility. Normally, the process for examining every document/evidence is 2 (two) pronged. First, the relevance of the document is ascertained. Once the document is held to be relevant, then comes the issue of proving the document and its contents.[27]

When the citizenship status of a person is questioned by the government, it is incumbent upon such person to disclose material facts (in his pleadings) which are thereafter required to be proved by adducing cogent and reliable evidence. Failure to disclose such material at the first instance may result in drawing an adverse inference against the person.[28]

Long stay in the country and enrolment in the voters list would not confer any right to an alien to continue to stay in the country

25 The written statement of the proceedee is the foundation of his defence. Failure to disclose material particulars in the written statement will raise a serious question mark on the citizenship status of the proceedee. Ayesha Khatun v. Union of India, (2017) 3 CLR 820. The expression 'written statement' as used in the proceedings before the Foreigners Tribunal, is a misnomer, which is not to be confounded with 'written statement' as understood under the Code of Civil Procedure, 1908 (CPC). The principles contained in the CPC relating to the scope of written statement and limitations placed thereon cannot be strictly applied to proceedings before the Foreigners Tribunal, though the principles may generally be applied. *See* Haider Ali v. Union of India, W.P. (C) No. 1818/2019 (30.03.2021, Guwahati High Court).

26 Rashminara Begum v. Union of India, (2017) 4 CLR 282.

27 *See* Farida Khatun v. Union of India, W.P. (C) No. 1455/2020 (10.06.2020, Guwahati High Court). Even admission of a document in evidence does not amount to its proof, in other words, mere marking of exhibit of a document does not dispense with its proof, which is required to be done in accordance with law. It is the duty of the proceedee to prove the documents in accordance with law. Under the law of evidence also, it is necessary that contents of documents are required to be proved either by primary or by secondary evidence. At the most, admission of documents may amounts to admission of contents but not its truth. Khatoon Nessa v. Union of India, W.P. (C) No. 2098/2013 (30.08.2013, Guwahati High Court). *See also* LIC of India v. Ram Pal Singh Bisen, (2010) 4 SCC 491.

28 Chanda Paul v. Union of India, W.P. (C) No. 4634/2017 (12.01.2018, Guwahati High Court); Jehirul Islam v. Union of India, W.P. (C) No. 7347/2016 (16.05.2017, Guwahati High Court).

or make the alien eligible for grant of citizenship.[29] In fact, mere long stay, even if authorised by the concerned authorities, does not confer citizenship rights.[30] Persons who are not Indian citizens but have been living in India for a long time would continue to be governed by the provisions of the (Indian) Foreigners laws.[31]

Government Role in Proceedings

There has been some debate in the past as to the nature of role of the government in connection with proceedings regarding determination of citizenship.

Courts observe that while the burden of proof is on the concerned person, there still exits a basic responsibility of the government to proceed only against persons who are 'reasonably' suspected to be foreigners. This aspect has been elaborated by the Guwahati High Court in the case of **State of Assam v. Moslem Mondal**,[32] in the following manner:

a) The primary onus would be on the state and once the Foreigners Tribunal has satisfied itself about the existence of grounds to suspect a person to be a foreigner, then the burden of proof would be on the concerned person.
b) The grounds based on which a suspicion of a person's nationality is raised should be reasonable and relevant to the issue of being a foreigner. For instance, grounds such as 'this

29 *See* Bhanwaroo Khan v. Union of India, W.P. (C) No. 737/1995 (02.04.2002, Supreme Court of India).

30 *See* Shishuwala Pal v. Union of India, Misc. Petition No. 246/1984 (31.10.1988, Madhya Pradesh High Court). In the said matter, certain persons who were permitted to enter India as refugees and residing in India in such capacity staked claim to Indian citizenship. In this context the Madhya Pradesh High Court observed that even if any humanitarian considerations were involved, the same would be considered only by the central government which was the appropriate authority in this regard.

31 *See generally* Bawalkhan v. B.C. Shah, AIR 1960 Bom 27.

32 *supra*

person wears a particular dress or possesses a particular feature' may not qualify to be reasonable enough.

Prosecution under the Foreigners Act

No criminal proceedings can be instituted in courts against a person under the Foreigners Act without a determination of his 'citizenship status' by the central government.[33] In case the citizenship is suspect, then a determination should follow.[34]

Penalty for Contravention of the Foreigners Act

Contravention of any provision of the Foreigners Act is punishable with imprisonment for a term which may extend to 5 (five) years and shall also be liable to fine.[35]

THE FOREIGNERS TRIBUNAL ORDER, 1964

The Foreigners Act empowers the central government to make provisions, either generally or specifically for prohibiting or regulating the movements of foreigners in India, including placing conditions on their entry to or departure from India or their presence in India.[36] The Foreigners Act contains merely a skeleton of the policy. It is left to the central government to provide its sinews, by means of statutory orders.[37] This has been done through the Foreigners Order, 1948 and Foreigners Tribunal Order, 1964.

---

33 Barsa v. State of Rajasthan, 2011 Cri LJ 2503.

34 No prosecution against an Indian citizen can be made under the Foreigners Act without a prior determination of his 'foreigner status' (and consequent cancellation of Indian citizenship) by the central government. *See* Md. Elahi v. State of West Bengal, C.R.R No. 1354/2008 (12.11.2008, Calcutta High Court). *See also* State of U.P. v. Rehmatullah, 1971 Cri LJ 1103.

35 S. 13 & 14 of the Foreigners Act.

36 S. 3 of the Foreigners Act.

37 Tudor Gunasekhar Jayavardene v. The Government of India, W.P. No. 2538/1981 (10.07.1981, Madras High Court).

The Foreigners Tribunal Order, 1964 (**Foreigners Tribunal Order**) has been enacted in furtherance of the Foreigners Act, for the purpose of making a determination, as to the 'nationality status' of a 'perceived' foreigner. The salient features of the Foreigners Tribunals Order are described below.

Constitution of Foreigners Tribunal

The Foreigners Tribunal Order provides for constitution of Foreigners Tribunal(s) for determining the 'citizenship status' of persons who are proceeded against under the provisions of Foreigners Act. The Foreigners Tribunals have been constituted by the central government for the purpose of exercising its powers under the Foreigners Act. The members of the Foreigners Tribunal are appointed by the central government.[38] The proceedings before the Foreigners Tribunal are summary in nature.[39]

Jurisdiction of Foreigners Tribunal

The principal objective of the Foreigners Tribunal is to ascertain whether a given person is a foreigner or not. Typically, a Foreigners Tribunal gives its opinion on the issue of 'foreigner status' only on a reference made by the competent authority. A matter can reach the Foreigners Tribunal in any of the following ways:[40]

a) By means of a reference by the central government, state government, union territory administration, District Collector or District Magistrate.
b) By means of a reference by the concerned registering authority under Section 6A of the Citizenship Act and Rule 19 of the Citizenship Rules, to verify whether the proceedee is eligible to be registered thereunder or not.

---

38 Order 2 of the Foreigners Tribunal Order.

39 State of Assam v. Jamait-E-Ulema-E-Hind, 2018 (4) GLT 264.

40 Order 2 (1), (1A) & (1B) of the Foreigners Tribunal Order.

c) A challenge to the order of the Local Registrar for excluding a person from the draft NRC in Assam (discussed in later chapters).

The opinion of the Foreigners Tribunal constitutes a quasi-judicial order (and not an administrative order).[41] The determination has civil consequences.[42]

Procedure for Opinion

The Foreigners Tribunal Order provides the framework for making a determination as to the citizenship status of a proceedee. This is summarised below.[43]

Power of Regulate Procedure

The Foreigners Tribunal has the power to regulate its own procedure.

Pre Referral Investigation

Any referral to a Foreigners Tribunal must be preceded by a 'pre-referral investigation' by the referring authorities (indicated above). The reference to the Foreigners Tribunal by the referring authority should not be mechanical in nature.

The referring authority has to apply its mind on the materials collected by the investigating officer during the investigation. Persons residing in the locality of the proceedee as well as the

41 *See generally* Jahir Ali v. Union of India, W.P. (C) No. 3402/2020 (03.03.2021, Guwahati High Court).

42 The expression 'quasi-judicial order' means a verdict in writing which determines and decides contesting issues and question by a forum other than a court. *See* Indian National Congress (I) v. Institute of Social Welfare, (2002) 5 SCC 685 for the meaning of the expression 'quasi-judicial body'. *See also* Shrimati Ujjambai v. State of Uttar Pradesh, AIR 1962 SC 1621 which holds that the principles of res judicata apply to quasi-judicial bodies.

43 Order 3 of the Foreigners Tribunal Order.

proceedee himself should be examined wherever possible. In case the concerned person is not available at the addresses (available on record), then in such case, reasonable efforts should be made by the investigating agency to trace him. The reference should be made only on being fully satisfied that there exist valid grounds for making such reference. The referring authority, however, need not pass a detailed order recording his satisfaction. An order agreeing with the investigation would suffice.

The referring authority also, while making the reference, shall produce all the materials collected during investigation before the Foreigners Tribunal, as the Foreigners Tribunal is required to *prima facie* satisfy itself about the existence of valid grounds before issuing notice to the proceedee.[44]

Opportunity of Representation

The proceedee shall be granted a reasonable opportunity to represent his case before the Foreigners Tribunal.[45]

Service of Notice

An important aspect of the proceeding is just and proper 'service of notice' to the procedee, without which the proceedee cannot have a fair opportunity to substantiate his case before the Foreigners Tribunal.[46] The following aspects are relevant in this regard:

a) The proceedee should be served with a copy of the main grounds on which he is alleged to be a foreigner and be provided with an opportunity of making a representation and producing evidence in support of his case.

44 *See generally* Rina Rani Das v. Union of India W.P. (C) No. 2706/2019 (10.03.2021, Guwahati High Court); Moslem Mondal, *supra*

45 *See* Rahima Khatun v. Union of India, W.P. (C) No. 8284/2019 (08.04.2021, Guwahati High Court).

46 Moslem Mondal, *supra*

b) The grounds need not be mentioned separately and elaborately. It would suffice if the grounds are mentioned in the notice itself, which need not be detailed or elaborate.[47]
c) A mistake in the notice which is not jurisdictional, does not invalidate the proceeding, if it is otherwise valid.[48]
d) Non-mentioning of the stream of foreigners in the notice would not vitiate the final conclusion reached by the Foreigners Tribunal.[49]

Proper notice to the proceedee assumes great importance in the proceedings before the Foreigners Tribunal, in as much as such proceedings can result in grave consequences i.e a person being declared a 'foreigner' and eventually being subjected to 'detention and deportation'. The Guwahati High Court in **Moslem Mondal** framed the following procedure in the matter of service of notice by the Foreigners Tribunal on the proceedee:

i. The proceedee shall be served with the notice, together with the main grounds on which he is suspected to be a foreigner, as far as practicable, personally, whose signature/thumb impression, as proof of service, is to be obtained.
ii. Such notice shall be issued in the address where the proceedee last resided or reportedly resides or works for gain. In case of change of place of residence, which has been duly intimated in writing to the investigating agency by the proceedee, the Tribunal shall issue notice in such changed address.

---

47 Bela Rani Devi v. Union of India, W.P. (C) No. 5852/2016 (10.05.2018, Guwahati High Court).

48 Bela Rani Devi v. Union of India, *supra*

49 *See* Ananda Ghosh v. Union of India, 2017 (3) GLR 815 & Bela Rani Devi v. Union of India, *supra*

iii. The notice shall be issued by the Tribunal in the official language of the State also indicating that the burden is on the proceedee to prove that he is an Indian citizen and not a foreigner.

iv. The service of notice on any adult member of the family of the proceedee, in case he is found to be not present at the time of service, shall constitute the service on the proceedee. In token of such service the name and signature/thumb impression of such adult member shall be obtained. In case such adult member refuses to put the signature or thumb impression, a report in that regard shall be submitted.

v. If the proceedee or any available adult member of his family refuses to accept the notice, the process server has to give a report in that regard along with the name and address of a person of the locality, who was present at the time of making such an effort to get the notices served, provided such person is available and willing to be a witness to such service. The signature/thumb impression of such witness, if present and willing, must be obtained.

vi. In case the proceedee has changed the place of residence or place of work, without intimation to the investigating agency, a report in that regard shall be submitted by the process server. A copy of the notice shall then be affixed in a conspicuous place where the proceedee last resided or reportedly resided or worked for gain, containing the name and address of a respectable person of the locality, if available and willing to be a witness for that purpose. The signature/thumb impression of such person, in that case, shall also be obtained in the said report.

vii. Where the proceedee or any adult member of his family are not found in the residence, a copy of the notice shall be pasted in a conspicuous place of his residence, witnessed by 1(one) respectable person of the locality, subject to his availability and willingness to be a witness in that regard. In that case the signature or thumb impression of that person shall also be obtained in proof of the manner in which such service is effected.

viii. Where the proceedee resides outside the jurisdiction of the Tribunal, the notice has to be sent for service to the officer-in-charge of the police station within whose jurisdiction the proceedee resides or last resided or last known to have been resided or works for gain. The process server shall then cause the service of notice in the manner as provided herein above.

ix. In case no person is available or willing to be the witness of service of notice, as mentioned above, or refused to put his signature or thumb impression, a signed certificate/verification is to be filed by the process server to that effect, which shall be sufficient proof of such non-availability, unwillingness and refusal.

It is pertinent to point out that the notice issued to the proceedee is in the form of a *simplicitor* statement informing him that he is an illegal entrant to Assam (and India) without any further facts or documents. After issuing summons to the proceedee, the Foreigners Tribunal does not examine any of the persons who had made the reference or had conducted the investigation. Thus, the proceedee is totally in the dark as to how he came to be considered as a foreigner and not an Indian citizen. The issue as to whether a proceeding is entitled to more than a mere notice is an open issue which requires consideration by courts.[50]

50 *See* Haider Ali v. Union of India, W.P. (C) No. 1818/2019 (30.03.2021, Guwahati High Court).

Investigation and Trial

The right to fair trial is a basic fundamental and human right. Fair trial also encompasses a fair investigation. Unfair investigation is a precursor to an unfair trial which results in miscarriage of justice. The concept of fair investigation and fair trial has great significance in the matter of detection and deportation of foreigners under the (Indian) Foreigner law regime, especially in view of the fact that the 'burden of proof' primarily rests on the concerned individual to show that he is not a foreigner.[51]

The investigation should be fair and the report of such investigation should be proper with all the material facts.[52] The report of the investigative agency (on which reference is made to the Foreigners Tribunal) must be exhaustive enough to show application of mind and reasonable efforts to ascertain the citizenship status of the concerned person.[53]

Supply of Documents to the Proceedee

Fair trial also includes within its fold, assisting a proceedee to address his defence by facilitating supply of the certified record of any public document, including the copy of the relevant electoral rolls (documents which are recognised in law for establishing the 'Indian citizenship' of a person). Certified copies of such documents, if applied for, must be supplied promptly. The interest of justice, therefore, requires supply of the certified copies of such documents, that too promptly, whenever asked for.[54]

---

51 Mondel Muslim, *supra*

52 Moslem Mondal, *supra*

53 Such investigation, while required to be reasonably exhaustive and detailed, need not be as comprehensive as an investigation which is normally conducted in criminal cases.

54 Moslem Mondal, *supra*

Reliance on Previous Opinion of Foreigners Tribunal

The previous opinion of the Foreigners Tribunal on the citizenship status of a member of the family of the proceedee (which is living together) or of 'blood relatives' generally cannot be ignored and must be given due weightage.[55] For instance, in **Pratap Sakharu v. Union of India,**[56] while relying on the Foreigners Tribunal's previous opinion on the proceedee's parents, he was held to be an Indian.

When two conflicting opinions are given by the same Foreigners Tribunal on the claim of legacy traceable to the same person and if these opinions relate to the blood relations (such as brothers or sisters) then the one favourable to either of the siblings can be applied to the other.[57]

The Standard of Proof

The standard of proof to be adopted by a Foreigners Tribunal by making a determination of forming an opinion as to the citizenship status of the proceedee is 'preponderance of probability'.[58]

If on appraisal of evidence on record, the proceedee is able to make out a case which is more favourable than the one made out by the government, then the Foreigners Tribunal should lean in favour of the proceedee.[59]

Minor inconsistencies in the evidence of the proceedee would not result in rejection of his case before the Foreigners

55 Rofikul Islam v. Union of India, W.P. (C) No. 6993/2018 (23.03.2021, Guwahati High Court).

56 W.P. (C) No. 6594/2019 (19.02.2020, Gauhati High Court).

57 Rofikul Islam v. Union of India, *supra*

58 The expression 'preponderance of probability' generally implies that the probability of the event taking place is more than the probability of it not taking place. At the other end of the spectrum is the rule of 'beyond reasonable doubt' which is the threshold required to be met by the prosecution in criminal matters.

59 Rofikul Islam v. Union of India, *supra*

Tribunal.[60] The more evidence one adduces, the better. But there is no law that if the proceedee does not disclose the names of all his other relatives (other than what matters) and does not produce all relevant evidence (other than what matters), then his evidence cannot be believed.[61]

Every opportunity should be given to a proceedee to enable him to produce new facts or documents (to substantiate his case) even at a later stage, so long as the same do not contradict his statement or stance taken in his written statement before the Foreigners Tribunal.[62] No pedantic view should be taken, if there has been some delay in producing documents or if the written statement does not provide reference to such documents. No adverse inference should be drawn against a proceedee for filing documents at a later stage.[63]

Applicability of the Principle of Res Judicata

The proceedings before the Foreigners Tribunal are quasi-judicial in nature having civil consequences and hence, the doctrine of res judicata operates to a determination made by the Foreigners Tribunal.[64] Thus, if a decision or determination has already

---

60 *See* Sirajul Haque v. State of Assam 2019 (5) SCC 534. In this case, certain typographical errors in some documents (filed by the proceedee in an effort to prove his Indian citizenship) were held to be minor inconsistencies. No adverse inference was drawn by the court on this count.

61 *See* Haider Ali v. Union of India, *supra*

62 In a proceeding under Section 9 of the Foreigners Act 1946, the state does not discharge any burden, except to the extent that a proper investigation has been conducted before the reference is made to the Foreigners Tribunal. In such a situation, as the onus is on the proceedee, he must be afforded every opportunity to put forth his evidence. Therefore, if certain facts are introduced subsequently, which do not contradict his statement or stance taken previously, introduction of the said facts should not be denied. *See* Haider Ali v. Union of India, *supra*

63 *See* Haider Ali v. Union of India, *supra*

64 The term 'res judicata' means 'no man should be vexed twice for the same cause'. The principle of 'res judicata' is founded on sound public policy and is of universal application. *See* Burn & Co, Calcutta v. Their Employees, Civil Appeal No. 325/1955 (11.10.1956, Supreme Court of India).

been made by the Foreigners Tribunal in respect of a particular person regarding the citizenship, then, on an application of the principle of res judicata that decision would act as a bar on any subsequent proceeding against the same person as regards the issue of his citizenship.[65]

Fate of Reference in case of absence of Procedee

Often a proceedee 'disappears' at the time of or during the course of investigation during the pendency of the proceedings before the Foreigners Tribunal. A logical question arises for consideration at this point is 'what should be the fate of the reference pending before the Foreigners Tribunal in absence of the proceedee'. The Guwahati High Court, in this regard, opined that a reference made to a Foreigners Tribunal seeking its opinion on whether the proceedee is a foreigner or not, cannot be 'abated' or 'adjourned indefinitely' on the grounds of non-availability of the proceedee. A Foreigners Tribunal cannot put a reference in cold storage if the proceedee is not traceable. The tribunal should continue with the proceedings regardless.[66]

Judicial Review

An opinion or order of the Foreigners Tribunal, can be challenged before the jurisdictional High Court by way of writ proceedings.[67] The High Court exercising its power of judicial review cannot sit in

65 Jahir Ali v. Union of India, W.P. (C) No. 3402/2020 (03.03.2021, Guwahati High Court). In the said matter, the Foreigners Tribunal, while ignoring its earlier opinion given on an earlier occasion (wherein a person had been held to be an Indian citizen), embarked on a fresh determination exercise against the same person and declared him a foreigner. The aggrieved person, in appellate proceedings, successfully contended that his case could not be re-determined or re-considered by the Foreigners Tribunal in view of its earlier opinion declaring him to be an Indian citizen. *See also* Amina Khatun v. Union of India, W.P. (C) 7339/2015 (19.04.2018, Guwahati High Court).

66 Tuta Mia v. Union of India, W.P. (C) No. 6280 & 7088/2016 (14.05.2018, Guwahati High Court).

67 Abdul Kuddus v. Union of India, AIR 2019 SC 2834.

appeal over the finding of facts recorded by the Foreigners Tribunal. The High Court will normally interfere only where the tribunal has acted illegally or failed to exercise jurisdiction or exceeded its jurisdiction.[68] The High Court may intervene if it is shown that it is a case of no evidence at all.[69] Separately, an error apparent on the face of record may also be interfered with by the High Court.[70]

Consequence of a Determination by a Foreigners Tribunal

The persons detected and determined to be foreigners by the Foreigners Tribunal shall be taken into custody immediately and kept in detention camp(s) till they are deported from India.[71]

THE FOREIGNERS ORDER, 1948

The Foreigners Order, 1948 regulates the entry and exit of foreigners in India.[72] It invests in the central government, the authority to determine as to who shall be permitted to enter or leave the country. The Foreigners Order, 1948 empowers the competent authority to examine any person who seeks permission to enter India or to depart therefrom or during his stay in India for the purpose of Foreigners Act, 1946 or of any order made thereunder, and it shall be the duty of every such person to furnish to the authority, such information in such manner and at such times, as that authority may require.[73]

The Foreigners Order, 1948 requires every foreigner entering India to obtain a permit from the competent authorities which shall, *inter alia,* indicate the period of stay, places of stay etc. The

68 Md. Ajijul Hoque v. The Union of India, W.P (C) No. 1488/2013 (30.08.2013, Guwahati High Court).

69 Md. Ajijul Hoque v. Union of India, *supra*

70 Moslem Mondal, *supra*

71 Moslem Mondal, *supra*

72 Ss. 3 & 5 of the Foreigners Order, 1948.

73 S. 5A of the Foreigners Order, 1948.

competent authorities may regulate the stay of the foreigner in India *via* the said permit.[74]

The provisions of the Foreigners Order, 1948 give wide powers to the competent authority including the power to impose restrictions on movements of a foreigner.[75] In **Reza Abdullatif Saboonchi v. The State of Maharashtra,**[76] the Bombay High Court upheld the order of the competent authority restraining certain Iranian nationals from moving out of the limits of South Mumbai on the premise that they were involved in a criminal case and there existed an apprehension that such persons may try to go underground and evade trial. Similarly, in **Maheswaran v. State of Tamil Nadu,**[77] the Madras High Court did not find any infirmity with an order of the competent authority requiring a Sri Lankan national to reside at a particular camp. The authority is not required to hold an inquiry against whom a restriction order is proposed to be passed or grant pre-decisional hearings.[78] Further, the authority is not expected to pass reasoned orders, much less, detail reasons when reliance is placed on reports of security agencies.

The central government has issued circulars from time to time requiring an investigation on illegal stay of foreigners in India and for their deportation.[79]

---

74 S. 7 of the Foreigners Order, 1948. This provision of the Foreigners Order, 1948 applies only with respect to persons who enter India as foreigners. *See generally* Rahmat Ullah v. State, AIR 1969 All 165.

75 S. 11 of the Foreigners Order, 1948. *See also* Rajesh P. Mankad v. State of Gujarat, Civil Application No. 497/2010 (22.04.2011, Gujarat High Court).

76 CDJ 2012 BHC 1634.

77 H.C.P. No. 1208/2005, (21.03.2006, Madras High Court).

78 Satish Nambiar v. Union of India, 2007 (5) Bom. C.R. 247. *See also* Reza Abdullatif Saboonchi v. State of Maharashtra, CDJ 2012 BHC 1634.

79 *See generally* Rajesh P. Mankad v. State of Gujarat, Civil Application No. 497/2010 (22.04.2011, Gujarat High Court).

REGISTRATION OF FOREIGNERS IN INDIA

Indian law contains provisions for regulation for foreigners who intend to stay in India for longer periods of time. The Registration of Foreigners Act, 1939 and the Registration of Foreigners Rules, 1992 provides for registration of certain categories of foreigners who intend to stay in India for long periods of time [i.e. more than 180 days (one hundred and eighty day)] or whose visa authorisation mandates a registration (such as foreigners from Pakistan and Afghanistan explained below).

The stated objective of these legislations is to maintain a record of foreigners who enter, stay/reside in and depart from India. Highlighted below are the salient features of these legislations.

Residential Permit

A residential permit is issued to foreigners, its validity being the period of stay specified in the visa. An application for extension of the permit is permissible in certain situations and has to be made to the appropriate foreigners registration office in the prescribed form and manner, at least 2 (two) months before its expiry.

Arrival

Every foreigner entering India is required to complete and present the disembarkation card or arrival card in the prescribed form. This arrival card contains particulars of the foreigner as to his name, nationality, age, sex, place of birth and address/ intended address in India. An immigration check is carried out for all passengers at the port of arrival in India.

A foreigner who is a PIO/OCI card holder can enter India upon presentation of his PIO/OCI card along with his valid foreign passport.

Typically, a registration is required to be made with the jurisdictional Foreigners Regional Registration Officer (**FRRO**)/ Foreigners Registration Office (**FRO**) within a period of 14 (fourteen) days from arrival.[80] However, Pakistani foreigners are required to obtain a registration within a period of 24 (twenty four) hours from arrival. The foreigners are required to report in person or through authorised representatives to the concerned FRRO or FRO. Normally, the registration process is completed within 1 (one) day. Generally, the following documents are required for the registration process:

a) A valid passport and visa.
b) Residence proof of the foreigner.
c) In case of an employment visa, the employment letter of the foreigner, a forwarding letter from the concerned employer and PAN/application for PAN.
d) In case of a student visa, a certificate from the concerned academic institution.
e) In case of a medical visa, a letter from the concerned hospital where the treatment is being taken along with supporting medical test reports/medical certificates indicating a tentative period of treatment.

No fee is chargeable for registration. However late registration attracts penalty, ranging between Rs. 500/- (Rupees Five Hundred) and Rs. 20,000/- (Rupees Twenty Thousand), depending on the days of delay. Similarly, overstay in India, beyond the permissible period, also attracts penalty, ranging between Rs. 10,000/- (Rupees Ten Thousand) and Rs. 50,000/- (Rupees Fifty Thousand), depending on the days of overstay.[81]

80 The Foreigners Regional Registration Officers are based at Calcutta, Mumbai, New Delhi, Amritsar, Chennai, Bangalore and Hyderabad. Insofar as other districts in the country are concerned, the District Superintendents of Police have been vested with the powers of the FRRO. *See generally* https://www.mea.gov.in/cpv.htm

81 *See generally* https://www.mea.gov.in/cpv.htm

Every registered foreigner is obligated to produce his certificate of registration for inspection, when demanded by a registration officer, a magistrate or a police officer not below the rank of a head constable.

In case the certificate of registration is lost or destroyed, then the foreigner (whom it was issued) shall be required to send to the concerned registration officer, an application for issuance of a duplicate copy of the certificate of registration, along with a report of the circumstances in which the certificate was lost or destroyed and a copy of the police report regarding such loss.

Visa

In common parlance, visa may be described as the travel authority which is required to be obtained prior to a journey, except in case of countries where a 'visa on arrival' option is available. Foreigners entering India are typically required to possess a valid passport and visa, except in cases where, a 'visa on arrival' facility is extended by the government.[82]

---

82 The Government of India has launched the Tourist Visa on Arrival (TVOA) Scheme. Initially, in January 2010 this scheme was introduced for citizens of 5 (five) countries, namely Finland, Japan, Luxembourg, New Zealand and Singapore. In January 2011, the scheme was extended to citizens of 6 (six) more countries, *viz.* Cambodia, Vietnam, Philippines, Laos, Indonesia and Myanmar. The main objective of this scheme is to attract more foreign tourists and to encourage them to plan their travel to India at a short notice. A tourist visa on arrival can be granted to citizens of the aforementioned countries in case the following conditions are met: (i) The sole objective of the foreigner in visiting India is recreation, sightseeing, casual visit to meet friends or relatives, short duration medical treatment or casual business visit etc. (ii) The foreigner does not have a residence or occupation in India. (iii) the foreigner holds a passport with a minimum validity of six months and a re-entry permit, if that is required under the law of his country. (iv) The foreigner is a person of a strong financial standing. This facility is not applicable to the holders of Diplomatic/Official Passports or to foreigners who have a permanent residence or occupation in India. The validity of the visa shall be 30 (thirty) days. This type of visa is neither extendable nor convertible into any other type of visa. A 'visa on arrival' is available only at international airports of Delhi, Mumbai, Chennai, Kolkata, Kochi, Thiruvananthapuram, Hyderabad and Bengaluru. *See generally* https://www.india.gov.in/spotlight/encouraging-inbound-tourism-tourist-visa-arrival-tvoa-scheme#tvoa2

Expiry or Non Extension of Visa

There exists a divergence of opinion in the manner in which a foreigner (who has arrived in India) on a valid visa, should be removed/deported in case his stay in India subsequently becomes illegal for unauthorised overstay (i.e. non-extension of visa etc.).[83]

An admitted foreigner at the time of entry into India who unauthorisedly overstays (without extension of visa), is required to be deported and in such case there is no need for any enquiry or determination by the central government (under Section 9 of the Citizenship Act). The act of illegal overstay, by itself, constitutes a contravention of Section 3 of the Foreigners Act and Foreigners Order, 1948 inviting punishment under Section 14 of the Foreigners Act. Notice to leave India is also not necessary under the Foreigners Act or the Foreigners Order as a condition precedent to prosecution. There is no provision in the Foreigners Act or the Foreigners Order enjoining that before a person is prosecuted a notice calling upon him to leave India must precede the prosecution.[84] In the case of a foreigner, who stays in India beyond the prescribed or permitted time period may not be able to use the benefit of the principles of natural justice.[85]

83 The appropriate course of action against a foreigner who does not leave India on expiry of his visa, is to remove him from India; punishing him and sending him to jail would be quite the reverse of his fulfilling the obligation to depart from India. If he is bound to depart from India, it would be useless to let him remain in India, even in jail. Wahid Mian Haddin v. The State, AIR 1961 All 111.

84 State of U.P. v. Shamsul Huda, 1971 Crl. LJ 977; State of Assam v. Jilkadar Ali, 1972 (2) SCC 320.

85 Tasleem Murad v. Government of A.P., 2002 (5) ALD 307. 'Entry into India' and 'Stay in India' are two different concepts. Once the entry of a person into India is permitted then, after the initial entry, his stay in India will be subject to the issuance of a visa. If the person violates the terms and conditions of his visa, then a 'Leave India Notice' may be issued and he may be subject to further proceedings as per law. *See* Mohammad Hassan Jafari Naeimi v. Union of India, Writ Petition No. 1316/2012 (06.09.2013, Bombay High Court).

The Supreme Court of India, in **Hasan Ali Raihany v. Union of India,**[86] opined that, barring cases involving national security *et al*, if the foreigner had entered India legally, then typically in such case, fairness demanded that the competent authority inform him the reasons for his deportation, followed by an opportunity to submit a representation, post which the competent authority may take a final decision in the matter. Observance of 'due process' or 'procedural due process' should be kept in mind when dealing with foreigners who have come to India legally or have been residing in India legally.[87]

Extension of Visa

Extensions of visa may be granted by the relevant authorities on a case to case basis. A foreigner seeking an extension must ensure that he prefers an appropriate application for extension along with supporting documents well before the expiry of the visa. Different categories of visas have different preconditions and require different supporting documents. In case of no extension of visa, the foreigner is bound to leave the country within the time prescribed, failing which he is liable to be deported.[88]

86 W.P. (Crl) No. 17/2006 (09.03.2006, Supreme Court of India).

87 Foreigners do not have a right to 'live in India' but have the right to be subjected to proper process in case of their removal from the country. Past conduct of the foreigner is also important. In the present case, a Pakistani national, married to an Indian citizen, was residing in India for a long time on a perfectly valid long term visa. Her visa had been renewed multiple times and she had, on several occasions, travelled to and fro India. Under such circumstances, it was opined by court, that competent authorities are duty bound to comply with due process of law prior to eviction from the country. *See* Mohd. Javed and Ors. v. Union of India and Ors., LPA 168/2019 (28.05.2019, Delhi High Court). A reasonable procedure is required to be followed in a case involving curtailment of the period of authorization granted by a residence permit. Mohammad Sediq v. Union of India, (1998) 47 DRJ 74.

88 Mere preferring an application for extension of visa before the appropriate authorities is not sufficient. If on the date of expiry of the visa, no extension is granted to the foreigner, then his stay in India becomes illegal inviting penal consequences under Section 14 of the Foreigners Act. *See generally* State of Kerala v. C.K. Kunju, Crl. Appeal No. 602/1987 (13.10.1988, Kerala High Court).

Intimation to the Authorities

Generally speaking, foreigners are required to report their arrival, details of their movement within India and their departure.[89] It is the responsibility of every registered foreigner to keep the authorities abreast of his address in India. Any change of address is also required to be intimated to the authorities.

Restriction on Movement

A foreigner is not permitted to either visit or reside in any prohibited place, declared as such, under the provisions of the Official Secrets Act, 1920 without the permission of the concerned authority. Further, in case the foreigner wishes to visit a protected/restricted/cantonment area,[90] a prior permission of the competent authority would be required.[91]

Departure

A registered foreigner who is about to depart from India is required to surrender his certificate of registration. Generally, it

---

In a case where a foreigner overstays in India (thereby violating Section 14 of the Foreigners Act) no prior notice 'to leave India' is required to be given to him and he may be removed from India straightaway. *See* State of Uttar Pradesh v. Shamsul Huda, (1971) 41 AWR 498.

89 A foreigner who stays at a hotel, guesthouse or such similar place, is required to furnish with the foreigners office the relevant particulars of his stay, on arrival as well at the time of departure.

90 The Protected Areas are as follows: (i) parts of the states of Manipur, Mizoram, Arunachal Pradesh, Uttaranchal, Jammu and Kashmir, Rajasthan, Himachal Pradesh; and (ii) whole of the states of Nagaland and Sikkim. The Restricted Areas are as follows: (i) whole of the union territory of Andaman and Nicobar Islands; and (ii) part of the state of Sikkim. Cantonment area is an area which houses a permanent military base/station of the Indian Armed Forces. In India there are numerous cantonment areas spread across the country, especially along the border towns/cities.

91 The competent authority in this regard is the Ministry of Home Affairs, Government of India. Please note that powers have been delegated to the FRRO to grant permit(s) to a group of foreigners, who wish to visit for tourist purposes, upon payment of a fee/levy, provided such foreigners are accompanied by a recognised travel agent. *See generally* https://www.mea.gov.in/cpv.htm

is not necessary for a foreigner (except the citizen of Pakistan or Afghanistan) to seek and exit/departure clearance from the concerned registration office.

Exemptions

The following categories of foreigners are exempted from obtaining registration on their arrival to and during their stay in India:

a) Foreign diplomatic and/or consular officials (and their families) who have been assigned to India are exempt from registration (on a reciprocal basis). However, this exemption is not available to the members of the staff of the missions of the Arab Republic of Egypt and Syria.
b) Officials (and their families) of the United Nations (and its specialized agencies) who come to India on duty.
c) Foreigner children below the age of 16 (sixteen) years.

Temporary and Collective Landing Permit

A temporary landing permit facility, up to a maximum period of 3 (three) days, may be extended by the Indian authorities to a foreigner, without a valid visa, under emergent circumstances (death, sudden illness) provided the immigration authorities are satisfied regarding the *bona fides* of the foreigner.

Foreigners arriving in groups of 4 (four) or more, for tourist purposes, may, upon satisfaction of certain conditions, be granted a collective landing permit for a maximum period of 60 (sixty) days, with multiple entry facility, so as to enable them to visit a neighbouring country. This facility (of collective landing permit) is available only at select airports and seaports.[92] However, the facility of temporary landing

92 The facility is available at the airports of Delhi, Mumbai, Chennai, Kolkata, Bangalore, Hyderabad, Kochi, Thiruvananthapuram and Goa; and at the

permits or collective landing permit is not available to citizens of Afghanistan, China, Ethiopia, Iraq, Iran, Nigeria, Pakistan, Somalia, Sri Lanka; and persons of Pakistani origin.

Nepal & Bhutan

Normally, foreigners coming to India are required to possess a genuine and valid passport or any other internationally recognised travel document. However, the Indian government has extended certain relaxations for the citizens of Nepal and Bhutan coming into India. Nationals of these countries do not require a passport or visa for entering into India. They however, are required to possess a proper authorised identity proof.[93] In case such persons enter India from a place other than their own country or exit India to a country other than their own, then in such an eventuality, the requirement of producing a valid passport becomes mandatory. Further, in case such persons enter India from China, Macau, Hong Kong, Pakistan or Maldives, then, in such case, they will require a valid passport and a visa.

Pakistan

Typically, citizens of Pakistan require a visa for entering India (along with their passport). Further, such persons are required to report at the relevant foreigner's office (based on the place of stay) within a period of 24 (twenty four) hours of arrival in India.

---

seaports of Goa, Kochi, Calicut, Thiruvananthapuram, Mumbai, Chennai, Kolkata and Nhava Sheva.

93 The following documents will serve as an appropriate identity proof: (i) passport; (ii) citizenship certificate; (iii) voter identification card issued by their nation's election commission; (iv) limited validity photo identity certificate issued by their nation's mission in India; (v) for children between the age group of 10 to 18, a photo identity card issued by their school principal, if accompanied by parents having valid travel documents. No document necessary for children below the age group of 10 (ten) years.

A visa on arrival facility is available for Pakistan citizens only at Attari Immigration Point[94] subject to the following terms and conditions:

a) The facility is available to a Pakistani national who is more than 65 (sixty five) years old, is crossing Attari on foot and (i) his objective of visiting India is to meet friends or relatives;[95] (ii) he does not have a residence or occupation in India; (iii) he holds a passport with minimum validity of 6 (six) months; (iv) he does not hold a diplomatic or official passport; (v) he exits India only from Attari on foot.
b) The facility is available for a maximum of 2 (two) times in a calendar year for single entry, a maximum of 45 (forty five) days stay, and for visit to a maximum of 5 (five) places in India.[96] 'A visa on arrival' is not available for visiting the restricted/protected areas, the containment areas, and the states of Jammu and Kashmir, Punjab and Kerala.
c) A 'visa on arrival' is neither extendable nor convertible, except with the prior approval of the Foreigners Division, Ministry of Home Affairs, Government of India.

Afghanistan

Citizens of Afghanistan require a visa for entering India (along with their passport). They are further required to get themselves registered with the relevant foreigner's office, within a period of 14 (fourteen) days of their arrival. The following documents are required for the registration: (i) passport; (ii) residence proof; (iii) duly completed temporary resident permit form. Persons

94 Attari is located at about 30 (thirty) kilometres from Amritsar in Punjab on the India-Pakistan Border. Wagha is the corresponding place in Pakistan.

95 Visit to India for business, medical, conference or pilgrimage purposes requires a visa from the relevant India mission/post.

96 A Pakistani national who wishes to travel to India for a longer duration is required to apply for a visa with the relevant India mission/post.

holding Indian visa which are valid for less than 30 (thirty) days are exempt from the above registration process.

Normally, exit permission is also required by citizens of Afghanistan from the concerned foreigners office, except where they leave India within the validity of the visa, or where they arrive in India holding a visa for a maximum period of 30 (thirty) days.

CHAPTER 4

The Indian Passport Law Regime

INTRODUCTION

The present chapter extensively deals with the Indian passport law regime. Passport laws are an integral element of foreign travel and immigration. This law applies (without exception) to all forms of international movement.

Generally speaking, a passport may be described as a document of identity issued to an Indian citizen and essential for his travel outside India and for his return to India. A passport serves as a document of identity and constitutes *prima facie* evidence of nationality.[1]

The Passport Law Regime

In India, the law governing passports is the Passports Act, 1967 (**Passports Act**) and the Passport Rules, 1980 (**Passport Rules**).

The Passports Act is the primary legislation in the Indian passports law regime regulating foreign travel. The Passport Rules act as a supplement to the Passports Act and regulate the mechanism relating to issue/renewal of passports and travel documents. The said rules also regulate other ancillary aspects such as varying entries in passports, making additional endorsements etc.

1 Devadasan Dayalal v. Collector of Customs, 1986 (9) ECR 558.

Additionally, the Passport (Entry into India) Act, 1920 and Passport (Entry into India) Rules, 1950 focus on the passport requirements for all persons who enter India.

Each of the above mentioned enactments are discussed in this chapter.

Historical Evolution of the Passports Act

The Passports Act was enacted subsequent to the judgement delivered in **Satwant Singh Sawhney v. D. Ramarathnam, Assistant Passport Officer, New Delhi and Others**[2] wherein the Supreme Court had held that the right to travel abroad is a fundamental right and deprivation of such right violates Articles 14 and 21 of the Constitution. The Supreme Court also held that since at that time, there was no law regulating or depriving a person of such rights or travel abroad, refusal to give passport or withdrawal of one already given violates the provisions of the Constitution. While doing so, the Supreme Court also rejected the government's claim for absolute discretion in the matter of issuance of passports to Indian citizens.

Previously, passports were issued by the Government of India in the exercise of its executive power to conduct foreign relations. Upon passing of the above-mentioned judgement of Satwant Singh Sawhney, the Parliament felt it imperative to enact a law to regulate foreign travel and issuance of travel documents. Since, at the relevant point of time, the Parliament was not in session, an ordinance, namely the Passports Ordinance, 1967 was promulgated for the said purpose. Subsequently, the Passports Act[3] was enacted, which, to this day, remains the primary legislation regulating the issuance and utilisation of passports and travel documents.

---

2 AIR 1967 SC 1836.

3 The Passports Act received the assent of the President of India on 24.06.1967.

Salient Features of the Passport Act

Some salient aspects of the Passport Act and the Passport Rules are discussed below.

Passport only for Citizens

Only Indian citizens can obtain a passport under the Passports Act.[4] A passport issued to a non-Indian citizen is liable to be impounded or revoked.[5]

No Departure without Passport

As per the Passports Act, no person (whether an Indian citizen or a foreigner) is permitted to depart from India without a valid passport or travel document.

Passport: Property of the Government

A passport or travel document issued by the passport authority is and remains the property of the central government.[6] A passport holder is not the owner of the passport and cannot offer his passport to any third person as security, pledge or guarantee etc.[7]

Grant of Passport

This section summarises the procedure for issuance of a passport to an Indian citizen by a passport authority.

An application for issue of a passport or travel document, or for issuance of an endorsement on a passport or travel

4 The Passports Act prohibits a person from departing (or attempting to depart) from India without a valid passport or travel document. S. 3 of the Passports Act.

5 S. 6 (2) & 10 of the Passports Act. *See also* S. 20 of the Passports Act which provides that the central government is, in exceptional situations (public interest), empowered to issue a passport to a person who is not a citizen of India.

6 S. 17 of the Passports Act.

7 *See generally* N. Venkata Ram Babu v. State of Kerala and Ors., Crl. Mic. No. 4252/2015 (18.03.2016, Kerala High Court).

document, is required to be made to the passport authority in the prescribed form and manner.[8] This is followed by an enquiry by the passport authority.[9]

At the outset, it is pertinent to point out that the right of a citizen to travel overseas is an integral part of his fundamental right, therefore any restriction imposed thereupon must always be interpreted objectively and in the perspective of public interest. This principle forms the touchstone for examining the conditions with respect to issuance, impounding, suspension and revocation of passports, imposed by the Passports Act.[10]

The Scope of Enquiry

The scope of enquiry (made by the passport authority) is to be confined within the contours of the Passports Act and the Passport Rules. The power of conducting enquiry under Section 5(2) of the Passports Act cannot be stretched so far as to mean that it would include the power to pronounce upon the legality, or otherwise, of an adoption, while dealing with an application for issue/renewal of a passport.[11]

It is no doubt true that under Section 5 (2) of the Passports Act, a passport officer is entitled to make an enquiry, if warranted, on an application filed for issue of a passport. However, this power should be reasonably and expeditiously exercised and mere

8 S. 5 (1) & (1A) of the Passports Act.

9 S. 5 (2) of the Passports Act.

10 Kulvir Singh v. Union of India, 2015 (147) DRJ 295.

11 Patel Mukeshkumar Karshanbhai v. Regional Passport Officer, 2012 GLH (1) 682. In the said matter, the application of the applicant for renewal of his passport, incorporating therein the name of his adoptive father, was rejected by the passport authority on the ground that, as per the passport authority, his adoption had not been done in compliance with the provisions of the Hindu Adoption and Maintenance Act, 1956. The High Court, *inter alia*, observed that the passport authority was not the competent authority to adjudicate upon the issue, of an adoption, irrespective of its views and analysis of the applicable law on the said subject.

suspicion or conjectured issues of national security or potential undefined criminality cannot by themselves stall the processing of an application for issue of a passport for an unreasonably long and undefined period of time.[12]

The passport authority shall, post an enquiry, either allow or refuse the application.[13] Any order for refusal is required to contain reasons. Further, a copy of the order is required to be furnished to the applicant, except where the passport authority is of the opinion that it will not be in the interests of the sovereignty and integrity of India, the security of India, friendly relations of India with any foreign country or in the interests of the general public to furnish such copy.[14]

No Objection for Government Employees

There is no legal requirement for an applicant of a passport, to secure or append to the application for grant of passport, a no-objection from his seniors in employment or service, even if he were to be a government official (centre or state government), an employee of a statutory body or public undertaking or a member of the armed forces. An intimation to the senior officer would suffice.[15]

Expeditious Disposal of Applications

Applications for issuance/renewal of passports should not be kept pending by the passport authority for a long period of time

12 Rehana Ali v. Union of India and Ors., S.B. W.P. (C) No. 15/2013 (26.11.2015, Rajasthan High Court). In this matter, an application for issue of passport continued to remain pending with the passport authority for almost 29 (twenty nine) months, and the said conduct was deprecated by the High Court.

13 S. 5 (2) of the Passports Act. The passport authority is entitled to seek additional information, documents or certificates, as may be considered necessary, for proper disposal of the application. *See generally* Regional Passport Officer v. Kokilaben, AIR 2009 Guj 59.

14 S. 5 (3) of the Passports Act.

15 *See generally* P. Shibu Kumar v. The Deputy Inspector General of Police, 2010 (5) ALD 732.

in as much as it affects the fundamental rights of the citizens.[16] The passport officer cannot indefinitely withhold consideration of the question of issuance/renewal/re-issue of a passport or travel document.[17]

Refusal of Passport

There exist various reasons contemplated under the statute due to which a person's application for grant of a passport may be refused by the concerned authorities. This section summarises such grounds.

An applicant may be refused a passport or travel document, by the passport authority, on any of the following grounds:[18]

a) The applicant is not a citizen of India.[19]
b) The applicant may, or is likely to, engage outside India in activities prejudicial to the sovereignty and integrity of India.[20]
c) The departure of the applicant from India is likely to be detrimental to the security of India.[21]
d) The presence of the applicant outside India is likely to prejudice the friendly relations of India with any foreign country.[22]

16 Deepak Dwarkasingh Chhabria v. Union of India, AIR 1997 Bom 181.

17 Anwar-ul-Haq v. Union of India, AIR 2008 J&K 35.

18 S.6(2) of the Passports Act. A passport can be denied only on the grounds specified in the Passports Act. Prabhleen Kaur v. Union of India, W.P. (C) No. 7974/2017 (03.10.2018, Delhi High Court).

19 S. 6 (2) (a) of the Passports Act. A doubt raised regarding nationality of a citizen is not a ground for refusal of a passport. The authorities must arrive at a definite conclusion on the 'citizenship status' of the applicant. Prabhleen Kaur v. Union of India, *supra*

20 S. 6 (2) (b) of the Passports Act.

21 S. 6 (2) (c) of the Passports Act.

22 S. 6 (2) (d) of the Passports Act.

e) The applicant has, in the previous 5 (five) years, been convicted by a court (for an offence involving moral turpitude) and sentenced to imprisonment for a minimum period of 2 (two) years.[23]

f) Proceedings in respect of an offence alleged to have been committed by the applicant are pending before a criminal court in India.[24]

g) A warrant or summons for appearance, or a warrant for arrest, of the applicant has been issued by a court of law or an order prohibiting the applicant's departure from India has been made by such court.[25]

h) The applicant has been repatriated and has not reimbursed the expenditure for such repatriation.[26]

i) That in the opinion of the central government, the issue of a passport or travel document to the applicant will not be in public interest.[27]

An applicant may be restrained (from visiting any foreign country) by the passport authority on any of the following grounds:[28]

a) The applicant may or is likely to engage in activities prejudicial to the sovereignty and integrity of India.

b) The presence of the applicant in the country sought to be visited is likely to be detrimental to the security of India.

---

23 S. 6 (2) (e) of the Passports Act. The rigor of this provision is applicable only for a period of 5 (five) years after such conviction. Ashok Kumar Sharma v. Regional Passport Officer, 2019 (173) DRJ 427.

24 S. 6 (2) (f) of the Passports Act.

25 S. 6 (2) (g) of the Passports Act.

26 S. 6 (2) (h) of the Passports Act.

27 S. 6 (2) (i) of the Passports Act.

28 S. 6 (1) of the Passports Act.

c) The presence of the applicant in the country sought to be visited is likely to prejudice the friendly relations of India with that or any other country.
d) That in the opinion of the central government, the presence of the applicant in the country sought to be visited is not in public interest.

An order of the passport authority restraining a person from travel should be supported by reasons. The applicant is to be supplied with a copy of the order except where the passport authority is of the opinion that it will not be in the interests of the sovereignty and integrity of India, the security of India, friendly relations of India with any foreign country or in the interests of the general public to furnish such copy.[29]

Activities Prejudicial to the Sovereignty & Integrity of India

Section 6 (2) (b) of the Passports Act empowers the passport authority to refuse to issue a passport on the grounds that the applicant may, or is likely to, engage outside India in activities prejudicial to the sovereignty and integrity of India.

The expression 'prejudicial to the sovereignty and integrity of India' used in this provision ordinarily implies secessionist activities, such as, burning of the constitution, refusal to take the oath of allegiance, raising a flag in any way simulating the flag of a foreign state with a view to encouraging feelings of allegiance to such state and gathering people to have such allegiance.[30] The expression must be read to mean activities that are derogatory to and/or could possibly result in affecting the sovereignty and integrity of India. The essential test to be applied is whether such an act is derogatory to the supremacy of the constitution or

29 S. 10 (5) of the Passports Act.

30 Union of India v. Satnam Singh, AIR 2018 Del 72.

is prejudicial to India's power of self-governance, such as inciting divisive forces in India et cetera.[31]

This provision must receive a strict construction in as much as the consequences are serious (i.e. denial of permission to travel abroad).[32] There must exist some reasonable and cogent material in possession of the passport authorities to show involvement of the applicant in such activities. The expression, 'likely to' appearing in this provision cannot be treated so lightly as to include every activity and relationship to be prejudicial to the sovereignty of the state. The 'likelihood' may take in its fold the apprehension which essentially must be borne from record or based on a reasonable cause. For example surveillance, maintenance of appropriate registers under the Police Rules, entry of the name of the person therein and at least some reasonable analytical examination by the concerned quarters in the Union of India would normally be the records which should substantiate such reasonable apprehension.[33] The court can examine the material produced by the passport authority to satisfy its conscience whether denial of the passport is in consonance with the provisions of Section 6 (2) of the Passports Act. The court may not go into the aspect of sufficiency of the material produced. However, the court may interfere in a case where there is either no material or totally irrelevant metrial.[34]

The act of an Indian citizen in seeking political asylum in a foreign country, by itself, does not create a valid apprehension that such person does not owe allegiance to the sovereignty and integrity of India.[35] Generally, political asylum in a foreign

31 Kulvir Singh v. Union of India, 2015 (147) DRJ 295.

32 *See* Naresh Lalchand Bhagchandani v. Union of India, 2007 SCC OnLine Bom 376.

33 Rajinder Kaur and Ors. v. Union of India, AIR 2004 P&H 347.

34 *ibid*

35 Union of India v. Satnam Singh, *supra*

country is sought by persons who fear persecution in their own country and are therefore unwilling to return. Such an act may bring disrepute to India. Regardless of how condemnable the act of seeking political asylum in a foreign land may be, it *ipso facto* (i.e. by itself, and without any other facts showing that the applicant had involved himself with activities of any individual or groups that plot, or had conspired, or are conspiring violence and other such activities to undermine the establishments in India or a section of its people) cannot possibly be a ground to deny a passport under Section 6 of the Passports Act.[36]

Conviction for Offence involving Moral Turpitude

Conviction for an offence involving moral turpitude and imprisonment for a period of 2 (two) years is another ground for denial of a passport.

The term 'moral turpitude' is not defined in the Passports Act. As per the dictionary meaning, the term 'moral' means 'conforming to or required or justified by consciousness, if not law' and the term 'turpitude' means 'baseness'.[37]

In a case where the applicant had committed the single offence which involved moral turpitude, but was sentenced to imprisonment for less than 2 (two) years, Section 6(2)(e) of the Passports Act would have no applicability. The same

---

But see Harjit Singh v. Union of India, 2008 (2) ILR 188 (P&H). In the said matter, the passport authorities had denied a passport to an Indian citizen who had previously sought political asylum in Germany. While upholding the decision of the passport authorities, the High Court observed that since political asylum is normally sought by persons by representing to another country that they fear persecution and oppression in their own country, the apprehension of the authorities that the person did not owe allegiance to the sovereignity and integrity of India was not entirely unjustified.

36 Union of India v. Satnam Singh, *supra*

37 J.R. Parikh v. The Director (PV) Chief Passport Officer, 1970 (2) ILR Delhi 378. An offence under the provisions of the Prevention of Corruption Act would qualify to be an offence involving moral turpitude. *See generally* M. Natarajan v. The Regional Passport Officer, 2012 (4) CTC 709.

would be the position if the applicant had committed a number of offences involving moral turpitude, for each of which he was sentenced to imprisonment for less than 2 (two) years. The intention of the legislature behind Section 6(2)(e) of the Passports Act appears to be that it is only when the applicant commits an offence involving moral turpitude which deserves a sentence of imprisonment for not less than 2 (two) years, that he should be refused the grant of a passport. In other words, even where the applicant had committed a number of offences involving moral turpitude, but was sentenced for each of the said offences, to imprisonment for less than 2 (two) years, it is the sentence for each offence that needs to be taken into consideration for the purposes of applicability of Section 6 (2) (e) of the Passports Act, and not the aggregate of the sentences for the various offences, and it is immaterial whether the sentences have been directed to run concurrently or consecutively.[38]

Criminal Court

Pendency of criminal proceedings can be another ground for denial/refusal of a passport. For the purposes of applicability of Section 6 (2) (f) of the Passports Act, the proceedings should be pending before a 'criminal court'. It would therefore be important to understand the meaning of the expression 'criminal court', used in this provision. In **Nilesh Heda v. Union of India**,[39] the High Court, while analysing this issue, observed that the expression 'criminal court' would normally refer to courts of ordinary criminal justice i.e. trial courts, which are constituted under the CRPC and other enactments to try offences. High Courts and other superior courts exercising appellate jurisdiction may not

38 J.R. Parikh v. The Director (PV) Chief Passport Officer, *supra*

39 W.P. (C) No. 14683/2015 (14.10.2015, Rajasthan High Court).

typically qualify to be criminal courts for the purposes of Section 6 (2) (f) of the Passports Act.[40]

The MEA Notification of 1993

As discussed above, under section 6 (2) (f) of the Passports Act, the passport authority can refuse to issue a passport to a person against whom criminal proceedings are pending in a court of law. However, there exist certain exemptions to this rule. Notification No. G.S.R. 570 (E), dated 25.08.1993 issued by the Ministry of External Affairs, Government of India (**MEA Notification**) granted certain exemptions with respect to applicability of this provision in certain specific situations and subject to certain specific conditions.[41] As per the said notification, the central government, in public interest, has exempted Indian citizens (against whom criminal proceedings were pending in India and who produced orders from the concerned court permitting them to depart from India) from the operation of Section 6 (2) (f) of the Passports Act subject to the satisfaction of the following conditions:

a) The passport shall be issued: (i) for the period specified in the order of the court; or (ii) if no period either for issue of

40 In this judgement, the Rajasthan High Court further observed that an appeal from a judgement of acquittal before the High Court would not qualify to be 'proceedings pending in a criminal court' for the purposes of Section 6 (2) (f) of the Passports Act. The pendency of such proceedings would not entitle the passport authority to refuse an application for issue of a passport or its renewal. *But see* Subhas Chandra Bose Mandava v. Union of India, 2018 (5) ALD 664, where the Andhra Pradesh High Court, in the context of an appeal pending against an order of acquittal, took a view that pendency of proceedings in an appellate court (the High Court in this case) in respect of an offence alleged to have been committed by the applicant would be sufficient ground for the passport authority to refuse issuance of a passport under section 6 (2) (f) of the Passports Act.

41 Published in the Gazette of India, Extra., Part II, Section 3 (i), dated 25.08.1993, pp. 2-3, Sl. No. 289 [No. VI/401/37/79]. The power of the central government to grant exemptions is traceable to Section 22 of the Passports Act. *See generally* Matbar Khan v. Union of India, W.P. (C) No. 33067 (M/B)/2018 (05.04.2019, Allahabad High Court, Lucknow Bench).

the passport or for travel abroad is specified in the order, then the passport shall be issued for a period of 1 (one) year;[42] or (iii) if the order gives permission to travel abroad for a period less than 1 (one) year, but it does not specify the period of validity of the passport, then the passport shall be issued for 1 (one) year; or (iv) if the order gives permission to travel abroad for a period exceeding 1 (one) year, and does not specify the validity of the passport, then the passport shall be issued for the period of travel abroad specified in the order.

b) Any passport issued in terms of the immediately preceding point (a) (ii) and (a) (iii) above can be renewed for 1 (one) year at a time, provided the applicant has not travelled abroad for the period sanctioned by the court; and in the meantime, the order of the court is not cancelled or modified.

c) Any passport issued in terms of the point (a) (i) above can be renewed only on the basis of a fresh court order specifying a further period of validity of the passport or a period for travel abroad.

d) The applicant shall give a written undertaking to the passport authority that he shall, if required by the concerned court, appear before it at any time during the currency of the passport so issued.

The object behind incorporating Section 6 (2) (f) to the Passports Act as one of the grounds for refusal of the issuance of a passport appears to be that permitting a person facing criminal charges to go abroad is against the interests of the country and the society at

42 Merely because an order of the court is silent about the time limit, the applicant cannot claim a right for issuance of the passport for the the the full validity period. Though it is open to the applicant to seek further extension, there is no logic in contending that in the absence of fixation of any time limit by the court, it has to be presumed that the court has allowed issuance of the passport for full validity period. Prashant Bhushan v. Union of India, 2016 (154) DRJ 385.

large. However, such restriction is not absolute and can be relaxed in appropriate cases, with the permission of the court, in the manner specified above.[43] No hard and fast straitjacket formula can be laid down regarding issuance of permission by the court in this regard.[44] If the applicant obtains permission from the concerned court then the passport authority will be duty-bound to issue the passport in terms of the order passed by the said court, subject to the terms of the notification.[45] It is the obligation of the passport authority to bring the notification to the attention of the applicant.[46] Even if the applicant has not received summons from the criminal court it will be open to him to prefer an appropriate application to that court, for issuance of necessary orders in terms of the above notification. Considering the fact that the matter involves the fundamental right of the applicant, the concerned court shall decide such application as expeditiously as possible, after notice to the prosecution.[47]

Section 6 (2) (f) of the Passports Act does not offend the constitutional mandate in any way. It also does not vest the authorities with arbitrary power. Pendency of a case before the criminal court, seen in the light of the police report, would be a sufficient ground for the authorities to act and in its wisdom even decline issuance of the passport. Exercise of such jurisdiction would hardly be open to judicial review unless such decision was palpably erroneous or was offending the basic rule of law. If the element of arbitrariness *ex-facie* vitiates the order, then alone it may be a case for interference by the High Court in exercise of its writ jurisdiction.[48]

---

43 Madhu Tyagi v. State of Uttar Pradesh, 2019 SCC OnLine All 6909.

44 *ibid*

45 Deepak Dwarkasingh Chhabria v. Union of India, AIR 1997 Bom 181.

46 *ibid. See also* Dhiren Baxi v. Regional Passport Officer, AIR 2003 Guj 108.

47 *ibid*

48 Ranjit Bajaj v. Regional Passport Authority, AIR 2004 P&H 327.

Meaning of the Expression 'Concerned Court'

A question arises as to the meaning of the expression 'concerned court' used in the MEA Notification. The words 'concerned court' refers only to the court where the case is presently pending and not any other court.[49] Only such court shall take a decision on the basis of applicable law.

Parameters for Determination by the 'Concerned Court'

While determining whether a permission should be given to the applicant (under the MEA Notification), the court may, inter alia, take into account the following considerations: (i) The present stage of investigation or trial of the case, as the case may be; (ii) Whether the presence of the accused is required for identification purpose; (iii) The time required for the culmination of the case in normal course; (iv) The purpose or necessity for the visit of the applicant in the foreign country;[50] (v) The consequence or difficulties that may be caused to the applicant on its refusal; (vi) The delay that may normally happen in disposal of a criminal case. In this context, a duty is also cast upon the court to take into account the fact that the pendency of a criminal case shall not stand in the way or cause hindrance to decide the future of an applicant.[51]

Pendency of Criminal Proceedings

Section 6(2)(f) of the Passports Act (discussed above) is applicable only in cases where criminal proceedings are pending in respect of an allegation of an offence. The said provision is inapplicable where the criminal proceedings have culminated in a conviction

49 Akhilesh v. State of Kerala, Crl. Misc. No. 185/2021 (01.03.2021, Kerala High Court).

50 Typically, permission to travel abroad may be given by the court if the applicant is able to show an emergent or compulsive need to travel, such as medical treatment et cetera. *See generally* Surinder Kaur v. State of Punjab, 2011 (1) RCC (Criminal) 358.

51 Akhilesh v. State of Kerala, *supra*

and the offence alleged to have been committed has been established.[52]

A proceeding can be said to be pending in a criminal court as soon as 'cognizance of the offence' is taken by the court.[53] Generally speaking, in terms of the provisions of the CRPC, cognizance may be said to be taken by the court in either of the following ways: (i) Pursuant to filing of a final report or charge sheet by the police authorities under Section 173 of the CRPC; (ii) upon the complaint made to the magistrate under Section 190 of the CRPC.

Mere registration or pendency of an FIR does not attract Section 6 (2) (f) of the Passports Act or Section 10 (3) (e) of the Passports Act.[54] Filing of a final report or charge sheet by the police authorities under Section 173 of the CRPC may not result in 'initiation of criminal proceedings' until the magistrate has taken cognizance of the same.[55] Separately, proceedings which reach a higher or superior court 'in the course of investigation' or 'prior to completion of an investigation' would not qualify the provisions of Section 6 (2) (f) of the Passports Act until filing of the final report with the concerned court and such concerned court taking

52 Ashok Kumar Sharma v. Regional Passport Officer, 2019 (173) DRJ 427. As per the author, even if there is a stay of conviction by the appellate court, then in such case, Section 6 (2) (f) of the Passports Act may be applicable. An order for stay of conviction (as well an order for suspension of sentence) can be passed under Section 389 (1) of the CRPC by an appellate court. In a case where the execution of the sentence is stayed by the court, the conviction would still continue to operate. Only once a conviction is stayed by court, would it cease to be operative during the subsistence of the stay order. *See generally* Ravikant S. Patil v. Sarvabhouma S. Bagali, 2007 (1) SCC 673; State of Maharashtra v. Gajanan, 2003 (12) SCC 432; Rama Narang v. Ramesh Narang, 1995 (2) SCC 513; Navjot Singh Sidhu v. State of Punjab, 2007 (93) DRJ 661 (SC). The power to stay a conviction should be exercised only in exceptional circumstances.

53 *See* S. 200 of the CRPC. *See generally* Abhijit Sen v. Superintendent (Administration) Regional Passport Officer, 2004 (1) CHN 66.

54 Sarath v. Regional Passport Officer, W.P. (MD) No. 18609/2018 (04.09.2018, Madras High Court, Madurai Bench).

55 *See generally* Abhijit Sen v. Superintendent (Administration) Regional Passport Officer, *supra*; Anand Tewari v. Union of India, 2014 (1) JCC 186.

cognizance of the offence.[56] The magistrate can take cognizance of an offence and direct the issue of process upon receipt of a police report, and until that stage is reached, he is said to be acting only as a magistrate controlling the investigation made by the police.[57]

The relevant date for the purpose of Section 6 (2) (f) of the Passports Act is the date of filing an application for issue of a passport. Any criminal proceedings initiated on a later date (i.e. after a determination has already been made by the passport authorities on the said application) will be considered separately and independently by the passport authorities in accordance with the prescribed procedures.[58] In appropriate cases, in case the criminal proceedings culminate in an acquittal of the passport holder, then in such case, he may be permitted to apply for a fresh passport for the purposes of scoring out any adverse entry or endorsement inserted against him in his passport by the passport authorities, during the pendency of the said criminal proceedings.[59] Further, the court may, in appropriate cases, order expunction of entries/endorsements from a passport if they are found to have been made in violation of law.[60]

Office Memorandum of 2019

The Ministry of External Affairs, Government of India,

56 W. Jaihar William v. State of Tamil Nadu, 2014 (8) MLJ 61.

57 Mathumari China Venkatareddy v. State of Andhra Pradesh, 1994 Cri. LJ 257 (A.P).

58 Anitha R. Radhakrishnan v. The Regional Passport Officer, Passport Office, W.P. (MD) No. 1547/2012 (03.09.2012, Madras High Court).

59 Gurpreet Singh Bal v. Union of India, 2008 (2) PLR 746.

60 Vikram Sharma v. Union of India, 2010 (171) DLT 671. In this matter, the passport authority, on the request of the National Commission of Women (NCW), issued a Look Out Circular (LOC) against the petitioner, and subsequently, while impounding his passport, inserted an endorsement 'off loaded (criminal complaint)' in the passport. The High Court, upon concluding that the act of the NCW in writing to the passport authority for issuance of a LOC against the petitioner was without authority of law, directed an expunction of the above-mentioned endorsement from the passport of the petitioner.

issued an office memorandum dated 10.10.2019 bearing No. VI/401/1/5/2019 on the subject of issuance of passports to persons against whom criminal proceedings were pending in a court of law. In the said memorandum, after taking note of the MEA Notification, the following additional instructions were issued to the passport authorities for processing passport applications in respect of applicants against whom criminal proceedings were pending before a criminal court in India:

a) The MEA Notification must be strictly applied in all cases.

b) The applicant must ensure that the undertaking (prescribed under the MEA Notification) was complete and correct in all respects.

c) The applications are to be processed on a pre police verification mode only.

d) In case the first pre police verification is found to be 'adverse', then in such case, a secondary police verification may be made. Separately, the passport authorities may also call for a discreet enquiry through the police authorities in the matter.

e) If the undertaking is found to be incomplete or misleading or the applicant is found to have suppressed details of criminal cases against him, then a show cause notice should be issued to the applicant and action initiated under the provisions of Section 12 of the Passports Act. In case the above-mentioned wrongdoing on the part of the applicant is detected after the passport has been issued, then in such case the passport may be impounded or revoked in accordance with Section 10 (3) (b) of the Passports Act, after following due procedure.

f) If the details mentioned in the police report and the undertaking submitted by the applicant are matching, then the 'no objection certificate' issued by a court of law would take precedence over any 'adverse' report submitted by the police authorities.

g) If the details mentioned in the police verification report and the undertaking submitted by the applicant are at variance, then a notice may be issued to the applicant seeking a clarification on this aspect.

h) If it comes to the attention of the passport authorities that the applicant has criminal proceedings pending against him before several courts of law, then the applicant may be advised to procure a 'no objection certificate' from all the concerned courts.

In the said office memorandum, a revised undertaking (to be filed by the applicant) was also annexed.

Court Prescribed Parameters

Further, recently in **Thadevoose Sebastian v. The Regional Passport Office**[61] the Kerala High Court, while taking note of the MEA Notification and the office memorandum dated 10.10.2019, formulated the following parameters which should govern the grant of permission by criminal courts in such matters:

a) The stage of the criminal proceeding and the duration of time within which the trial may take place.

b) The criminal antecedents and past conduct of the applicant.

c) The nature and gravity of the crime; offences under statutes dealing with acts of terrorism and acts of smuggling should require a different consideration.

d) In henious crimes, if the court decides to grant permission, the period for which permission is granted can be limited.

e) Chances of the applicant fleeing or evading trial.

61 2021 (5) KLT 531

f) The mode in which the presence of the applicant can be ensured during trial, alluding stipulating conditions like providing the address, change of address in the country of residence abroad, either with the Indian consulate at the country of residence abroad or with the court where the trial is pending.

g) The courts may, if deemed fit, fix the period for which the applicant can be granted permission to travel.

Effect of an Order of Probation

A question arises as to the interplay between an order of release under the provisions of the Probation of Offenders Act, 1958 (**Probation Act**) and the disqualification (for issuance of a passport) envisaged under Section 6(2)(f) of the Passports Act. In **Dalwinder Singh v. Union of India,**[62] the Punjab and Haryana High Court, while examining the provisions of the Probation Act and the Passports Act, observed that a release of the accused on good conduct under the provisions of the Probation Act will not relieve him of the disqualification envisaged under Section 6 of the Passports Act. Thus, an accused convicted of an offence by a criminal court and subsequently released on probation will not be entitled to issuance/renewal of his passport (on the basis of the said release) until the term/tenure and the conditions of the release/probation are fulfilled.[63]

62 2012 (2) ILR P&H 133.

63 The High Court, in the judgement, adverted to the following provisions of the Probation Act, which, to its mind, would be rendered nugatory in case the accused is issued a passport on the basis of which he leaves the country: (i) Section 4 (1) of the Probation Act which provides that an order of release on probation can be passed only if the offender or the surety has a fixed place of residence over which the court has effective jurisdiction. A person who takes a passport and leaves the country actually goes outside the jurisdiction of the jurisdictional court which has ordered the release; (ii) Section 4 (3) of the Probation Act which empowers the court ordering the release to pass an order of supervision of the offender by a probation officer. There cannot be an effective supervision of an offender who leaves the country using the

Types and Classes of Passports

The Passports Rules prescribe various types of passports or travel documents which can be issued to different classes of persons. This may be briefly summarised as follows:[64]

PASSPORTS		
S. No.	**Type of Passport**	**Class of Person**
1	Ordinary Passport	• Citizens of India
2	India, Sri Lanka Passports	• Persons who have been granted Indian citizenship under the India-Sri Lanka repatriation agreements of 1964 and 1974.*
3	Official Passports	• Government Officials whose passage is paid for by the government; • Officials of the Reserve Bank of India, State Bank of India, nationalised banks, corporations, undertakings and other institutions owned or controlled by the state, proceeding out of India on official work of their respective organisations; • Government officials sponsored by the Government of India for attending international conferences, seminars, meets, trainings et cetera.
4	Diplomatic Passports	• Officers of the Indian Foreign Service when proceeding out of India on official business.

passport; (iii) Section 9 of the Probation Act which provides that a probation order can be cancelled by court in case of failure on the part of the offender in complying with the conditions of probation. The High Court further observed that the passport holders will be entitled to prefer an appropriate application for renewal after the period of probation is completed.

64 R. 4 & Schedule II of the Passports Rules.

* On 30.10.1964, the governments of India and Sri Lanka signed an Agreement on Persons of Indian Origin in Ceylon (also known as the Sirima–Shastri Pact) for the purpose of determining the status and future of persons of Indian origin living

TRAVEL DOCUMENTS		
S. No.	Type of Travel Document	Class of Person
1	Emergency Certificate	• Indian citizens abroad who have been refused a passport, or whose passport is impounded or revoked or who have to be repatriated to India; • Indian citizens abroad whose passports are lost, stolen or damaged, and to whom you passports cannot be issued without verification by the passport authorities; • Persons who have produced a *prima facie* evidence of Indian citizenship but such evidence is considered insufficient and requires a further verification; • Persons of Indian origin abroad when allowed to come to India for settling down in India.
2	Certificate of Identity	• Stateless persons residing in India; • Foreigners, whose country is not represented in India, or whose national status is in doubt.
3	Haj Pilgrims	• Persons holding Haj allotment number for the relevant year from the Haj Committee.

in Ceylon. A chief feature of this agreement was India accepting repatriation of about 5.25 lakh persons of Indian origin (along with the natural increase to this number) from Ceylon over a span of 15 (fifteen) years, in an evenly phased manner. In the said agreement, it was also decided that a decision with respect to another lot of 1,50,000 (one lakh fifty thousand) persons of Indian origin (at Ceylon) would be taken at a later point in time. Subsequently, in the year 1974, the governments of both countries entered into another round of deliberations with respect to the above said 1.5 lakh persons. In this regard, inter alia, it was mutually decided that out of the said 1,50,000 (one lakh fifty thousand) persons, 75,000 (seventy five thousand) persons would be repatriated to India, in a phased manner across 2 (two) years, and granted Indian citizenship. An agreement in this regard came into being through a correspondence exchange dated 27.01.1974 between the then prime ministers of India and Sri Lanka.

Conditions of Passport

The issuance of a passport or travel document comes with various terms and conditions which if violated, can result in impounding or revocation of the passport. These terms and conditions are comprised in the Passport Rules and are summarised below:[65]

a) The passport or travel document ought to be used for travel only to the countries specified therein and must not be utilised for travel to other countries.
b) The passport or travel document must not be used for travel to countries not recognised by the Government of India.
c) The passport or travel document should not be sent out of any country by post.
d) The passport or travel document should not be allowed to pass into the possession of any unauthorised person.
e) The holder of the passport or travel document is personally responsible for its safe custody. It must not be wilfully lost, damaged or destroyed. In the event of its unintentional loss or destruction, the facts and circumstances of the case should be immediately reported to the nearest passport authority in India or to the nearest Indian mission or post (if the passport holder is abroad); and to the local police.
f) The passport or travel document must neither be altered nor mutilated in any way nor should any endorsement be made in it by any person other than a duly authorised official.
g) If the particulars of children are included in the passport or travel document of the parent or guardian, as the case may be, then the children shall not travel alone.
h) Children should apply for a separate passport on attaining the age of 15 (fifteen) years.
i) Where an Indian citizen abroad is to be repatriated to India

65 R. 19 & Schedule V of the Passports Rules.

at the expense of the Government of India, he shall surrender his passport or travel document to the Indian mission or post repatriating him and obtain an emergency certificate for direct return to India.

j) The holder of an emergency certificate, on arrival in India, shall surrender the certificate to the immigration check post.
k) The holder of a passport or travel document should be surrender it to the passport authority in case he ceases to be eligible to hold it.
l) A diplomatic or official passport shall automatically cease to be valid if the person to whom it was issued, ceases to exercise the functions which rendered him eligible to receive a diplomatic or official passport. In such event, the passport is required to be surrendered to the passport authority.

Duration of a Passport

The Passport Rules provide the period or duration of subsistence of a passport.[66] Post completion of this period or duration, the passport is required to be renewed.

a) An ordinary passport (for persons other than children below the age of 15 (fifteen) years)[67] remains in force for a period of 10 (ten) years from the date of its issue.
b) An emergency certificate remains in force for a period of 3 (three) months from the date of its issue.
c) A certificate of identity remains in force for a period of 10 (ten) years from the date of its issue.
d) A diplomatic and an official passport remains in force for a period to be decided by the central government or the passport

66 R. 12 of the Passports Rules.

67 An ordinary passport for a child below the age of 15 (fifteen) years, shall be in force for a period of 5 (five) years from the date of its issue or until the child attains the age of 15 (fifteen) years, whichever is earlier.

authority. In any case, the total life of the diplomatic or the official passport is 10 (ten) years from the date of its issue.

e) A passport issued to Haj pilgrims remains in force for a period of 8 (eight) months from the date of its issue.[68]

One Person: One Passport

The general rule is that one person is entitled to only one passport or travel document. A person holding a passport or travel document is not entitled to another passport or travel document unless he surrenders the one already held by him. However, if found necessary by the competent authorities, separate passports or travel documents may be issued to the same person in respect of different countries.[69]

Variation, Impounding and Revocation of Passport

The passport authority may, either on a *suo moto* application of the holder or with prior approval of the central government, vary or cancel the conditions under which the passport or travel document has been issued.[70] Further, the passport authority may, with prior approval of the central government, impound or revoke a passport or travel document in any of the following situations:[71]

a) If the passport authority is satisfied that the holder of the passport or travel document is in wrongful possession thereof.
b) If the passport or travel document was obtained by suppression of material information or on the basis of wrong

68 The practice of issuing temporary passports for Haj pilgrimage appears to have been discontinued by the government. *See* Unstarred Question No. 1904, Rajya Sabha available at https://www.mea.gov.in/press-releases.htm?dtl/21380/Q+1904+DISCONTINUATION+OF+TEMPORARY+PASSPORT+FOR+HAJ+PILGRIMS

69 R. 13 of the Passports Rules.

70 S. 10 (2) & (4) of the Passports Act.

71 S. 10 (3) of the Passport Act.

information provided by the holder of the passport travel document (or by any other person on his behalf).

c) If the passport authority deems it necessary, in the interests of the sovereignty and integrity of India, the security of India, friendly relations of India with any foreign country, or in the interests of the general public.[72]

d) If the holder of the passport or travel document has, post the issuance of the passport or travel document, been convicted by a court in India for an offence involving moral turpitude and sentenced to imprisonment for a minimum period of 2 (two) years.[73]

e) If criminal proceedings (with respect to an offence alleged to be committed by the holder of the passport or travel

---

72 Aspects such as the applicants being related to a militant or an extremist leader may, on its own, appear to be an irrelevant consideration for denying or impounding a passport. However such aspect must be taken into consideration in conjunction with other relevant factors. *See generally* Union of India v. Smt. Chiranjit Kaur, 1987 SCC (1) 671; Abid Hussain v. Union of India, AIR 2013 J & K 90. Merely because the applicant's father and uncle had a criminal record would not, *per se*, be sufficient to deny her a passport, especially when there is nothing on record to show her association or nexus with the crime syndicate of her relatives. *See* Akansksha Amar Naik v. Government of India, Ministry of External Affairs & Others, 2007 Cri LJ 575 (Bom). Clauses (a) to (c) of Section 10 (3) of the Passports Act contemplate a situation where a determination would have to be made either based on information available with the passport authority or, on the inputs of other statutory authorities. For instance, if it is a case of identity theft under clause (a) or under clause (b) some information has been suppressed or incorrectly provided, say for example, with regard to the address or details of parentage, inputs of other departments may have to be taken into account. Similarly, as to whether sovereignty and integrity or the security of the country is endangered, or the effect on the country's relationship with other countries is in issue, reliance may have to be placed on inputs provided by other wings of the Government of India. The same yardstick can be applied to the aspect of 'interests of the general public' in Section 10 (3) (c) of the Passports Act. As long as the inputs received from other authorities are actionable in nature, no fault can be found with the passport authorities taking recourse of the said aspect to impound a passport. Lalit Kr. Modi v. Union of India, 2013 (IV) ILR Del 2484.

73 Mere suspension of sentence of imprisonment, by the appellate court, or release of the convict on bail neither erases the conviction nor makes the conviction inoperative. *See generally* M. Natarajan v. The Regional Passport Officer, 2012 (4) CTC 709.

document) are pending against him before a court in India.[74]

f) If the holder of the passport or travel document has violated any conditions of the passport or travel document.

g) If the holder of the passport or travel document fails to comply with the notice issued under Section 6 (1) or Section 19 of the Passports Act requiring him to deliver up the same.[75]

h) If it is brought to the notice (and satisfaction) of the passport authority that a warrant or summons for the appearance, or a warrant for the arrest of the holder of the passport or travel

---

74 Pendency of a prosecution, besides being a ground for impounding of the passport under Section 10 (3) (e) is also a ground for refusal of issuance of a passport under Section 6 (2) (f) of the Act. Pendency of a criminal case is not ipso facto a ground under Section 10 (3) (e) of the Passports Act for impounding of the passport. it is not in all cases that pendency of proceedings in a Criminal Court will entail impounding of a passport; the Passport Authority is expected to apply its mind whether in the facts and circumstances of the case, a case of impounding of the passport is made out or not. Though the MEA Notification does not refer to Section 10(3) (e) which makes pendency of prosecution a ground for rejection of Passport but once persons against whom prosecution is pending are exempted from applicability of Section 6(2) (f), they would also be exempted from applicability of Section 10 (3) (e). Siddhartha Ashish Dey v. Union of India, W.P (C) No.7339/2015 (08.12.2015, Delhi High Court). Preventing persons with crime pending, to travel abroad, is to avoid fugitiveness. The nature of the crime assumes importance. Mere property disputes, family disputes or neighbourhood disputes masqueraded as crimes cannot be within the legislative contemplation to deprive a person of his fundamental right to travel. Here comes into play the passport authority's discretion in evaluating the nature, gravity and the depravity of the crime for deciding whether the pending crime should result in variation, impounding or revocation of the passport or travel document. Jayan v. Union of India, 2019 ILR (1) Kerala 56; Shashank Gupta v. Union of India, AIR 2018 All 253.

75 The notice must be specific to Section 6 (1) of the Passports Act (i.e. activities prejudicial to the sovereignty and integrity of India, presence detrimental to the security of India, presence prejudicial to the friendly relations of India with the other country) or to Section 19 of the Passports Act (i.e. pursuant to a notification of the central government prohibiting travel to an enemy state). A show cause notice calling upon the holder of a passport requiring him to show cause why the passport should not be impounded, does not qualify to be a notice as contemplated under Section 10 (1) to attract the provision of Section 10 (1) (g) of the Passports Act. *See generally* Jayan v. Union of India, 2019 ILR (1) Ker 56; Muhammed v. Union of India, 2018 (4) KHC 945.

document has been issued by a court under applicable law or an order has been made by a court prohibiting the departure of the holder of the passport or travel document from India.[76]

Section 10(3) of the Passports Act vests a fair amount of discretion in the passport authority whether to impound or not to impound the passport. Once a passport is issued by the passport authority for a particular period and certain developments subsequently come to its notice, then there are only 3 (three) options available to the passport authority i.e. (i) variation of the endorsements made on the passport under Section 10 (1) of the Passports Act; (ii) impounding of the passport under Section 10(3) of the Passports Act; or (iii) suspension of the passport under section 10 A of the Passports Act.[77]

Impounding & Revocation of Passport

There is a nuanced distinction between the concepts of 'impounding' and 'revocation' of a passport. In simple terms, the expression 'impound' means 'to seize or take into custody of law'. The expression 'revocation' on the other hand, refers to 'the withdrawal or recall of some power, authority or thing granted' or 'the undoing of or making void a thing granted'.

A passport, on its impounding, does not cease to exist. Only its possession in custody changes hands and it is placed in the hands of the relevant authorities. A passport, upon being revoked gets invalidated or is rendered *non-est*.[78]

---

76 Section 10 (3) (h) of the Passports Act gives power to the passport authority to impound the passport if any warrant of arrest is pending against passport holder. Issuance of non-bailable warrants by a court is sufficient to qualify Section 10 (3) (h) of the Passports Act. K. Sowmya v. Regional Passport Officer, Secunderabad and Ors., W.P. No. 4370/2015 (16.08.2016, Hyderabad High Court). A summons issued by Commission of Enquiry cannot form part of an impounding order under Section 10 (3) (h) of the Passports Act. *See* Menaka Gandhi v. Union of India, 1978 (1) SCC 248.

77 Venkatesh Kandasamy v. Government of India, AIR 2015 Mad 3.

78 *See generally* Aditya Khanna v. The Regional Passport Officer, 2009 (156) DLT 172.

While impounding is an interim measure which may be invoked during the pendency of the proceedings for revocation, revocation is the final punishment. Revocation of an earlier passport does not debar the passport holder from applying for a fresh passport, though it may be a consideration in issuance of a fresh passport.[79]

Power to Impound: Passport Authority

Only the 'passport authority', as defined under the Passports Act, is empowered to impound a passport.[80] Put differently, it is only under the provisions of the Passports Act that the revocation or impounding is possible.[81] Neither the police nor the court has the power to impound a passport.[82] No executing court has the power to impound the passport of the judgement debtor.[83] An order of court to deposit passport (and visa) as a condition of bail may not be sustainable.[84] There is no provision in the Passports Act which authorises an employer to retain the passport of the employee, even

79 Mohd. Irfan Gani v. Union of India, W.P. (C) No. 3605/2011 (30.09.2011, Delhi High Court).

80 S. 2 of the Passports Act and R. 3 of the Passport Rules along with Entry 27 of Schedule I thereto indicates as to who qualifies to be a passport authority under Indian law. *See also* Luingam Luithui v. Union of India, W.P. (C) No. 1546/2014 (23.08.2017, Delhi High Court).

81 Arockia Jeyabalan v. The Regional Passport Officer, W.P. Nos. 18637 & 22205/2014 (15.09.2014, Madras High Court).

82 Suresh Nanda v. Central Bureau of Investigation, (2008) 3 SCC 674. *See also* Abdul Majeed v. The State of Telangana, Criminal Petition No. 5266/2019 (01.04.2021, Telangana High Court); Shaik Abdul Jabbar v. State of A.P., 2019 (1) ALT (Crl.) 130 (AP).

83 Jose Peter v. C.K. Vijaya Kumar, W.P. (C) No. 8217/2009 (O) (18.06.2009, Kerala High Court).

84 Pushpal Swarnkar v. State of Chhattisgarh, Criminal Revision No. 715/2008 (03.12.2008, Chhattisgarh High Court). *But see* Krushnakant Kantilal Pancholi v. State of Gujarat, Criminal Application No. 5047/2008 (05.09.2008, Gujarat High Court) which suggests that a criminal court, while releasing an accused on bail, has power to impose condition to deposit/surrender passport.

if disciplinary proceedings or any other investigations are pending against the employee.[85]

While the police may have power to seize a passport under the provisions of the Criminal Procedure Code (CRPC), it does not have power to retain or impound the same, because that can only be done by the passport authority. Hence, if the police seize a passport, it must send the same along with a letter to the passport authority clearly stating that the seized passport deserves to be impounded for one of the reasons mentioned in Section 10 (3) of the Act. Thereafter, the passport authority would decide whether to impound the passport or not.[86]

When there exists a situation warranting impounding of a passport, there is no necessity to pass an independent order requiring a surrender of the passport since the expression 'impounding' includes within its meaning seizure of passport.[87]

It is impermissible to impound a passport (in the garb of public interest) to compel a settlement between disputing parties or to enforce recovery of money. Such action, even if taken *bona fide*, would not be countenanced by courts.[88]

The authority of courts and other governmental authorities to order for impounding/surrender of passports have been a subject to debate and deliberation. Various high courts have delivered conflicting decisions on this aspect. While some high courts observe that the power to impound solely vests in the passport authorities, other high courts observe that

85 *See* Norman Swaroop Issac v. State Bank of India, AIR 2007 AP 40.

86 Suresh Nanda, 2008 (3) SCC 674; Jae Young Chung v. State of A.P., W.P. No. 25639/2020 (05.01.2021, Andhra Pradesh High Court). All contingencies contemplated under Section 10 of the Passports Act are discretionary. If a passport has already been issued, its variation, impounding, or revocation is not automatic, even if a crime is found pending against the passport holder. Jayan v. Union of India, 2019 ILR (1) Ker 56.

87 *See generally* Hitesh Kapoor v. Union of India, 2012 (4) RCR (Civil) 135.

88 *See generally* Rohit Goswami v. Ministry of External Affairs, W.P. (C) No. 7706/2016 (18.09.2017, Delhi High Court).

in appropriate situations, even courts and other authorities (such as customs authorities etc.) can pass orders for deposit/surrender of passports. This section summarises some of the various judicial precedents on this issue.

Power to Impound: Courts

This section discusses the various precedents which allow for impounding or surrender of a passport by a court. At the time of adjudicating a bail application, in exercise of the judicial discretion vested with the court to secure the accused passport holder's presence for investigation, and also trial, it is open to the court to pass appropriate orders, including imposition of a condition directing the accused to produce and surrender his passport.[89] If, according to the prosecution, the passport is a vital document to be exhibited in the trial to prove the charges against the accused, then in such case, the prosecution can consider using certified copies of the passport for the trial.[90]

If the passport has no relevance to the criminal proceedings or the passport bears no nexus with the crime alleged to be committed by the accused, then the police have no authority to retain a passport especially when the investigation process is also over.[91]

The power of the passport authority to impound passport under Section 10(3)(e) of the Passports Act does not deprive the power and authority of a criminal court to enforce its order by appropriate directions.[92] The power granted to a criminal

89 Lijeesh v. State of Kerala, 2012 (3) KLJ 240. In the said matter, bail was granted by a criminal court to the accused subject to certain conditions, including surrender of his passport. This condition regarding surrender of passport was assailed by the accused before the High Court.

90 Veenita Gupta v. State, 2011 (1) RCR (Crl.) 915 (Ker). In the said matter, during the course of criminal proceedings, the prosecution wanted to use some of the entries in the passport as evidence for proving the charges against the accused.

91 *See generally* Ajeit Saksena v. The Deputy Director Directorate of Enforcement, 2018 (2) Crimes 227 (Mad).

92 V.A. Mohammed Rafeek v. Union of India, 2011 (3) KJL 183.

court under Section 437 of the CRPC to impose conditions for bail, including restriction of movement, can be taken as a procedure established by law as required under Article 21 of the Constitution.[93]

However, criminal courts must take extreme care in imposing such conditions regarding surrender of passport. It cannot mechanically, and in every case where an accused has a passport, impose a condition for its surrender. The criminal court has to consider the possibility of the accused, if released on bail, fleeing justice. The court has to decide whether, notwithstanding the personal liberty of the accused, interest of justice demands that his right of movement should be restricted during the pendency of the case, by directing him to surrender his passport.[94]

Power to Impound: Customs & Other Authorities

Typically, the customs authorities are not authorised to impound the passport of a person (a power solely vested with the passport authorities). However, the customs authorities have the power to detain a passport if it is relevant for any enquiry or proceedings under the Customs Act.[95] However, the procedure envisaged under Section 110 of the Customs Act must be followed and proper reasons must be afforded by the customs authority for retaining the passport as required under Section 110(3) of the Customs Act. The passport ought to be returned when not required by the customs authorities for the above said purpose.[96]

93 The function of a criminal court under section 437 of the CRPC is not merely to impose a condition in the bond that the accused to whom bail is being granted, is required to be present before the court or the concerned officer. The court has to ensure that the condition is complied with and enforced. The court has to ensure that the accused who is released on bail and who has a passport does not flee from justice.

94 V.A. Mohammed Rafeek v. Union of India, 2011 (3) KJL 183.

95 S. 110 of the Customs Act.

96 Bangantavida Nazir v. Inspector of Customs, W.P. (C) No. 32496/2014 (11.12.2014, Kerala High Court). *But see* Shahid Ali v. Commissioner of Customs, Airport and Administration and Ors., W.P. No. 641/2012 (25.09.2012, Calcutta High Court)

Section 14 of the Passports Act can be invoked for the purpose of dealing with the offences or illegalities committed in regard to the issuance of passports or the misuse of the same. If the passport is seized on the ground that it is useful or relevant for the proceeding under the Customs Act, the proper action to be taken is provided under Section 110 of the Customs Act and not under Section 14 of the Passports Act.[97] Where the passport or travel documents itself forms the basis of the offence imputed against the passport holder, then the investigating agency can retain such document for the purposes of fair investigation of the crime.[98]

In the context of the Foreign Exchange Management Act, 1999, Delhi High Court has observed that the power to seize a passport is not exclusive to the passport authority. The provisions of the Passports Act do not, in any manner, control or limit provisions in other laws which empower other authorities to independently impound or detain passports in furtherance of the specified objectives of such enactments.[99]

---

which indicates that there is no provision under the Customs Act, 1962 under which customs authorities can withhold a passport.

97 Santha Kumar v. Collector of Customs & Ors., 1990 (29) ECR 46 (Ker). A passport answers the description of 'document' under Section 110 (3) of the Customs Act. Devadasan Dayalal v. Collector of Customs, 1986 (9) ECR 558.

98 Niyas v. State of Kerala, 2011 (3) ILR 981 (Ker). In the said matter, the imputation against the passport holder was alleged production of a forged visa before the immigration department of an international airport, for travelling to a foreign country. Apparently, there appeared a close nexus between the passport and the offence committed by the accused. The court further observed that the investigating agency had to be given an opportunity to examine the alleged forged documents for ascertaining commission of an offence.

99 Suman Sehgal v. Union of India, 2006 (88) DRJ 721. In the said matter, the Delhi High Court discussed the provisions of Section 37 and 38 of the Foreign Exchange Management Act, 1999 (FEMA), a special law relating to foreign exchange, which permitted the competent authorities to seize documents, in specific situations. The Delhi High Court, while examining the conspectus of the passports act, *inter alia*, made the following observations: (i) the provisions of the passports act, provides for a comprehensive law dealing with the conditions under which passports can be issued, revoked and impounded; (ii) Nevertheless, the Passports Act cannot be considered to override the provisions contained in other enactments conferring independent powers upon other authorities to impound

Rules of Natural Justice

The passport authority is statutorily empowered to vary or cancel an endorsement on the passport only with the previous approval of the central government.[100] Rules of natural justice would be applicable while exercising the power to impound or revoke a passport or a travel document. Typically, a pre-decisional hearing should be given to the passport holder prior to taking steps to impound a passport or travel document.[101] In extreme or emergent situations, the passport authorities may impound a passport without affording a prior opportunity to the concerned person (where the exercise of power itself may be frustrated by giving a prior notice of hearing etc.) however, such hearing then must be given immediately after the order is passed.[102] The passport authority must apply its mind on the material available and thereafter take a decision on this aspect.[103]

A person cannot be deprived of his right to travel except in accordance with the procedure established by law.[104] It is incumbent upon the passport authority to record in writing a brief statement of reasons for making an order of impounding of passport and to furnish such ground and statement to the

---

passports and documents, in exercise of the jurisdiction; (iii) Reliance was also placed on Section 23 of the Passports Act which indicates that the provisions of the Passports Act are in addition to and not in derogation of other enactments including laws relating to foreigners and foreign exchange.

100 *See* Adishri Saisha Manan v. Union of India, W.P. (C) No. 8682/2005 (31.05.2005, Delhi High Court).

101 *See generally* Maneka Gandhi v. Union of India, AIR 1978 SC 597; Institute of Chartered Accountants of India v. L.K. Ratna, (1087) 164 ITR 1 (SC); Aditya Khanna v. The Regional Passport Officer, 2009 (156) DLT 172.

102 *See generally* Maneka Gandhi v. Union of India, AIR 1978 SC 597; Aditya Khanna v. The Regional Passport Officer, 2009 (156) DLT 172.

103 Abid Hussain v. Union of India, AIR 2013 J & K 90; DTC v. DTC Mazdoor Congress, (1991) I LLJ 395 SC.

104 Satwant Singh Sawhney v. D. Ramarathnam, Assistant Passport Officer, AIR 1967 SC 1836. The Passports Act is 'procedure established by law' within the meaning of Article 21 of the Constitution. Peter Samouel Wallace v. The Regional Passport Officer, 1972 (8) DLT 433.

concerned person,[105] unless the passport authority opines that furnishing the same to the concerned person would not be in the interests of the sovereignty and integrity of India, friendly relations of India with any foreign country or in the interests of the general public.[106] Reasons for impounding and refusal of issuance of a passport should be communicated to the applicant.[107]

The procedure for impounding a passport is not dependent on the subjective satisfaction of the passport authority. The passport authority is required to record in writing a brief statement of reasons for impounding the passport and, save in exceptional circumstances, to supply a copy of such statement to the affected person, so that he can challenge the decision before a higher authority which can then examine and evaluate the reasons so recorded for impounding.[108]

The requirement of giving reasons acts as a healthy check against abuse or misuse of power.[109] If the reasons adduced for impounding are, in the opinion of the court, irrelevant or extraneous or if there exists no nexus between the reasons and the ground on which the passport is impounded, then the court may strike down the order of impounding.[110] Impounding of a passport has civil consequences and therefore, the competent

105 Sunil Jaiswal v. Union of India, 2010 (3) GLT 775. *See also* S. 10 (3) and 10 (5) of the Passport Act.

106 The exception contained in Section 10 (5) the Passports Act results in exclusion of principles of natural justice by necessary implication. This exception should normally be invoked only in special circumstances, such as urgency, emergency, need for secrecy, possibility of the person concerned thwarting remedial or preventive action, where promptitude is of great importance et cetera. *See generally* Minoo Maneckshaw Khalifa v. Union of India, 1974 (76) Bom LR 788.

107 Hajra Iqbal Memon v. Union of India, 1997 (41) DRJ 108. *See also* Adishri Saisha Manan v. Union of India, W.P. (C) No. 8682/2005 (31.05.2005, Delhi High Court).

108 Maneka Gandhi v. Union of India, AIR 1978 SC 597.

109 An appeal challenging an unreasoned order of compounding/revocation is really inconsequential in as much as, the aggrieved is incapable of effectively assailing the order. Manish Kumar Mittal v. Chief Passport Officer, 2013 (202) DLT 317.

110 Menaka Gandhi v. Union of India, *supra*

authorities are duty bound to afford an opportunity of hearing to the concerned person.[111]

Normally the material on the basis of which are decision to impound is taken, should have a rational nexus with the decision itself.[112] In the event the alleged 'nexus' between the material and the ground is problematic, fanciful or too remote, then it may be held to be 'no real nexus' at all.[113]

Orders under Section 10 (3) of the Passports Act must be based on some material, even if the material relates to reasonable suspicion arising from certain credible assertions made by reliable individuals.[114]

Since impounding of a passport has civil consequences, the passport authority must give an opportunity of hearing to the person concerned before impounding his passport. It is well settled that any order which has civil consequences must be passed after giving opportunity of hearing to a party.[115] The procedure for impounding of a passport prescribed in the Passports Act must be strictly followed.[116] The show cause issued to the applicant in case of an intended impounding/revocation by the passport authority, should typically specify the specific provision under which an impounding/revocation is sought to be made.[117] An order of revocation of

111 Suresh Nanda, *supra*

112 *See generally* Minoo Maneckshaw Khalifa v. Union of India, 1974 (76) Bom LR 788.

113 Minoo Maneckshaw Khalifa, *supra*

114 DTC v. DTC Mazdoor Congress, (1991) I LLJ 395 SC.

115 State of Orissa v. Binapani Dei, AIR 1967 SC 1269. *See generally* Jae Young Chung v. State of A.P., W.P. No. 25639/2020 (05.01.2021, Andhra Pradesh High Court).

116 Gilden Jacob v. The Foreigners Regional Registration Officer, W.P. (MD) No. 24591/2018 (11.02.2020, Madrah High Court, Madurai Bench).

117 In Monika Karmakar v. Union of India, W.P. No. 24020(W)/2015 (01.10.2015, Calcutta High Court), the petitioner was asked to show cause by the passport authorities as to why her passport should not be revoked under Section 10 (3) (a) of the Passports Act, but the decision to revoke her passport was ultimately

a passport without issuance of a show cause notice is liable to be set aside.[118]

It is impermissible for the passport authority to *simplicitor* retain a passport without impounding the same or taking recourse to applicable law for its impounding.[119] When no order for impounding the passport is passed, it may not be proper for the passport authority to withhold the passport.[120]

If a passport has not been impounded on any of the grounds specified in the Passports Act, it is impermissible for the passport authority to withhold issuance of a passport clearance certificate for travel abroad.[121]

Pendency of a criminal offence against the holder of the passport would not automatically result in impounding of the passport.[122] Non-disclosure of pendency of a minor criminal case should not be taken by the competent authorities to be a material suppression of fact warranting impounding of the passport.[123]

---

taken under Section 10 (3) (b) of the Passports Act. In that context, the court held that the passport authorities should have allowed the petitioner to raise a defence under the changed provision. No order for revocation of passport can be passed on the ground which is not previously put to the applicant.

118 Rajbardhan Singh Rajpoot v. Union of India, W.P. (C) No. 6679/2013 (18.12.2013, Delhi High Court).

119 Asit Kumar Rout v. Principal Secretary to Government of Odisha, 2014 (II) OLR 248.

120 Gilden Jacob v. The Foreigners Regional Registration Officer, *supra*

121 *See* Bhupinder Singh Cheema v. The State of Haryana, 2012 (5) RCR (Civil) 286. In the said matter, when the petitioner (the holder of a valid subsisting passport) applied to the passport authority for issuance of a passport clearance certificate (as required by the US Embassy), the same was denied to him by the passport authority on the pretext that his name had been included in the surveillance list on account of the fact that his brother and brother-in-law were perceived to be terrorists. However, no separate steps for impounding or revocation of the petitioner's passport were (or had been) taken by the passport authority. The High Court *inter alia* held that sans an impounding or a revocation of a passport (in compliance with law) a passport clearance certificate cannot be denied to a passport holder.

122 Neera Chandra v. Union of India, 2019 (9) ADJ 791.

123 *ibid*

Interplay between Section 6 and 10 of the Passports Act

Pertinently, the ground of 'pendency of criminal proceeding' is found both under section 6 and section 10 of the Passports Act. In other words, Pendency of a prosecution, besides being a ground for impounding of the passport under Section 10 (3)(e) may also be a ground for refusal of issuance of a passport under Section 6(2)(f) of the Passports Act. Section 6 of the Passports Act lays down the threshold for issuance of passports. On the other hand, Section 10 of the Passports Act deals with passports already issued.

Though the MEA Notification does not refer to Section 10 (3)(e), which makes pendency of prosecution a ground for rejection of passport, however, once persons against whom prosecution is pending are exempted from applicability of Section 6 (2)(f) of the Passports Act, they would also be exempted from applicability of Section 10 (3) (e) of the Passports Act.[124]

A passport cannot be refused or cancelled only on the ground of registration of an FIR.[125] The act of the applicant in not revealing a crime, when the matter is at the stage of police investigation, may not amount to suppression, either for the purposes of Section 10 (3) (b) or Section 10 (3) (e) of the Passports Act or Section 12 (1) of the Passports Act.[126]

Courts observe that a person cannot be deprived of his livelihood by seizing his passport, merely because he is involved in a criminal case. A holistic view of the matter should be taken by the authorities. In one instance, the applicant was in active service in a foreign country even before the charge sheet had been submitted

---

124 Siddhartha Ashish Dey v. Union of India, W.P. (C) No.7339/2015 (08.12.2015, Delhi High Court).

125 Sahib Jaskaran Singh v. Union of India and Ors., C.W.P. No. 19551/2015 (O&M) (13.10.2015, Punjab & Haryana High Court); Daler Singh v. Union of India and Ors., C.W.P. No. 12143/2015 (O&M) (01.10.2015, Punjab & Haryana High Court).

126 Jayan v. Union of India, 2019 ILR (1) Kerala 56; Muhammed v. Union of India, 2018 (4) KHC 945.

against him. Thereafter, he had attended court on each and every date; his visa was about to expire and he was in a position of losing his employment if he did not go back to the foreign country.[127] The court directed for issuance of a passport to him.

Public Interest

The expression 'in the interest of the general public' appearing in Section 10 (3) (c) of the Passports Act has been generally interpreted to mean 'for the benefit of general public and for a public purpose'.[128] Any restriction placed in the interest of the general public may be interpreted to include any fetters placed 'in furtherance of social or economic policy' and 'for common good'. Any action which impinges on a citizen's fundamental right to travel has to be justified by overwhelming public good and larger public interest, so as to fall within the scope of the expression 'in the interest of the general public' as employed in Section 10 (3) (c) of the Passports Act.[129] Typically, a court will not sit in appeal over the satisfaction of the government on this aspect and even if there is *prima facie* evidence on which a reasonable body of persons may hold that it is in public interest

---

127 Pawan Kumar v. State of Rajasthan, Crl. Misc. Petition No. 69/2000 (16.02.2000, Rajasthan High Court).

128 The expression 'interest of the general public' has wide connotation and takes within its sweep all kinds of interests of the general public. *See generally* Aditya Khanna v. The Regional Passport Officer, 2009 (156) DLT 172. Any action taken by the passport authorities in connection with any violation with respect to the Foreign Exchange Management Act, 1999 (FEMA), a special law relating to foreign exchange, and involving large sums of money, may be considered to be in the realm of public interest. Lalit Kr. Modi v. Union of India, 2013 (IV) ILR Delhi 2484. A passport may not be suspended or revoked under Section 10 (3) of the Passports Act merely on account of non-appearance before the investigation proceedings under FEMA. *See generally* Junaid Iqbal Mohammed Memon v. Union of India, AIR 2019 Delhi 142.

129 Rohit Goswami v. Ministry of External Affairs, W.P. (C) 7706/2016 (18.09.2017, Delhi High Court). *See also* State of Bihar v. Kameshwar Singh, AIR 1952 SC 252 which observes that the expression 'public interest' would also take a look from the statute.

to impound the passport, the requirements of law would be said to be fulfilled.[130]

Security of India

The expression 'security of India' used in Section 10 (3) (c) of the Passports Act would refer to 'any aggravated form of prejudicial activities which endanger the very existence of the state' or 'in the very least, threaten the life and limb of its citizens'.[131]

This expression must be construed in keeping with the accompanying words in the said provision, namely, 'sovereignty and integrity of India'. Consequently, the words 'security of India' will not include or encompass 'economic or financial security of India'.[132]

Warrant or Summons issued by a Court

Where the notice issued by the Debt Recovery Tribunal provides an option to the passport holder to either appear in person or through an authorised representative, then such notice cannot be construed as a 'summons' or 'warrant' in terms of Section 10 (3(h) of the Passports Act. Section 10 (3 (h) of the Passports Act has been devised in larger public interest. It cannot be called in aid for settling civil disputes by aggrieved persons. This provision does not give any right to a person who has civil claims against the passport holder, to seek impounding of his passport.[133]

130 *See generally* Minoo Maneckshaw Khalifa, *supra*

131 *See generally* Priya Parameswaran Pillai v. Union of India, 2015 (VII) AD Del 10.

132 Faisal P.A. and Ors. v. Regional Passport Officer and Ors., 2019 (369) ELT 184 (Ker).

133 ICICI Limited v. The Passport Office, AIR 2002 Kar 118. In the said matter, the petitioner, a financial institution, had lent money to certain persons who had defaulted in their repayment obligations, resulting in the financial institution commencing recovery proceedings in the relevant Debt Recovery Tribunal. In the meanwhile, the petitioner, based on an apprehension that the defaulting persons may flee the country and defeat the recovery process, requested the passport office to impound their passports in furtherance of Section 10 (3) (h) of the Passports Act, however the passport office did not take any action. The question before the

Prohibition of Travel by a Court Order

The power or the Court under Section 10 (3) (h) of the Passports Act to pass an order prohibiting the departure of a person from India has to be made only in exceptional and rare cases where there are necessary grounds and reasons and that power cannot be exercised liberally.[134]

Suspension of Passport

The Passports Act permits the central government (or any designated officer) to temporarily suspend or invalidate a passport or travel document, if it is satisfied that the said passport or travel document is likely to be impounded or caused to be impounded or revoked under Section 10 (3) (c) of the Passports Act. (i.e. in the interests of the sovereignty and integrity of India, the security of India, friendly relations of India with any foreign country, or in the interests of the general public); and that it is necessary in public interest to do so.[135] Such order of suspension/ invalidation of a passport or travel document is further subject to the following conditions:

a) The suspension order shall be valid for a period not exceeding 4 (four) weeks. This period may be extended by an order and for reasons to be recorded in writing, until the proceedings

---

high court was whether, in the facts and circumstances of the case, the petitioner could, as a matter of right, require the passport authorities to impound a passport in accordance with section 10 (3) (h) of the Passports Act. *But see* Annai Jayabharathi v. The Debt Recovery Tribunal, 2005 (1) KLJ 737 which distinguishes the above judgement of ICICI Ltd. and observes that the powers of execution granted to the Debt Recovery Tribunal to arrest the judgement debtor and to detain him in prison for enforcing the realisation of a debt carries with it an incidental power to prevent a person from going abroad, as an interim measure, so as to give effect to the power of ordering the arrest of the judgement debtor and his detention in prison conferred on the Debt Recovery Tribunal in terms of the applicable statute.

134 C.T. Abraham v. J.R. James and Ors., C.M.P. No. 11866/1992 in A.S. No. 874/1991 (17.11.1992, Madras High Court).

135 S. 10A of the Passports Act.

relating to variation, impounding or revocation of the passport or travel document are concluded.[136]

b) The affected person shall be granted an opportunity of hearing within a period of not later than 8 (eight) weeks (to be reckoned from the date of passing of the order), pursuant to which, the central government may, if necessary, by order in writing, modify or revoke the earlier order.[137]

An order for suspension/invalidation of a passport or travel document would be in the nature of an emergent action, having a limited time span, and further subject to the conditions described above.[138] In the absence of reasons for suspension of the passport, the right to hearing available to the applicant would be reduced to an empty formality.[139] The requirement of giving reasons for the extension of the suspension/invalidation order is a vital safeguard against such suspension/invalidation being whimsical or arbitrary; and this requirement cannot be defeated by mechanically passing an order of extension.[140] The power of suspension/

136 Retention of a passport by the central government under Section 10A of the Passports Act can only be initially for a period of 4 (four) weeks. Thereafter, the passport can be retained only pursuant to an order passed by the competent authority. Suresh Nanda v. Central Bureau of Investigation, (2008) 3 SCC 674.

137 It is well settled that a show cause notice should contain the particulars to enable the noticee to address the allegations made against him. Absence of relevant materials/information on the show cause notice may result in such notice getting vitiated. *See* Faizal Ibrahim v. Union of India, W.P. (C) No. 2109/2017 (12.09.2017, Delhi High Court). It is desirable that a show cause notice should be a self-contained document spelling out the case to be met. There can be no illegality or infirmity in a show cause notice which refers to or incorporates certain contents from accompanying documents, so long as the concerned party receives the complete text of such accompanying documents also. *See generally* R.M. Tufail v. Union of India, 2002 (64) DRJ 22 (DB).

138 Rajiv Saxena v. Union of India, 276 (2021) DLT 245.

139 Sikandar Khan v. Union of India, W.P. (C) No. 5315/2017 (06.07.2017, Delhi High Court).

140 Faizal Ibrahim v. Union of India, *supra*

invalidation of a passport is a serious restriction on the fundamental rights of a citizen of India and the same cannot be resorted to without sufficient cause, without complying with the express conditions as indicated in law and without following the principles of natural justice.[141] Framing of a show cause notice without application of mind or making bald allegations (as a cause for the suspension) would result in deprivation of rights of the applicant.[142]

It is impermissible to pass an indefinite order of suspension while not proceeding further with the proceeding under Section 10 of the Passports Act.[143] It is essential that the order is communicated to the affected person before that person can be bound by that order.[144] If no step(s) are taken by the passport authority for impounding or revoking a passport, then the passport cannot even be suspended under Section 10 A of the Passports Act.[145]

Look Out Circular

A Look-Out-Circular (**LOC**) is issued by government authorities for keeping a watch on arrival/departure of Indians and foreigners. The principal objective of the LOC is to ensure that a person is available for interrogation, trial or enquiry.[146] Under Indian law, issuance of LOC is governed by executive instructions issued by the Ministry of Home Affairs (Foreigners Division), Government of India. In the context of the Passports

141 Sikandar Khan *supra*

142 Sikandar Khan *supra*

143 Rajiv Saxena v. Union of India, 276 (2021) DLT 245.

144 Bachhittar Singh v. The State of Punjab, AIR 1963 SC 395. *See also* Rajiv Saxena v. Union of India, 276 (2021) DLT 245.

145 Ashok Muthana v. The Regional Passport Officer, W.P. No. 33546/2013 (24.09.2014, Madras High Court).

146 Asifkhader v. Central Bureau of Investigation, W.P. No. 55157/2018 (04.04.2019, Karnataka High Court).

Act, the power to issue a LOC is traceable to Sections 10A and 10B thereof.[147]

A LOC is issued by the Ministry of Home Affairs, Government of India as well as certain other authorities such as Ministry of External Affairs, Government of India; Customs Department; Income Tax Department; Directorate of Revenue Intelligence; Central Bureau of Investigation; Interpol; Regional Passport Officers; Police Authorities in various states et cetera.[148] Statutory bodies like the National Commission for Human Rights are not empowered or authorised to issue LOCs.[149] Recently the central government has permitted heads of public sector banks to request for opening of a LOC against wilful defaulters attempting to flee India.[150] The evolution of the concept of LOC in India is discussed briefly below.

The Office Memorandum of 1979

The earliest set of instructions/directives with respect to LOC's was issued by the Ministry of Home Affairs *vide* Office Memorandum No. 25022/13/78 - F1, dated 05.09.1979. As per the said communication, the authorities authorised to issue a LOC included the Ministry of External Affairs, Customs Department, Income Tax Department, Directorate of Revenue

147 *ibid*

148 Karti P. Chidambaram v. Bureau of Immigration, Ministry of Home Affairs, Government of India, W.P. No. 21305 & 20798/2017 (23.07.2018, Madras High Court).

149 Vikram Sharma v. Union of India, W.P. (C) No. 10180/2009 (27.07.2010, Delhi High Court). In OM No. 25016/31/2010-Imm dated 27.10.2010 issued by the Ministry of Home Affairs, statutory bodies like NCW, NHRC, National Commission for Protection of Children's Rights etc. can now make a request for issuance of a LOC in accordance with the procedure prescribed therein.

150 *See* Unstarred Question No. 1317 answered by the Ministry of Home Affairs, Government of India available at https://www.mha.gov.in/MHA1/Par2017/pdfs/par2018-pdfs/ls-18122018/1317.pdf. As per the knowledge of the author, the said decision of the central government to allow banks to request for LOCs has been assailed in various high courts, including the Delhi & Bombay High Court and the matter is *sub judice*.

Intelligence, Central Bureau of Investigation, Interpol, Regional Passport Officers, Police Authorities in various states etc. The said communication further provided that the period of validity of the LOC should be clearly specified therein, failing which the LOC shall be considered valid only for a period of one year from the date of issue, and the same shall be maintained by the person concerned at the immigration check posts only for the said period.

The Office Memorandum of 2000

Subsequently, the Ministry of Home Affairs issued another OM No. 25022/20/98 – FIV dated 27.12.2000 which, *inter alia*, specified the steps required to be taken for opening a LOC in respect of an Indian citizen, which included the following: (i) making a request for opening an LOC, in the prescribed proforma, to the immigration check posts, to an officer not below the rank of deputy secretary to the government of India/joint secretary in the state government/concerned superintendent of police at district level; and (ii) provision of complete identifying particulars of the concerned person (in respect of whom the LOC is to be opened).

The said OM further provided that an LOC would be initially valid for a period of 1 (one) year and would be automatically closed upon completion of the said period, absent an extension (pursuant to a request by the concerned authority).

The Delhi High Court Guidelines

In the year 2010, in **Sumer Singh Salkan v. Assistant Director,**[151] the Delhi High Court formulated the following guidelines with respect to issuance of a LOC:

a) Recourse to a LOC can be taken by an investigating agency in case of cognizable offences under the Indian Penal Code or other penal laws, where the accused is deliberately evading

151 2010 (6) ILR Del 706.

arrest or not appearing in the trial court despite non-bailable warrants and other coercive measures; and there is a likelihood of the accused leaving the country to evade trial/arrest.

b) The investigating officer shall make a written request for issuance of a LOC to the notified officer in the Ministry of Home Affairs, Government of India, giving details and reasons for seeking issuance of a LOC.[152] The said notified officer alone shall give directions for issuing/opening LOC by passing an order in this respect.

c) The person against whom the LOC is issued must join investigation by appearing before the investigating officer or should surrender before the concerned court or should satisfy the court that the LOC was wrongly issued against him. He may also approach the notified officer who issued the LOC to explain how the LOC was wrongly issued against him. A LOC can be withdrawn by the authority that issued it and can also be rescinded by the trial court (where the case against the accused is pending) or by the concerned trial court having jurisdiction over the concerned police station, on an application being preferred by the accused.

d) A LOC is a coercive measure to make a person surrender to the investigating agency or the court of law. The trial court's jurisdiction in affirming or cancelling a LOC is commensurate with its jurisdiction in affirming or cancelling non-bailable warrants.

The Office Memorandum of 2010

In the year 2010, subsequent to the above-mentioned judgement of the Delhi High Court, the Ministry of Home Affairs issued another detailed office memorandum on the subject (OM No. 25016/31/2010-Imm dated 27.10.2010) wherein detailed

152 Existence of reasons is a condition precedent for issuance of a LOC, which should be disclosed in the request form/proforma. Karti P. Chidambaram, *supra*

guidelines were laid down regarding issuance of an LOC in respect of Indian citizens and foreigners. Some of the pertinent guidelines are summarised below.

a) The request for opening a LOC is required to be made by the originating agency to the Deputy Director, Bureau of Immigration, in the prescribed pro-forma.
b) The request for opening a LOC must be issued only with the approval of an officer of a certain rank, not below the grades mentioned in the OM.
c) The originating agency must provide complete identifying particulars (apart from sex and nationality) of the concerned person (in respect of whom an LOC is to be opened). A LOC can be issued if the name and passport particulars of the concerned person are made available. The originating agency is obligated to proactively provide additional identification parameters to minimise harassment to genuine passengers.
d) In exceptional cases, LOCs can be issued without complete parameters or case details against terrorists, antinational elements etc, in larger national interest.[153]
e) The legal liability of the action taken by the immigration authorities in furtherance of a LOC rests with the originating agency.
f) The originating agency is mandated to provide the reasons for opening the LOC.
g) Recourse to LOC is to be taken in case of cognizable offences under the provisions of the Indian Penal Code or other penal laws.

153 In Priya Parameswaran Pillai v. Union of India, 2015 (VII) AD Del 10, the Delhi High Court examined as to who would qualify to be an 'anti-national element' under the said OM. The Delhi High Court, post a detailed discussion, concluded that the said expression would refer to a person who projects a present and imminent danger to the national interest.

h) In cases where there is no cognizable offence under the provisions of the Indian Penal Code or other penal laws, the concerned person cannot be detained/arrested or prevented from leaving the country. At best, the originating agency can be informed about the arrival/departure of the concerned person.
i) The LOC will be valid for a period of 1 (one) year from the date of its issue and the name of the concerned person shall be automatically removed from the list unless the concerned agency requests for its renewal before the expiry of the 1 (one) year period. However, there shall be no automatic deletion in the following cases: (i) Ban-Entry LOCs issued for watching arrival of wanted persons; (ii) Loss of passport LOCs; (iii) LOCs regarding impounding of passports; (iv) LOCs issued at the behest of courts and Interpol.
j) Statutory bodies such as the NCW, NHRC, National Commission for Protection of Children's Rights may make a request for preventing any Indian or foreigner from leaving India subject to the fulfilment of the following conditions: (i) The request (along with all necessary facts) are to be brought to the notice of the law enforcement agencies; (ii) The concerned Superintendent of Police will assess the situation and make a request for issuance of the LOC in accordance with the procedure prescribed in the OM; (iii) Further, the immigration authorities will open the LOC in accordance with the OM.

Renewal of Passport

There is no express provision in the Passports Act which deals with the aspect of renewal of a passport. An application for renewal of a passport is to be considered only in accordance with Section 5 of the Passports Act. In other words, the terms renewal, extension or re-issue, of a passport after the expiry of the normal period as originally prescribed, should be construed as the issue of passport.[154]

Once a passport is issued for a particular period, there are only three options open to the passport authority namely: (a) Variation of the endorsements made on the passport under Section 10 (1); or (b) the impounding of the passport under Section 10 (3); or (c) the suspension of the passport under Section 10A.[155]

Surrender of Passport

A person holding a passport or travel document, in special circumstances, shall not be entitled to another passport or travel document unless he surrenders to the passport authority, the passport or travel document already held by him.[156]

Change of Name and Birth Details in the Passport

Generally, it is permissible for the passport authorities to accept and consider applications for rectification/correction in the passport, including a change in the date of birth, place of birth etc. However, in case of a dispute/difference in the documents of the applicant, the passport authority may require the applicant to obtain a proper declaration from a civil court before a rectification is made.

Various circulars have been issued from time to time by the Ministry of External Affairs, Government of India, setting out parameters for effecting a change in the passport details, including a change in the date of birth, place of birth et cetera.[157] One such specific circular is Circular No. 18.04.2001 issued by the Ministry

154 Venkatesh Kandasamy v. Government of India, AIR 2015 Mad 3; Ashok Muthana v. The Regional Passport Officer, W.P. No. 33546/2013 (24.09.2014, Madras High Court).

155 Ashok Muthana, *supra*

156 R. 13 of the Passport Rules. See also Tenzin Passang v. Union of India, 2017 (164) DRJ 100.

157 *See for example* Circular No. VI/401/2/5/2001, dated 29.10.2007 issued by the MEA. *See generally* Musthafa Nambiamkulam Abdulkader v. Ministry of External Affairs, 2013 (4) KLT 527; Mohd. Nasrullah Khan v. Regional Passport Officer, 2005 (1) ALD 95.

of External Affairs, Government of India, wherein the following instructions have been issued to the passport authorities:[158]

a) Where an applicant is seeking rectification/correction of a mistake in the entry on the date of birth/place of birth in the passport, the passport authority may, after verifying/satisfying itself, affect the correction treating the same as a technical correction. There is no need for a declaratory order from a civil court in such cases.
b) Where a competent authority issuing a birth certificate were to issue any correction/amendment, the passport authority may affect the necessary amendment in the passport without insisting on a court order.
c) Where the initial entry has been made on the basis of a supportive document issued by one competent authority i.e. school/educational authority and the applicant subsequently requests for a change on the basis of a certificate issued by another competent authority i.e. municipal authorities, resulting in conflicting sources of valid proof, the passport authority should direct the applicant to obtain an order from a civil court certifying the valid date of birth/place of birth.

The above circular dated 18.04.2001 was subsequently amended by another circular dated 29.10.2007 wherein the following clarifications were made by the Ministry of External Affairs, Government of India, as regards change in date/place of birth in a passport:[159]

a) Where an applicant claims a clerical/technical mistake in the entry relating to date of birth/place of birth in the passport and

158 Circular No. 18.04.2001 issued by the Ministry of External Affairs, Government of India. *See generally* Siddiqui Suraiya Bano v. The Regional Passport Officer, 2007 (6) ALD 568.

159 The parameters set out in the above-mentioned Circular dated 29.10.2007 were upheld in Union of India v. Sunil Kumar, 2015 (3) KLT 501.

asks for a rectification/correction, the documents produced by the applicant earlier as proof of date of birth/place of birth, at the time of issue of the passport, may be produced by the passport authorities. If it is found that there is a clerical mistake either made by the applicant or by the passport authorities, then the date/place of birth may be corrected. There is no need for a declaratory court order in such cases.

b) Where the competent authority which issued a birth certificate or an educational certificate (presented by the applicant to the passport authorities at the time of issuance of the passport), issues any correction or amendment in the date/place of birth, then the passport authority may affect a corresponding change/amendment in the passport without insisting on a court order.

c) In case files/documents have been destroyed, the passport authorities can use their discretion in making a correction of date of birth without a court order, where such correction does not exceed 2 (two) years, and the applicant provides as satisfactory explanation that the concerned document was indeed produced by him at the time of issuance of the passport.

d) Where the initial entry in the passport has been made on the basis of a document issued by one competent authority i.e. school/educational institution, and the applicant subsequently makes a request for change on the basis of a certificate issued by another competent authority i.e. municipal authorities et cetera, resulting in conflicting documents for valid proof, the passport authorities should accept the birth certificate as the correct date of birth. However, suspicious documents should be verified from the issuing competent authority.

The passport authority is not expected to make its own independent enquiry when there is a dispute or difference with regard to the date of birth, place of birth or name entered in the passport, especially when entries were once made on the basis of records produced by the passport holder. Passport authorities are always competent to direct the parties to produce relevant records either from the authorities functioning under the Register of Births and Deaths or from the judicial magistrate or from the civil courts, as the case may be.[160] The passport authority would be well within its jurisdiction to satisfy itself as to the genuineness of a certificate produced (such as certificate from the Registrar of Births and Deaths, matriculation certificate etc.) to substantiate a change in the details of the passport in case the documents appear to be suspicious, manipulated or procured, the passport authority would be justified in relegating the party to approach a civil court to seek a declaration, as to his date of birth.[161] On production of adequate documents, the passport authorities will immediately carry out necessary correction in the passport.[162] Criminal courts are not competent to issue declaratory orders regarding change in date of birth or place of birth. This power vests only with civil courts.[163]

Seizure & Impounding

There is a difference between 'seizing of a document' and 'impounding of a document'. A seizure is made at a particular moment when a person or authority takes into its possession

160 Regional Passport Officer v. Kokilaben, AIR 2009 Guj 59.

161 The passport authority should not routinely direct applicants to approach civil courts. If there appears to be a conflict between the entries in the birth certificate issued by the Registrar of Births and Deaths, and the entry of birth in a school leaving certificate, the entry in the birth certificate issued by the Registrar of Births and Deaths would prevail. Unless the certificate appears to be unreliable, suspicious, procured or manipulated, parties should not be relegated to civil courts in a mechanical manner. *See generally* Resham Singh v. Union of India, (2008) 149 PLR 621.

162 Regional Passport Officer v. Kokilaben, AIR 2009 Guj 59

163 Raveendran Pillai G. v. Vice Consulate General of India, 2011 (3) KLT 652). Aboo Chettiyanthodi v. Regional Passport Officer, 2008 (1) KLT 992.

some property which was earlier not in its possession. Hence, a seizure is done at a particular moment of time. However if, after seizing of the property or document, the said property or document is retained for some period of time, then such retention amounts to impounding of the property or document.[164]

Physical seizure of a passport may not be possible if the passport holder is outside India. However, impounding can be done even in the absence of the physical passport, even if the passport holder is outside India. Upon impounding, the continued stay of the passport holder in a foreign country becomes unlawful inasmuch as his passport or travel document becomes invalid.[165]

THE APPELLATE MECHANISM

Appealable Orders

The following orders passed by the passport authority are appealable before the appellate authority:

a) Refusal of the passport authority to issue a passport or travel document to an applicant or refusal to make any endorsement on the (issued) passport or travel document of the applicant.[166]
b) Refusal of the passport authority to make an endorsement of travel (for the passport holder) in respect of some foreign countries.[167]
c) Issuance of a passport or travel document by the passport authority to the applicant for a period/duration shorter than

164 Suresh Nanda *supra*

165 *See generally* S.M. Sobha v. The Joint Secretary, 2016 (3) LW 850 Madras.

166 S. 5 (2) (c) of the Passports Act.

167 S. 5 (2) (c) of the Passports Act.

what is generally prescribed under Rule 12 of the Passport Rules.[168]

d) Variation of the endorsements, conditions of issuance of passport and/or issuance of notice for delivery-up of the passport to the passport authority, under Section 10 (1) of the Passports Act.

e) Impounding or revocation of a passport or travel document by the passport authority (or by an authority superior to the passport authority)[169] for any of the reasons specified under Section 10 (3) of the Passports Act.

Non-Appealable Orders

An order made by the central government is not appealable.[170]

Alternate Remedy

Despite the availability of the statutory appeal mechanism under Section 11 of the Passports Act (discussed here), an aggrieved person may directly approach the concerned jurisdictional High Court[171] under writ jurisdiction[172] in the following 3 (three) contingencies: (i) where the writ petition seeks enforcement of any fundamental rights; (ii) in the event of failure of any principles of natural justice; (iii) where the orders or proceedings are wholly without jurisdiction or the *vires* of a statute is challenged.[173]

---

168 *Proviso* b of S. 7 of the Passports Act & R. 12 of the Passports Rules.

169 S. 10 (6) of the Passports Act.

170 Proviso to S. 11 (1) of the Passports Act. Such an order of the central government may be challenged by the aggrieved, by preferring an appropriate writ before the jurisdictional High Court.

171 *See generally* Sterling Agro Industries Ltd v. Union of India, W.P. No. 6570/2010 (01.0.2011, Delhi High Court) for a detailed discussion on, *inter alia*, the following aspects relating to writ jurisdiction: (i) territorial jurisdiction of High Courts in writ jurisdiction; (ii) cause of action; (iii) forum convenience.

172 Article 226 of the Constitution of India.

173 *See generally* Harbanslal Sahnia v. Indian Oil Corporation, AIR 2003 SC 212;

The Appellate Authority

The Passport Rules has designated the following officers as the appellate authority for the purposes of the Passports Act and Passport Rules.

a) The Chief Passport Officer, Ministry of External Affairs, New Delhi, for the purpose of challenging an order passed by the passport authority under the following provisions of the Passports Act: Section 5 (2) (b); Section 5 (2) (c); Proviso (b) to Section 7; Section 10 (1) & Section 10 (3).
b) The Additional Secretary or Secretary, Ministry of External affairs, New Delhi for the purpose of challenging an order passed under Section 10 (6) of the Passports Act.

Limitation Act

An appeal against any of the above mentioned orders is required to be filed within a period of 30 (thirty) days from the date the order is communicated to the appellant.[174] An appeal filed beyond the above stated period of 30 (thirty) days may be admitted provided the appellant is able to satisfy the appellate authority about the existence of sufficient cause for not preferring the appeal within the above said period.[175] The provisions of the Limitation Act, 1963 shall apply to the appellate procedures envisaged under the Passports Act.[176]

Aditya Khanna v. The Regional Passport Officer, 2009 (156) DLT 172. Orders that are passed either on no evidence or evidence which is irrelevant or evidence which does not exist, may be interfered with by the high court under judicial review. Hazram Imam v. Union of India, (1999) 80 DLT 19.

174 R. 14 of the Passports Rules.

175 S. 11 (2) of the Passports Act.

176 S. 11 (3) of the Passports Act.

Procedure for Appeal

Every appeal shall be made in writing and be accompanied by a copy of the statement of reasons of challenge.[177] Every appeal shall also be accompanied by the prescribed fee.[178]

The Appellate Authority, while adjudicating the appeal, shall follow the prescribed procedure.[179] The Appellate Authority has the power to call for records of the case from the relevant passport authority, which passed the order under challenge.[180]

The appellant shall be given a reasonable opportunity of representing his case before the appellate authority.[181] There exists no prohibition for lawyers to appear before the Appellate Authority to represent the case of the appellant. Failure of the Appellate Authority to afford an opportunity of hearing to the appellant, prior to disposal of the appeal, shall have the effect of vitiating the order itself.[182]

The Appellate Authority cannot exercise any power under Section 6 (2) of the Passports Act inasmuch as such powers are to be exercised by the passport authority and the Appellate Authority does not qualify to be a passport authority under the provisions of the Passports Act. The Appellate Authority is only required to confirm, modify or reverse the order of the passport authority.[183]

An order of the passport authority (passed at the instance of an authority which is superior to the prescribed appellate authority) may not be subject to a meaningful challenge under

---

177 S. 11 (4) of the Passports Act.

178 R. 15 of the Passports Rules.

179 S. 11 (5) of the Passports Act.

180 R. 16 of the Passports Rules.

181 S. 11 (5) of the Passports Act & R. 16 of the Passports Rules.

182 *See* Alex Varghese v. The Chief Passport Officer and Ors., W.A. No. 1104/2007 (29.05.2007, Kerala High Court).

183 *See generally* Deepak Sadashiv Nikalje v. Union of India, AIR 2003 Bom 255.

Section 11 of the Passports Act, inasmuch as, in such a situation, the Appellate Authority may not reasonably be in a position to apply its independent mind to the matter.[184] An impugned order of the passport authority which is bereft of reasons may be set aside by the Appellate Authority.[185]

Offences and Penalties

The following offences (committed by a citizen or a foreigner) are punishable with imprisonment which may extend to 2 (two) years or with fine which may extend to Rs. 5000/- or with both:[186]

a) Contravention of the provisions of Section 3 of the Passports Act.
b) Knowingly furnishing any false information or suppressing any material information[187] with a view to obtaining a passport or travel document; or without lawful authority, altering or attempting to alter or causing to alter entries in a passport or travel document.[188]

---

184 *See generally* Aditya Khanna v. The Regional Passport Officer, 2009 (156) DLT 172.

185 A statutory right of appeal (available to a passport holder) under Section 11 of the Passports Act can be meaningfully utilised only if reasons and grounds behind passing of the impugned order are available with the passport holder. *See generally* Aditya Khanna v. The Regional Passport Officer, 2009 (156) DLT 172.

186 S. 12 (1) of the Passports Act. This provision is applicable to citizens and foreigners alike. Non-mentioning of proper educational qualification cannot be stated to be a material information for the purposes of Section 12 (1) of the Passports Act. *See* Shymesh v. State of Kerala, 2014 (3) KLJ 632.

187 Non-disclosure about the existence of a crime in relation to which cognizance has not been taken by a criminal court, may not amount to 'suppression'. In fact, in certain cases, non-disclosure of pendency of a criminal case which does not relate to any heinous offences may also be ignored by the passport authorities. *See generally* Shabu Kottoli Parambil Adimaikutty v. The Regional Passport Officer, 2019 (1) Writ LR 156.

188 Mere pasting of plain sheet on a blank page of the passport, without anything else, would not amount to violation of Section 12 (1) (b) of the Passports Act. *See* Balwinder Singh v. State, Crl. Misc. No. 3630/2006 (09.10.2006, Delhi High Court). Non-mentioning of proper educational qualifications cannot qualify to be 'material information' for the purposes of Section 12 (1) (b) of the Passports Act. Differences in spelling of the name of the petitioner and his educational

c) Failing to produce for inspection the passport or travel document (whether issued under the Passports Act or not) when called upon to do so by the prescribed authority.
d) Knowingly using another person's passport or travel document.
e) Knowingly allowing another person to use a passport or travel document issued to him.[189]

The following offences (committed by a foreigner) are punishable with imprisonment for a term which shall not be less than 1 (one) year (but which may extend to 5 (five) years) and with fine which shall not be less than Rs. 10,000/- (Rupees Ten Thousand) but may extend to Rs. 50,000/- (Rupees Fifty Thousand):

a) Making an application for a passport or obtaining a passport by suppressing information about his nationality.
b) Holding a forged passport or travel document.

Offences under Section 12 of the Passports Act are cognizable offences, in as much as, *inter alia,* the police are empowered to arrest without warrant,[190] and only a certain class of police officers are empowered to arrest.[191] The offence under Section 12 (1) of the Passports Act is bailable.[192]

---

qualification or making an incorrect statement as regards marital status, may not qualify to be 'suppression of material information with a view to obtain a passport' under Section 12 (1) (b) of the Passports Act. Dr. Madas Venkat Goud v. State of Andhra Pradesh, 2010 KHC 7572,
Mens rea is an essential element of Section 12 (1) (b) of the Passports Act. Twisha Prasad v. Union of India, 2014 (134) AIC 380 (Pat).

189 Whoever abets any offence punishable under Section 12 (1) or 12 (1A) of the Passports Act shall be punished in like fashion. S. 12 (2) of the Passports Act.

190 Maganlal Bagti v. Emperor, AIR 1934 Nagpur 71; Noufal M.H v. State of Kerala, 2017 (3) KLT 660.

191 *See generally* State of Gujarat v. Lal Singh Kishan Singh, AIR 1981 SC 368; Union of India v. IC Lala, AIR 1973 SC 2204. *But see* Mohammed Hussain Pangadan v. State of Kerala, Crl. M.C. No. 493/2015 (10.06.2015, Kerala High Court).

192 Vijayan v. State of Kerala, 2009 (4) ILR 864 (Ker). The Kerala High Court, in the

Rules of Circumstantial Evidence

Establishment of *mens rea* is mandatory in order to successfully prove an offence under Section 12 (1) of the Passports Act. While direct evidence for the offence would be ideal, in the absence of the same, circumstantial evidence may be relied up by the prosecution, which may involve, *inter alia*, proving the following:[193]

a) The circumstances from which an inference of guilt is sought to be brought must be cogently and firmly established.
b) Those circumstances should be of a definite tendency unerringly pointing towards guilt of the accused.
c) The circumstances taken cumulatively should form a chain so complete that there is no scope from the conclusion that within all human probability the crime was committed by the accused and none else.
d) The circumstantial evidence in order to sustain conviction must be complete and incapable of explanation of any other hypothesis other than that of the guilt of the accused and such evidence should not only be consistent with the guilt of the accused but should also be inconsistent with his innocence.

Penalties for other Offences

Contravention of any condition of a passport or travel document or of any provision of the Passports Act (or rules made thereunder) for which no specific punishment is provided elsewhere, shall be punishable with imprisonment for a term which may extend to 3 (three) months or with fine which may extend to Rs. 500/- (Rupees Five Hundred) or with both.[194]

---

said judgement, had suggested that lawmakers consider suitably amending the punishment provisions under Section 12 (1) of the Passports Act so as to make the offence a non-bailable one.

193 *See generally* Public Prosecutor, High Court of A.P. v. Gopichetty Rajendran and Ors. 2004 (11) CCR 438; Pedda Veera Reddy v. The State of A.P., AIR 1990 SC 79.

194 S. 12 (3) of the Passports Act.

Penalties for Recidivists

A person who having been convicted of an offence under the Passports Act, is again convicted of an offence under the same, shall, on the subsequent occasion, be punished with double the penalty provided for the latter offence.[195]

Power of Arrest, Search and Seizure

Any officer of the customs (authorised by an order of the central government) and any officer of police or emigration officer (not below the rank of a sub-inspector) may arrest without warrant, any person against whom a reasonable suspicion exists that he has committed any offence punishable under Section 12 the Passports Act, and shall, as soon as may be, inform him of the grounds for such arrest.[196] Once the arrest is made, the accused shall be sent to the jurisdictional magistrate or to the officer in charge of the nearest police station and the provisions of the CRPC shall apply to such arrest.[197]

Any officer of the customs (authorised by an order of the central government) and any officer of police or emigration officer (not below the rank of a sub- inspector) may search any place and seize any passport or travel document from any person against whom a reasonable suspicion exists that he has committed any offence punishable under Section 12 of the Passports Act. The provisions of the CRPC relating to searches and seizures, shall apply.[198] While the customs authorities are empowered to seize a passport under this provision, the action of impounding can be taken only by the competent authority i.e. passport authority.[199]

195 S. 12 (4) of the Passports Act.

196 S. 13 (1) of the Passports Act.

197 S. 13 (2) of the Passports Act.

198 S. 14 of the Passports Act.

199 Kaja Mohaideen v. The Senior Intelligence Officer, 2013 (1) LW 114 Mad.

Prosecution with Sanction of Central Government

No prosecution shall be instituted against any person in respect of any offence under the Passports Act, without the previous sanction of the central government.[200] The central government has authorised all state governments and administrators of the union territories to sanction prosecution in respect of offences under Section 12 of the Passports Act within their respective territorial jurisdiction.[201]

The language of Section 15 of the Passports Act is quite clear, in that, the very initiation of prosecution is barred without the required sanction.[202] Absence of a prior sanction from the central government, results in the prosecution getting vitiated.[203] Prosecution launched without a valid sanction is a nullity.[204]

Obtaining a sanction is a mandatory and not a mere technical requirement. It should not be regarded as an automatic formality. It shall be imperative for the authorities to obtain a sanction before the prosecution is commenced. A sanction obtained *ex post facto* (post-commencement of prosecution) would not suffice.[205] If sanction is subsequently given, new proceedings should be commenced *ab initio*.[206]

To 'prosecute' means to institute and pursue a criminal action against a person.[207] A person can be prosecuted in a court only by instituting a case. The expression 'institution of a case' refers to

200 S. 15 of the Passports Act.

201 *See* Order No. VI/401/17/75, dated 01.12.1979 issued by the Ministry of External Affairs, Government of India.

202 Mary v. State of Kerala, Crl. Rev. Pet. No. 3265/2005 (25.01.2018, Kerala High Court).

203 *See generally* State of Gujarat v. Iliyasbhai Adambhai Vohra and Ors., Criminal Appeal No. 867/2000 (03.08.2016, Gujarat High Court).

204 Shymesh v. State of Kerala, *supra*

205 *See generally* Basdeo Agarwalla v. Emperor, 1945 (47) Bom LR 392.

206 *ibid*

207 *See generally* Noufal M.H v. State of Kerala, 2017 (3) KLT 660.

the point when the court take cognizance of the offence alleged therein.[208] In other words, it is imperative to obtain sanction of the central government (for the purposes of this provision) prior to filing of the charge-sheet/final report/complaint, as the case may be, and taking of cognizance by the competent court.[209]

Travel to Enemy States

The central government is empowered to order a passport or travel document to become inoperative for travel to a foreign country: (i) which commits external aggression against India; (ii) which assists another country in committing external aggression against India; (iii) where armed hostilities are in progress; or (iv) to which travel must be restricted in public interest for preventing a serious impairment in the conduct of foreign affairs of the government of India.[210]

Issue of Passport to Non-Citizens

The Passports Act empowers the central government to issue a passport or travel document to a person who is not a citizen of India, if in the opinion of the government, it is necessary to do so, in public interest.[211]

Typically, this provision of the Passports Act may be triggered in situations where political asylum is provided by the government of India to a non-citizen. It may also be kicked into operation where extraditions and deportations

208 Jamuna Singh v. Bhadai Shah, AIR 1964 SC 1541; Noufal M.H v. State of Kerala, 2017 (3) KLT 660. *See also* Shereef v. State of Kerala, 2019 (1) KHC 702 which indicates that a sanction is not required for registration of the case or investigation of the same, but is required before filing of the charge sheet. *But see* Shymesh v. State of Kerala, *supra* which appears to suggest that a previous sanction of the central government is necessary even for registration of the case.

209 *See generally* Shereef v. State of Kerala, *supra*

210 S. 19 of the Passports Act.

211 S. 20 of the Passports Act.

are involved, keeping with the best interests of the nation. A child born in India to foreign citizens (of Indian origin) cannot be said to be entitled to a passport under Section 20 of the Passports Act in as much as there is no 'public interest' element involved.[212]

The Passport (Entry into India) Act

The Passport (Entry into India) Act, 1920 regulate the entry in India of foreign nationals. Foreigners entering India require a specific authorisation (visas) on their valid travel documents/ passports for entering India. The grant of such authorisation is essentially governed by the Passport (Entry into India) Act, 1920 along with the Passport (Entry into India) Rules, 1950.

PASSPORT (ENTRY INTO INDIA) RULES, 1950

Restriction of Entry into India

Generally speaking, the Passport (Entry into India) Rules, 1950 (**Passport Entry Rules**) prohibits a person from entering or attempting to enter India (by air, water or land) without a valid passport.[213] A violation invites punishment in the form of imprisonment (up to 5 [five] years) or fine [up to Rs. 50,000/- (Fifty Thousand)] or both.[214] Repeat offenders are liable for double of the said punishment.[215]

There are however, certain exceptions to the said entry rule such as entry of persons of the armed forces on government transport, Nepalese and Bhutanese entering India over the Nepalese or Bhutanese frontier etc.[216]

---

212 Seana Shanth v. Union of India, AIR 2017 Ker 17.

213 R. 3 of the Passport Entry Rules.

214 R. 6 of the Passport Entry Rules.

215 R. 6A of the Passport Entry Rules.

216 R. 5 of the Passport Entry Rules.

The Permit to Enter India

The Passport Entry Rules describes, in detail, the various aspects relating to issuance of a visa or permit from the government authorities with respect to persons who have passports of foreign countries.[217] The Schedule to the Passport Entry Rules contains a model form of the permit which is required to be issued by the government authorities for authorising the entry of such persons in India.

Conditions of a Valid Passport

The Passport Entry Rules enunciates the conditions which are necessary for a valid passport.[218] These include the following: (i) it should be issued/renewed by the government of the country of which the concerned person is a national; (ii) it should have the photograph of the concerned person duly authenticated by the issuing authority; (iii) passport issued by the government of a foreign country should bear the endorsement by the concerned government authority permitting entry into India (visa or permit); (iv) it should not have been obtained by misrepresentation or fraud. Apart from the above, various other specific preconditions are laid down with respect to passports which are issued by governments of Pakistan, Bangladesh and Nepal.

---

217 R. 4 of the Passport Entry Rules.

218 R. 5 of the Passport Entry Rules.

CHAPTER 5

The Emigration Law Regime

INTRODUCTION

The Emigration Act, 1983 (**Emigration Act**) has been enacted to protect and regulate Indian workers with respect to their employment in a foreign land. The Emigration Act provides a regulatory framework for movement of Indian workers who wish to take contractual overseas employment and further seeks to safeguard their interests and ensure their welfare.

SCOPE OF THE EMIGRATION ACT

A principal object of the Emigration Act is to deal with concerns relating to matters of exploitation of Indian workers by recruiting agents and employers; and streamlining the entire system in that no person can recruit an Indian worker for a foreign employment without registration and no Indian worker can travel abroad for employment purposes without an appropriate authorisation from the relevant authorities. The Emigration Act had its genesis in a judgement of the Supreme Court titled **Erach Sam Kanga and Others v. Union of India,**[1] wherein the Supreme Court issued several guidelines for regulating foreign employment of Indian citizens.[2] This judgement ultimately led to the passing of

1 W.P. No. 2632/1978 (20.03.1979, Supreme Court of India).

2 *See generally* https://www.mea.gov.in/Images/attach/20_Emigration_and_You.pdf

the Emigration Act and the Emigration Rules, 1983 for setting up an emigration management mechanism for governing certain types of overseas employment of Indian nationals.

Emigrant

Simply speaking, the Emigration Act applies to Indian citizens[3] who travel to foreign countries for certain types of employment. The provisions of the Emigration Act apply only to citizens who fit the description of an 'emigrant'. The Emigration Act defines the expression 'emigrant' as a citizen of India who intends to emigrate, or emigrants to a foreign country.[4]

The expression 'to emigrate' above refers to the departure to a foreign country for the purpose of taking up an 'employment' (whether or not under an agreement, with or without the assistance of a recruiting agent or employer).[5] In this regard, the expression 'employment'[6] refers to service, occupation or engagement (excluding government service) in any of the following kinds of work, for earning wages or reward:[7]

a) Any unskilled work, including any form of industrial and agricultural labour.
b) Any domestic service.
c) Any service (not in a managerial capacity) hotel, restaurant, teahouse or other place of public resort.
d) Work as a driver of a truck or other vehicle, mechanic, technician or skilled labourer or artisan.

3 This legislation does not apply to emigrants who are not citizens of India. S. 42 of the Emigration Act.

4 S. 2 (d) of the Emigration Act.

5 S. 2 (f) of the Emigration Act.

6 S. 2 (h) of the Emigration Act.

7 S. 2 (o) of the Emigration Act.

e) Work as an office assistant, accountant, typist, stenographer, salesman, nurse or operator of any machine.
f) Work in connection with, or for the purposes of, any cinema, exhibition or entertainment.
g) Any such work which the central government may specify through a notification.

In essence, an emigrant is an Indian citizen who travels abroad for taking up specific kinds of work mainly of a non-managerial capacity.

At the outset, it is important to highlight that while the Emigration Act is administered by the Ministry of External Affairs, Government of India, its provisions are enforced by an authority constituted thereunder called the Protector of Emigrants (discussed below in detail).

No Indian citizen (unless exempted) can emigrate without obtaining emigration clearance from the concerned Protector of Emigrants. The Protector of Emigrants is, *inter alia,* tasked with the responsibility of determining whether an Indian citizen intending to depart from India for employment purposes answers the description of an 'emigrant'. The said determination is to be made by holding a proper enquiry and considering all relevant evidence.[8]

This enquiry by the Protector of Emigrants is to be made on the following parameters:[9]

a) Requisition of presence of the concerned person on an appointed day and time.
b) Requisition of evidence from the person on the following aspects: (i) his present occupation; (ii) his financial status

8 S. 29 of the Emigration Act.

9 R. 22 of the Emigration Rules.

and income; (iii) documents regarding sponsorship; (iv) the source of financing of the journey; (v) the source of receipt of foreign exchange.

c) The Protector of Emigrants is required to pass a speaking order and supply a copy of the same to the concerned person, along with an endorsement to this effect in the person's passport.

The Emigration Authority: Protector of Emigrants

The Protector General of Emigrants (and its subordinate Protectors of Emigrants)[10] are the principal authorities (appointed by the central government)[11] for protecting the interests of Indian workers (or emigrants) going abroad.

The central government also appoints such other officers to assist the Protector General of Emigrants and the Protectors of Emigrants, in the performance of their duties.[12] All officers appointed by the central government under the provisions of the Emigration Act shall be considered public servants (within the meaning of Section 21 of the Indian Penal Code).[13]

General Duties of Protector of Emigrants

The general duties of a Protector of Emigrants are as follows:[14]

a) Protect and aid all emigrants with his advice.

---

10 The Protectors of Emigrants perform their functions under the general superintendents and control of the Protector General of Emigrants. S. 3 (3) of the Emigration Act.

11 The central government may, by general or special order, define the area to which the authority of a Protector of Emigrants so appointed shall extend and, where 2 (two) or more Protectors of Emigrants are appointed for the same area, also provide, by such order, for the distribution and allocation of the work to be performed under the Emigration Act and in relation to such area. S. 3 (1) & (2) of the Emigration Act.

12 S. 7 of the Emigration Act.

13 S. 8 of the Emigration Act.

14 S. 4 of the Emigration Act.

b) Cause all provisions of the Emigration Act to be complied with.
c) Inspect any emigration conveyance or any other conveyance if he has reason to believe that any emigrant is proceeding from or returning to India by such other conveyance.
d) Inquire into the treatment received by an emigrant during his journey, in the country of employment, as the case may be.
e) Aid and advise all emigrants who have returned to India.

Recruiting Agent

For better regulation of emigrants, the Emigration Act has granted to 'recruiting agents' the exclusive authority to recruit Indians for overseas employment.[15]

Under the Emigration Act, a 'recruiting agent' means a person engaged in India in the business of recruitment[16] for an employer (discussed below) in representing such employer with respect to any matter in relation to such recruitment, including dealings with persons who are recruited or desire to be so recruited (emigrants).[17] Recruiting agents require a registration for conduct of business (discussed below).[18]

Registration of Recruiting Agents

No recruiting agent can commence or carry on the business

15 A direct recruitment may be made by a foreign employer provided a permit for the same is obtained from the Protector General of Emigrants.

16 Under the Emigration Act, the expression 'recruitment' includes the issuing of any advertisement for the purpose of recruitment, the offering by advertisement to secure or assist in securing any employment in any country or place outside India and the entering into any correspondence, negotiation, agreement or arrangement with any individual for or in relation to the employment of such individual in any country or place outside India. S. 2 (m) of the Emigration Act.

17 S. 2 (l) of the Emigration Act. A recruiting agent cannot undertake the business of recruitment, without an offer from an employer, for recruitment. Mohd. Faruq Kureshi v. State of Rajasthan, 2016 (1) RLW 252 (Raj).

18 For detailed recruitment procedures *see* https://www.mea.gov.in/Images/attach/20_Emigration_and_You.pdf

of recruitment without a registration certificate issued by the competent registering authority.[19]

Procedure for Registration

An application for registration shall be made by a person intending to engage in the business of recruitment in the prescribed Form I along with the prescribed fee and shall contain particulars as prescribed, including as to the following aspects: (i) the applicant's financial status and trustworthiness; (ii) the details of premises from where the business is intended to be carried out; (iii) facilities at the disposal of the applicant for the recruitment; (iv) the applicant's antecedents (including details of any past allocation and cancellation of a registration certificate); (v) past experience, if any, of recruitment.[20] Specifically, the application shall contain the following particulars:[21]

a) Educational qualifications of the applicant.
b) Certified copy of the balance sheet for the previous financial year or a statement of accounts showing the assets and liabilities of the applicant.
c) Copy of the income tax returns of the applicant for the last 3 (three) consecutive years.
d) An affidavit in the prescribed form executed before a magistrate or notary public.

Deposit of Security Deposit for Registration Certificate

Under the Emigration Act, every prospective recruiting agent

19 S. 10 of the Emigration Act. Where a *prima facie* violation of S. 10 of the Emigration Act is established, courts will normally not interfere to quash the FIR at the stage of investigation. *See* M.D.K. Immigration Consultant, Chandigarh v. Union of India, 1999 (4) RCR (C) 535.

20 S. 11 (1) of the Emigration Act.

21 R. 7 of the Emigration Rules. There is no limit to the number of registration certificates which can be issued by a registering authority. J.M. International v. Union of India, W.P. (C) 6284/2011 (29.08.2011, Delhi High Court).

is required to make a 'security deposit' as a precondition to grant of a registration certificate. The concept of a 'security amount' is envisaged for the following purposes: (i) securing due performance of the terms and conditions of the registration certificate (proposed to be granted to the applicant); (ii) securing compliance of the provisions of the Emigration Act or Emigration Rules; (iii) meeting expenses which may have to be incurred in the event of repatriation of any emigrant to India.

In the event the registration application (above) is found complete in all respects and the applicant is eligible for grant of a registration, then the registering authority shall (post an opportunity of hearing to the applicant) determine the amount of security deposit to be made by the applicant.[22] Upon furnishing of the security amount within the time prescribed, a registration certificate shall be issued to the applicant. In case the applicant fails to deposit the security amount within the time prescribed, his application shall be deemed to be rejected.[23]

Quantum of Security Deposit

Generally, the security deposit is in the form of a bank guarantee for an amount of Rs. 25,00,000/- (Rupees Twenty Five Lakhs) with a validity period of 8 ½ (eight and a half) years.

A recruiting agent may be permitted to furnish a reduced security of Rs. 4 (four) Lakhs with the condition that he shall be permitted to recruit only 100 (one hundred) workers during the period of registration. A recruiting agent may be permitted to continue recruitment of additional workers, in tranches of 100 (one hundred) workers, on furnishing additional security of Rs. 4,00,000/- (Rupees Four Lakhs) per additional 100 (one hundred) workers.[24]

22 S. 11 (2) of the Emigration Act. If the application is incomplete or if it is not in the prescribed form, then the same shall be returned to the applicant.

23 S. 11 (4) & (5) of the Emigration Act.

24 R. 8 of the Emigration Rules.

Terms and Conditions of Registration

The registration certificate shall be issued by the registering authority in the prescribed Form V and shall be subject to, *inter alia,* the following terms and conditions:[25]

a) The certificate shall be valid for the period specified therein.
b) The certificate shall be non-transferable.
c) The certificate holder shall conduct the business under his own hand and seal.
d) The certificate holder shall not employ sub-agents for the conduct of the business.
e) A copy of the certificate shall be displayed prominently at a conspicuous place of business. The certificate holder shall conduct the business from the place indicated in the certificate. For opening a recruitment centre at a place other than the place indicated in the certificate, the certificate holder shall obtain a prior permission of the competent authorities.
f) The certificate shall be made available for inspection to all stakeholders including the emigration authorities, law enforcement authorities and the employers. The certificate shall be produced on demand, for satisfaction of the *bona fides* of the recruiting agent.
g) The certificate holder shall maintain, *inter alia,* the following records at his place of business and make them available for inspection on demand by the competent authorities: (i) a register of receipt of charges from emigrants recruited; (ii) a register and records of the amounts received from the employers; (iii) a register containing details of expenses incurred on the recruitment of emigrants; (iv) bio-data of each emigrant recruited; (v) copies of employment contracts of each emigrant; (vi) original demand letter, power of attorney and correspondence with the employers; (vii) all documents

25 S. 12 of the Emigration Act & R. 10 of the Emigration Rules.

relating to the recruitment of emigrants; (viii) a register of visas received from the employers; (ix) a register of claims made for all compensations (including for injury or death) made by the emigrants or their dependents, recruited by the certificate holder, along with proof of payment of compensation.

h) The certificate holder shall file a monthly return in the prescribed Form IV with the relevant emigration authorities.

i) A copy of each advertisement for recruitment of emigrants shall be endorsed to the Protector of Emigrants.

j) The certificate holder shall ensure that the employer observes the terms and conditions of the contracts.

k) The certificate holder shall not charge any amount from the emigrants towards repatriation expenses.

l) The certificate holder shall have the following additional duties: (i) to provide details of employment, including contract conditions, to the intending emigrants, before recruitment; (ii) to endeavour to ensure proper reception of the emigrant by the employer in the country of employment; (iii) to endeavour to ensure that subsequent to the employment, the employer does not alter the terms of the employment contract; (iv) to endeavour to ensure that the employer takes timely action for renewal of documents authorising the stay of the emigrant in the country of employment; (v) to facilitate amicable settlement of disputes between the employer and the emigrant, should they arise; (vi) to issue a receipt for the payments received from the emigrant; (vii) to issue only such advertisements that are genuine and factually correct and to refrain from any inducement or misrepresentation in this regard; (viii) to provide copies of all advertisements to the Protector General of Emigrants immediately after their publication or release.[26]

26 A recruiting agent is mandated to conduct his business strictly in accordance with the conditions imposed under the registration certificate. Any breach of the conditions of the registration certificate would invite penalty in accordance with the provisions of the Emigration Act. Typically, no advertisement can be

m) The certificate holder shall be required to maintain the following: (i) an office premises of prescribed space, with sitting of at least 30 (thirty) persons along with all necessary facilities in this regard; (ii) workstations for the office personnel; (iii) Internet facility, email accounts and a web portal containing detailed information about the recruiting agent and the recruitment business, including the validity status of the registration certificate, the services offered, the cost of services, job vacancies etc; (iv) adequate and trained staff; (v) a sign board to be displayed at a conspicuous place indicating the name and the registration number of the recruiting agent, and the period of validity of the registration certificate.

n) The recruiting agent shall maintain registers and other records (as prescribed) and submit them to the prescribed authorities, when called for.[27]

Validity of Registration Certificate

A registration certificate shall be initially valid for a period of 10 (ten) years, with an option of being renewed by the holder, for a further period of 10 (ten) years.[28]

Renewal of Registration Certificate

A registration certificate may be renewed by the certificate holder in accordance with applicable law.[29] Renewal of a registration certificate cannot be sought by the certificate holder as a matter of right. While discretion is vested in the registering authority, however, the same ought to be exercised on considerations which are germane and relevant to the objectives sought to be

---

issued by a recruiting agent without a corresponding offer from an employer. *See generally* Mohd. Faruq Kureshi v. State of Rajasthan, *supra*

27 S. 36 of the Emigration Act.

28 R. 9 of the Emigration Rules.

29 S. 13 of the Emigration Act.

achieved. A renewal should be refused only for reasons which are objective, cogent and fair.[30]

An application for renewal of the registration certificate shall be made in the prescribed Form II-A, accompanied by a fee of Rs. 25,000/- (Rupees Twenty Five Thousand).[31] The application for renewal is required to be made at least 3 (three) months prior to the date of expiry of the certificate,[32] except where the certificate holder is able to satisfy the registering authority that he had sufficient cause for not making such application before the said period.[33]

Cancellation of Registration Certificate

A registration certificate issued to a recruiting agent may be cancelled by the registering authority[7] on any of the following grounds:[34]

a) If the recruiting agent is considered unfit to continue to hold the registration certificate, having regard to the manner in which he has carried out his business or to any deterioration in his financial position or in any of the facilities at his disposal for recruitment.
b) If the recruiting agent has recruited emigrants for purposes prejudicial to the interests of India or for purposes contrary to public policy.
c) If the recruiting agent, subsequent to the issue of the registration certificate, has been convicted in India for any offence involving moral turpitude.

30 Ashim and Brothers v. Union of India, W.P. (C) No. 2695/2012 (11.10.2013, Delhi High Court).

31 R. 9A of the Emigration Rules.

32 S. 13 of the Emigration Act.

33 *Proviso* to S. 13 of the Emigration Act.

34 S. 14 of the Emigration Act.

d) If the recruiting agent, subsequent to the issue of the registration certificate, has been convicted by a court in India for any offence under the Emigration Act or any other law relating to passports, foreign exchange, drugs, narcotics smuggling, and sentenced to imprisonment for not less than 6 (six) months.
e) If the recruiting agent obtains or renews the registration certificate based on misrepresentation or suppression of any material fact.
f) If the recruiting agent violates any term or condition of the registration certificate.
g) If in the opinion of the central government, it is necessary in the interests of foreign relations of India with any foreign country or in the interests of the general public, to cancel the registration certificate.

Cancellation of Registration Certificate by Court

A court (including an appellate and revisional court) convicting a recruiting agent for an offence under the Emigration Act may also cancel his registration certificate. However, if the conviction is set aside in appeal or otherwise, such cancellation (by court) shall become void.[35]

The cancelling authority (registering authority or court), prior to making an order for cancellation (or suspension) of the registration certificate, would be required to consider the question as to provisions and arrangements which should be made for safeguarding the interests of emigrants and other persons with whom the recruiting agent transacted during the course of his business and would be required to pass appropriate orders in this regard (including orders permitting the recruiting agent to continue to carry on his business with respect to all or any such emigrants and other persons).[36]

35 S. 14 (3) & (4) of the Emigration Act.

36 S. 14 (5) of the Emigration Act.

Cooling Off Period

A recruiting agent, whose registration certificate is cancelled, shall not be eligible for making a fresh application for another registration certificate, until the expiry of a period of 2 (two) years from the date of such cancellation.[37]

Suspension of Registration Certificate

During the pendency of the question of cancellation of any registration certificate, if the registering authority is satisfied that it is necessary to suspend the registration certificate of a recruiting agent, then it may suspend the same, for reasons recorded in writing, for a period not exceeding 30 (thirty) days. Further, the registering authority shall require the registering agent to show cause as to why the suspension of the registration certificate should not be extended until the final determination of the issue of cancellation.[38] The registering authority may, during the subsistence of an order of suspension, withdraw the registration certificate from the recruiting agent.[39]

Service Charges

The Emigration Act regulates the quantum of service charge which can be levied by a recruiting agent on an emigrant for the recruitment related services. A recruiting agent is not permitted to charge, from an emigrant, service charge of more than Rs. 30,000/- (Rupees Thirty Thousand), against a proper receipt, which shall include the following: (i) scouting and selecting candidates; (ii) cost

37 S. 14 (6) of the Emigration Act.

38 S. 14 (2) of the Emigration Act. For extension of suspension, an independent show cause notice would be required to be issued to the concerned recruiting agent. It is impermissible for the registering authority to disregard compliance of this provision (for extending a suspension) by contending that no separate notice (for suspension) is required to be given once a show cause notice has already been issued for cancellation of the registration certificate of the agent. Habsons Jobsup Ltd. v. Union of India, W.P. (C) No. 5980/2011 (25.08.2011, Delhi High Court).

39 R. 26A of the Emigration Rules.

of advertisements; (iii) costs of trade test fee, wherever applicable; (iv) cost of domestic travel, lodging and boarding for conduct of interviews by the recruiting agent; (v) recurring annual cost of enhanced bank guarantee, wherever applicable; (vi) cancellation charges imposed by foreign employers on recruiting agents where emigrants refuse to travel and want early repatriation; (vii) administrative cost of running offices by the recruiting agent for conduct of the recruitment exercise.[40]

The above service charge shall, however, not include the following: (i) Embassy or consular visa fee; (ii) pre-employment medical check-up cost; (iii) air ticket to destination country; (iv) boarding and lodging charges of the emigrant before deployment, if any; (v) the goods and services tax, as applicable.[41]

Employer

The Emigration Act defines an 'employer' as a person who provides or offers to provide employment to emigrants in any country outside India.[42] A recruiting agent recruits emigrants for employers. Further, an employer may directly recruit emigrants by availing a permit from the competent authorities.

Employer Permits

Every employer who wishes to recruit emigrants can do so only after obtaining a permit for the same in the prescribed manner from the competent authorities.

The Competent Authority

The central government is empowered to appoint the Protector General of Emigrants (or any other officer of higher rank) to be the

40 R. 25 (1) & (2) of the Emigration Rules.

41 R. 25 (3) of the Emigration Rules.

42 S. 2 (g) of the Emigration Act.

competent authority for issuing permits (**Competent Authority**).[43] Further, the central government is also authorised to appoint any person (under its employ) in a foreign country to exercise the powers of the Competent Authority for the purpose of issuing permits to employers who are not citizens of India but seek to recruit emigrants for employment in such foreign country.[44]

The Recruitment Process

No employer shall recruit an emigrant for employment in any country outside India except: (i) through a duly authorised recruiting agent; or (ii) in accordance with a valid permit.[45]

Power of Attorney to Recruiting Agent

An employer can authorise a (duly registered) recruiting agent, through a power of attorney, for the purpose of recruitment of emigrants.[46]

Procedure for Obtaining a Permit

An employer desiring to obtain a permit shall be required to make an application in the prescribed form[47] with the competent authority, along with the prescribed fee.[48]

On receipt of the application, the Competent Authority may verify the facts contained in the application and further may make inquiries on the following aspects so as to ensure that the

43 S. 15 (1) of the Emigration Act.

44 S. 15 (2) of the Emigration Act. A permit issued under S. 15 (2) of the Emigration Act shall not be valid unless a certified copy of the same is filed with the Protector of Emigrants. S. 19 of the Emigration Act.

45 S. 16 of the Emigration Act.

46 R. 5 of the Emigration Rules.

47 The application for issue of permits for recruitment by foreign employers shall be in Form VI and the application for issue of permits for recruitment by Indian employers for foreign jobs shall be in Form VII.

48 S. 17 (1) of the Emigration Act & R. 11 of the Emigration Rules.

terms and conditions of employment (to be offered to emigrants) are not discriminatory or exploitative: (i) the basis on which the demand for employment has been computed; (ii) the principles on which the skills have been classified; (iii) the job contents of the post required to be filled; (iv) the future prospects in various categories of jobs; (v) the structure of supervisory control; (vi) the grievance procedure followed; (vii) the general reputation of the applicant and reports of specific misconduct, if any.

The Competent Authority may, prior to grant of permit, require the applicant to comply with certain conditions in the interests of the emigrants, including furnishing of a security deposit.

Denial of Permit

An application for grant of permit may be denied or rejected for any of the following reasons:[49]

a) The application is incomplete or if some of the material particulars furnished in the application are untrue.
b) The terms and conditions of employment offered or proposed to be offered to the emigrants are discriminatory or exploitative.
c) The employment offered to the emigrants involves work of a nature which is unlawful under Indian law, or offends public policy of India, or is violative of the norms of human dignity and decency.
d) That having regard to the antecedents of the applicant, his financial standing, the facilities at his disposal, the working and living conditions of emigrants employed by him in the past, it is not in public interest or in the interests of the emigrants to issue a permit.
e) That having regard to the prevailing circumstances in the country of employment, it would not be in the interests of the emigrants to take up the employment.

49 S. 17 (3) of the Emigration Act.

An order of rejection by the Competent Authority shall typically contain reasons and a copy of the same shall be provided to the applicant. However, in case the Competent Authority is of the opinion that it is in the interests of friendly relations with a foreign country or in the interests of the general public to do so, then it may refuse to provide a copy of the order to the applicant or only furnish such parts of the order as it may deem fit.[50]

Conditions of Permit

The permit shall be issued in the prescribed Form VII[51] and shall be subject to, *inter alia*, the following conditions:[52]

a) The permit shall be non-transferable.
b) Emigrants recruited on the strength of the permit shall not be repatriated on the ground that they do not possess the required skill(s).
c) The permit holder shall not obtain the assistance of the recruiting agent in any manner.
d) The employment contract with the emigrant shall be signed by the permit holder.
e) The permit holder shall treat the contract (executed with the emigrant) as enforceable under the applicable labour laws of the country of employment. The permit holder shall file copies of the executed contract with the relevant authorities in the country of employment.
f) The permit holder shall not supply manpower recruited on the strength of the permit to any other agency or concern.
g) The permit holder shall be responsible for the general welfare of the emigrants recruited on the strength of the permit, during the subsistence of the contract.

50 S. 17 (4) of the Emigration Act.

51 R. 13 (2) of the Emigration Rules.

52 R. 12 of the Emigration Rules.

h) The permit holder shall not extend the services of the emigrant, post the expiry of the contract, without extending the said contract or executing a fresh contract.

i) In case of death or disability of the emigrant, the permit holder shall notify the Indian mission (in the country of employment) within a period of 48 (forty eight) hours of the incident. Further, the next-of-kin of the emigrant in India should also be intimated within the said period of 48 (forty eight) hours.

j) The permit holder shall not supply manpower to a country other than the country for which the permit is issued.

k) The permit holder shall have the following further obligations: (i) providing details of employment, including contract conditions, to the intending emigrants before recruitment; (ii) ensuring proper reception of the emigrant in the country of employment; (iii) ensuring that subsequent to the employment, the terms of the contract are not altered; (iv) ensuring timely action for the renewal of documents authorising stay of the emigrant in the country of employment; (v) ensuring that the emigrant is not deprived of the custody of his travel and employment documents; (vi) ensuring genuineness of the recruitment related advertisements, released by the permit holder; (vii) filing copies of all recruitment advertisements to the Protector General of Emigrants immediately after their publication/release.

The permit shall be issued only after the applicant furnishes a bank guarantee of Rs. 10,000/- (Rupees Ten Thousand) for every person intended to be recruited, subject to a minimum of 1,00,000/- (Rupees One Lakh) and a maximum of Rs. 20,00,000/- (Rupees Twenty Lakhs), valid for a period of 1 (one) year over and above the duration of the employment contract.[53]

53 R. 13 (2A) of the Emigration Rules.

Validity of a Permit

Generally, the permit is valid for a period of 1 (one) year from the date of its issue or till the recruitment of the persons (for whose recruitment such permit was issued, is completed) whichever is earlier.[54]

Cancellation and Suspension of a Permit

The provisions of the Emigration Act relating to cancellation and suspension of a registration certificate shall apply *mutatis mutandis* (but with modifications as may be deemed necessary) to the case of permits as well.[55]

Emigration Clearance

Generally, no Indian citizen who intends to emigrate, can do so without an authorisation (or emigration clearance) from the Protector of Emigrants[56] unless exempted from this requirement (discussed below).

Procedure for obtaining Emigration Clearance

An application for emigration clearance shall be made in the prescribed Form IX directly, or through a recruiting agent (if any) or through the employer, along with the prescribed fee and the following documents/information:[57]

a) A true copy of the demand, verified and authenticated by the Indian mission in the country of employment.
b) A true copy of the power of attorney given by the employer to the recruiting agent, verified and authenticated by the Indian mission in the country of employment.

54 R. 13 (2) of the Emigration Rules.

55 S. 20 of the Emigration Act.

56 S. 22 (1) of the Emigration Act.

57 S. 22 (3) of the Emigration Act & R. 15 of the Emigration Rules. The requirements of this provision are mandatory nature. Union of India v. Roopesh, 2015 (1) KLJ 398.

c) A true copy of the employment contract, verified and authenticated by the Indian mission in the country of employment.[58]
d) A statement setting out the particulars of matters (required to be provided in the employment contract, explained above), if not provided in the employment contract.
e) A statement of additional conditions, if any.
f) A statement as to provision for meeting the expenses which may be incurred in case it becomes necessary to arrange for the repatriation to India of the emigrant. Such statement shall be verified and authenticated by the recruiting agent in case the emigrant is recruited by him.
g) An insurance policy providing insurance cover for the emigrant, for the period of the employment contract.

If the application is complete in all respects and accurate, then the Protector of Emigrants shall issue the emigration clearance to the concerned emigrant. Typically, emigration clearance is issued on the same day on which the application is preferred.[59]

Denial of Emigration Clearance

An application for emigration clearance may be rejected by the Protector of Emigrants, on any of the following grounds:[60]

58 The employment contract should provide for the following aspects: (i) period of employment and place of employment; (ii) wages and other conditions of service; (iii) free food or food allowance provision; (iv) free accommodation; (v) provision in regard to disposal, or transportation to India, of dead body of the emigrant; (vi) working hours, overtime allowance, other working conditions, leave and social security benefits as per local labour laws; (vii) to-and-fro passage at the employers cost; (viii) mode of settlement of disputes.

59 For more on clearance procedures *see* https://www.mea.gov.in/Images/attach/20_Emigration_and_You.pdf

60 S. 22 (5) of the Emigration Act.

a) The terms and conditions of employment which the applicant proposes to take up are discriminatory or exploitative.
b) The employment which the applicant proposes to take up involves work of a nature which is unlawful under Indian law, or offends public policy of India, or is violative of the norms of human dignity and decency.
c) The applicant will have to work or live in substandard working and living conditions.
d) That having regard to the prevailing circumstances in the country or in the proposed country of employment, it would not be in the interests of the applicant to take up the employment.
e) That no provision or arrangement has been made for meeting the expenses which may be incurred in case it becomes necessary to arrange for the repatriation to India of the applicant, or that the provision or arrangement made in this behalf are not adequate for the purpose.

An order rejecting an application for emigration clearance shall be speaking and shall set out the grounds/reasons as well as the facts and circumstances on which such grounds are based.

The Exceptions to Emigration Clearance

The general rule requires an emigration clearance for emigrants. This rule is however subject to various exemptions. There are certain categories of persons who have been exempted from this requirement. Further, there are certain countries travel to which does not require an emigration clearance. This category is also called 'Emigration Check Not Required Category' (ECNR). Typically, every passport requiring an emigration clearance will carry a notation to this effect. As a corollary, a passport not containing such a notation will be considered a ECNR passport.

ECNR Persons

The ECNR persons who are not required to obtain any emigration clearance before seeking employment abroad are: (i) holders of diplomatic passports; (ii) all gazetted government servants; (iii) income-tax payers (including agricultural income tax payers) in their individual capacity; (iv) professional degree holders, such as doctors holding MBBS degrees or degrees in Ayurveda or Homoeopathy; accredited journalists; engineers; chartered accountants; lecturers; teachers; scientists; advocates etc.; (v) spouses and dependent children of category of persons listed from (ii) to (iv) above; (vi) persons holding class 10th or higher qualification; (vii) seamen who are sea cadets or desk cadets; (viii) persons holding permanent immigration visas, such as the visas of UK, USA and Australia; (ix) persons possessing 2 (two) years diploma from any institute recognized by the National Council for Vocational Training or State Council of Vocational Training or persons holding 3 (three) years diploma/equivalent degree from institutions like polytechnics recognized by central/state governments; (x) nurses possessing qualification recognized under the Indian Nursing Council Act, 1947; (xi) persons above the age of 50 (fifty) years; (xii) persons who have been staying abroad for more than a consolidated period of 3 (three) years and their spouses; (xiii) children below 18 (eighteen) years of age.

ECNR Countries

Presently, travel to these countries does not require emigration clearance: Albania, Algeria, Andorra, Angola, Antigua and Barbuda, Argentina, Armenia, Australia, Austria, Azerbaijan, Bahamas, Bangladesh, Barbados, Belarus, Belgium, Belize, Benin, Bhutan, Bolivia, Bosnia and Herzegovina, Botswana, Brazil, Bulgaria, Burkina Faso, Burundi, Cambodia, Cameroon, Canada, Cape Verde, Central African Republic, Chad, Chile, China, Colombia, Comoros, Congo, Costa Rica, Cote d'lvoire, Croatia, Cuba, Cyprus, Czech

Republic, Democratic People's Republic of Korea, Democratic Republic of the Congo, Denmark, Djibouti, Dominica, Dominican Republic, Ecuador, Egypt, El Salvador, Equatorial Guinea, Eritrea, Estonia, Ethiopia, Fiji, Finland, France, Gabon, Gambia, Georgia, Germany, Ghana, Greece, Grenada, Guatemala, Guinea, Guinea Bissau, Guyana, Haiti, Honduras, Hungary, Iceland, Iran, Ireland, Israel, Italy, Jamaica, Japan, Kazakhstan, Kenya, Kiribati, Kyrgyzstan, Lao, People's Democratic Republic, Latvia, Lesotho, Liberia, Liechtenstein, Lithuania, Luxembourg, Madagascar, Malawi, Maldives, Mali, Malta, Marshall Islands, Mauritania, Mauritius, Mexico, Micronesia, Moldova, Monaco, Mongolia, Montenegro, Morocco, Mozambique, Myanmar, Namibia, Nauru, Nepal, Netherlands, New Zealand, Nicaragua, Niger, Nigeria.

ECR Countries

At present, the ECR passport holders and nurses travelling to the below mentioned 18 (eighteen) countries for work are required to obtain emigration clearance. As a special case, persons going to Iraq for employment purposes after 30.09.2019 irrespective of their passport category, are also required to obtain emigration clearance.

The 18 (eighteen) countries are as follows: Afghanistan, Bahrain, Indonesia, Iraq, Jordan, Kuwait, Lebanon, Libya, Malaysia, Oman, Qatar, Kingdom of Saudi Arabia, Sudan , South Sudan, Syria, Thailand, United Arab Emirates and Yemen.[61]

Exemptions for ECR Category in Emergent Situations

Immigration officers may allow the following persons (who otherwise require an emigration clearance) to travel abroad under emergent circumstances:[62]

61 Press Release dated 03.01.2020 issued by the Ministry of External Affairs, Government of India.

62 *See* https://www.mea.gov.in/Images/attach/20_Emigration_and_You.pdf

a) VIP persons (like ministers, MPs, MLAs etc.) and their families.
b) Students going abroad for higher studies provided they furnish proof of their admission.
c) Persons going abroad due to sudden demise of their relatives in a foreign country.
d) Persons going abroad for their or their relative's medical treatment.
e) Sports persons representing the country in international events, provided their foreign visit is approved by the Ministry of Youth Affairs and Sports.

The Appellate Mechanism

Orders passed under the provisions of the Emigration Act can be appealed against by the aggrieved person. This section briefly describes the appellate mechanism under the (Indian) emigration law.

Appealable Orders

Under the Emigration Act, the following orders can be appealed against by an aggrieved person to the central government:[63]

a) An order passed by the registering authority in the following contexts of a recruiting agent: (i) rejecting an application for registration certificate; or (ii) suspending a registration certificate; or (iii) cancelling a registration certificate; or (iv) refusing to renew a registration certificate; or (v) requiring the agent to furnish any security; or (vi) directing the agent to comply with a term or condition which is not a prescribed term or condition of the registration certificate.
b) An order of the Competent Authority in the context of an employer: (i) rejecting an application for grant of permit; or

63 The Secretary, Ministry of External Affairs, Government of India has been notified as the appellate authority.

(ii) suspending a permit; or (iii) cancelling a permit; or (iv) refusing to extend the validity of a permit; or (v) requiring an employer to comply with a term or condition which is not a prescribed term or condition of the permit.

c) An order passed by the Protector of Emigrants rejecting the application for grant of emigration clearance.

d) An order of the relevant authority directing furnishing of any security, additional security or fresh security under the Emigration Act; or forfeiting or rejecting a claim for refund of any security (whether wholly or in part).

Limitation for Appeal

An appeal is required to be filed by the aggrieved person within a period of 30 (thirty) days from the date of receipt of the order.[64] An appeal preferred after the expiry of the above mentioned limitation period will not be entertained unless the appellant is able to satisfy the central government about the existence of 'sufficient cause' for not being able to prefer the appeal within time.[65] Medical illness of the appellant, supported by adequate evidence (such as genuine medical certificate/records) may constitute 'sufficient cause'.[66] While the appellate authority has the discretion in deciding an application for condonation of delay (in filing the appeal), however, the approach of the appellate authority in this regard must be reasonable, in accordance with the statutory provisions and the principles of natural justice. Further, courts suggest a liberal approach of the appellate authority on this aspect.[67]

---

64 R. 18 (3) of the Emigration Rules.

65 S. 23 (2) of the Emigration Act & R. 18 (3) of the Emigration Rules.

66 J.M. International v. Union of India, W.P. (C) No. 6284/2011 (29.08.2011, Delhi High Court).

67 Al-Haman Exports & Imports v. Union of India, W.P. (C) No. 9053/2008 (08.04.2009, Delhi High Court).

Form of Appeal

a) An appeal shall be in the form of a memorandum signed by the appellant, in triplicate, along with the prescribed fee.[68]

b) The memorandum shall set out the grounds of objection of the impugned order along with other necessary particulars, such as date of the impugned order, address of the appellant etc.[69]

Adjudication of the Appeal

The proceedure for adjudication of an appeal is summerized below:

a) The appellate authority/central government shall issue notice to the authority which passed the impugned order.

b) The appellant shall be provided a reasonable opportunity of representing his case.[70] The appellant may either appear on his own or appoint a pleader/advocate.[71]

c) Every order made on an appeal confirming, modifying or reversing the impugned order shall be final.[72]

d) The order of the appellate authority/central government shall be in writing, signed and briefly state the grounds for the decision.[73]

Offences and Penalties

Violation of the provisions of the Emigration Act and the Emigration Rules invites punishment. This section summarises the various penalties and punishments prescribed under the Emigration Act.

---

68 R. 18 (1) of the Emigration Rules.

69 R. 18 (2) of the Emigration Rules.

70 S. 23 (5) of the Emigration Act.

71 R. 21 of the Emigration Rules.

72 S. 23 (6) of the Emigration Act.

73 R. 20 of the Emigration Rules.

Punishment for Offences

Commission of (or an attempt to commit) the below mentioned offences (by any person) is punishable with imprisonment for a minimum term of 6 (six) months, extendable to 2 (two) years; and with minimum fine of Rs. 1000/- (Rupees One Thousand), extendable to Rs. 2000/- (Rupees Two Thousand). The minimum punishment may be reduced for any special and adequate reasons (to be specified by the court in the judgement).[74]

a) Emigrating to a foreign country except in conformity with the provisions of the Emigration Act.
b) Contravening the provisions of Section 10 or Section 16 of the Emigration Act.
c) Intentionally furnishing any false information or suppressing any material information, for obtaining a registration certificate, a permit or an emigration clearance (under the provisions of the Emigration Act).
d) Making or causing to be made any alteration in a registration certificate, a permit or an emigration clearance related document (or endorsement) issued under the provisions of the Emigration Act.
e) Disobeying or neglecting to comply with any order of the Protector of Emigrants.
f) Collecting from an emigrant any charges in excess of the limits prescribed under the Emigration Act.
g) Cheating any emigrant.[75]

---

74 S. 24 of the Emigration Act.

75 The same set of facts, in conceivable cases, can constitute an offence under 2 (two) different laws and trial thereon would not amount to double jeopardy. Thus, an offence under Section 24 (1) (g) of the Emigration may also be an offence under Section 420 of the Indian Penal Code. *See generally* State v. Anil Grover, Crl.M.C 2087/2010 (06.01.2017, Delhi High Court).

Residuary Punishment Provision

A person who contravenes any term or condition of the emigration clearance shall, if no other punishment is provided elsewhere in the Emigration Act for such contravention, be punishable with imprisonment for a term which may extend to 1 (one) year or with fine which may extend to Rs. 2000/- (Rupees Two Thousand) or with both.[76]

Abetment of an Offence

A person who abets any offence punishable under the Emigration Act, shall be punished with the punishment provided for that offence.[77]

Punishment for Recidivists

A person who having been convicted of an offence under the Emigration Act, is again convicted of an offence (under the same provision), shall be punished (for the second and each subsequent offence) with double the penalty provided for that offence.[78]

Offences by Companies

Where an offence under the Emigration Act is committed by a company, every person who, at the time of commission of the offence, was in charge of, and was responsible to the company for the conduct of its business, as well as the company, shall be deemed to be guilty of the offence and shall be liable to be proceeded with accordingly. However, where a person proves that the offence was committed without his knowledge or that he had exercised all due

76 S. 24 (3) of the Emigration Act.

77 S. 24 (4) of the Emigration Act.

78 S. 23 (5) of the Emigration Act.

diligence to prevent the commission of the offence, he shall not be considered liable for the offence.[79]

Where an offence under the Emigration Act is committed by a company, and it is proved that the offence has been committed with the consent of connivance of, or is attributable to any neglect on the part of any director,[80] manager, secretary or other officer of the company, such director, manager, secretary or other officer shall be deemed to be guilty of that offence and shall be liable to be proceeded with accordingly.[81]

Offences to be Cognizable

All offences under the Emigration Act are cognizable in nature.[82]

Prior Sanction of Central Government

No prosecution shall be instituted against any person in respect of any offence under the Emigration Act, without the previous sanction of the central government[83] or of the officers/authority authorised by the central government in that behalf.[84] However, no sanction shall be required in case of an offence committed in respect of an emigrant and a complaint is filed by such emigrant (or on his behalf by his immediate family member).[85]

---

79 S. 25 (1) of the Emigration Act.

80 The expression 'director' in relation to a firm, shall mean a partner in the firm.

81 S. 25 (2) of the Emigration Act.

82 S. 26 of the Emigration Act.

83 This sanction is a mandatory requirement. B.T. Deva Varma v. State of A.P, 2002 (2) ALD (Cri) 371.

84 Mere filing of a FIR (First Information Report) against an accused may not amount to prosecution. See also the discussion on Section 14 of the Passports Act.

85 S. 27 of the Emigration Act. Section 27 of the Emigration Act and Section 14 of the Passports Act are similarly worded.

PROHIBITION OF EMIGRATION BY THE CENTRAL GOVERNMENT

The central government is empowered to prohibit emigration to any country in certain select circumstances and situations.

Public Interest

The central government is empowered to prohibit emigration to any country having regard to the following aspects: (i) sovereignty and integrity of India; (ii) security of India; (iii) friendly relations of India with any foreign country; (iv) in the interests of the general public.

The prohibition shall be made by means of a notification which, typically, shall have a validity period of 6 (six) months, unless extended by the central government from time to time.[86]

Further, the central government is, in the interests of the general public, authorised to prohibit emigration of any class or category of persons, (to any country) having regard to their age, sex or other relevant factors. The prohibition shall be made by means of a notification which, typically, shall have a validity period of 6 (six) months, unless extended by the central government from time to time.[87]

Outbreak of Epidemics & Civil Disturbances

The central government is, in the interests of the life of emigrants, empowered to prohibit emigration of intending immigrants, in the following cases: (i) where there exists a serious risk to life of intending immigrants by reason of outbreak of any disease or grave

86 S. 30 of the Emigration Act. In Mohd. Faruq Kureshi v. State of Rajasthan, 2016 (1) RLW 252 (Raj), the Rajasthan High Court, *inter alia*, appeared to suggest that an offence committed with respect to an emigrant can be prosecuted with prior sanction of central government even where no complaint is filed by the concerned emigrant. This view may not be correct. *Proviso* to Section 30 of the Emigration Act (which exempts prior sanction of the central government) essentially has 2 (two) parts which must be satisfied collectively, namely: (i) commission of offence in respect of an emigrant; (ii) filing a complaint by the emigrant or his representative. Hence, no sanction is required only when both the above aspects are collectively satisfied. In all other cases, prior governmental sanction would be necessary.

87 S. 32 of the Emigration Act.

pollution of environment in the country of employment; or outbreak of hostilities or civil war or civil commotion or political disturbances; (ii) where by reason of India not being in diplomatic relations with the concerned country, it would not be possible to protect the emigrants from discrimination, maltreatment and exploitation. The prohibition shall be made by means of a notification which, typically, shall have a validity period of 6 (six) months, unless extended by the central government from time to time.[88]

Powers of Search, Seizure and Detention

The officers and authorities appointed/designated under the Emigration Act shall have the powers of search, seizure and detention, as are available with officers of customs authorities (under the provisions of the Customs Act, 1962).[89]

Powers of Civil Court

All authorities and officers appointed or designated under the provisions of the Emigration Act shall have the same powers as are vested in a court (under the Code of Civil Procedure, 1908) while trying a suit, in respect of the following matters:[90]

a) Summoning and enforcing the attendance of witnesses.
b) Requiring any public record or copy thereof, from any court or office.
c) Requisitioning any public record or copy thereof, from any court or office.
d) Receiving evidence on affidavits.
e) Issuing commissions for the examination of witnesses or documents.

88 S. 31 of the Emigration Act.

89 S. 35 of the Emigration Act.

90 R. 24 of the Emigration Rules.

Effect of other Laws

The provisions of the Emigration Act have a dual attribute i.e. they have an overriding effect over (other) inconsistent laws; and have a supplemental effect where there exists no inconsistency with other laws. This may be described as follows:[91]

a) The provisions of the Emigration Act (and its accompanying rules) shall have effect notwithstanding anything inconsistent contained in any other law/enactment.
b) Except as aforesaid (in point a), the provisions of the Emigration Act shall be in addition to and not in derogation of any other law/enactment.

Security Deposit

As discussed above, the law requires furnishing/deposit of security by recruiting agents and employers, at the time of issuance of registration certificate and permit, respectively. This section describes the relevant provisions with respect to the conditions of deposit, forfeiture and refund of security deposit.

Deposit of Security Deposit

Any security required to be furnished under the provisions of the Emigration Act shall be reasonable, having regard to the purpose for which it is required to be furnished.[92]

Forfeiture of Security Deposit

Where the competent authority has reason to believe that it is expedient to forfeit the whole or any part of the security furnished by any person (under the provisions of the Emigration Act), for

91 S. 39 of the Emigration Act.

92 S. 33 (1) of the Emigration Act.

being utilised for such purpose and in such manner as may be specified in the order, then he may, after giving a notice to this effect (and an opportunity of hearing) to the concerned person, forfeit the whole or any part of the security.[93] A security deposit can be forfeited only by a specific order indicating the purpose for which such security may be utilised.[94] The amount recovered by encashment of the security deposit can only be utilised for a purpose which has a direct bearing on the allegations made against the recruiting agent.[95] The question, as to how the sums recovered by forfeiture are required to be utilised, rests with the Protector General of Emigrants.[96]

Refund of Security

A security furnished under the provisions of the Emigration Act (if not forfeited in the manner described above) shall be refunded or released when no longer required for the purpose for which it was furnished.[97]

GOVERNMENT SCHEMES FOR EMIGRANTS

The Government of India has, from time to time, introduced various schemes and policies, in an effort to better regulate and to protect the interests of Indians who are overseas, including

---

93 S. 33 (2) of the Emigration Act & R. 23 of the Emigration Rules. The requirment of notice and prior hearing is mandatory. Suneer E v. Union of India, 2012 (111) AIC 588.

94 S.J. Overseas v. Union of India, 2019 (174) DRJ 533. There can be no forfeiture of security without indicating the purpose and without utilising the same for the said purpose. *See* Malkit Singh Bamrha v. Union of India, W.P. (C) No. 9263/2016 (05.02.2019, Delhi High Court).

95 S.J. Overseas v. Union of India, 2019 (174) DRJ 533. For instance, where forfeiture is made on account of complaints against the recruiting agent for overcharging from intending immigrants, it would be necessary for the relevant authorities to ensure that such recovered sums are utilised for the redress of such complaints. Malkit Singh Bamrha v. Union of India, W.P. (C) No. 9263/2016 (05.02.2019, Delhi High Court).

96 Malkit Singh Bamrha v. Union of India, *supra*

97 S. 34 of the Emigration Act.

emigrants. This section briefly describes some of the principal schemes introduced by the government in this regard. These schemes have been discussed in detail in a recent judgment of the Madras High Court in **Lawyers Beyond Borders (LBB) India & Others v. Union of India & Others**.[98]

Indian Community Welfare Fund

The Indian Community Welfare Fund (**ICWF**), set up in 2009, is aimed at assisting overseas Indian nationals in times of distress and emergency on a means-tested basis. ICWF has also been a critical support in emergency evacuation of Indian nationals from conflict zones, countries affected by natural disasters and other challenging situations. Over 1,60,000 (one lakh and sixty thousand) people have benefited from ICWF.

The recent revisions in the ICWF guidelines (in 01.09.2017) have expanded their scope. By virtue of the said guidelines, Indian Missions and posts have now been provided with greater flexibility in swiftly addressing requests for assistance by Indian nationals abroad. The extant guidelines cover 3 (three) key areas: (i) assisting overseas Indian nationals in distress situations; (ii) support for community welfare activities; and (iii) improvement in consular services. These are described below in turn.

a) Assisting overseas Indian nationals in distress situations
   i. Boarding and lodging for deserving distressed Indian nationals abroad on a means-tested basis in budget category or shelters run by Mission/Post or NGOs empanelled with Mission.
   ii. Air passage to India to stranded Overseas Indian nationals.
   iii. Legal Assistance on a means-tested basis to deserving overseas Indian nationals who have committed minor

98 W.P. (C) No. 13444/2020 (S) & W.P. (C) No.14496/2020 (S), (25.08.2020, Kerala High Court).

crimes, offences or have been falsely implicated by their employer and put in jails; fishermen / seamen / sailors / Indian students in distress.

iv. Legal/financial assistance to Indian women abandoned/ cheated / abused by their NRI/PIO or foreign spouses (up to seven years after their marriage).

v. Payment for small fines and penalties in respect of Indian nationals for minor offences/crimes; for illegal stay in the host country where *prima facie* the worker is not at fault, and to enable release of Indian nationals from jail/ detention centre.

vi. Transportation of mortal remains and expenditure on incidentals of deceased Indian nationals to India or local cremation/burial of deceased in such cases where the employer, sponsor or insurance company is unable or unwilling to do so as per the contract and the family is unable to meet the cost.

vii. Emergency Medical Care on means-tested basis to overseas Indians who are involved in an accident (with serious life threatening injuries) have life-threatening medical conditions or suffer a serious disability.

b) Support for community welfare activities Indian Missions and Posts abroad, subject to availability of funds. Expenditure may be incurred on community activities pertaining to the Indian community such as:

i. To promote Indian culture by organizing cultural programmes by recognized Indian Diaspora organizations at major Indian Festivals, National Days of India, Indian culture programs by recognized local artists or Indian artists based in India etc.

ii. Payment of honorarium for teachers/faculty teaching Indian languages, art forms.

iii. Welfare activities for Indian students towards organizing annual day for Indian students at universities/ educational institutions to discuss problems, issues faced by Indian students, including their visa, residence status, work permit, financial, welfare and other issues with participation of students.

c) Improvement in consular services, Indian missions and Posts abroad, subject to availability of funds. Expenditure may be incurred on schemes/welfare measures etc. for the following purposes:

   i. Hiring of limited additional staff for rendering various consular services.
   ii. Hiring vehicles on a need basis for visits to jails, police stations.
   iii. Detention centres; labour camps; welfare camps; shelters for distressed Indians; prisons; hospitals; morgues and travel to airports for deportation/repatriation of distressed Indian nationals.
   iv. Hiring of local interpreters on a case-to-case basis for consular visits.
   v. Design, publication, translation costs of pamphlets by Mission/Post about local labour laws, regulations, norms, dos & don'ts, welfare measures pertaining to overseas employment in the host country.
   vi. Organizing labour camps / consular camps for interacting with Indian migrant workers and informing them about issues related to overseas employment; labour laws; welfare and protection measures of the government.
   vii. Setting up 24 x 7 toll-free helplines, walk-in resource centres for providing information, advice, guidance on problems faced by distressed Indian nationals; and helping them register their grievance with the Mission/Post.

viii. Development of e-Governance solutions, applications to address Consular/ welfare matters.

ICWF can also be utilised to provide legal assistance to deserving overseas Indian nationals who have committed minor crimes, offences or have been falsely implicated by their employer and put in jails.

Criteria for Utilisation of the Fund

The ICWF can be utilised subject to the following conditions:

a) ICWF funds can be used to assist only Indian citizens residing in the host country or those in distress while visiting a foreign country. Persons of Indian Origin (PIO) and Overseas Citizens of India (OCI) cardholders are not eligible for individual financial assistance from ICWF.
b) ICWF can be utilized for the benefit of Indian nationals in distress on a means tested basis provided the officer approving ICWF expenditure has satisfied himself that the beneficiary deserves to be assisted.
c) Ordinarily, only such Indian national(s) who have entered the host country legally shall be eligible to receive benefits under this Fund. In cases where it is not so, assistance may be provided after the Head of Mission/Head of Post has recorded his satisfaction to the effect that the circumstances of the case necessitate providing assistance under ICWF.
d) A record of all beneficiaries of the ICWF is maintained. Generally, an endorsement is made in the passport of the beneficiaries.

Pravasi Bharatiya Bima Yojana

Pravasi Bharatiya Bima Yojana (**PBBY**) is a mandatory insurance scheme for all Emigration Check Required (ECR) category workers going to ECR countries. The scheme provides an insurance cover of Rs. 10,00,000/- (Rupees Ten Lakhs) in case of accidental death or permanent disability and few other benefits at a nominal insurance premiums. This scheme, initially launched in 2003, has been amended from time to time with the overarching objective of expanding its benefits for migrant workers. This scheme is applicable to all persons who answer the description of 'emigrants' under the Emigration Act.

The scheme, comprehensively revamped with effect from 01.08.2017, has been made simpler and more beneficial for migrant workers. It provides for, *inter alia,* the following:[99]

a) Global coverage irrespective of change of employer, employee's location and place of work.
b) Acceptance by insurance companies of certification of accidental death/permanent disability by Indian missions/posts abroad.
c) Facility for online renewal and copy of insurance policy is to be made available to the nominee(s). The Government promptly takes up the matter with the concerned insurance companies whenever any representation regarding settlement of claims is received.
d) Maternity benefits for women emigrants.
e) Medical cover and cashless hospitalisation provided the medical treatment is taken in India.

Since the launch of the e-Migrate portal in 2014, the competent authorities have been issuing online Emigration Clearance. As per information available in public domain, premiums of Rs. 9,211.8 Lakhs (ninety-two crores, eleven lakhs and eighty thousand) have been paid by the emigrants and 877 (eight hundred and seventy seven) have been settled.

---

99 For detailed features of PBBY *see* https://www.mea.gov.in/Images/attach/20_Emigration_and_You.pdf

Madad

The Madad portal, launched on 21.02.2015, is an online consular grievances monitoring system to extend a helping hand to Indians abroad requiring consular assistance. MADAD seeks to address grievances on issues related to a variety of cases including the following: (i) asylum cases; (ii) compensation; (iii) domestic help; (iv) fraudulent calls/emails; (v) marital disputes; (vi) NORI (no obligation to return to India) certificate; (vii) passport issues abroad; (viii) recruiting agent; (ix) salary/dues; (x) student issues; (xi) physical or sexual abuse; (xii) worker abuse; (xiii) birth certificate; (xiv) contract problems; (xv) dubious job letter/employer/company; (xvi) imprisonment abroad; (xvii) mortal remains; (xviii) OCI related issues; (xix) repatriation; (xx) Seafarer issues; (xxi) sponsor problems; (xxii) whereabouts unknown. The grievances/queries with regard to visa, passport, emergency travel documents and attestation of documents are not within the scope of the Madad portal.

The Madad portal enables online forwarding, filing, tracking and escalation of grievances by members of the public and effective tracking of the entire grievance handling process all the way until the redressal of the grievance. All Indian Missions and Posts abroad have been linked to this portal for consular grievance tracking and follow-up. In addition, the names and contact details of all officers in Missions and Posts are available on their respective websites. The Madad portal also stands integrated with e-Migrate system. On Madad portal, from its commencement in February 2015 till 14.08.2020, a total 64,311 (sixty four thousand three hundred and eleven) grievances have been filed, out of which 55,299 (fifty five thousand two hundred and ninety nine) have been resolved/replied to.

E-Migrate

The e-Migrate project was implemented in all Protector of Emigrants offices with effect from 25.09.2014. The project is designed for facilitating emigration of ECR category emigrants going to notified countries for employment purposes. The project helps in making the recruitment of workers a smooth process and mitigates the scope for malpractices. The e-Migrate system provides the government a comprehensive and online database of emigrants, Missions, recruiting agents, foreign employers, insurance agencies to make the whole emigration cycle faster, transparent and allows authentication/verification of credentials of all the stakeholders. The portal is integrated with Passport Seva Project (PSP) for validation of passport details of ECR category workers. The system is also integrated with Bureau of Immigration, Ministry of Home Affairs, and is used at Immigration Check Post (ICP) at airports for online validation of the emigration clearance granted by Protector of Emigrants. Nurses and seafarers have also been brought under emigration clearance.

Pravasi Bharatiya Sahayata Kendras

Pravasi Bharatiya Sahayata Kendras (**PBSKs**) and other support Pravasi Bharatiya Sahayata Kendras have been set up at Riyadh, Jeddah, Dubai, and Kuala Lumpur that provide guidance and counseling on all matters pertaining to overseas Indian workers. Shelter homes for distressed Indian nationals have been set up in Bahrain, Kingdom of Saudi Arabia, Kuwait, Qatar, UAE and Malaysia. Missions in Gulf countries also conduct Open Houses on a regular basis where workers can convey their grievances. Toll-free helplines are also available with the concerned Missions/ Posts. Kshetriya Pravasi Sahayata Kendras have also been set up in Kochi, Hyderabad, Delhi, Chennai and Lucknow. Grievances of migrant workers can also be registered with the Pravasi Bharatiya

Sahayata Kendra (PBSK) at New Delhi which provides assistance through a multilingual round-the-clock helpline.

Some noteworthy features of PBSK are as follows:

a) A round-the-clock helpline in the PBSKs which have been receiving, registering and monitoring grievance petitions of Indians and providing necessary advice / resolution / clarification. Cases unresolved thorugh the helpline are escalated to the Embassy / Consulate for further resolution.
b) Providing counseling sessions on legal, financial, medical and psychological matters.
c) Awareness camps that are conducted in labour camps which educates the workers on various issues they face during their employment, health related talks by experts, various schemes of the Government of India for the welfare of the workers.
d) Liaising with help-groups, individuals, social workers and related bodies to offer assistance to Indian Community Members.
e) To verify the genuineness of job offers received by Indians from companies in foreign countries.

Centralised Public Grievances Redress and Monitoring System

This government run portal aims at providing the citizens with a platform for redress of their grievances. The Department of Administrative Reforms & Public Grievances is the nodal agency to formulate policy guidelines for citizen-centric governance in the country. The grievances received by the department are forwarded to the concerned ministries/departments/state governments/ union territories, for redress under intimation to the complainant.

CHAPTER 6

National Register of Citizens (NRC)

INTRODUCTION

Any discourse on the Indian Citizenship Law regime and the CAA would be incomplete without an examination of the concept of the National Register of Citizens. Simply speaking, the National Register of Citizens (**NRC** or **National Register**) is a register of all Indian citizens. Its primary purpose is to document all the legal citizens of India. The NRC may be described as a record collation exercise where information about Indian citizens can be inscribed at one place.

The NRC is a concept which is somewhat intertwined with the CAA and is often a subject of discussion along with the CAA. As per the author, the genesis of the concept of the NRC appears to be in the Assam Accord of 1985 which was the first instrument aimed towards identifying and deporting illegal migrants (specifically from the state of Assam).[1] Since then, this concept of the NRC appears to have been expanded with the objective of extending it throughout the country. To the best of knowledge of the author, the only time that a

1 The Assam Accord, amongst other things, mandates the government to detect and deport all foreigners from the state of Assam who had entered 25.03.1971 onwards. The Assam Accord was signed for the principal purpose of checking the extensive problem of 'illegal migration' in Assam from Bangladesh. The Assam Accord has been discussed extensively in the previous chapters.

national register was ever prepared was in the year 1951 in connection with the census of 1951.[2]

This chapter describes the concept and framework of the NRC in general. Further, this chapter also delves into those facets of the NRC which are specific to the state of Assam.

THE LEGAL FRAMEWORK OF NRC

The legal framework for the NRC can be found in Section 14 A of the Citizenship Act and the Citizenship (Registration of Citizens and Issue of National Identity Cards) Rules, 2003. These two statutory developments will be discussed in turn.

Section 14 A to the Citizenship Act

The Statement of Objects & Reasons for the Citizenship (Amendment) Bill clearly spelt out the objective i.e. to provide for compulsory registration and issuance of national identity cards to all citizens of India.[3] Section 14 A of the Citizenship Act was formally introduced to the statute book through the Citizenship (Amendment) Act, 2003 and was given effect to on 03.12.2004.

Section 14 A of the Citizenship Act provides for compulsory registration of every Indian citizen and issuance of a National Identity Card to him.

Section 14A of the Citizenship Act empowers the central government to create and maintain a national register of Indian citizens, to establish a national registration authority

2 *See generally* https://assam.gov.in/en/main/NRC. As per available information, this exercise was carried out on account of large-scale illegal migration from East Pakistan (now Bangladesh) into India. Historically, a citizen counting exercise has been carried out by the Indian government action in an effort to check the problem of illegal migration.

3 In the year 2003 a Parliamentary Standing Committee on Home Affairs consisting of 15 (fifteen) members of Rajya Sabha and 30 (thirty) members of Lok Sabha under the Chairmanship of Shri Pranab Mukherjee had examined the Citizenship (Amendment) Bill, 2003.

and to carry out compulsory registration of the Indian citizens. The National Identity Card is to be provided to all Indian citizens.

Section 14 A is reproduced below for ready reference:

14A. Issue of National Identity Cards

(l) The Central Government may compulsorily register every citizen of India and issue national identity card to him.

(2) The Central Government may maintain a National Register of Indian Citizens and for that purpose establish a National Registration Authority.

(3) On and from the date of commencement of the Citizenship (Amendment) Act, 2003, the Registrar General, India, appointed under subsection (1) of section 3 of the Registration of Births and Deaths Act, 1969 (18 of 1969) shall act as the National Registration Authority and he shall function as the Registrar General of Citizen Registration.

(4) The Central Government may appoint such other officers and staff as may be required to assist the Registrar General of Citizen Registration in discharging his functions and responsibilities.

(5) The procedure to be followed in compulsory registration of the citizens of India shall be such as may be prescribed.

The National Identity Card Rules

In furtherance of and in connection with the above Section 14A of the Citizenship Act, the Citizenship (Registration of Citizens and Issue of National Identity Cards) Rules, 2003 (**NIC Rules**) were formulated and notified by the government on 10.12.2003.[4]

The NIC Rules prescribe the manner of preparation of the

4 The NIC Rules were actually notified prior to Section 14 A of the Citizenship Act.

National Register of Citizens. The NIC Rules also contain special provisions with respect to the creation of the NRC in Assam. The salient features of the NIC Rules are mentioned below.

National Register of Indian Citizens

The NIC Rules contemplate establishment and maintenance of a register containing details of all Indian citizens called the National Register.[5] The NRC shall contain the following information/details:

a) Name
b) Name of Father
c) Name of Mother
d) Sex
e) Date of Birth
f) Place of Birth
g) Residential Address
h) Marital Status
i) Visible Identification Mark
j) Date of Registration of Citizen
k) Serial No. of registration
l) National Identity No.

Constituents of the National Register

The National Register shall be divided into various parts comprising the State Register, the District Register, Sub-District Register and Local Register. This system shall be hierarchal, starting from the local levels and moving though sub-district, district and state levels, finally to the national level.

The said registers shall contain such details which the central government may specify in consultation with the Registrar General of Citizen Registration[6] (**Registrar General**).

5 R. 3 of the NIC Rules.

6 A Registrar General is appointed under the Registration of Births and Deaths Act, 1969.

As the name suggests, a State Register shall contain details of Indian citizens residing in the state; a District Register shall contain details of Indian citizens residing in the district; a Sub-District Register shall contain details of Indian citizens usually residing in a taluk of the sub-district; a Local Register shall contain details of Indian citizens usually residing in a village or rural area or town or ward or demarcated area (demarcated by the Registrar General) within a ward in a town or urban area.[7] Each of the above-mentioned registers shall have a registrar, who shall act as a supervising authority thereof.

The collection of information etc. shall be first made at the local level and the results of the same shall be transferred to the higher levels of the register. Post the conclusion of the process (described below), the final results shall be transferred to the National Register.

The Population Register

Separately, the NIC Rules also contemplate preparation of a Population Register which shall contain details of persons who fall in the jurisdiction of the Local Register. The population register is discussed in more detail in the latter part of this chapter.

PREPARATION OF NATIONAL REGISTER

This section summarises the mode and manner of creation of a National Register.

The Process

Broadly speaking, preparation of the National Register shall be a 3 (three) step process:[8]

7 *See* R. 2 of the NIC Rules.

8 Rule 4 of the NIC Rules.

i. A house-to-house enumeration for collection of the relevant particulars (including citizenship status) relating to each family and individual.
ii. A verification and scrutinization process of every family and individual.
iii. Enquiry of persons whose citizenship is considered doubtful (pursuant to the verification and scrutinization process)

The Enquiry

During the course of enquiry of doubtful cases, an opportunity shall be granted to the concerned persons before a final decision is taken on their inclusion (or exclusion) from the register. Such decision making shall be made in writing within a period of 90 (ninety) days or such further reasonable time for which reasons shall be recorded.

The Publication of the Register(s)

Post the above-mentioned enquiry and decision making, the draft of the local register shall be published for the following purposes: (i) inviting objections, if any; (ii) for inclusion of any name therein; or (iii) corrections in the family or individual particulars. The above objections/challenge are required to be filed within a period of 30 (thirty) days from the date of the publication in the form and manner prescribed. A decision shall be made on the said objections/challenge within a period of 90 (ninety) days. An appeal thereagainst may be made within a period of 30 (thirty) days from the order, which shall be decided within a period of 90 (ninety) days after giving the parties an opportunity of being heard.

Post a final decision, the finalised version of the Local Register shall move up the hierarchal pyramid and ultimately become a part of the National Register.

Initialization of the National Register

The concerned authorities shall notify the date on which the National Register shall be initialized throughout the country. Once initialized, the preparation of the National Register shall commence (in the manner described above). It shall be the duty of every individual to get himself registered with the Local Register during the period of initialization.[9]

Citizen Assistance for National Register

Every Indian citizen is mandated to assist the concerned officials in the preparation of the National Register and to get himself registered in the Local Register during the said period of initialization. Further, it shall be the duty of every head of the family to provide correct information (about himself and his family members) in connection with the preparation of the Local Register.[10]

Deletion from the National Register

The name and particulars of a citizen may, by order of the appropriate authority, be removed from the National Register upon the happening of any of the following:

a) Death of the citizen.
b) Cessation of Indian citizenship by renunciation.
c) Cessation of Indian citizenship by acquisition of foreign citizenship.
d) Provision of any incorrect particulars by the concerned person which affects his citizenship status.

An order of deletion of name from the National Register shall be intimated by the authority to the concerned person, or his

9 R. 6 of the NIC Rules.

10 R. 7 of the NIC Rules.

nearest relative, as the case may be, within a period of 30 (thirty) days. A person aggrieved from such order can prefer an appeal within a period of 30 (thirty) days from such intimation. The said appeal shall be decided by the concerned authority after giving to the aggrieved person an opportunity of hearing and permission to produce any documentary or oral evidence in support of his case.[11]

Modification in the National Register

A modification in the National Register (post verification) would be permissible in any of the following situations:[12]

a) Change of Name.
b) Change of Residential Address.
c) Change of Marital Status.
d) Change of Sex.
e) Change in parents, name in case of adoption under applicable law.

Maintenance and Updation of the National Register

The National Register shall be maintained and updated continuously on the basis of various registers discussed above. It shall be the responsibility of the head of every family to ensure that the particulars of his family members are updated in the concerned Local Register.[13]

National Identity Cards

A National Identity Card (**Identity Card**) shall be issued by the authorities to every person whose name and particulars are entered in the National Register. The Identity Card shall be the

11 R. 10 of the NIC Rules.

12 R. 12 of the NIC Rules.

13 R. 11 of the NIC Rules.

property of the central government and shall not be wilfully destroyed, altered or transferred.[14]

Surrender of the National Identity Card

In case of deletion of a person from the National Register, his Identity Card shall be surrendered to the appropriate authorities.[15]

Loss of the National Identity Card

Loss of the Identity Card is required to be immediately reported to the nearest police station and the concerned authorities.[16]

Violation of the Rules

Violation of the NIC Rules attract a fine of Rs. 1,000/- (One Thousand only).

NATIONAL REGISTER OF CITIZENS: ASSAM CONTEXT

Introduction

The preceding section of the chapter discusses the general framework of the NRC and the NIC Rules. This section of the chapter discusses the subject specifically in the context of Assam.

The National Identity Card Rules for Assam

The NIC Rules contain special provisions as to the National Register for the state of Assam (**Assam NRC**).[17] This special procedure has been prescribed (under Rule 4A & Schedule of the NIC Rules) for the purpose of preparation of the Assam NRC.[18]

---

14 R. 13 & 14 of the NIC Rules.

15 R. 14 (3) of the NIC Rules.

16 R. 14 (4) of the NIC Rules.

17 R. 4 A & Schedule of the NIC Rules.

18 A special category of 'deemed' citizens is created in the context of Assam. R. 4A is a departure from the other rules (which deal with preparation of NRC of

It is noteworthy that the sole test for inclusion for a person in the NRC is 'citizenship' (as per the Indian Constitution and Section 6A of the Citizenship Act). No special privilege is to be given to indigenous persons of Assam in this regard.[19]

Salient Features of NIC Rules with respect to the Assam NRC

The NIC Rules contains a special schedule which describes the procedure and processes to be followed with respect to preparation of the Assam NRC. The said provisions are discussed below in brief.

Invitation of Applications

The process of preparation of the Assam NRC would commence by inviting applications from all residents of Assam for collection of specified particulars relating to each individual, including the information available in the NRC of 1951 and the Rolls of 1971 (defined below).

Publication

The District Magistrate shall cause to be published copies of the National Register of Citizens 1951 (**NRC of 1951**) along with the electoral rolls up to the midnight of 24.03.1971 (**Rolls of 1971**), as available, and send the same to the Local Register for wide circulation and public inspection in each village and ward.

The Local Registrar shall select centrally located public places for display of records and for issue and receipt of the applications. The Local Registrar shall be the custodian of records of his area and shall be responsible for its display during office hours.

Indian citizens from the rest of the country). This procedure has been followed in the Assam NRC exercise. *See generally* Assam Public Works v. Union of India, W.P. (C) No. 274/2009 (Order dated 13.08.2019, Supreme Court of India). For more on the Assam NRC exercise, see Chapter Nos. 8 & 9.

19 Kamalakhya Dey Purkayastha and Others v. Union of India, W.P. (C) No. 1020/2017 (05.12.2017, Supreme Court of India).

Scrutiny of Applications

Post receipt of the applications, the Local Registrar shall scrutinize the applications and post verification, prepare a consolidated list which shall contain the names of the following persons: (i) persons whose name appear in the NRC of 1951 and the Rolls of 1971; (ii) the descendants of persons mentioned in the preceding serial no. (i). The scrutiny shall be made by comparing the information stated in the application form along with the official records. All persons whose information is found in order shall make the cut. The said consolidated list shall be prepared village and ward wise.

The Local Registrar is authorised to use inter-state correspondence or inter-district correspondence for verifying information relating to persons who were residing outside Assam or had shifted to another district within Assam up to midnight of 24.03.1971.[20]

Investigation by District Magistrate

The Local Registrar is empowered to refer doubtful cases to the District Magistrate for investigation and decision-making. Such referral shall be informed to the concerned person as well.

The Exceptions

The persons declared as 'illegal migrants' or 'foreigners' by the competent authority shall not be included in the list.

However, persons who came to Assam between 1966 and 25.03.1971; and got themselves registered with the Foreigner Registration Regional Officer shall be eligible to be included in the list provided they have not been declared as 'illegal migrants' or 'foreigners' by the competent authority.[21]

20 Clause 3(5) of the Schedule. Indian citizens, including their children and descendants, who may have moved to the State of Assam subsequent to 24.03.1971 would be eligible for inclusion in the NRC on adducing satisfactory proof of residence in any part of the country (outside Assam) as on 24.03.1971. *See* Assam Sanmilita Mahasangha v. Union of India, W.P. (C) No. 562/2012 (21.07.2015, Supreme Court of India).

21 Clause 3 (2) of the Schedule.

Separately, persons who are originally inhabitants of Assam, and their children, and descendants who are citizens of India shall be included in the list if their citizenship is ascertained beyond reasonable doubt and to the satisfaction of the concerned authorities.[22]

Publication of the List

The District Magistrate shall publish the list as the 'Draft Assam NRC'. A public notice with regard to the said publication shall also be issued in the local newspaper having wide circulation in the concerned areas. Objections and suggestions shall be invited to the draft Assam NRC.

Continued Verification

The Local Registrar is authorised to cause a verification of names of persons as considered necessary, until the final publication of the Assam NRC. This mechanism allows the government authorities to re-verify cases in case the need arises or the situation demands. However, such authorisation of 'continuing verification' is likely to result in 'undue harassment' of the persons. In this regard, the Local Registrar is required to take special care in attending to instances of allegation of 'undue harassment' if brought to his attention during the conduct of the verification exercise.

The report of verification shall be examined by the District Registrar who shall pass an order (with reasons) on the said report.

---

22 Clause 3 (3) of the Schedule provides for identification of persons entitled to be included in the Assam NRC by a process different from what is enumerated under Clause 3 (2). Clause 3 (3) contemplates a less strict and vigorous process for deciding claims for inclusion in the NRC in so far as persons who are originally inhabitants of the state of Assam are concerned. Identification of persons who are originally inhabitants of the state of Assam is to be done solely on the basis of citizenship proof.

Publication of Additional List

Post the above-mentioned order by the District Registrar, an additional list of the Draft Assam NRC shall be published.

Claims and Objections

Objections can be filed by the following persons within a period of 30 (thirty) days from the date of the publication of the draft list, with the Local Registrar: (i) persons whose names are not included in the draft list; (ii) persons who object to the inclusion of any name in the draft list.

The Local Registrar shall decide the objections after giving the concerned parties an opportunity to file supporting documents and an opportunity of hearing.

Publication of Supplementary List

Post disposal of the above-mentioned objections, the Local Registrar shall publish a supplementary list and subsequently, the final Assam NRC shall be published.

Appeal

Any person dissatisfied with the decision of the Local Registrar on the objections may prefer an appeal before the appropriate Foreigners Tribunal [established under the Foreigners (Tribunals) Order, 1964] within a period of 60 (sixty) days from the date of the order. No further challenge or appeal is prescribed in this regard.[23]

However, where the issue and question of nationality has been determined previously by the Foreigners Tribunal, then the appeal would not be maintainable. The determination would be final and binding on the Registering Authority and the Local Registrar. There cannot be a second round of litigation before the same tribunal.[24]

---

23 Clause 8 of the Schedule.

24 Abdul Kuddus v. Union of India AIR 2019 SC 2834. *See also* Chapter 3 for more

Opinion of the Foreigners Tribunal

Even in case where no appeal is preferred by an aggrieved person, the District Magistrate is still empowered to make a suo moto reference to the Foreigners Tribunal for its opinion on the 'status' of the concerned person.[25] Simply put, a decision by the authorities on the 'status' of a person can be got cross-verified by the District Magistrate *via* a reference to the Foreigners Tribunal.

As long as the name of the citizenship status of a person is 'doubtful' or 'disputed', he will be prohibited from casting his vote in any election (to the house of people or the state legislative assembly). This includes the period during which his case remains pending with the Foreigners Tribunal.[26]

Procedure for Appeal

The Foreigners (Tribunals) Order, 1964 provides the procedure for preferring and adjudication of an appeal. The brief procedure(s) of appeal are discussed below.

a) Notice to the District Magistrate: The Foreigners Tribunal shall issue a notice to the District Magistrate for production

---

on the procedures and processes of an adjudication or determination by a Foreigners Tribunal.

25 Order 3A (6) of the Foreigners (Tribunal) Order, 1964.

26 *See generally* Biswajit Debnath v. Union of India, W.P. (C) No. 4497/2019 (12.03.2021, Guwahati High Court). *See also* HRA Choudhury v. Election Commission of India, 2002 (1) GLT 1, wherein the Guwahati High Court upheld an order of the Election Commission of India which had held that the persons (whose names were a part of the electoral rolls) but had been subsequently labelled as 'doubtful' or 'disputed' would not be permitted to cast their votes in the election so long as their citizenship status was not decided favourably by an appropriate tribunal. The court further observed that any decision with regard to the status of a person marked as 'doubtful' can only be decided by the Foreigners Tribunal. The court also made reference to the provisions of the Representation of the People Act, 1950 and the Registration of Electors Rules, 1960 to observe as follows: (i) A citizen of India alone and no one else, is eligible to vote at elections to the house of the people and the state legislative assemblies; (ii) Where the Foreigners Tribunal decides that a person is not a citizen of India, then such persons name is liable to be deleted from the electoral roll in accordance with Rule 21 A of the Registration of Electors Rules, 1960.

of the relevant records (including the application form along with documents filed therewith, and the orders passed by the relevant authorities in the matter) within a period of 30 (thirty) days. A copy of the said notice shall also be issued to the parties.

b) Notice for Hearing: Upon examination of the produced records, if the Foreigners Tribunal finds merit in the appeal, then it shall issue a notice of hearing to the aggrieved as well as the District Magistrate. The grounds need not be mentioned separately and elaborately. It would suffice if the grounds are mentioned in the notice itself, which need not be detailed or elaborate.[27] A mistake in the notice which is not jurisdictional, does not invalidate a proceeding, if it is otherwise valid.[28] Non-mentioning of the stream of foreigners in the notice would not vitiate the final conclusion reached by the Foreigners Tribunal.[29]

c) Opportunity of Hearing: Both parties shall be granted a reasonable opportunity of being heard by the Foreigners Tribunal.

d) Findings of the Foreigners Tribunal: During the disposal of the appeal, the Foreigners Tribunal shall give a clear finding as to whether the aggrieved is a foreigner or not.

e) Contents of the Final Order: The final order of the Foreigners Tribunal is required to be clear, concise and reasoned. The order shall also contain the tribunal's opinion as to whether the aggrieved person is eligible for inclusion in the NRC or not.

f) No Right of Appeal: No appeal shall lie in the following cases: (i) where a reference (above) has already been made

---

27 Bela Rani Devi v. Union of India, W.P. (C) No. 5852/2016 (10.05.2018, Guwahati High Court).

28 Bela Rani Devi v. Union of India, *supra*

29 *See* Ananda Ghosh v. Union of India, 2017 (3) GLR 815 & Bela Rani Devi v. Union of India, *supra*

to the Foreigners Tribunal (with regard to the concerned person) by the competent authority; or (ii) where an opinion of the Foreigners Tribunal has previously been sought and obtained as to the citizenship status of the concerned person.

THE NATIONAL POPULATION REGISTER

Another analogous term which requires a brief discussion is the National Population Register. The National Population Register (**NPR**) may be commonly described as a register of usual residents of the country. Put differently, the NPR is a record of biographical data of 'usual residents' (which includes both citizens and non-citizens) residing in a particular area. It is required to be prepared at the local (Village/Sub-Town), Sub-District, District, State and National level under provisions of the Citizenship Act, 1955 and the Citizenship (Registration of Citizens and issue of National Identity Cards) Rules, 2003.

Simply put, the NPR is a collection of personal details of all 'usual residents' of the country, regardless of their nationality.[30] The prime purpose of the NPR is creation of a comprehensive identity database in the country. It is envisioned that the a properly created NPR would not only strengthen the security of the country but also help in better targeting of the benefits and services under the government schemes apart from improving planning.

The contents of the NPR are also used for the purposes of preparation of the Local Register and consequently the National Register. The preparation of the NPR is considered by many to be the first step towards a nation wide NRC.

30 A usual resident is defined for the purposes of NPR as a person who has resided in a local area for the past 6 (six) months or more or a person who intends to reside in that area for the next 6 (six) months or more. *See* http://censusindia.gov.in/2011-Common/IntroductionToNpr.html

Preparation of the National Population Register

On 31.07.2019, by means of a notification, the central government announced the preparation of the NPR.[31] Subsequently, an instruction manual was also issued by the government (i.e. the office of the Registrar & Census Commissioner, India, Ministry of Home Affairs) in connection with the preparation of the NPR (**NPR Manual**).

Updation of NPR

The NPR for India had been prepared for the first time in the year 2010 followed by an updation in the year 2015. A proposal for updation of the NPR (on a national wise basis) has been approved by the union cabinet at a cost of Rs. 3,941.35 crores along with the Census of India for 2021.[32]

The NRC Protests

The proposed implementation of a nation-wide NRC has seen stiff opposition from various sections of the Indian society. A chief argument against the NPR is that it is part and parcel of the NRC exercise and carries all the alleged vices of the NRC.

THE ASSAM NRC EXERCISE

The Supreme Court, in **Assam Public Works v. Union of India** (the Assam NRC Judgement) directed that the NRC exercise be carried out for the state of Assam (under its supervision). The final draft of the Assam NRC was published on 31.08.2019 but about 19 (nineteen) lakh people have been excluded from the list. Various issues with respect to the Assam NRC have cropped up and been dealt with. The Assam NRC and its implementation have been discussed in some detail in subsequent chapters.

31 As per information available in public domain, presently the preparation of the NPR is on hold on account of the global pandemic.

32 *See generally* https://pib.gov.in/PressReleasePage.aspx?PRID=1597350

CHAPTER 7

The Amendments to the Citizenship Act (CAA)

INTRODUCTION

As noted in the previous chapters, the Citizenship Act has been amended on various occasions, in keeping with the needs of the hour. Amongst other things, various provisions of the Citizenship Act (as also the Foreigners Act etc.) have been tightened and made more stringent over time especially in the context of 'illegal migration'.

The Citizenship (Amendment) Act, 2019 (**CAA**) has, by far, been the most significant (and perhaps most controversial) of all amendments. Simply put, the CAA relaxes requirements and simplifies procedures with respect to grant of Indian citizenship to certain classes of migrants from certain neighbouring countries who are facing or are susceptible to persecution on the basis of religion.

The benefit of the CAA to thousands of its beneficiaries cannot be understated. However, the CAA comes with a host of questions and challenges on various counts, from various sections of the Indian society. Some people view this to be a purely religious and political propaganda of the current dispensation; and an attempt to 'persecute' muslims in India. It is being argued that the underlying intention of the CAA is to take away citizenship of certain communities in India. Most people opposing the CAA contend that the CAA violates various provisions of the Indian Constitution, including Article 14 (right to equality). They contend that the selective nature or character of the CAA is proof enough of its latent objective. Although the government has made various public statements seeking to clarify various issues relating to the CAA, the critics are not impressed or assuaged.

More than a hundred petitions have been filed in the Supreme Court of India, by various groups (and state governments) challenging the constitutionality of the CAA. The government has also filed a response justifying the CAA and clarifying various aspects related thereto. The matter is pending in the Supreme Court.

This chapter attempts a detailed exposition of the amendments which have been brought about by the CAA. The author urges the readers to read the present chapter with the immediately succeeding chapter, *in seriatim,* for a complete discourse on the subject.

The CAA: In a Nutshell

In a nutshell, the CAA amends the citizenship law to state that persons belonging to six minority communities (namely Hindus, Sikhs, Parsis, Jains, Buddhists and Christians in Afghanistan, Bangladesh and Pakistan) (hereinafter the **Classified Communities**) who were compelled to seek shelter in India due to religious persecution or fear of religious persecution in these countries, would no longer be regarded as 'illegal migrants' and would be given an opportunity to get their 'irregular' status regularised by applying for Indian citizenship through naturalisation.

A BACKGROUND NOTE: PRECURSORS TO THE CAA

Over the last few decades, a number of Afghani, Bangladeshi and Pakistani nationals belonging to 6 (six) minority communities namely Hindus, Sikhs, Buddhists, Jains, Parsis and Christians have sought long shelter in India due to persecution on grounds of religion or for fear of such persecution, many without valid travel documents. Ideally, under Indian law, such persons would be classified as 'illegal migrants' and be liable for deportation. However, while recognizing their plight, and with a view to facilitate the entry of such people into India and to grant them some basic amenities for their wellbeing, the Ministry of Home Affairs, Government of India enacted the Passport (Entry into India) Amendment Rules, 2015 & The Foreigners (Amendment) Order, 2015 allowing persons (who entered into India latest by 31.12.2014) permission to reside in India. This is discussed below.

The Regularisation Notifications

In the years 2015 and 2016, the Ministry of Home Affairs, Government of India tweaked the passport and foreigner laws regularising stay of persons from the Classified Communities (who had entered India on or before 2014 without valid documents). Such amendments were made *via* Notifications issued by the Ministry of Home Affairs bearing Nos. G.S.R. 685 (E) dated 07.09.2015, G.S.R. No. 686 (E) dated 07.09.2015, G.S.R. No. 702 (E) dated 18.07.2016 & G.S.R. No. 703 (E) dated 18.07.2016 (collectively **Regularisation Notifications** for ease of reference).

Amendment to the Passport Rules

Typically, Indian law requires that every person entering India should possess a passport or other valid travel document.[1] On 07.09.2015, the Passport (Entry into India) Amendment Rules, 2015 were promulgated to exclude the Classified Communities of Bangladesh and Pakistan (who had come to India by 31.12.2014 due to religious persecution or fear of religious persecution)

1 R. 3 of the Passport (Entry into India) Rules, 2015.

from the scope of the above legal requirement. The relevant excerpt of the said notification is as follows:

G.S.R. 685(E).- In exercise of the powers conferred by section 3 of the Passport (Entry into India) Act, 1920 (34 of 1920), the Central Government hereby makes the following rules further to amend the Passport (Entry into India) Rules, 1950, namely:

> I. (I) These rules may be called the Passport (Entry into India) Amendment Rules, 2015.
>
> (2) They shall come into force on the date of their publication in the Official Gazette.
>
> 2. In the Passport (Entry into India) Rules, 1950, in rule 4, in sub-rule (I), after clause (h), the following clause shall be inserted, namely:
>
> (ha) persons belonging to minority communities in Bangladesh and Pakistan, namely, Hindus, Sikhs, Buddhists, Jains, Parsis and Christians who were compelled to seek shelter in India due to religious persecution or fear of religious persecution and entered into India on or before the 31st December, 2014
>
> (i) without valid documents including passport or other travel documents; or
>
> (ii) with valid documents including passport or other travel document and the validity of any of such documents has expired:
>
> Provided that provision of this clause shall take effect from the date of publication of this notification in the Official Gazette.

Subsequently, *vide* notification dated G.S.R. No. 702 (E) dated 18.07.2016 the Classified Communities from Afghanistan were also extended the same benefits.

Amendment to the Foreigners Order

Similarly, on 07.09.2015, the Foreigners (Amendment) Order, 2015 was promulgated to exempt the Classified Communities from Pakistan, Bangladesh and Afghanistan (who had come to India by 31.12.2014 due to religious persecution or fear of religious persecution) from the purview of the Foreigners Act, 1946.

In effect, this meant that the 'illegal migrants' from the Classified Communities were granted immunity from legal proceedings under the Foreigners Act, 1946 as well as the Passports Act. As a natural corollary, the beneficiaries of the Regularisation Notifications would not be proceeded against and deported, despite being an 'illegal migrant'. This virtually amounts to 'regularisation' of their stay in India. The relevant excerpt is as follows:

> GSR 686(E) - In exercise of the powers conferred by section 3 of the Foreigners Act, 1946, the Central Government hereby makes the following order further to amend the Foreigners Order, 1948, namely:-
>
> 1. (1) This Order may be called the Foreigners (Amendment) Order, 2015.
>   (2) It shall come into force on the date of its publication in the Official Gazette.
> 2. In the Foreigners Order, 1948, after paragraph 3, the following paragraph shall be inserted, namely -
> 3. A. Exemption of certain class of foreigners - (1) Persons belonging to minority communities in Bangladesh and Pakistan, namely, Hindus, Sikhs, Jains, Parsis and Christians who were compelled to seek shelter in India due to religious persecution or fear of religious persecution and entered into India on or before the 31st December, 2014-

(a) without valid documents including passport or other travel documents and who have been exempted under rule 4 from the provisions of rule 3 of the Passport (Entry into India) Rules, 1950 made under section 3 of the Passport (Entry into India) Act, 1920 (34 of 1920); or-

(b) with valid documents including passport or other travel document and the validity of any of such documents has expired, are hereby granted exemption from the application of the Foreigners Act, 1946 and the orders made thereunder in respect of their stay in India without such documents or after the expiry of those documents, as the case may be, from the date of publication of this order in the Official Gazette.

Subsequently, *vide* notification dated G.S.R. No. 703 (E) dated 18.07.2016 the Classified Communities from Afghanistan were also extended the same benefits.

The *sine qua non* for invoking the Regularisation Notifications was that the person is required to be from the Classified Communities from a Classified Country and is taking shelter in India due to religious persecution.[2] The Guwahati High Court, while examining the Regularisation Notifications has also opined that the basis for relief thereunder is establishment of 'religious persecution'.[3]

Clearly, the Regularisation Notifications are interconnected with the CAA. The CAA appears to be the next logical step by affording a 'full and legitimate recognition' to the beneficiaries

2 Falu Das v. Union of India, W.P. (C) No. 1157/2018 (09.04.2018, Guwahati High Court); Subhash Chandra Roy v. State of Assam, Rev. Petition No. 86/2016 (17.11.2016, Guwahati High Court).

3 *See generally* Falu Das v. Union of India, *supra;* Subhash Chandra Roy v. State of Assam, *supra*

of the Regularisation Notifications by giving to them a fast track option of availing Indian citizenship.[4]

The Effect of the Regularisation Notifications

Through the Regularisation Notifications, the central government 'regularised' the entry and stay of illegal migrants from the Classified Communities from Pakistan, Bangladesh and Afghanistan. The expression 'regularisation' here denotes 'immunity' from prosecution under the Indian passport and foreigners laws.

The Regularisation Notifications were truly a precursor to the CAA. In fact, post such notifications, all that remained was to give full citizenship rights to persons who had been 'sheltered' in India, which is now sought to be through the CAA. Ergo, it may be said that the CAA is an extension of the Regularisation Notifications.

Gaps in the Regularisation Notifications

In **Ranjit Kumar Mazumder v. The State of West Bengal**[5] the Calcutta High Court, while examining the Regularisation Notifications, made certain observations, which, as per the author, reveal the following gaps:

a) The notifications do not specify or designate any authority before which the possibility of facing religious persecution has to be factually established in order to get shelter in India.
b) The notifications do not provide any screening procedure which tells the genuine cases from the non-genuine ones. The true intent of the notifications is to afford protection only to

4 Even if a beneficiary of the CAA does not avail of the fast track channel for Indian citizenship (provided under the CAA), he would still be protected (in the sense that he would be permitted continue to 'legitimately' reside in India).

5 C.R.M No. 10076/2015 (09.03.2016, Calcutta High Court).

cases where there actually exists religious persecution or a real likelihood of religious persecution. Absence of proper screening procedure makes the notifications susceptible to misuse.

It is important to point out that the Regularisation Notifications are subject to challenge before the Supreme Court of India in the challenge petitions. Further, the above aspects may be addressed in the CAA rules which are presently under deliberation.

The Procedure for Obtaining Citizenship

As discussed above, the Regularisation Notifications gave legal immunity to certain 'irregular' migrants. To further the objectives of the Regularisation Notifications, the central government introduced Notification No. S.O. 4132 (E) dated 23.12.2016 for the purpose of establishing a mechanism for determination of citizenship applications of the Classified Communities. The said notification does the following: (a) designate authorities for deciding claims of citizenship of the Classified Communities; (b) specifies the procedures for adjudication of the claims of citizenship, such as the process of making the application, the verification exercise, the inquiry process and maintenance of records. Recently, another notification dated 28.05.2021 was issued by the central government authorising the collectors of 13 (thirteen) districts in India to accept and process applications for citizenship made by the beneficiaries of the CAA. These districts are Morbi, Rajkot, Patan and Vadodara in Gujarat; Durg and Balodabazar in Chhattisgarh; Jalore, Udaipur, Pali, Barmer and Sirohi in Rajasthan; Faridabad in Haryana and Jalandhar in Punjab. To the understanding of the author, no citizenship applications have been processed till date.

Permission to the Classified Communities to purchase Immovable Property in India

In the year 2018, another step was taken to further accommodate the beneficiaries of the Regularisation Notifications. The Reserve Bank of India granted permission to them to purchase immovable property in India, for residential and self-employment purposes, subject to certain conditions.

The Reserve Bank of India, through its Notification No. FEMA 21 (R)/2018 - RB, dated 26.03.2018, titled 'Foreign Exchange Management (Acquisition and Transfer of Immovable Property in India) Regulations, 2018, provided that a person, being a citizen of Afghanistan, Bangladesh or Pakistan, belonging to minority communities in those countries, namely, Hindus, Sikhs, Buddhists, Jains, Parsis and Christians, who are residing in India and have been granted a Long-Term Visa (LTV) by the government,[6] may purchase 1 (one) residential immovable property for self-occupation and 1 (one) immovable property for carrying out self-employment, subject to the following conditions:[7]

a) The property should not be located in or around restricted/protected/cantonment areas.
b) The person shall submit a declaration in the prescribed form and manner, to the revenue authority of the district where the property is located, specifying the source of funds and details of the LTV.
c) The person shall submit a copy of the property papers with

6 Under Indian law, a long-term visa is required by a foreigner who intends to stay in India for a period of more than 180 (one hundred and eighty) days. The Ministry of Home Affairs, Government of India, has issued detailed guidelines pertaining to grant of long-term visa for citizens of Pakistan, Bangladesh and Afghanistan seeking permanent settlement in India, with a view to acquire Indian citizenship. *See generally* https://www.mha.gov.in/PDF_Other/AnnexVI_01022018.pdf.

7 Reg. 7 of Foreign Exchange Management (Acquisition and Transfer of Immovable Property in India) Regulations, 2018.

the concerned foreigners office and the Ministry of Home Affairs (Foreigners Division), Government of India.

d) The property would be liable to be attached/confiscated in the event of the person indulging in anti-India activities.

e) The person would be eligible to sell the property only after acquiring Indian citizenship. Transfer of the property prior to acquisition of Indian citizenship would require prior approval of the concerned foreigner's office.

The above regulation however only pertained to persons who had come to India with valid travel documents.

Clearly, this regulation was in the form of a step-in-aid, with the ultimate objective being grant of Indian citizenship to the beneficiaries of the CAA.

THE CITIZENSHIP AMENDMENT BILL

The process of amending the Citizenship Act started with the introduction of the Citizenship (Amendment) Bill, 2016 in the Lok Sabha on 19.07.2016 (**Bill**). A motion was moved and adopted by the Lok Sabha on 11.08.2016 for the constitution of a Joint Parliamentary Committee which would examine the Bill and file a report thereon in the winter session of 2016. Thereafter, a Joint Parliamentary Committee (**JPC**) consisting 20 (twenty) members from the Lok Sabha and 10 (ten) members from the Rajya Sabha under the Chairpersonship of Dr Satyapal Singh, was constituted on 23.08.2016 to examine the Bill and make a report.

In the process of the examination of the Bill, the JPC issued a Press Communique on 17.09.2016 inviting views/suggestions from the Stakeholders/Experts/Public at large on the proposed amendments contained in the Bill. In response to that, more than 9000 (nine thousand) memoranda were received and scrutinised by the JPC. The JPC submitted its report on 07.01.2019. The

Bill was taken into consideration and passed by Lok Sabha on 08.01.2019 and moved to the Rajya Sabha. The Bill however lapsed consequent to the dissolution of the Lok Sabha.

Post the central elections of 2019 and re-formation of the Lok Sabha, the Bill was cleared on 04.12.2019 for introduction in the Parliament. The Bill was passed by the Lok Sabha on 10.12.2019 and by the Rajya Sabha on 11.12.2019. The Bill received the assent from the President of India on 12.12.2019 and came into force on 10.01.2020.

THE OBJECTS OF THE CAA

The Statement of Objects and Reasons to the CAA succinctly explain its purport. The relevant excerpt is reproduced below:

> 1. The Citizenship Act, 1955 (57 of 1955) was enacted to provide for the acquisition and determination of Indian citizenship.
> 2. It is a historical fact that trans-border migration of population has been happening continuously between the territories of India and the areas presently comprised in Pakistan, Afghanistan and Bangladesh. Millions of citizens of undivided India belonging to various faiths were staying in the said areas of Pakistan and Bangladesh when India was partitioned in 1947. The constitutions of Pakistan, Afghanistan and Bangladesh provide for a specific state religion. As a result, many persons belonging to Hindu, Sikh, Buddhist, Jain, Parsi and Christian communities have faced persecution on grounds of religion in those countries. Some of them also have fears about such persecution in their day-to-day life where right to practice, profess and propagate their religion has been

obstructed and restricted. Many such persons have fled to India to seek shelter and continued to stay in India even if their travel documents have expired or they have incomplete or no documents.

3. Under the existing provisions of the Act, migrants from Hindu, Sikh, Buddhist, Jain, Parsi or Christian communities from Afghanistan, Pakistan or Bangladesh who entered into India without valid travel documents or if the validity of their documents has expired are regarded as illegal migrants and ineligible to apply for Indian citizenship under section 5 or section 6 of the Act.
4. The Central Government exempted the said migrants from the adverse penal consequences of the Passport (Entry into India) Act, 1920 and the Foreigners Act, 1946 and rules or orders made thereunder vide notifications, dated 07.09.2015 and dated 18.07.2016. Subsequently, the Central Government also made them eligible for long term visa to stay in India, vide, orders dated 08.01.2016 and 14.09.2016. Now, it is proposed to make the said migrants eligible for Indian Citizenship.
5. The illegal migrants who have entered into India up to the cut off date of 31.12.2014 need a special regime to govern their citizenship matters. For this purpose the Central Government or an authority specified by it, shall grant the certificate of registration or certificate of naturalisation subject to such conditions, restrictions and manner as may be prescribed. Since many of them have entered into India long back, they may be given the citizenship of India from the date of their entry in India if they fulfil conditions for Indian citizenship specified in section 5 or the qualifications for the naturalisation under the provisions of the Third Schedule to the Act.

6. The Bill further seeks to grant immunity to the migrants of the aforesaid Hindu, Sikh, Buddhist, Jain, Parsi and Christian communities so that any proceedings against them in respect of their status of migration or citizenship does not bar them from applying for Indian citizenship. The competent authority, to be prescribed under the Act, shall not take into account any proceedings initiated against such persons regarding their status as illegal migrant or their citizenship matter while considering their application under section 5 or section 6 of the Act, if they fulfil all the conditions for grant of citizenship.
7. Many persons of Indian origin including persons belonging to the said minority communities from the aforesaid countries have been applying for citizenship under section 5 of the Citizenship Act, 1955 but they are unable to produce proof of their Indian origin. Hence, they are forced to apply for citizenship by naturalisation under section 6 of the said Act, which, inter alia, prescribes twelve years residency as a qualification for naturalisation in terms of the Third Schedule to the Act. This denies them many opportunities and advantages that may accrue only to the citizens of India, even though they are likely to stay in India permanently. Therefore, it is proposed to amend the Third Schedule to the Act to make applicants belonging to the said communities from the aforesaid countries eligible for citizenship by naturalisation if they can establish their residency in India for five years instead of the existing eleven years.
8. Presently, there is no specific provision in section 7D of the Act to cancel the registration of Overseas Citizen of India Cardholder who violates any provisions of the Act or any other law for the time being in force. It is

also proposed to amend the said section 7D so as to empower the Central Government to cancel registration as Overseas Citizen of India Cardholder in case of violation of any provisions of the Act or any other law for the time being in force.

9. Since there is no specific provision in the Act at present to provide an opportunity of being heard to the Overseas Citizen of India Cardholder before cancellation of the Overseas Citizen of India Card under section 7D, it is proposed to provide the opportunity of being heard to the Overseas Citizen of India Cardholder before the cancellation of the Overseas Citizen of India Card.
10. The Bill further seeks to protect the constitutional guarantee given to indigenous populations of North Eastern States covered under the Sixth Schedule to the Constitution and the statutory protection given to areas covered under "The Inner Line" system of the Bengal Eastern Frontier Regulation, 1873.
11. The Bill seeks to achieve the above objectives.

THE CAA: EXPLAINED

The CAA came into force with effect from 10.01.2020. The principal objective of the CAA is to provide protection to certain communities who face persecution on religious grounds in neighbouring theocratic states, and to facilitate the grant of citizenship to such persons.

The government stance behind the CAA finds mention in the Joint Committee Report, the relevant part of which is reproduced below.

> .....the first amendment aims to redress problems faced by the members of the minority community from Afghanistan,

> Bangladesh and Pakistan, who having entered India on a valid visa could not return to their countries for fear of religious persecution…"
>
> "Representations were received seeking extension of their visas and also permitting such individuals to apply for long-term visas. In the absence of this facility they were termed as illegal migrants and even deprived of basic amenities necessary for their wellbeing"
>
> "Against this backdrop the Ministry of Home Affairs vide its notification of 7th September, 2015, namely the Passport (Entry Into India) Amendments Rules, 2015 and the Foreigners (Amendment) Order, 2015 regularised the stay of such people who entered into India on or before 31st December, 2014. This was essentially in the nature of a one-time waiver or amnesty granted to these migrants from minority communities. The proposed amendment is a natural corollary to MHA's notification of 7th September, 2015.

Putting it succinctly, the CAA grants an opportunity to the Classified Communities from the Classified Countries to apply for and avail Indian Citizenship. For the ease of understanding, the critical aspects of the CAA have been dissected into parts and discussed below.

The Classified Communities

The beneficiaries under the CAA are select communities *viz.* Hindus, Sikhs, Buddhists, Jains, Parsis and Christians (the Classified Communities).

The purpose is to enable acquisition of Indian citizenship by members of minority communities namely Hindus, Sikhs, Buddhists, Jains, Parsis and Christians from Afghanistan, Bangladesh and Pakistan who were forced or compelled to seek shelter in India due to religious persecution or fear of religious persecution in their countries.[8]

The Classified Countries

The CAA extends to Classified Communities coming only from Pakistan, Bangladesh and Afghanistan (**Classified Countries**).

The fundamental reasoning of the central government behind selection of only 3 (three) neighbouring countries *viz.* Pakistan, Bangladesh and Afghanistan under the CAA is that these counties are essentially theocratic states with Islam as their state religion and the Classified Communities are a minority in such countries. Further, while these countries have provisions in their constitutions guaranteeing certain (limited) rights to non-muslims, however, in practice, the non-muslims in these countries have faced discrimination and persecution along the lines of religion.

In sum, the following persons fall outside the scope of the CAA: (i) persons from Bangladesh, Pakistan and Afghanistan who are not from the Hindu, Jain, Sikh, Buddhist, Christian, Parsi or Sikh faith; and (ii) persons of any faith from any countries other than the above mentioned 3 (three) countries.

The relevant excerpt of the CAA is reproduced below:

> Section 2 –Interpretation
>
> "illegal migrant" means a foreigner who has entered into India – (i) without a valid passport or other travel documents and such other document or authority as may be prescribed by or under any law in that behalf; or (ii) with a valid passport or other travel documents and such other document or authority as may be prescribed by or under any

8 *See Joint Committee Report.*

law in that behalf but remains therein beyond the permitted period of time;

Provided that any person belonging to Hindu, Sikh, Buddhist, Jain, Parsi or Christian community from Afghanistan, Bangladesh or Pakistan, who entered into India on or before the 31st day of December, 2014 and who has been exempted by the Central Government by or under clause (c) of sub-section (2) of section 3 of the Passport (Entry into India) Act, 1920 or from the application of the provisions of the Foreigners Act, 1946 or any rule or order made thereunder, shall not be treated as illegal migrant for the purposes of this Act; (emphasis supplied by the author)

The Cut Off Date

The application of the CAA has a time/date based restriction (or a cut-off date) i.e. 31.12.2014. Therefore, only the Classified Communities who had entered India until 31.12.2014 would be entitled to benefit from the CAA.

Interestingly, the Statement of Objects and Reasons of the CAA does not offer any reasoning behind the selection of this cut-off date. However, the *Joint Committee Report* connects the cut-off date with the Regularisation Notifications which had regularised the stay of the Classified Communities in India who had arrived in India until 31.12.2014 (discussed above).

Illegal Migrants

The general position with regard to Indian citizenship law is that persons who qualify to be 'illegal migrants' under the provisions of the Citizenship Act are ineligible to apply for Indian citizenship. This position is sought to be reversed by the CAA for its beneficiaries (described below).

The Citizenship Act defines an 'illegal migrant' as a person who has entered into India: (i) without a valid passport or other prescribed travel documents; or (ii) with a valid passport or prescribed travel document but overstays beyond the permitted time period.[9] Simply put, the Citizenship Act defines an 'illegal migrant' as a foreigner (i.e. non-Indian citizen) who has either entered India illegally or has overstayed illegally. Under Indian law, the uniform treatment for all 'illegal migrants' is detention and deportation.[10]

Under Indian law, an 'illegal migrant' is not fit to apply for or be granted Indian citizenship. The CAA regularises the status of the Classified Communities (who qualify) by stating that they are not to be considered as 'illegal migrants'. This regularisation of status hence makes them eligible to apply for Indian citizenship under the provisions of the Citizenship Act.

As per the *Joint Committee Report*, the immediate beneficiaries of the CAA are about 31,313 (thirty-one thousand, three hundred and thirteen) people: 25,447 (twenty-five thousand, four hundred and forty-seven) Hindus, 5,807 (five thousand, eight hundred and seven) Sikhs, 55 (fifty-five) Christians, 2 (two) Buddhists and 2 (two) Parsis.

The relevant excerpt of the CAA in this regard is reproduced below:

> 6B. - Special provisions as to citizenship of person covered by proviso to clause (b) of sub-section (1) of section 2.
>
> (1) The Central Government or an authority specified by it in this behalf may, subject to such conditions, restrictions and manner as may be prescribed, on an application made in this behalf, grant a certificate

---

9 S. 2 (b) of the Citizenship Act.

10 Note that the term 'illegal migrant' is religion neutral i.e. illegal migration by a person of any religion, faith or ethnic background would be meted out the same treatment under applicable law. There is no classification on the basis of religion.

of registration or certificate of naturalisation to a person referred to in the proviso to clause (b) of sub-section (1) of section 2.

(2) Subject to fulfilment of the conditions specified in section 5 or the qualifications for naturalisation under the provisions of the Third Schedule, a person granted the certificate of registration or certificate of naturalisation under sub-section (1) shall be deemed to be a citizen of India from the date of his entry into India.

(3) On and from the date of commencement of the Citizenship (Amendment) Act, 2019, any proceeding pending against a person under this section in respect of illegal migration or citizenship shall stand abated on conferment of citizenship to him: Provided that such person shall not be disqualified for making application for citizenship under this section on the ground that the proceeding is pending against him and the Central Government or authority specified by it in this behalf shall not reject his application on that ground if he is otherwise found qualified for grant of citizenship under this section:

Provided further that the person who makes the application for citizenship under this section shall not be deprived of his rights and privileges to which he was entitled on the date of receipt of his application on the ground of making such application.

(4) Nothing in this section shall apply to tribal areas of Assam, Meghalaya, Mizoram or Tripura as included in the Sixth Schedule to the Constitution and the area covered under "The Inner Line" notified under the Bengal Eastern Frontier Regulation, 1873.

Legal and Illegal Migrant

Needless to point out, both legal and illegal migrants are entitled to avail the benefits of the CAA (provided they satisfy all eligibility criteria discussed above). The expression 'legal migrant' is not specifically defined under Indian law. In this context, the *Joint Committee Report* records the government's stance as to an illegal migrant and a legal migrant in the following words:

> As per Section 2(1)(b) of the Citizenship Act, 1955 'illegal migrant' means a foreigner who has entered into India without a valid passport or other travel documents and such other documents or authority as may be prescribed by or under any law in that behalf; or with a valid passport or other travel documents and such other document or authority as may be prescribed by or under any law in that behalf but remains therein beyond the permitted period of time. Those who enter into India on valid travel documents and are registered with FRRO/FRO and possess valid residential permit/visa have a legal right to stay in India and are termed as legal, otherwise they are illegal immigrants.

Citizenship by Naturalisation

As discussed in Chapter 2, under Indian law, an application for obtaining citizenship by naturalisation can be preferred only after the applicant has, amongst others, resided in India for a set number of years. Generally speaking, this time period is 12 (twelve) months immediately preceding the date of the application, coupled with a minimum stay of 11 (eleven) years of the previous 14 (fourteen) years.

This key requirement (of residence) for citizenship by naturalisation has been significantly relaxed by the CAA. The

CAA has reduced the said time period of 11 (eleven) years to 5 (five) years for its beneficiaries. The relevant excerpt of the CAA in this regard is reproduced below:

> THE THIRD SCHEDULE (see section 6(1))
> QUALIFICATIONS FOR NATURALISATION
>
> The qualifications for naturalisation of a person are:
>
> (a) that he is not a subject or citizen of any country where citizens of India are prevented by law or practice of that country from becoming subjects or citizens of that country by naturalisation;
>
> (b) that, if he is a citizen of any country, he undertakes to renounce the citizenship of that country in the event of his application for Indian citizenship being accepted;
>
> (c) that he has either resided in India or been in the service of a Government in India or partly the one and partly the other, throughout the period of twelve months immediately preceding the date of the application;
> Provided that if the Central Government is satisfied that special circumstances exist, it may, after recording the circumstances in writing, relax the period of twelve months up to a maximum of thirty days which may be in different breaks.
>
> (d) that during the fourteen years immediately preceding the said period of twelve months, he has either resided in India or been in the service of a Government in India, or partly the one and partly the other, for periods amounting in the aggregate to not less than eleven year;
> <u>Provided that for the person belonging to Hindu, Sikh, Buddhist, Jain, Parsi or Christian community in Afghanistan, Bangladesh or Pakistan, the aggregate</u>

period of residence or service of Government in India as required under this clause shall be read as not less than five years in place of not less than eleven years.

(e) that he is of good character;

(f) that he has an adequate knowledge of a language specified in the Eighth Schedule to the Constitution; and

(g) that in the event of a certificate of naturalisation being granted to him, he intends to reside in India, or to enter into, or continue in, service under a Government in India or under an international organisation of which India is a member or under a society, company or body of persons established in India:

Provided that the Central Government may, if in the special circumstances of any particular case it thinks fit.

(i) allow a continuous period of twelve months ending not more than six months before the date of the application to be reckoned, for the purposes of clause (c) above, as if it had immediately preceded that date;

(ii) allow periods of residence or service earlier than fifteen years before the date of the application to be reckoned in computing the aggregate mentioned in clause (d) above.

(emphasis supplied by the author)

Naturalisation: The Selected Medium

The government appears to have moved on the assessment that the most suitable manner for obtaining citizenship for the Classified Communities is the process of naturalisation and hence the rigors of this process needs to be relaxed. This is explained in the *Joint Committee Report* in the following words:

> *The government also felt that many of these foreign nationals of Indian origin, who were applying for citizenship under Section 5(1)(a) of Citizenship Act, 1955 requiring seven years of residency period, were not able to provide the birth proof of their parents for establishing that they were born in undivided India in support of their claim for being of Indian origin. They were, therefore, compelled to apply under Section 6(1) of The Citizenship Act, 1955 which needs a minimum of twelve years residency period in India.*

Separately, on this score, the *Joint Committee Report* also records the government's stance that a relaxation in the residency period requirement will facilitate and aid the grant of citizenship to the persons who are not able to provide adequate documentary proof in support of their claim of 'Indian Origin'.

This part of the amendment is required to be read with the amendment to the definition of 'illegal migrant' (described above) as well as the cut-off date of 31.12.2014. The cumulative effect of this is that the eligible migrants under the CAA would be in a position to immediately apply for citizenship for naturalisation (subject to qualifying the other criteria in the naturalisation process).

Overseas Citizens

As discussed in Chapter 2, 'overseas citizenship of India' is a concept prevalent under Indian law wherein foreigners having moorings in India or an Indian origin can get themselves registered to gain various benefits such as life time visa to India, parity with Non-Resident Indians on various aspects etc.

Pithily speaking, an overseas citizenship is a notch below full Indian citizenship and grants various benefits to its holders, the benefits of which are determined by the government from time to time.

A person who qualifies to be an overseas citizen is required to apply and get himself registered with the relevant authorities.

Upon such registration, a registration card/booklet is issued. However, the law also authorises the government to cancel such registration in case of violation(s) by the overseas citizen. Section 7D of The Citizenship Act, 1955 states that the central government has the power to cancel a person's registration as an overseas citizen if he is found involved in false representation, concealment of any material fact, fraudulently obtaining the OCI card, showing dissatisfaction towards the Indian Constitution, indulging in anti-India activities etc.[11]

The CAA appears to 'more clearly clarify' the power of the central government regarding cancellation of OCI cards. The amendment provides that registration of an OCI holder can be cancelled if the concerned person violates any provisions of the Citizenship Act or of any other applicable India law. It also adds that an opportunity of hearing shall be granted to the concerned person before the cancellation.

The relevant excerpt of the CAA in this regard reads thus:

> 7D. - Cancellation of registration as Overseas Citizen of India Cardholders:
>
> The Central Government may, by order, cancel the registration granted under sub-section (1) of section 7A, if it is satisfied that:
>
> (a) the registration as an Overseas Citizen of India Cardholder was obtained by means of fraud, false representation or the concealment of any material fact; or
>
> (b) the Overseas Citizen of India Cardholder has shown disaffection towards the Constitution, as by law established; or
>
> (c) the Overseas Citizen of India Cardholder has, during any war in which India may be engaged, unlawfully traded

11 *See* Chapter 2 for a detailed discussion on OCI.

or communicated with an enemy or been engaged in, or associated with, any business or commercial activity that was to his knowledge carried on in such manner as to assist an enemy in that war; or

(d) the Overseas Citizen of India Cardholder has, within five years after registration under sub-section (1) of section 7A, been sentenced to imprisonment for a term of not less than two years; or

(a) the Overseas Citizen of India Cardholder has violated any of the provisions of this Act or provisions of any other law for time being in force as may be specified by the Central Government in the notification published in the Official Gazette; or

(e) it is necessary so to do in the interests of the sovereignty and integrity of India, the security of India, friendly relations of India with any foreign country, or in the interests of the general public; or

(f) the marriage of an Overseas Citizen of India Cardholder, who has obtained such Card under clause (d) of sub-section (1) of section 7A,

(i) has been dissolved by a competent court of law or otherwise; or

(ii) has not been dissolved but, during the subsistence of such marriage, he has solemnised marriage with any other person;

Provided that no order under this section shall be passed unless the Overseas Citizen of India Cardholder has been given a reasonable opportunity of being heard. (emphasis supplied by the author)

As per the author, the said amendment appears to be ambiguous and broad based. To justify cancellation of OCI registration on the basis of violation of 'any' applicable Indian law seems to be very wide and discomforting for OCI cardholders. Ideally, some limits on this authority would be required to prevent unbridled and arbitrary use of the law. This would prevent abuse of this provision.[12]

The Exempted Regions

The CAA is region specific. Certain Indian regions are excluded from the scope and applicability of the CAA, namely (i) The tribal areas of Assam, Meghalaya, Mizoram or Tripura as included in the Sixth Schedule to the Constitution; and (ii) Areas covered under 'The Inner Line' notified under the Bengal Eastern Frontier Regulation, 1873.

Sixth Schedule of the Constitution

The purpose behind the Sixth Schedule of the Constitution was to aid the development of tribal areas, to protect the indigenous population of the area and to preserve their distinct customs. This special provision is provided under Articles 244 and 275 of the Constitution.

In Assam, the Bodo, Karbi, and Dimasa areas fall under the Sixth Schedule of the Constitution, so the CAA will be inapplicable to such regions as well.

The Inner Line

The Inner Line refers to areas which have been declared to be protected by the state. A permit (called the Inner Line Permit or ILP)[13] is required from the government to visit these areas,

---

12 The JPC in the *Joint Committee Report*, in the context of the amendment to Section 7D of the Citizenship Act, had opined that it would be prudent to restrict the scope of the suggested expression 'violations of the provisions of any other law' therein lest it results in misuse of the provisions and harassment of OCI cardholders even for very minor or petty violation of law like traffic violations etc.

13 An ILP is a travel document which is issued under the provisions of the Bengal Eastern Frontier Regulations, 1873.

by both Indian citizens as well as foreigners. The ILP is akin to a visa required to visit the designated place. There are various kinds of permits, i.e. a tourist permit, long term permit, permit for employment purposes etc.

The following areas fall within the scope of the Inner Line: Arunachal Pradesh, Mizoram and Nagaland and parts of Tripura. Further, Manipur has also been added to this list in December 2019.

As per the author, a joint reading of this part of the amendment and the Regularisation Notifications gives rise to an anomaly. Evidently, the Regularisation Notifications (which also regularise the stay of illegal migrants) is not region specific, it operates throughout the territory of India. Hence, illegal migrants from the Classified Communities and Classified Countries residing in the above described exempted regions, while being unable to take the benefit of the CAA, may nevertheless be entitled to the benefit of the Regularisation Notifications. Consequently, while such persons may not be in a position to obtain Indian citizenship, they would still be entitled to reside in India without fear of being prosecuted under Indian law.

THE EXCLUSIONS UNDER THE CAA

There are various categories of communities and regions which have been excluded from the scope of the CAA. Mentioned below are some notable exclusions.

Exclusion of Muslims

Muslims from the Classified Countries (and everywhere else) have been excluded from the ambit of the CAA. Put differently, muslims in India possessing an 'illegal migrant' status will not be entitled to get their status regularised and will not get an opportunity to apply for and claim Indian citizenship. Even otherwise, muslims from the Classified Countries residing in India on valid travel documents will not be able to get the benefit of the CAA and will have to apply for Indian citizenship through the normal procedure/ channel under the Citizenship Act.

Exclusion of Neighbouring Countries

Several neighbouring countries (such as Sri Lanka, Myanmar, Bhutan, Nepal etc.) have been excluded from the CAA. As per the government, migrants from these excluded neighbouring countries will have to continue to take the benefit of the SOP of 2011 for continuing stay in India. The *Joint Committee Report* also records this in the following words:

> Government of India has issued a Standard Operating Procedure (SOP) vide letter dated 29.12.2011 for dealing with foreign nationals in India who claim to be refugees. These guidelines are applicable to refugees from various countries including Sri Lanka, Myanmar etc"

Exclusion of 'Religiously Persecuted' Muslims

It is a well-known fact that the problem of 'religious persecution' exists inter-se various sects of the muslim community, such as the Ahmadiyas in Pakistan and the Hazaras in Afghanistan. While the Statement of Objects and Reasons of the CAA refers to the issue of 'religious persecution' as one of the basis of its introduction, it however restricts itself only to 'religious persecution' of the minority groups in the Classified Countries. The CAA appears to move on the premise that muslims in Islamic states (like Pakistan, Bangladesh and Afghanistan) are unlikely to face religious persecution and even if they do, then shelter may be taken in (other) Islamic states of the world such as countries in the Middle East and Africa, etc.

Exclusion of other Persecuted Communities

As discussed above, the ambit of the CAA is limited to the minorities in the muslim-dominated/centric neighbouring countries. It also does not take into account the persecuted categories of muslims in such countries.

Additionally, it is noteworthy that the CAA does not include migrants from other non-muslim neighbouring countries who have a history of fleeing to India to escape persecution, including religious persecution. Some notable exclusions in this regard are as follows:

a) Hindus from Sri Lanka: Buddhism is the state religion of Sri Lanka and the long standing persecution of the Tamil Ealams (a minority) at the hands of the Sinhalese is also well known. However, this section of persons does not make it to the CAA.
b) Rohingyas in Myanmar: The majority in Myanmar practice Buddhism and the persecution of the Rohingya muslims (a minority) is well known. Presently, there are about 40,000 Rohingyas in India spread across states like Uttar Pradesh, West Bengal, Andhra Pradesh, Kerala, Assam, Jammu and Kashmir and Delhi. This group is not within the scope of the CAA.[14]
c) Buddhists from Tibet: Tibetan influx in India began in the 1960s. Tibetans in India have a 'stateless' status. Although they have been given refugee status in India through executive orders, however, they do not enjoy citizenship rights.

Effect of Exclusion from the CAA

Another question which arises is to the fate of migrants who

14 The stance of the government is that the SOP of 29.12.2011 (as amended from time to time) would take care of the migrants/refugees from other countries including Sri Lanka and Myanmar.

are excluded from the scope and ambit of the CAA. As per the author, the following would be the impact of the CAA on the excluded migrants:

a) Persons who qualify to be 'illegal migrants' would never be able to obtain Indian citizenship. This is because the general law on citizenship clearly states that 'illegal migrants' are disqualified from obtaining citizenship. The CAA provides to its beneficiaries (irrespective of whether they are legal and illegal migrants), an exception to this general law and in effect, regularises their entry and stay in India with and added opportunity to apply for Indian citizenship. Non-beneficiaries of the CAA cannot avail of this exception.
b) Persons who do not qualify under the CAA but qualify to be 'legal migrants' (i.e. those who entered and stay in India legally) would be permitted to apply for Indian citizenship in accordance with the regular procedure/channel prescribed under the Citizenship Act. The 'fast track' procedure for obtaining citizenship (available to the CAA beneficiaries) would not apply to them.

Inclusion of Afghanistan

Afghanistan (one of the beneficiary countries under the CAA) is a surprise inclusion. While Pakistan and Bangladesh have historical ties with India (they were a part of undivided India), no connection as such exists with Afghanistan. Afghanistan is, at best, a neighbouring country, with Islam as its state religion.

The Statement of Objects and Reasons of the CAA (reproduced above) also makes reference to undivided India. However, there appears to be no explanation therein for inclusion of Afghanistan. However, the *Joint Committee Report* offers the following rationale for adding Afghanistan with countries like Bangladesh and Pakistan, which were a part of India in the pre-Independence era:

> There have been multiple attacks against Indian interests in Afghanistan by the Pakistan establishment sponsored LET, Haqqani Network and Taliban. Besides, minority communities in Afghanistan had migrated to Afghanistan from Pakistan region during pre-independence India. They are facing continuous atrocities due to their Indian origin.
> A number of persons belonging to minority communities in Afghanistan have also come to India on account of religious persecution or fear of religious persecution. Hence, it was decided to include Afghanistan within the ambit of the Notification issued on the 7 September, 2015 by issuing two more Notifications on the 18 July, 2016

In the Afghanistan context, the largest beneficiaries are going to be Sikhs, who are in 'small minority' there.

To sum up, as per the author, the CAA seeks to be viewed as an 'amnesty scheme' with an 'eligibility criteria'. Persons falling outside such 'eligibility criteria' would continue to be governed by the (unamended) law of citizenship in India. If the (unamended) law grants them an opportunity to apply for and procure citizenship, then such persons will be able to take a shot at Indian citizenship albeit without the benefit of the 'simplified' processes provided under the CAA.

Religious Persecution

Religious prosecution is one of the central points of the CAA. As the term suggests, religious persecution is harassment on the grounds of religion or on religious lines. A more technical meaning of religious persecution is the systematic mistreatment of an individual or a group of individuals as a response to their religious beliefs or affiliations or their lack thereof, often intended to deprive minorities of political rights and force them to assimilate, leave, or live as second-class citizens. Some examples of religious persecution (faced by minorities in Pakistan) which were highlighted in the *Joint Committee Report* are as follows:

a) Forced conversion to Islam.
b) Compelling minorities to dress up in muslim attire (such as muslim dresses, skull caps etc.).
c) Absence of representation in judiciary.
d) Absence of representation in government positions.
e) Compelling students to study Islam. Urdu is the medium of instruction in most schools.
f) Minorities normally addressed as 'kafirs'. In many cases, in a bid to evade harassment, the minorities had to change their names which sounded similar to muslim names.
g) Little or no access to temples or other places of worship for the minorities. No facilities provided for conducting religious prayers and ceremonies.
h) Unavailability of cremation ground.
i) Offences such as snatching, theft, kidnapping, dacoity committed on minorities.

The Element of Religious Persecution

Some sections of the society argue that the claim of the central government that the CAA has been enacted to protect 'persons facing religious persecution' is not correct because the expression 'religious persecution' does not find specific mention in the language of the CAA.

The central government has however maintained that the CAA has been promulgated for the benefit of certain select sects who are suffering from or at a risk of 'religious persecution'. While the language of the CAA does not specifically mention the term 'religious persecution' anywhere, however, this aspect does find mention in the Statement of Objects and Reasons of the Citizenship Amendment Bill.

It is settled law that the Statement of Objects and Reasons accompanying a Bill, when introduced in Parliament, can be used for the purpose of understanding the background and the antecedent state of affairs leading up to the legislation.[15] For the purpose of appreciating the background and the antecedent factual matrix leading to the legislation, it is permissible to look into the Statement of Objects and Reasons of the Bill which actuated the step to provide a remedy for the then existing malady.[16] As per the author, the intent of the government appears to have been brought out in the Statement of Objects and Reasons of the CAA. Also, the CAA is interlinked/interconnected with the Regularisation Notifications which used the expression 'religious persecution'.

Proving Religious Persecution

The Regularisation Notifications and the CAA are only aimed at migrants who have either faced or fear 'religious persecution' in Pakistan, Bangladesh and Afghanistan. It therefore becomes pertinent for an applicant to establish 'religious persecution' and for the authorities to be satisfied about the same, before proceeding to grant benefit under the CAA.

A fundamental question which arises is to the manner in which the government authorities would or may ascertain the veracity of a claim of 'religious persecution' of the applicant. The *Joint Committee Report* contains some guidance on this aspect, which is reproduced below:

> Asked to state the mechanism available with the government to establish religious persecution in a foreign land, the MHA

15 State of West Bengal v. Union of India, AIR 1963 SC 1241.

16 Shashikant Laxman Kale v. Union of India, (1990) 2 SCR 441. *See also* Hiral P. Harsora v. Kusum Narottamdas Harsora, Civil Appeal No. 10084/2016 (06.10.2016, Supreme Court of India).

responded as under: Inputs from security agencies along with other corroborative evidence in the print/electronic media would help to establish religious persecution in a foreign land.

As regards authentic verification of the claims of the applicants for Indian citizenship that they have been victims of religious persecution in their respective countries, the Intelligence Bureau (IB) submitted as under:

The individuals claiming religious persecution and seeking Indian citizenship had entered India decades ago, mostly in the aftermath of Partition of the country when a largescale migration between India and Pakistan took place. It is not possible to verify their claim now. However, for recent cases, if any, due verification would be made before their claim for Indian Citizenship is entertained. As per the Standard Operating Procedure (SOP) under preparation by MHA, for an applicant who applies with an affidavit mentioning that he/she was compelled to migrate to India due to religious persecution or fear of religious persecution, along with other supporting documents, a detailed enquiry will be conducted by Foreigners Regional Registration Office (FRRO)/ Foreigners Registration Office (FRO) concerned to verify his/ her claim. If the affidavit is not supported by documents, the case will be referred to Foreigners Tribunals to be constituted for this purpose under the Foreigners (Tribunals) Order, 1964 for verification of the claim regarding religious persecution.

Asked to state the fate of other people belonging to minority communities who have come to India from the three countries under reference due to religious persecution but have not declared so at the time of their arrival in India, the Intelligence Bureau submitted as under: For others to apply for Indian Citizenship under this category, they will have to prove that they came to India due to religious persecution.

> If they had not declared so at that time of their arrival in India, it would be difficult for them to make such a claim now. Any future claim will be enquired into, including through R&AW before a decision is taken.

Therefore, the government basically seeks to rely on various layers of internal investigation(s) to check the truthfulness or otherwise of a claim of 'religious persecution'. It is apposite to mention that checking the antecedents of and the veracity of the claims of migrants (seeking the benefit of the CAA) would be an arduous task. In fact, one of the challenges to the CAA in the Supreme Court includes absence of proper standards and safeguards on the aspect of determination and cross-verification of a claim of 'religious persecution' made by a potential beneficiary of the CAA. Further clarification and direction on this count may be required from the government.

CHAPTER 8

The Assam History

INTRODUCTION

Since independence, Assam has been the hotspot of illegal migration from (predominantly) Bangladesh. There exists sufficient public database to suggest that approximately 40% (forty percent) of the illegal migrants from Bangladesh have settled down in Assam. While, various steps have been taken by the Government of India at various points of time over the last several decades to stem the migration, the problem however continues to persist.

The indigenous people of Assam have an independent set of grievances against the CAA. To understand and appreciate these grievance(s) better, it is first imperative to understand the history of the Assam migration, the Assam Accord and its overall relationship with the NRC.

This chapter describes the history/background of the Assam Accord and its relationship with the NRC.

THE BACKGROUND TO ASSAM MIGRATION

Prior to Independence, Assam was a Governor's Province. At the time of Independence, Pakistan had 2 (two) parts i.e. West Pakistan (present day Pakistan) and East Pakistan (present day Bangladesh). There was large scale illegal migration from East Pakistan into Assam.

In 1950, the Immigrants (Expulsion from Assam) Act, 1950 was enacted to protect the indigenous inhabitants of Assam. The Statement of objects and reasons of the said legislation clearly recognised the need to check the large scale influx of people from East Bengal (now Bangladesh) into Assam, which was disturbing the economy of the region and causing serious law and order problems. Subsequently, in the census of 1951, a National Register of Citizens for Assam was prepared under the directions of the Ministry of Home Affairs which consisted of detailed area wise information about the inhabitants of Assam.

In 1971, the liberation war between East and West Pakistan (with India siding with East Pakistan) led to birth of a new nation (Bangladesh). The illegal migration, however, continued.

Around 1980, the All Assam Students Union submitted a memorandum/representation to the then Prime Minister of India requesting a solution to this problem. As a consequence of such representation, the Illegal Migrants (Determination by Tribunal) Act, 1983 was enacted (hereinafter **IMDT Act**) for the purpose of expediting the identification and deportation of illegal migrants from Assam, which legislation failed to stem the problem and was finally struck down by the Supreme Court of India (discussed later in the chapter).

A critical provision in the said law (which received flak) was that the responsibility of proving that a person was an illegal migrant rested on the government. This was an arduous and onerous obligation which ultimately led to the failure of the enactment.

The years 1980 to 1985 witnessed large scale agitations in Assam on the issue of illegal migration. While most of the agitations were peaceful, however some did turn violent. In other words, life in Assam was in some state of disarray during these times.

The Assam Accord

Finally, the 'Assam Accord' came into existence. The Assam Accord was an agreement executed on 15.08.1985 between the central and state governments, All Assam Students Union and the All Assam Gana Sangram Parishad. Some critical parts of the Assam Accord are reproduced below:

ASSAM ACCORD

15th August, 1985

(Accord between AASU, AAGSP, Central and State Government on the Foreigner Problem Issue)

MEMORANDUM of SETTLEMENT

1. Government have all along been most anxious to find a satisfactory solution to the problem of Foreigners in Assam. The All Assam Students' Union (AASU) and the All Assam Gana Sangram Parishad (AAGSP) have also expressed their keenness to find such a solution.
2. The AASU through their Memorandum dated 2nd February, 1980 presented to the Late Prime Minister Smt. Indira Gandhi, conveyed their profound sense of apprehensions regarding the continuing influx of foreign nationals into Assam and the fear about adverse affects upon the political, social, cultural and economic life of the State.
3. Being fully alive to the genuine apprehensions of the people of Assam, the then Prime Minister initiated the dialogue with the AASU/AAGSP. Subsequently, talks were held at the Prime Minister's and Home Ministers levels during the period 1980-83. Several rounds of informal talks were held during 1984. Formal discussions were resumed in March, 1985.
4. Keeping all aspects of the problem including constitutional and legal provision, international

agreements, national commitments and humanitarian considerations, it has been decided to proceed as follows:

5. Foreigners Issue:

5.1 For purposes of detection and deletion of foreigners, 1.1.1966 shall be the base date and year.

5.2 All persons who came to Assam prior to 1.1.1966, including those amongst them whose name appeared on the electoral rolls used in 1967 elections, shall be regularized.

5.3 Foreigners who came to Assam after 1.1.1966 (inclusive) and upto 24th March 1971 shall be detected in accordance with the provisions of the Foreigners Act, 1946 and the Foreigners (Tribunals) Order 1964.

5.4 Names of Foreigners so detected will be deleted from the electoral rolls in force. Such persons will be required to register themselves before the Registration Officers of the respective districts in accordance with the provisions of the Registration of Foreigners Act, 1939 and the Registration of Foreigners Rules, 1939.

5.5 For this purpose, Government of India will undertake suitable strengthening of the governmental machinery.

5.6 On the expiry of a period of ten year following the date of detection, the names of all such persons which have been deleted from the electoral rolls shall be restored.

5.7 All persons who were expelled, earlier, but have since re-entered illegally into Assam, shall be expelled.

5.8 Foreigners who came to Assam on or after March 25, 1971 shall continue to be detected, deleted and expelled in accordance with law. Immediate and practical steps shall be taken to expel such foreigners.

5.9 The Government will give due consideration to certain difficulties expressed by the AASU/AAGSP regarding the implementation of the Illegal Migrants (Determination by Tribunals) Act, 1983.

6. Constitutional, legislative and administrative safeguards:

   Constitutional, legislative and administrative safeguards, as may be appropriate, shall be provided to protect, preserve and promote the cultural, social, linguistic identity and heritage of the Assamese people.

7. Economic development:

   The Government takes this opportunity to renew their commitment for the speedy all round economic development of Assam, so as to improve the standard of living of the people. Special emphasis will be placed on education and science & technology through establishment of national institutions.

8. Other Issues:

8.1 The Government will arrange for the issue of citizenship certificates in future only by the authorities of the Central Government.

8.2 Specific complaints that may be made by the AASU/ AAGSP about irregular issuance of Indian Citizenship Certificates (ICC) will be looked into.

9. Security of International Border

9.1 The international border shall be made secured against future infiltration by erection of physical barriers like walls, barbed wire fencing and other obstacles at appropriate places. Patrolling by security forces on land and riverine routes all along international border shall be adequately intensified. In order to further strengthen the security arrangements, to prevent effectively future infiltration, an adequate number of check posts shall be set up.

9.2 Besides the arrangements mentioned above and keeping in view security considerations, a road all along the international border shall be constructed so as to facilitate patrolling by security forces. Land between border and the road would be kept free of human habitation, wherever possible. Riverine patrolling along the international border would be intensified. All effective measures would be adopted to prevent infiltrators crossing or attempting to crass the international border.

10. Prevention of Encroachment of Government Lands

    It will be ensured that relevant laws for prevention of encroachment of Government lands and lands in tribal belts and blocks are strictly enforced and unauthorized encroachers evicted as laid down under such laws.

11. Restricting Accusation of Immovable Property by Foreigners

    It will be ensured that the relevant law restricting acquisition of immovable property by foreigners in Assam is strictly enforced.

12. Registration of Births and Deaths

    It will be ensured that Birth and Death Registers are duly maintained.

    Restoration of Normalcy

13. The All Assam Students Union (AASU) and the All Assam Gana Sangram Parishad (AAGSP) call off the agitation assure full co-operation and dedicate themselves towards the development of the country.

14. The Central and the State Government have agreed to:

(a) Review with sympathy and withdraw cases of disciplinary action taken against employees in the context of the agitation and to ensure that there is no victimization;

(b) Frame a scheme for ex-gratia payment to next of kin of those who killed in the course of the agitation;

(c) Give sympathetic consideration to proposal for

relaxation of upper age limit for employment in public services in Assam, having regard to exceptional situation that prevailed in holding of academic and competitive examinations, etc. in the context of agitation in Assam;

(d) Undertake review of detention cases, if any, as well as cases against persons charged with criminal offences in connection with the agitation, except those charged with commission of heinous offences;

(e) Consider withdrawal of the prohibitory orders/ notifications in force, if any.

15. The Ministry of Home Affairs will be the nodal Ministry for the implementation of the above.

Sd/-
(P.K. Mahanta)
President
All Assam Students' Union

Sd/-
(B.K. Phukan)
General Secretary
All Assam Students' Union

Sd/-
(Biraj Sharma)
Convenor
All Assam Students' Union

Sd/-
(R.D. Pradhan)
Home Secretary
Government of India

Sd/-
(Smt. P.P. Trivedi)
Chief Secretary
Government of Assam

In the Presence of

Sd/-
(Rajiv Gandhi)
Prime Minister of India

Date: 15th August, 1985
Place: New Delhi

Features of The Assam Accord

The objective of the 'Assam Accord' was to take appropriate steps towards arresting and containing the illegal migration of foreigners into the state of Assam. Broadly speaking, the Assam Accord provided the following:

a) The cut-off date for detection and deletion of foreigners was fixed at 01.01.1966. Therefore, persons who came to Assam prior to 01.01.1966 were outside the Assam Accord and were to be regularised.
b) Persons who came to Assam between 01.01.1966 and 24.03.1971 were to be detected in accordance with the Foreigners Act and the Foreigners Tribunals Order. The names of such 'detected' persons would be deleted from the electoral rolls and they would be required to get themselves registered with the relevant registration offices. After a period of 10 (ten) years from the date of detection, the names of such persons would be restored to the electoral rolls.

c) Essentially, all illegal migrants who had come to Assam 25.03.1971 onwards would be expelled from India. All persons who were expelled earlier but have since re-entered into Assam shall be expelled again.
d) Provisions were made for adequate constitutional, legislative and administrative safeguards to protect, preserve and promote cultural, social, linguistic identity and heritage of the Assamese people.
e) Provisions in the Assam Accord included securement of India's international border(s) with Bangladesh by taking appropriate steps such as erection of physical barriers like walls, wire fencing etc. at appropriate places, increased patrolling by security forces along the international border, increasing the number of check posts to prevent future infiltration. All necessary steps were to be undertaken to prevent infiltration, including construction of roads to facilitate patrolling, intensification of riverine patrolling etc.
f) Enforcement of law restricting acquisition of immovable property by foreigners in Assam.
g) Joint efforts of all stakeholders towards development and growth of Assam and the nation.

Introduction of Section 6A to the Citizenship Act

The execution of the Assam Accord was followed up by the introduction of Section 6A to the Citizenship Act in the year 1985 (*via* the Citizenship Amendment Act, 1985). The objective behind introduction of Section 6A was to give effect to certain parts of the Assam Accord, more particularly aspects relating to detection and determination of foreigners and grant of citizenship.

The statement of objects and reasons of this amendment indicated that it's purpose was to give effect to the Assam Accord and to grant deemed citizenship to all persons of Indian origin who came to Assam before 01.01.1966, including persons whose names were included in the electoral roll used for the purpose of general election of 1967 and who have been ordinarily resident in Assam ever since. The further object of such amendment was to grant deemed citizenship (through a process of registration) to those persons of Indian origin who came to Assam on or after 01.01.1966 but before 25.03.1971 from Bangladesh and have been ordinarily residents in Assam ever since.[1]

Section 6A of the Citizenship Act is reproduced below for the sake of ready reference:

> 6A. Special provisions as to citizenship of persons covered by the Assam Accord-
>
> (1) For the purposes of this section-
>
> (a) "Assam" means the territories included in the State of Assam immediately before the commencement of the Citizenship (Amendment) Act, 1985;
>
> (b) "detected to be a foreigner" means detected to be a foreigner in accordance with the provisions of the Foreigners Act, 1946 (31 of 1946) and the Foreigners (Tribunals)Order, 1946 by a Tribunal constituted under the said Order;
>
> (c) "specified territory" means the territories included in Bangladesh immediately before the commencement of the Citizenship (Amendment) Act, 1985;
>
> (d) a person shall be deemed to be of Indian origin, if he, or either of his parents for any of his grandparents was born in undivided India;

1 Moslem Mondal, *infra*

(e) a person shall be deemed to have been detected to be a foreigner on the date on which a Tribunal constituted under the Foreigners (Tribunals) Order, 1964 submits its opinion to the effect that he is a foreigner to the officer or authority concerned.

(2) Subject to the provisions of the sub-sections (6) and (7), all persons of Indian origin who came before the 1st day of January, 1966 to Assam from the specified territory (including such of those whose names were included in the electoral rolls used for the purposes of the General Election to the House of the People held in 1967) and who have been ordinarily resident in Assam since the dates of their entry into Assam shall be deemed to be citizens of India as from the 1st day of January, 1966.

(3) Subject to the provisions of sub-sections (6) and (7), every person of Indian origin who-

(a) came to Assam on or after the 1st day of January, 1966 but before the 25th day of March, 1971 from the specified territory; and

(b) has, since the date of his entry into Assam, been ordinarily resident in Assam; and

(c) has been detected to be a foreigner,

shall register himself in accordance with the rules made by the Central Government in this behalf under section 18 with such authority (thereafter in this sub-section referred to as the registering authority) as may be specified in such rules and if his name is included in any electoral roll any Assembly or Parliamentary constituency in force on the date of such detection, his name shall be deleted therefrom.

Explanation.- In the case of every person seeking

registration under this sub-section, the opinion of the Tribunal constituted under the foreigners (Tribunals) Order, 1964 holding such person to be a foreigner, shall be deemed to be sufficient proof of the requirement under clause (c) of this sub-section and if any question arises as to whether such person complies with any other requirement under this sub-section, the registering authority shall,-

(i) if such opinion contains a finding with respect to such other requirement, decide the question in conformity with such finding;

(ii) if such opinion does not contain a finding with respect to such other requirement, refer the question to a Tribunal constituted under the said Order hang Jurisdiction in accordance with such rules as the Central Government may make in this behalf under section 18 and decide the question in conformity with the opinion received on such reference;

(4) A person registered under sub-section (3) shall have, as from the date on which he has been detected to be a foreigner and till the expiry of a period of ten years from that date, the same rights and obligations as a citizen of India(including the right to obtain a passport under the Passports Act, 1967 (15 of 1967) and the obligations connected therewith), but shall not be entitled to have his name included in any electoral roll for any Assembly or Parliamentary constituency at any time before the expiry of the said period of ten years.

(5) A person registered under sub-section (3) shall be deemed to be a citizen of India for all purposes as from the date of expiry of a period of ten years from the date on which he has been detected to be a foreigner.

(6) Without prejudice to the provisions of section 8-

(a) if any person referred to in sub-section (2) submits in the prescribed manner and form and to be prescribed authority within sixty days from the date of commencement of the Citizenship (Amendment) Act, 1985, for year a declaration that he does not wish to be citizen of India, such person shall not be deemed to have become a citizen of India under that sub-section;

(b) If any person referred to in this sub-section (3) submits in the prescribed manner and form and to the prescribed authority within sixty days from the date of commencement the Citizenship (Amendment) Act, 1985, for year or from the date on which he has been detected to be a foreigner, whichever is later, a declaration that he does not wish to be governed by the provisions of that sub-section and sub-sections (4) and (5), it shall not be necessary for such person to register himself under sub-section(3).

Explanation.- Where a person required to file a declaration under this sub-section does not have the capacity to enter into a contact, such declaration may be filed on his behalf by any person competent under the law for the time being in force to act on his behalf.

(7) Nothing in sub-sections (2) to (6) shall apply in relation to any person-

(a) who, immediately before the commencement of the Citizenship (Amendment) Act, 1985, for year is a citizen of India;

(b) who was expelled from India before the commencement of the Citizenship (Amendment)

Act, 1985, for year under the Foreigners Act, 1946 (31 of 1946).

(8) Save as otherwise expressly provided in this section, the provisions of this section shall have effect notwithstanding anything contained in any other law for the time being in force.

Features of Section 6A of the Citizenship Act

The salient features of Section 6A of the Citizenship Act are discussed below.

Region Specific Nature

Section 6A was specific to the state of Assam for the purposes of specifically addressing illegal migration from Bangladesh.[2]

Deemed Citizenship

All persons of Indian origin (from undivided India) who came from Bangladesh to Assam before 01.01.1966 and had since resided in Assam, were conferred 'deemed' Indian citizenship. Therefore, 01.01.1966 was the cut-off date for 'deemed Indian citizenship'.

2 Section 6A of the Citizenship Act is not intended to address issues of migration from nations other than Bangladesh. *See generally* Indira Newar and Ors. v. Union of India, W.P. (C) No. 8490/2018 (29.11.2019, Guwahati High Court). Only those persons who came from Bangladesh and are living in the state of Assam can be treated as persons migrating from the 'specified territory' envisaged under section 6 A of the Citizenship Act. The only cases of members of Gorkha community living in Assam, who do not fall in any of the categories specified in the notification dated 24.09.2018 issued by the Ministry of Home Affairs, Government of India, may be referred to the Foreigners Tribunal for its opinion as to whether the person is or is not a foreigner within the meaning of the Foreigners Act, 1946. Smt. Tika Devi v. The Union of India, W.P. (C) No. 6292/2019 (26.10.2021, Guwahati High Court). Section 6 A of the Citizenship Act is only applicable to 'persons who have come to Assam from the specified territory i.e. Bangladesh'. The children of such persons cannot take the benefit of Section 6 A of the Citizenship Act. Section 3 of the Citizenship Act would apply to the children. State v. Bikram Singha. F.T. case No. 129/2017 & Police Enquiry No. TD/3654/98 (10.09.2021, foreigners Tribunal II, Karimganj, Assam).

Registration

Persons, who came to Assam between 01.01.1966 and 25.03.1971 and had resided in Assam since, were required to get themselves registered with the appropriate registration authority. Further, such persons were to be disenfranchised for a period of 10 (ten) years.[3]

A core requirement for being eligible for registration was that the person should have come to Assam after 01.01.1966 but before 25.03.1971 and had resided continuously in Assam since then.[4] Hence, 'ordinary residence' in Assam was a condition precedent.[5]

Registration was a mandatory requirement and could be either voluntary or pursuant to an order of a Foreigners Tribunal (under the provisions of the Foreigners Act and the Foreigners Tribunal Order) declaring the concerned person to be a foreigner (**Declaration Order**).

Time Period for Registration

Registration was required to be made within the following prescribed timelines:

An application for registration was required to be made in the prescribed form by the registrant with the registering authority[6] within a period of 30 (thirty) days from date of receipt of the Declaration Order of the Foreigners Tribunal.

The said period of 30 (thirty) days could be extended by the registering authority, for reasons recorded in writing, to a maximum of 60 (sixty) days.[7]

---

3 Deprived of a right to vote.

4 The date of entry is a condition precedent for attraction of Section 6 A of the Citizenship Act. Anil Barman v. Union of India, W.P. (C) No. 266/2019 (10.06.2019, Guwahati High Court).

5 Ashma Khatun v. Union of India, W.P. (C) No. 8592/2018 (30.01.2019, Guwahati High Court).

6 The registering authority shall be an officer holding a rank not below that of an Additional District Judge. A registering authority shall be appointed for every district of the state of Assam. R. 19 (1) of the Citizenship Rules.

7 R. 19 (2) of the Citizenship Rules.

Extension of Time for Registration

During the course of the registration exercise, it came to the attention of the government that numerous persons who had been declared foreigners by the Foreigners Tribunal did not apply for registration in a timely manner (for various reasons such as non-receipt of the Declaration Order, lack of knowledge etc.). Consequently, applications of a large number of people were rejected for being belated. In fact, in some cases, post a Declaration Order, instead of obtaining a registration, these persons had somehow managed to get their names included in the electoral rolls. Such aspects came to light once 'quit India' notices were issued by the authorities to such persons.[8]

The above issues were addressed by the government by introduction of the following special one-time timelines (in the year 2013):[9]

Persons who had been declared a foreigner (prior to 16.07.2013) but not preferred an application on account of non-receipt of the order or whose application had been rejected on account of delay, would have a fresh opportunity for making the application (in the prescribed Form) within a period of 30 (thirty) days from the date of receipt of the order or from the date of publication of the notification.

The said period of 30 (thirty) could be extended by the registering authority, for reasons recorded in writing, to a maximum of 180 (one hundred and eighty) days.

Despite the aforementioned one-time special measures, some people still 'missed the bus' and subsequently approached court for seeking liberty to get themselves registered. In **Ashutosh Das v. Union of India,**[10] the Guwahati High Court

8 *See* Md. Samsul Haqu v. Member, Foreigner's Tribunal, W.P. (C) No. 464/2009 (07.08.2009, Guwahati High Court).

9 R. 19 (2A) was introduced in the Citizenship Rules with effect from 16.07.2013.

10 2019 (2) GLT 393.

held that in special cases, the High Court may, in exercise of writ jurisdiction, permit registration even at a later point in time. In the said matter, permission to apply for registration was granted even in the year 2018.

Receipt & Record of the Application

Post receipt of the registration application, a receiving/ acknowledgement was to be provided to the registrant by the registering authority.[11] Further, a copy of the said application was to be sent by the registering authority to the central government and the state government for record keeping.[12]

Consequences of Failure to Register

A person who does not register within the time limit fixed or within the time limit that may be extended by the registering authority, is liable to be deported from India in as much as he would be considered to have 'not acquired' the right of a citizen of India 'in the manner prescribed by law' and consequently would be considered a 'foreigner'.[13]

Regularisation post Registration

Every person registered (above) was to get disenfranchised and be granted a period of 10 (ten) years to regularise his status. During the said period of disenfranchisement, the registered person had the same rights as that of a 'regular' citizen (including the right to obtain an Indian passport) except one right i.e. the right to vote. Post completion of 10 (ten) years, the registered person was to be given 'full' citizenship.[14]

---

11 R. 19 (3) & (4) of the Citizenship Rules.

12 R. 19 (5) of the Citizenship Rules.

13 Moslem Mondal, *supra*

14 Moslem Mondel, *supra*

The Exclusion

The following categories of persons were/are beyond the purview of Section 6A of the Citizenship Act:

a) Persons who were citizens of India prior to introduction of Section 6A.
b) Persons who were expelled from India prior to introduction of Section 6A.

In sum, the mechanism for grant of citizenship in terms of the Assam Accord (and Section 6A of the Citizenship Act) was as follows: (i) All persons who had migrated to Assam prior to 01.01.1966 were to be granted 'immediate' citizenship; and (ii) All persons who had migrated to Assam between 1966 and 1971 were granted 'deferred' citizenship after 10 (ten) years provided they had qualified the parameters specified under Section 6A, namely, registering themselves with the registration authorities and 'settling down' in India.

The IMDT Act

The IMDT Illegal Migrants (Determination by Tribunals) Act, enacted in the year 1983, was a part of the 'special measures' sought to be taken by the government to tackle the illegal migration problem in Assam.

The Objective of the IMDT Act

The Statement of Objects and Reasons and the Preamble of IMDT Act provided the following reasons behind its enactment:

a) Influx of foreigners who illegally migrated to India across the borders of the eastern and north-eastern regions of the country and remained in the country pose a threat to the integrity and security of the said regions and a substantial number of such foreigners who migrated into India after 25.03.1971 had, by taking advantage of the circumstances of such migration and their ethnic similarity and other connections with the people of India, illegally remained in India without having in their possession lawful authority to do so giving rise to serious problems.

b) Continuance of such foreigners in India was recognized to be detrimental to the interest of the country.

Although this legislation was to have a nation-wide applicability, it was, however, brought into force in the state of Assam.

Overriding Effect of the IMDT Act

The provisions of the IMDT Act overrode and superseded the provisions of the Foreigners Act and the Passport Act.

Illegal Migrant under the IMDT Act

The IMDT Act defined an 'illegal migrant' on similar lines as the Citizenship Act. As per the IMDT Act, an 'illegal migrant' was a foreigner who entered India on or after 25.03.1971 without a valid passport or other travel documents or any other lawful authority.[15]

Special Tribunals under the IMDT Act

The Illegal Migrant Tribunals were constituted under the IMDT Act to hear and adjudicate references made by the central government on the issue as well as applications preferred directly by a resident of Assam. Additionally, Appellate Illegal Migrant Tribunals were also set up for deciding appeals against orders passed by the Illegal Migrant Tribunals.

The Assam Governor's Report of 1998

Despite the introduction of the IMDT Act and the Assam

15 S. 3 (1) (c) of the IMDT Act.

Accord, the problem of illegal migration into Assam could not be effectively curbed. In the year 1998, the then Governor of Assam submitted an extensive report to the then President of India on the grave threat posed by the influx of people from Bangladesh into Assam. The said report highlighted the dangerous consequences of the large scale migration from Bangladesh both for the people of Assam and the nation as a whole. The report warned that the results of such unchecked migration was that the indigenous people of Assam were being reduced to a minority in their own home state. Also, their cultural survival was in jeopardy, their political control weakened and their employment opportunities undermined. Some critical excerpts from the said report are reproduced below.

1. The unabated influx of illegal migrants from Bangladesh into Assam and the consequent perceptible change in the demographic pattern of the State has been a matter of grave concern. It threatens to reduce the Assamese people to a minority in their own State, as happened in Tripura and Sikkim.
2. Illegal migration into Assam was the core issue behind the Assam student movement. It was also the prime contributory factor behind the outbreak of insurgency in the State. Yet we have not made much tangible progress in dealing with this all important issue.
3. There is a tendency to view illegal migration into Assam as a regional matter affecting only the people of Assam. It's more dangerous dimensions of greatly undermining our national security, is ignored. The long cherished design of Greater East Pakistan/Bangladesh, making inroads into strategic land link of Assam with the rest of the country, can lead to severing the entire land mass of

the North East, with all its rich resources from the rest of the country. They will have disastrous strategic and economic consequences.

MIGRATION INTO ASSAM HISTORICAL BACKGROUND

7. Failure to get Assam included in East Pakistan in 1947 remained a source of abiding resentment in that country. Zulfikar Ali Bhutto in his book *Myths of Independence* wrote 'It would be a wrong that Kashmir is the only dispute that divides India and Pakistan, though undoubtedly the most significant. One at least is nearly as important as the Kashmir dispute, that of Assam and some district of India adjacent to East Pakistan. To these Pakistan has very good claims. Even a pro-India leader like Sheikh Mujibur Rahman in his book *Eastern Pakistan; its population & economics* observed, 'Because Eastern Pakistan must have sufficient land for its expansion and because Assam has abundant forests and mineral resources, coal, petroleum etc., Eastern Pakistan must include Assam to be financially and economically strong.'

CONTRIBUTORY FACTORS

10. Besides the above consideration, there are other contributory factors facilitating Infiltration from Bangladesh. Ethnic, linguistic and religious commonality between the illegal migrants and many people on our side of the border enables them to find shelter. It makes their detection difficult. Some political parties have been encouraging and even helping illegal migration with a view to building vote banks. These immigrants are hardworking and are prepared

to work as cheap labour and domestic help for lower remuneration than the local people. This makes them acceptable. Moreover, with corruption being all pervasive, corrupt officials are bribed to provide help. Recently, a racket has been busted in Lakhimpur. Four individuals were found to have been providing forged citizenship certificates and other documents to illegal migrants for the last 14 years.

ILLEGAL MIGRANTS

15. ... Mr. Mulan described this as invasion using military terminology which in present geostrategic context, underscores the strategic aspect of the problem. It is unfortunately that to this day, after half a century of independence, we have chosen to remain virtually oblivious to the grave danger to our national security arising from this unabated influx of illegal migrants. Third, the prophecy that except the Sibsagar district, the Assamese people will not find themselves at home in Assam, is well on its way to becoming true as reflected by the present demographic pattern of Assam.

16. Mr. Inderjit Gupta the then Home Minister of India stated in the Parliament on May 6, 1997 that there were 10 million illegal migrants residing in India. Quoting Home Ministry/Intelligence Bureau sources, the August 10 1998 issue of *India Today* has given the breakdown of these illegal migrants by States:

EXPLANATORY NOTE

...In the case of Muslims the Assam growth rate was much higher than the all India rate. This suggests continued large scale Muslim illegal migration into Assam.

(d) Muslim population in Assam has shown a rise 77.42 percent in 1991 from what it was in 1971. Hindu population has risen by nearly 41.89 percent in this period.

(e) Muslim population in Assam has risen from 24.68 percent in 1951 to 28.42 percent in 1999. As per 1991 census four districts (Dhubri, Goalpara, Barpeta and Hailakandi) have become Muslim majority district. Two more districts (Nagaon and Karimganj) should have become so by 1998 and one district Morigaon is fast approaching this position.

20. The growth of Muslim population has been emphasized in the previous paragraph to indicate the extent of illegal migration from Bangladesh to Assam because as stated earlier, the illegal migrants coming into India after 1971 have been almost exclusively Muslims.
21. Pakistan's ISI has been active in Bangladesh supporting militant movement in Assam. Muslim militant organization have mushroomed in Assam and there are reports of some 50 Assamese Muslim youths having gone for training to Afghanistan and Kashmir.

In the report, an emphasis was made on the dangerous consequences of large scale illegal migration from Bangladesh. It is pertinent to highlight here that the problem of illegal migration in Assam has, over the years, reached such heights that even courts have recognised and acknowledged the same and rued the lack of political will in remedying the situation. In **Sarabari Begum v. State of Assam,**[16] the Guwahati High Court had, in

16 *See generally* Sarabari Begum v. State of Assam W.P. (C) No. 1094/2008. One of the earliest arguments professing faith-based classifications of illegal migrants in Assam

the year 2008, suggested that the problem of Assam required a political solution. The High Court had emphasised that it was a known fact that illegal Bangladeshis had intruded every corner of Assam, including forest land. The court further stated that a strong political will was required to free Assam from illegal Bangladeshi intrusion.

Challenge to the IMDT Act: The Sonowal I Judgement

In the year 2004, a writ petition titled **Sarbananda Sonowal v. Union of India**[17] was filed in the Supreme Court of India, *inter alia*, questioning the constitutional validity of the IMDT Act and the IMDT Rules. The Supreme Court while striking down the IMDT Act (and its accompanying rules), made the following critical observations:

a) Post analysis of the provisions of the IMDT Act and the IMDT Rules, the Supreme Court held that they were highly complicated on the aspect of detention and deportation of illegal migrants when compared to the Foreigners Act, 1946 and the Foreigners Order, 1964. It was observed that the procedures established thereunder were difficult, cumbersome and time consuming; which would do injustice to the objectives sought to be achieved by the IMDT Act. Even securing conviction for a person in a criminal trial was perceived to be easier than establishing the 'illegal migrancy' of a person under the IMDT Act.
b) It was noticed that the IMDT Act did not contain any provision similar to Section 9 of the Foreigners Act (Section 9 of the

can be found in this judgement. In this matter, an argument was made that Hindu migrants from Bangladesh ought to be treated differently keeping in mind the aspect of partition and also since they would face oppression even if they were deported to Bangladesh. The High Court declined to make any comment on such an argument since it perceived it to be a political issue over which the court had nothing to say.

17 2005 (5) SCC 665.

Foreigners Act places the burden of proof upon the person who claims to be an Indian citizen). Hence, a very heavy burden was cast on the government to establish that a person qualified to be an 'illegal migrant' under the provisions of the IMDT Act. This was considered to be against the ethos of the objective sought to be achieved by the IMDT Act.[18]

c) The Supreme Court observed that the Union had failed to protect the state of Assam from 'external aggression' and 'internal disturbance' caused by illegal migration into Assam from Bangladesh thereby violating its constitutional obligations towards its states, including Article 355 of the Constitution.[19] The Supreme Court, amongst other things, took note of the Governor's Report of 1998 which elaborately dealt with the problem of illegal migration.
d) The Supreme Court observed that the IMDT Act not only fails to serve the objective of the Assam Accord but works to its detriment. It was also held that provisions of the IMDT Act were one sided and had been purposefully made so as to give shelter or protection to illegal migrants rather than to identify and deport them.
e) The Supreme Court observed that the provisions of the Foreigners Act, 1946 were far more effective in identification and deportation of illegal migrants. The court observed that the procedures prescribed under the Foreigners Act, 1946 and the Foreigners Order, 1964 were considered just, fair and reasonable by the court.

---

18 Section 9 of the Foreigners Act, 1946 regarding 'burden of proof' is basically on the same lines as the corresponding provisions in UK and some other western nations; and is based upon the legal principle that the facts which are peculiarly within the knowledge of a person should be required to prove it. The Supreme Court opined that in the absence of a provision in the IMDT Act (similar to Section 9 of the Foreigners Act, 1946) regarding burden of proof, the whole complexion of the case will change in favour of the illegal migrant.

19 Article 355 of the Constitution of India provides that it shall be the duty of the Union to protect every state against external aggression and internal disturbance.

f) The IMDT Act was also found to be violative of Article 14 of the Constitution on the premise that its application only to the state of Assam was bereft of any rational or reasonable nexus.
g) The Supreme Court held that promulgation of special laws and establishment of separate tribunals for determining issues relating to illegal migration specially for Assam was neither warranted nor desirable. The Supreme Court opined that there was absolutely no reason why the illegal migrants coming into the state of Assam should be treated differently from those who had migrated to the other parts of the country.

Directions of the Supreme Court

Ultimately, the Supreme Court issued the following directions in the matter:

a) The provisions of the IMDT Act were declared to be *ultra vires* the Constitution and were struck down.
b) The tribunals and the appellate tribunals constituted under the IMDT Act were ordered to cease functioning.
c) All cases pending before the tribunals under the IMDT Act would stand transferred to the tribunals constituted under the Foreigners Order, 1964 and would be decided in terms of the Foreigners Act, 1946 and the Foreigners Order, 1964.
d) The government authorities were permitted to initiate fresh proceedings under the Foreigners Act 1946 against persons whose cases were yet to be referred to the tribunals (under the IMDT Act) for any reason.
e) All appeals pending in the appellate tribunal (under the IMDT Act) were directed to be abated.
f) The government was directed to constitute sufficient number of tribunals under the Foreigners Order, 1964 to effectively

deal with the cases of foreigners who had illegally come to Assam from Bangladesh.

Effect of the Sonowal I Judgement on existing litigation

The directions (above) made by the Supreme Court in Sonowal I Judgement decided the fate of the following matters in connection with the IMDT Act:

a) Matters which were yet to be referred to the tribunals under the IMDT Act.
b) Matters which were pending adjudication before the tribunals under the IMDT Act.
c) Appeals pending before appellate tribunal(s) under the IMDT Act.

However, there was no observation in the above judgement with respect to petitions which, on the date of the said judgement, were pending in the Guwahati High Court (assailing the orders of the appellate tribunal under the IMDT Act). This issue came up before the Guwahati High Court in **Santi Ranjan Dey and Others v. State of Assam and Others.**[20] The question was how should the court deal with the petitions under the provisions of the IMDT Act once the said legislation itself ceased to exist. The High Court decided this controversy by ordering all such matters to be remanded to the tribunals under the Foreigners Act for a fresh adjudication.

Legality of Judgements passed under IMDT Act

Another peculiar situation arose before the Guwahati High Court in connection with the Sonowal I Judgement. The Sonowal I Judgement apparently omitted to decide the validity, applicability and fate of orders previously passed under the

20 2006(4) GLT 716.

IMDT Act. The question was whether matters wherein a person had been declared to be an 'illegal migrant' (under the provisions of the IMDT Act) would be required to be re-adjudicated under the Foreigners Act or whether the government could take such orders as gospel (and final) and proceed to deport the concerned person without further ado. This issue was deliberated upon by the Guwahati High Court in **Anowar Ali v. State of Assam**[21] wherein the court concluded as follows:

a) If a person was declared to be an illegal migrant, he was liable for deportation and such order would be binding upon him. Such orders would not be obliterated only because IMDT Act had been struck down. Final orders of the tribunals constituted under the IMDT Act were held to be conclusive. The court observed that any other view would be self-defeating and would run counter to the very objective of detection and deportation of illegal migrants.
b) Orders already passed by the tribunals constituted under the IMDT Act do not cease to exist with the striking down of the IMDT Act. Consequently, it does not necessarily follow that all cases already decided by the tribunals constituted under the IMDT Act prior to such declaration have to be decided afresh by the Foreigners Tribunal. Orders passed by the tribunals constituted under the IMDT Act can be assailed by way of a writ petition and each writ petition has to be considered on its own merits. If on consideration of the material on record, the court finds that the matter requires to be remanded for a fresh consideration, in that event, case will be remanded to the Foreigners Tribunal for disposal in accordance with Foreigners Act, 1946 and Foreigners Order, 1964. If the court upholds the order under challenge, then the illegal migrant would be deported. In

21 W.P. (C) No. 1043/2013 (13.06.2014, Guwahati High Court).

the event of dismissal of the petition of the illegal migrant, he would be deported.

c) The government would be entitled to proceed under the provisions of the Foreigners Act 1946 and the Foreigners Order 1964 and make a reference to the Foreigners Tribunal for adjudication even in respect of a person whose petition challenging an order declaring him to be an illegal migrant under the IMDT Act is set aside by the High Court.
d) The government would be at liberty to make a reference to the Foreigners Tribunal even in respect of those persons, who were not declared as illegal migrants by tribunals constituted under the IMDT Act.

The Foreigners (Tribunals for Assam) Order, 2006

Subsequent to the above, in a perceived bid to overcome various observations and directions of the Supreme Court in the Sonowal I Judgement, the Foreigners (Tribunals for Assam) Order, 2006 was promulgated on 10.02.2006 (**2006 Order**). The 2006 Order supplanted the Foreigners Order, 1964 in so far as Assam was concerned. In other words, the Foreigners Order, 1964 was made inapplicable to Assam and replaced with the 2006 Order.

The Sonowal II Judgement

The 2006 Order was challenged before the Supreme Court by Sarbananda Sonowal and finally the Supreme Court in what is commonly called the **Sonowal II Judgement**[22] struck down the 2006 Order for, amongst others, being arbitrary, unreasonable, adversative to the principles enshrined in the Assam Accord and violative of Article 14 of the Constitution. The following pertinent observations were made by the Supreme Court in Sonowal II Judgement:

22 (2007) 1 SCC 174.

a) The Supreme Court opined that it appeared that the 2006 Order had been issued just as a cover up for non-implementation of the directions issued in Sonowal I Judgement.
b) The 2006 Order was unnecessary in light of the Foreigners Act, 1946 and the orders made thereunder, as well as in view of the directions issued in Sonowal I Judgement.
c) The 2006 Order did not serve the purpose sought to be achieved by the Foreigners Act, 1946 or the Citizenship Act or the obligations cast on the central government to protect the nation in terms of Article 355 of the Constitution of India highlighted in Sonowal I Judgement.
d) The Supreme Court lamented that the conduct of the government in bringing out the 2006 Order exhibited a lack of will in ensuring that illegal migrants were evicted from the country.[23]
e) The Supreme Court opined that the government had simply refused to implement the Foreigners Act, 1946 and the Foreigners Order, 1964 in the state of Assam or to comply with the directions of the court in Sonowal I.
f) The Supreme Court also observed that while the Foreigners Act placed the 'burden of proof' on the concerned person to show that he was an Indian citizen (also discussed elaborately and upheld in Sonowal I), this legal position was sought to be significantly altered by the 2006 Order (which placed the burden on the tribunal itself to substantiate that a given person was a foreigner). This reversal in legal position was viewed by the Supreme Court as detrimental to the notion of removing illegal migrants from the country.
g) No rational reason or explanation had been put forward for excluding Assam from the ambit of the Foreigners Act, 1946

23 In Sonowal I Judgement, the Supreme Court had taken note of the lack of will on the part of the central government to proceed against the foreigners.

and the Foreigners Order, 1964; and supplanting it with the 2006 Order.

Finally, the Supreme Court quashed the 2006 Order and directed the government to forthwith implement its directions passed in Sonowal I Judgement.

The Thana Level Committee Episode

In the interregnum, in 2005, the Government of Assam had also issued a notification dated 27.05.2005 for constitution of a 'thana level committee' (**TLC**) purportedly for the purpose of avoidance of harassment to genuine Indian citizens in the name of detection of foreigners.[24] The TLC was required to have the following members:

1. Circle Officer (Revenue) of the area - Chairman
2. Officer in Charge of the Thana - Member Secretary
3. Inspector/Sub-Inspector of Border Branch - Member
4. Representative of recognized Political parties (one each) - Member
5. Elected member of Zila Parishad within the Thana Area - Member
6. Four leading citizens to be nominated by the Government
   (i) One Lady - Member
   (ii) One majority community - Member
   (iii) One religious minority community - Member
   (iv) One linguistic minority community - Member

The primary duties and responsibilities of the TLC were as follows:

24 *See generally* State of Assam v. Jamait-E-Ulema-E-Hind, Review Petition No. 5/2017 (13.07.2018, Guwahati High Court).

a) The TLC was to have an advisory role. It was required to keep strict vigil against rumour mongers and ensure that no genuine citizen was harassed in any way in the name of suspected foreigners.
b) Any person within the thana area could submit an application to the concerned officer regarding presence of illegal migrants in the area as per law.
c) On receipt of such an application, the relevant officer of the thana was first required to examine and verify the matter.
d) The jurisdictional police station was required to apprise the TLC of the action taken on such application.
e) The TLC was required to sit once in a month.
f) The TLC was obligated to take all necessary steps to ensure that there was no tension or misunderstanding amongst the different communities living within the thana area relating to the issue of illegal migrants.
g) The TLC was required to ensure that no person took law into his hands in the matter of detecting suspected illegal migrants.

However, the Guwahati High Court in **State of Assam v. Jamait-E-Ulema-E-Hind**[25] struck down the above notification dated 27.05.2005 and the constitution of TLC on the following principal premise: (i) After the declaration of the IMDT Act and IMDT Rules as unconstitutional, there was no scope for the concept of TLC; (ii) The Foreigners Act (which was applicable to the entire country, including Assam), left no room for a TLC; and (iii) The TLC has no legal force or authority to accept or verify petitions relating to illegal migrants.

The Assam NRC Judgement

In 2012, large scale riots took place in Assam which led to the filing of another set of petitions in the Supreme Court. In the said batch

25 2018 (4) GLT 264.

of petitions, amongst other things, Section 6A of the Citizenship Act was challenged. Other prayers in the said petitions included immediate deportation of illegal migrants from Assam and from India, updating of the Assam NRC by taking into account the NRC prepared in the year 1951, and taking the year 1951 as the base year for the purpose of detection of illegal migrants.[26]

The petitioners in the said petitions made a slew of contentions before the Supreme Court, which included the following:

a) Sovereignty and integrity of India were at stake on account of the massive influx of illegal migrants into India from a neighbouring country.
b) The said influx of migrants was a major cause of the periodic clashes in Assam thereby affecting the law and order situation, including loss of life and property.
c) The culture of an entire people was being eroded owing to large-scale illegal migration.

The Supreme Court made the following set of observations in the matter:

a) The Supreme Court discussed various issued highlighted in a White Paper dated 20.10.2012 prepared by the State of Assam on the foreigner's issue to hold that very little had been done to implement various promises set out in the Assam Accord. The following issues were highlighted in the White Paper:
   i. The set-up of the foreign tribunals and their performance was questioned. It was noted that there was a large

26 Judgement dated 17.12.2014 in a batch of petitions in the Supreme Court of Assam Sanmilita Mahasangha & Others v. Union of India, W.P. (C) No. 562/2012; Assam Public Works v. Union of India, W.P. (C) No. 274/2009; and All Assam Ahom Association & Ors. v. Union of India, W.P. (C) No. 876/2014.

cumulative pendency of cases in the tribunals which needed to be addressed.

ii. The White Paper rued the absence of a proper procedure between the governments of India and Bangladesh regarding deportation of illegal migrants. It was noted that the deportation was being carried out through the 'push back' method which was neither sufficient nor completely effective.

iii. The international borders with Bangladesh had not been secured. Large parts of the border were still porous and required fencing.

b) On the aspect of the Foreigners Tribunals, the Supreme Court observed that the number of tribunals set up were abysmally low resulting in low number of decisions by these tribunals. Further, even the 'push back mechanism' was not entirely successful because the 'pushed back' persons would be able to re-enter on account of porous borders.

c) On the aspect of porous borders, the Supreme Court observed that the large parts of the borders were unfenced. Apart from the Assam portion of the border, even the border with West Bengal and other north-eastern states was porous, thereby making it extremely easy to cross. This unhappy situation was contrasted with the Indo-Pakistan border which was not only properly fenced but also properly manned.

d) The Supreme Court directed the union and state governments to take effective and expeditious steps to check the above-mentioned issues which were resulting in mass illegal migration, including fencing of borders, creating proper border roads, installation of flood lights along the border, deployment of sufficient forces for proper patrolling etc. Additionally, the Supreme Court also requested the Gauhati High Court to expedite the selection process for members of the foreigner's tribunals and also monitor the functioning of the tribunals.

e) On the issue of deportation, the Supreme Court directed the union government to enter into discussions with the government of Bangladesh for streamlining the deportation procedure(s).

f) On the aspect of NRC for Assam, the Supreme Court directed the government to conclude updating of the NRC within a time bound manner.

g) Separate from the above, the Supreme Court stated that the issues pertaining to the challenge to the constitutionality of Section 6A of the Citizenship Act (which gave effect to certain parts of the Assam Accord) needed to be adjudicated by a 5 (five) judge bench of the Supreme Court.[27]

THE ASSAM NRC

Readers may be aware that the Assam NRC exercise commenced post the above discussed Supreme Court judgement and has since been carried out under its supervision. The entire exercise took about 5 (five) years and the final draft of the NRC was published in August 2019.[28] A summary of the Assam NRC exercise, along with the impediments faced by the government in conducting the exercise have been highlighted in a separate chapter. This sub topic explains the legal framework behind the NRC exercise and elucidates some of the extant legal provisions in connection therewith.

The legal framework for the NRC can be found in the Citizenship Act and Citizenship (Registration of Citizens and Issue

27 To the best of knowledge of the author, a 5 (five) judge bench of the Supreme Court is yet to be constituted.

28 Recently, the Foreigners Tribunals have taken a view that the NRC list of 2019 is the final NRC list. See for example State v. Bikram Singha. F.T. case No. 129/2017 & Police Enquiry No. TD/3654/98 (10.09.2021, Foreigners Tribunal II, Karimganj, Assam).

of National Identity Cards) Rules, 2003 (NIC Rules).[29] Speaking specifically about Assam, the genesis of the NRC can be found in the Assam Accord which, amongst other things, mandated the government to detect and deport all foreigners who had entered Assam post 25.03.1971. The NIC Rules contain special provisions with respect to the creation of an NRC for Assam.

National Identity Card

The starting point of the NRC can be found in Section 14A of the Citizenship Act which was introduced *vide* the Citizenship (Amendment) Act, 2003 and was given effect to on 03.12.2004. The said provision empowers the central government to create and maintain a national register of Indian citizens, to establish a national registration authority and to carry out compulsory registration of citizens.

The National Identity Card Rules

The NIC Rules contain special provisions as to the National Register for the state of Assam.[30] A special procedure was prescribed (under Rule 4A & Schedule of the NIC Rules) in the matter of preparation of the Assam NRC.[31]

At the outset, it is noteworthy that the sole test for inclusion for a person in the NRC is his Indian citizenship (as per applicable law). No further distinction or classifications exist in this regard.[32]

29 S. 14 A was introduced to the Citizenship Act with effect from 03.12.2004. The NIC Rules were brought into force on 10.12.2003.

30 R. 4 A & Schedule of the NIC Rules.

31 R. 4A is a departure from the other rules which deal with preparation of NRC of Indian citizens from the rest of the country. *See generally* Assam Public Works v. Union of India (UOI) W.P. (C) No. 2174/2009.

32 No distinction is to be made between persons who are original inhabitants of Assam and those who are not. No special privilege is to be given to indigenous persons of Assam in this regard. *See* Kamalakhya Dey Purkayastha and Others v. Union of India, W.P. (C) No. 1020/2017.

Salient Features of the NIC Rules with respect to the Assam NRC

The NIC Rules contain a special schedule which describes the procedure and process to be followed with respect to the preparation of the Assam NRC. The said provisions are discussed below in brief.

Invitation of Applications

The process of preparation of the Assam NRC commences by inviting applications from all residents of Assam, for collection of specified particulars relating to every individual, including the information available in the NRC of 1951 and the Electoral Rolls of 1971 (defined below).

Publication

The District Magistrate shall cause to be published copies of the National Register of Citizens 1951 (**NRC of 1951**) along with the electoral rolls up to the midnight of 24.03.1971 (**Rolls of 1971**), as available, and send the same to the Local Registrar for wide circulation and public inspection in each village and ward.

The Local Registrar shall select centrally located public places for display of records and for issue and receipt of the applications. The Local Registrar shall be the custodian of records of his area and shall be responsible for its display during office hours.

Scrutiny of Applications

Post receipt of the applications, the Local Registrar shall scrutinize the applications and after verification, prepare a consolidated list which shall contain the names of the following persons: (i) persons whose names appear in the NRC of 1951 and the Rolls of 1971; and (ii) the descendants of persons mentioned in the preceding serial no. (i). The scrutiny shall be made by comparing the information stated in the application form with the official records. All persons whose information is found in order shall make the cut. The said consolidated list shall be prepared village and ward wise.

Separately, the Local Registrar is authorised to use inter-state correspondence or inter-district correspondence for verifying information relating to persons who were residing outside Assam or had shifted to another district within Assam up to midnight of 24.03.1971.

Investigation by District Magistrate

The Local Registrar is empowered to refer doubtful cases to the District Magistrate for investigation and decision. Such referral shall be informed to the concerned person as well.

The Exceptions & Exclusions

The persons declared to be 'illegal migrants' or 'foreigners' shall not be included in the list. However, persons who came to Assam between 1966 and 25.03.1971; and got themselves registered with the Foreigner Registration Regional Officer shall be eligible to be included in the list provided they have not been declared as 'illegal migrants' or 'foreigners' by the competent authority.[33]

Separately, persons who are originally inhabitants of Assam and their children and descendants, who are citizens of India, shall be included in the list, if their citizenship is ascertained beyond reasonable doubt and to the satisfaction of the concerned authorities.[34]

33 Clause 3 (2) of the Schedule.

34 Clause 3 (3) of the Schedule. Clause 3 (3) of the Schedule provides for identification of persons entitled to be included in the Assam NRC by a process different from what is enumerated under Clause 3 (2). Clause 3 (3) contemplates a less stringent process for deciding claims for inclusion in the NRC in so far as persons who are originally inhabitants of the state of Assam are concerned. Identification of persons who are originally inhabitants of the state of Assam is to be done solely on the basis of citizenship proof.

Publication of the List: The Draft NRC

The District Magistrate shall publish the list as a draft Assam NRC. A public notice with regard to the said publication shall also be issued in local newspaper having wide circulation in the concerned areas. Objections and suggestions shall be invited to the draft Assam NRC.

Continued Verification

The Local Registrar is authorised to cause a verification of names of persons as considered necessary, until the final publication of the Assam NRC. This mechanism allows the government authorities to re-verify cases if the situation demands. However, such authorisation of 'continuing verification' is likely to result in 'undue harassment' of the Assam residents. Hence, special care should be taken by the Local Registrar in attending to instances of allegation of 'undue harassment' if brought to his attention during the conduct of the verification or re-verification exercise.

The report of verification shall be examined by the District Registrar who shall pass an order (with reasons) on the said report.

Publication of Additional List

Post the above-mentioned order by the District Registrar, an additional list of the draft Assam NRC shall be published.

Claims and Objections

Objections can be filed by the following persons within a period of 30 (thirty) days from the date of publication of the draft list, with the Local Registrar: (i) persons whose names are not included in the draft list; (ii) persons who object to the inclusion of any name in the draft list.

The Local Registrar shall decide the objections after giving the concerned parties an opportunity to file supporting documents and an opportunity of hearing.

Publication of Supplementary List

Post disposal of the above-mentioned objections, the Local Registrar shall publish a supplementary list and subsequently, the final Assam NRC shall be published.

Appeal

Any person dissatisfied with the decision of the Local Registrar on the objections, may prefer an appeal before the tribunal established under the Foreigners Order, 1964 within a period of 60 (sixty) days from the date of the order. No further challenge or appeal is prescribed in this regard.

CHAPTER 9

Assam National Register of Citizens & Assam Accord – Implementation

INTRODUCTION

The previous chapters discuss in detail the history of the Assam migration issue; the genesis of and the events leading to the Assam Accord. The Assam NRC has become a test case of sorts for the government. The Assam NRC exercise has given to the government (as well as the courts) an opportunity to understand the practical (and legal) aspects which need to be considered in a country like India whilst creating a detailed record of its populace.

This chapter summarises the manner in which the Assam NRC exercise was carried out by the government under the supervision and vigil of the Supreme Court. This chapter briefly highlights the various stages of the Assam NRC as well as some of the hurdles which were (and are being) faced by the government in connection with the implementation of the Assam NRC. A review of the orders passed by the Supreme Court (while monitoring the NRC exercise) also brings out the positive steps and efforts made (from time to time) in the interest of an effective implementation of the NRC exercise, which are also discussed herein.

Additionally, this chapter also summarises the steps which have been taken by the Assam government towards implementation of the provisions of the Assam Accord.

Assuming that the concept of NRC generally (Assam excepting) is able to withstand judicial scrutiny and a similar exercise is sought to be carried out for the entire country, then in such case, the experience of the Assam NRC will prove vital for the government as well as for the relevant authorities. The highlights of the NRC are discussed in a chronological manner.

Border Fencing

The Supreme Court appointed a committee to supervise the work of the border fencing (with Bangladesh). It is understood that the fencing work is currently ongoing. In fact, various new age devices are being used along the borders to prevent migration from Bangladesh.[1]

Verification of Applications

The draft version of the NRC was first published on 31.12.2017. Thereafter, an extended verification exercise was carried out. Initially, it was envisioned that the verification exercise would be completed by 31.05.2018 with another month for mop-up operations.[2] However, these timelines got extended for various reasons (briefly discussed below).

Verification at NRC Seva Kendras

NRC Seva Kendras were set up in various parts in Assam for the purpose of verification of the applications and documents which had been filed by the applicants. In order to expediate the entire process, it was proposed before the Supreme Court that the applicants be called to the respective NRC Seva

1 Re: Assam Public Works (Order dated 14.09.2017, Supreme Court of India).

2 Re: Assam Public Works (Order dated 20.02.2018, Supreme Court of India).

Kendras instead of going house to house in so far as the District Magistrate's investigation in respect of verification of documents was concerned. The said proposal was accepted and allowed by the Supreme Court.[3]

Overshooting Timelines

Additional time was sought from the Supreme Court for completing the verification exercise for the following reasons:[4]

a) The mop-up operations were taking longer than expected.
b) During the course of family tree investigations, discrepancies were found in a large number of cases which was consuming more time.
c) The quality control exercise had revealed errors with respect to about 20,000 (twenty thousand) persons.

The Draft NRC List

The draft NRC was again published on 30.07.2018 along with a district-wise break-up list of the persons who made (or could not make) the cut. In the said list, about 40 (forty) lakh people were excluded from the list. The government then commenced the process of preparing modalities in the form of standard operating procedures for consideration of claims and/or objections.[5]

Constitution of Judges Committee

The Supreme Court directed constitution of a judges committee (comprising of former judges of the High Court of Guwahati) for the purpose of taking care of any clarifications with respect to the

3 Re: Assam Public Works (Order dated 08.05.2018, Supreme Court of India).

4 Re: Assam Public Works (Order dated 02.07.2018, Supreme Court of India).

5 Re: Assam Public Works (Order dated 16.08.2018, Supreme Court of India).

modalities in the preparation of the NRC. The said judges committee was also tasked with the responsibility of making an enquiry on any complaint(s) received with regard to any obstruction in the matter of preparation or updating of the NRC by any person or authority; and submitting the said report (on such enquiry) with the Supreme Court so that necessary steps could be taken on the same.[6]

Access to Government Database

The Supreme Court was regularly apprised about the ongoing process and the difficulties faced by the state coordinator in connection with the NRC exercise. On one occasion, the state coordinator requested for access to the database of the population, from relevant authorities so that the verification of the documents (such as PAN Cards, Passports, Electoral records etc.) could be done expeditiously and effectively.

The Supreme Court directed the concerned authorities (in the Finance, Home and External Affairs Ministries) to provide the relevant database so that the verification exercise could be carried out expeditiously and seamlessly.[7] Further, the Supreme Court also directed the state governments to extend their cooperation by expeditiously responding to the verification requests of the state coordinator.

Information from State Governments

Another impediment faced by the state coordinator was that various documents (of applicants) had been sent to certain states for verification but their response was not forthcoming. The Supreme Court directed the concerned states to expedite the process of sending response to the state coordinator.[8]

6 Re: Assam Sanmilita Mahasangha (Order dated 21.07.2015, Supreme Court of India).

7 Re: Assam Sanmilita Mahasangha (Orders dated 01.12.2015 & 13.01.2016, Supreme Court of India).

8 Re: Assam Sanmilita Mahasangha (Order dated 13.01.2016, Supreme Court of India).

Securement of International Borders

One of the foremost steps taken by the Supreme Court in connection with the NRC exercise was to pass orders to secure the international borders between India and Bangladesh which included the following: (i) intensive patrolling on the riverine borders in Dhubri and Cachar sections; (ii) improvement of border roads; (iii) electrification of flood lights; (iv) strengthening of BSF battalions and also the other para-military forces that guard the international border. The central and state government were directed to take requisite steps in this regard. Further, the relevant officials were also requested to make visits of the international border to check the progress.[9]

The Supreme Court made further efforts to augment coordination between the central government and the state government to achieve this objective. Towards this end, the Supreme Court also directed constitution of a committee consisting of personnel from both the central and state governments, for thrashing out any and all differences between them and for chalking out a detailed time-bound action plan for securing the international borders.[10]

Adjudication of Claims & Publication of Final List

The process of filing of claims and objections was concluded on 31.12.2018. About 36 (thirty six) lakh claims and about 2 (two) lakh objections were filed. The hearings with respect to such claims and objections commenced in the month of February 2019 (with advance notice to the parties).[11]

The final NRC for Assam was published on 31.08.2019, after a span of approximately 5 (five) years from the date of passing of

9 Re: Assam Sanmilita Mahasangha (Order dated 14.07.2015, Supreme Court of India).

10 Re: Assam Sanmilita Mahasangha (Order dated 05.11.2015, Supreme Court of India).

11 Re: Assam Public Works (Order dated 24.01.2019, Supreme Court of India).

the NRC judgement by the Supreme Court. About 19 (nineteen) lakh persons were excluded from this final list. Presently, appeals filed by the excluded persons are pending adjudication at various levels and forums.

SUPREME COURT CLARIFICATIONS

Apart from the efforts as highlighted above, clarifications were also issued by the Supreme Court, from time to time, for clearance of the various impediments which regularly emerged during the course of the NRC exercise.

Validity of Orders under IMDT Act

In the month of August 2019, clarity was sought from the Supreme Court on the matter of validity of orders passed under the erstwhile Illegal Migrants (Determination by Tribunals) Act (**IMDT Act**).[12] The principal question before the Supreme Court was whether orders passed under the IMDT Act, which declared certain persons to be Indians, could be (or should be) taken into account while determining their citizenship status for the purposes of the NRC.[13]

The Supreme Court directed that the above said issue would be governed by the decision of the Guwahati High Court in **Anowar Ali v. State of Assam.**[14]

The Admissible Documents

Confusion arose amongst the authorities as to the documents which could be taken into account for the purpose of the NRC exercise.

12 *See* Chapter 8.

13 Several persons had submitted orders passed under IMDT Act which declared them to be Indians. A submission was sought to be made by these persons that they should be included in the NRC list solely on the basis of the orders passed in their favour under the IMDT Act.

14 2014 (3) GLT 500. *See also* Chapter 8

To resolve this issue, the Supreme Court categorised the below mentioned documents as 'legacy documents' which were 'admissible' for the purposes of establishing the claimant's (or his ancestor's) residence in Assam on or before 24.03.1971. Separately, certain other documents were also classified as 'supporting documents' for the same purpose.[15]

I. <u>List of Legacy Documents:</u>

a) Extract of NRC, 1951.
b) Extract/certified copy of Electoral Rolls up to the midnight of 24.03.1971 (midnight).
c) Land records including tenancy records of the relevant period up to 24.03.1971 (midnight).
d) Citizenship Certificate issued by competent authority up to 24.03.1971 (midnight).
e) Permanent Residential Certificate issued from outside the state up to 24.03.1971 (midnight) (which should all be verified from the issuing authority by the registering authority).
f) Refugee Registration Certificate issued up to 24.03.1971 (midnight).
g) Passport issued by the Government of India up to 24.03.1971 (midnight).
h) Life Insurance Corporation of India Insurance Policy (LIC) of relevant period up to 24.03.1971 (midnight).
i) Any license/certificate issued by any government authority during the relevant period i.e. up to 24.03.1971 (midnight).
j) Document showing service/employment under Government/Public Sector Undertaking up to 24.03.1971 (midnight).
k) Bank/Post Office Accounts of relevant period i.e. up to 24.03.1971 (midnight).

15 Re: Assam Public Works (Order dated 13.08.2019, Supreme Court of India).

l) Birth certificates issued by the competent authority up to 24.03.1971 (midnight).
m) Educational certificate issued by Board/Universities up to 24.03.1971 (midnight).
n) Records/processes pertaining to court up to 24.03.1971 (midnight).

II. <u>List of Supporting Documents</u>

Ration cards issued by the competent authority with official seal and signature up to 24.03.1971 (midnight).

Family Tree Hearings

During the course of the NRC exercise, it came to the attention of the relevant authorities that there were contradicting decisions of foreigners tribunals even in cases of near family members i.e. one member of the family being declared to be an Indian citizen by one Foreigners Tribunal and another close relation of the same family (now residing in another part of Assam) being declared a foreigner by another jurisdictional foreigners tribunal. To solve such a problem, the concept of 'family tree hearings' was evolved as per which adjudication with respect to one family tree was done by one foreigners tribunal only. This mechanism helped citizenship data collectors to segregate fabricated claims.

Priority to NRC Exercise

The Supreme Court had an important role to play in the timely completion of the NRC exercise. The Supreme Court closely monitored the process and on various occasions, stressed on the importance of the NRC exercise, further clarifying that the NRC exercise should be top priority and that the officials/employees of the state government engaged in this activity should continue to be primarily and principally engaged with the said work.[16]

16 Re: Assam Sanmilita Mahasangha (Order dated 01.12.2015 & 13.01.2016, Supreme Court of India).

On one occasion, permission was sought from the Supreme Court by the state government seeking temporary accommodation for the officers (involved in the NRC exercise) on the pretext of election work/duty (for the upcoming elections). The Supreme Court permitted such officers to carry out election work/duty but without affecting the primacy of the NRC work.[17] Hence, the Supreme Court required the state government to give precedence to the NRC exercise at all times.

The Doubtful Cases

During the course of the Assam NRC exercise, *inter alia*, the authorities were confronted with another peculiar situation. In many cases, while determining the status of certain persons (including children) it was found that one parent was a declared foreigner, doubtful voter (DV) [or his case/application pending in a court of law in accordance under the Citizenship Act (PFT)] while the other parent was found clear (from all angles) to be a citizen of India and eligible for inclusion in the NRC. A clarification was sought from the Supreme Court on how to deal with such situations since descendance could be drawn from either parent and in such cases the children were invoking the descendance from the parent who was in the clear. The Supreme Court, while placing reliance on the provisions of Section 3 (1) (b) & (c) of the Citizenship Act directed the following mechanism to be adopted:

a) For any NRC applications/claimants, if parent/legacy person through whom eligibility is sought to be established is a doubtful voter (DV) or DF or PFT, then such persons will not be included in NRC irrespective of the status of the other parent.
b) For those persons born before 03.12.2004, if the parent through whom legacy is drawn is not DV or DF or PFT

17 Re: Assam Sanmilita Mahasangha (Order dated 13.01.2016, Supreme Court of India).

and is found eligible for inclusion in NRC, but the other parent from whom legacy is not drawn is a DV or DF or PFT, then, such descendants may be included in NRC.

c) For those persons who are born on or after 03.12.2004, they will not be included in NRC if any of the parent is DV or DF or PFT even if the parent from whom legacy is drawn is clear from all angles.

The above course of action led to another peculiar situation. Many minor children of persons falling in point (c) above were excluded from the NRC. Now the consequence of exclusion from the NRC is 'being labelled a foreigner' and 'being confined to a 'detention centre'. This may also result in separation of children from their parents or the confinement of children to detention centres (if the separation is to be avoided). This peculiar issue was again brought to the attention of the Supreme Court and the government, at least as an interim measure, stated that no child would be separated from the parent and would not be committed to a detention centre.[18] This issue appears to be presently pending before the Supreme Court.

Treatment of Tea Tribes under the NIC Rules

Another issue which arose for consideration before the Supreme Court was the method of implementing the NRC with respect to the 'tea tribes' in Assam.[19]

---

18 Assam Public Works v. Union of India and Ors. (06.01.2020, Supreme Court of India).

19 'Tea-Tribe of Assam' is a term commonly used for the tea garden workers and their dependents who reside in labour quarters built inside the tea estates spread across Assam, while the expression 'Ex-Tea Tribe' refers to those who were once active as labourers but now have left the job and labour quarters for other employment opportunities. The terms 'Tea-Tribe' and 'Ex-Tea Tribe' are collectively used for those set of people who are the descendants of both tribals and backward caste Hindus, who were brought by the British colonial planters as indentured labourers from the predominantly tribal and backward caste-dominated regions of central India into colonial Assam during 1860–90s, in

On this aspect, the Supreme Court clarified that the expression 'original inhabitants of Assam' in Schedule of the NIC Rules would include the tea tribes and the inclusion of such original inhabitants to the NRC would be on the basis of proof to the satisfaction of the Registering Authority which establishes the citizenship of such persons beyond reasonable doubt.[20]

The Reverification Exercise

The Supreme Court after considering a report of the state coordinator (which specified a district-wise data of the percentage of the population who have been excluded from the final draft NRC), in its wisdom, directed a sample reverification exercise of at least 10% of the names included in the final draft of the NRC. The thought process of the court apparently was to ensure high precision or accuracy for the NRC exercise.[21]

Corruption Charges & Criminal Proceedings

The NRC exercise has also experienced its fair share of trouble, such as allegations of corruption, tampering, falsification of records et cetera.

Police Complaints against State Officials

Various criminal complaints have been filed against the erstwhile state coordinator (appointed for carrying out the Assam NRC exercise) by Assam Public Works, an NGO.

---

multiple phases, for the purpose of being employed in the tea gardens industry as labourers. The total population is estimated to be around 60 (sixty) lakh of which an estimated 40 (forty) lakh reside in residential quarters built inside tea estates. *See generally* http://teaworld.kkhsou.in/index.php

20 Assam Sanmilita Mahasangha v. Union of India (21.07.2015, Supreme Court of India). *See also* Chapter No. 8.

21 Assam Public Works v. Union of India and Ors. (28.08.2018, Supreme Court of India).

The allegations made against the state coordinator include 'tampering with the final NRC list published on August 31, 2019, making false documents, committing offences under cyber laws for altering /changing the public records by misusing his powers and positions'.[22] Police complaints have also been lodged against other officials interested with the NRC exercise. The issue is presently pending investigation.

Falsification of Claimant Records

During the course of the NRC exercise, numerous cases of falsification of records (by persons illegally attempting to project themselves as Indian citizens) have been detected by the authorities. Such falsifications include falsifying the name and age of parents, school certificates, forged certified documents. This has also led to the filing of criminal cases against the offenders. On numerous occasions, it is left to court to carry out a comprehensive examination and scrutiny of the documents in order to ascertain their veracity.[23]

Overburdening Litigation

The final list of the NRC is out which excludes approximately 19 (nineteen) lakh persons currently residing in Assam. The excluded persons are from various faiths (including Hindu, Christian and Muslims). The objections and appeals proferred by such excluded persons are currently pending adjudication at various levels of the judiciary, including the Foreigner Tribunals and the High Court. This has burdened courts with excessive litigation, which is an added burden on the government exchequer as well.

---

22 *See* https://indianexpress.com/article/north-east-india/assam/assam-firs-filed-against-prateek-hajela-former-nrc-employee-6267060/

23 *See generally* Abdur Rashid v. Union of India, W.P. (C) No. 7413/2016 (27.09.2018, Guwahati High Court).

IMPLEMENTATION OF THE ASSAM ACCORD

This section of the chapter briefly elucidates the steps which have been taken by the Assam government towards implementation of the Assam Accord. On the basis of the information available on the official website of the state government of Assam, the following progress has been made by the government on some of the critical aspects of the Assam Accord.[24]

The Foreigners Issue

Clause 5 of the Assam Accord contains provisions regarding detection and expulsion of foreigners from the state of Assam (who have entered or re-entered post 24.03.1971). It also provides for registration and regularisation of (Assam domiciled) foreigners who have entered Assam within the designated dates.

The progress made on this count is as follows:

a) The government has suitably strengthened its machinery for a more effective and expeditious foreigner's detection and government registration.
b) Thousands of re-infiltrators (from Bangladesh) have been detected and deported. This is a continuous and ongoing process.
c) There are about 100 (one hundred) Foreigners Tribunals functioning in the state of Assam for detection and deportation of foreigners.

Preservation and Promotion of the Cultural, Social, Linguistic Identity and Heritage of the Assamese People

Clause 6 of the Assam Accord requires provision of appropriate constitutional, legislative and administrative safeguards to

24 *See generally* https://assamaccord.assam.gov.in/portlets/assam-accord-and-its-clauses

protect, preserve and promote the cultural, social, linguistic identity and heritage of the Assamese population.

The progress made on this count is as follows:

a) Establishment of the Srimanta Sankardeva Kalakshetra Society which is committed to work for preservation, promotion and upliftment of culture of the people of Assam.
b) Modernisation of the Jyoti Chitraban Film Studio and efforts to make this film studio the film hub of the entire north-eastern region.
c) Financial assistance to *satras* of Assam as well to historic monuments for their protection, preservation and development.

Economic Development

Clause 7 of the Assam Accord requires the government to ensure an all-round economic development of Assam. The following steps have been taken in this regard:

a) Construction of rail-cum-road bridge(s) over various places.
b) Setting up of Numaligarh Refinery Limited, which has displayed creditable performance since its commencement in the year 1999 and has been conferred the status of a Mini Ratna PSU.
c) Reopening of the Shil Ghat Jute Mill.
d) Setting up of the Assam Gas Cracker Project.
e) Setting up of the Indian Institute of Technology and other Central and State Universities.
f) Upgrading of the Guwahati Medical College & Hospital.

Security of International Border

Clause 9 of the Assam Accord mandates the government to

secure the international borders to prevent infiltration from Bangladesh. This includes construction of physical barriers, fencing, patrolling, roads along the border etc.

The progress on this aspect is summarised below:

a) Out of the total length of about 280 (two hundred and eighty) kilometres of the Indo-Bangladesh in Assam, about 208 (two hundred and eight) kilometres has been fenced.
b) With respect to the riverine/char area of the border, a feasibility study is ongoing for use of 'high-tech physical and non-physical' barriers to seal these areas.
c) Floodlight work (along the border) is in progress.
d) Numerous border outposts have been set up.

Prevention of Encroachment of Government Land

Clause 10 of the Assam Accord mandates strict enforcement of laws to prevent encroachment of government lands and lands in the tribal belts & blocks; and to evict unauthorised encroachers.

In this regard, land administration (in the protected belts and blocks) is being done as per the relevant provisions of the Assam Land and Revenue Regulation 1886 and its rules.

Restricting Acquisition of Immovable Property

Clause 11 of the Assam Accord mandates strict enforcement of laws to restrict acquisition of immovable property by foreigners in Assam.

Efforts are being made (on an ongoing basis) to strictly implement the Assam Alienation of Land (Regulation) Act, 1980 (which, *inter alia*, restricts acquisition of immovable property by foreigners in Assam).

Registration of Births and Deaths

Clause 12 of the Assam Accord requires regular maintenance of birth and death registers.

About 700 (seven hundred) centres have been set up in Assam by the Health and Family Welfare Department to issue birth and death certificates. Additionally, steps are being taken to computerise the process and introduce an online system for the same.

CHAPTER 10

The CAA Debate

INTRODUCTION

The CAA, from day one, has been riddled with controversies. When the CAB was tabled in the Parliament, various features and aspects were sharply opposed and dissented by several factions and groups, including the members of the Parliament of the Lok Sabha and Rajya Sabha.

Post the enactment of the CAA, a clutch of petitions were proferred in the Supreme Court of India challenging (almost) every aspect of the CAA on a variety of grounds.[1] Additionally, various state governments (including Kerala, West Bengal, Punjab, etc) have also opposed the CAA as well as the NRC. The challenge to the CAA is in the domain of the Supreme Court of India and the matter is *sub judice*. The CAA also continues to be a subject of ongoing debate and discussion in the public realm.

The central government defends the CAA before the Supreme Court of India as well as in public domain through speeches, clarifications, interviews etc. Even the Parliamentary Joint Committee Report throws light on the government's position on various facets of the CAA.

---

1 Even the Exemption Notifications are under challenge before the Supreme Court of India and the challenge shall be decided by the court along with the challenge to the CAA.

While the previous chapters explain and describe the various amendments to the Indian citizenship law brought about by the CAA, this chapter attempts to bring out the various criticism(s) of the CAA and the justifications which have been made for them. This chapter attempts to summarise the principal arguments for and against the CAA. This chapter has been constructed on the basis of information available in public domain.

For the ease of reference and comprehension, this chapter has been broadly divided into 2 (two) parts. The first part of this chapter summarises the principal arguments against the CAA, and the second part of the chapter summarises the chief defences of the government

CAA: THE CRITICISM

This section attempts to describe the chief criticisms of the CAA,

Violation of Fundamental Rights

The first and foremost attack on the CAA is that it is inconsistent with the provisions of the Constitution of India and violates fundamental rights guaranteed thereunder.

Part III of the Constitution deals with fundamental rights. From the standpoint of applicability, fundamental rights can be broadly dissected into two parts i.e. those which are available only to 'citizens'[2], and those which are available to 'any person' (citizens and non-citizens).[3]

---

2 *See for example* Article 15 (prohibition from discrimination against any citizen on grounds of religion race, caste, etc., or from imposing any disability in respect of certain matters); Article 16 (equality of opportunity in matters of public employment). *See generally* State Trading Corporation of India Ltd. v. The Commercial Tax Officer, Visakhapatnam, AIR 1963 SC 1811.

3 *See for example* Article 14 (Equality before the law or equal protection of laws within the territory of India); Article 20 (protection against the enforcement of ex-post-facto laws or against double-jeopardy or against compulsion of self-incrimination); Article 21 (protection of life and personal liberty); Article 22 (protection against arrest and detention in certain cases); Article 27 (no person shall be compelled to pay any taxes for the promotion and maintenance of any

The Right to Equality

Article 14 of the Constitution is one principal fundamental right which essentially states that it is impermissible to discriminate amongst persons in application of law. Article 14 of the Constitution has a large expanse and does not restrict its application to citizens only, but commands the state not to deny equality before law or the equal protection of laws to any person.[4]

Article 14 of the Constitution provides that the state shall not deny to any person equality before the law or the equal protection of the laws within the territory of India. Right to equality is the basic tenet of Article 14 of the Constitution. Article 14 of the Constitution propagates like treatment to persons under like circumstances.

What, however, Article 14 does not prohibit, is a 'reasonable classification' being made between persons founded on 'intelligible differentia' which has a 'rational relation' or 'rational nexus' to the object sought to be achieved by the law or act in question.

The critics argue that the classification or dissections of religions and regions made under the CAA (discussed below) is 'unreasonable' and 'unintelligible' thereby making the CAA violative of Article 14 of the Constitution.

The Region Classification

Critics argue that the CAA does not provide any plausible explanation for including Afghanistan to the list of 'regions'. While the inclusion of Pakistan and Bangladesh may have a reasoning (both countries were a part of undivided India), the inclusion of Afghanistan does not appear to have any basis.

---

particular religious denomination); Article 28 (freedom to attend or not to attend religious instructions or religious worship in certain educational institutions) etc.

4 Satish Nambiar v. Union of India, 2007 (5) Bom CR 247.

This specific inclusion is 'inexplicable', especially when other neighbouring countries like Myanmar (part of the British province until the year 1937) and Sri Lanka have been left out.

The Religion Classification

The first opposition on this count is the 'unexplained' exclusion of Muslims from the list of beneficiary religions. As per the author, this is perhaps one of the biggest oppositions being faced by the CAA and is viewed as an attack on the social fabric of the nation.

A further extension of this criticism relates to 'selective application' of the concept of religious persecution. This is sought to be explained by taking the example of the various sects of Muslims in Pakistan such as Ahmadias and the Baloch who have historically been victims of religious persecution in Pakistan for a long time, but find no place in the CAA (discussed in some more detail later in the chapter).

Articles 15 & 19 of the Constitution

Critics argue that the CAA violates Articles 15 and 19 of the Constitution. Article 15 of the Constitution prohibits discrimination against any citizen on the grounds of religion, race, caste, sex, place of birth. Article 19 of the Constitution provides to the citizens, the following fundamental rights: (i) right to freedom and expression; (ii) right to assemble peacefully and without arms; (iii) right to form unions or associations; (iv) right to move freely throughout the territory of India; (v) right to reside and settle in any part of the territory of India; (vi) right to practice any profession, or the right to carry out any occupation, trade or business.

Article 21 of the Constitution

The opposition to the CAA argues that the non-beneficiaries of the CAA in India would continue to be 'illegal migrants' and face the threat of deportation, which in turn, violates Article 21 of the Constitution. Article 21 of the Constitution deals with the concept of protection of life and personal liberty and provides that no person shall be deprived of his life or personal liberty except according to procedure established by law.

The Religious Persecution Element

The critics have sought to hold the government guilty of failing to holistically appreciate the concept of element of 'religious persecution' which is an essential component of the CAA fabric. This is discussed in some detail below.

Religious Persecution: The Facets Overlooked

Critics argue that the problem of 'religious persecution' runs deep and has many facets which have been overlooked while constructing the CAA. It is argued that the legislature has not looked at the aspect of 'religious persecution' in a holistic manner but has adopted a selective approach with the objective of keeping the Muslim community out of the context. Put differently, the legislature has 'failed' to recognise the fact that the problem of 'religious persecution' is rampant even amongst the excluded faiths in the Classified Countries of Pakistan, Bangladesh and Afghanistan. An example is made of the various religious groups/sects which are considered 'religious minorities' in Pakistan (i.e. Ahmadias, Baloch, Hazara etc.) and also victims of 'religious persecution'. As per the critics, viewed strictly from a 'religious persecution' standpoint, these 'religious minorities' ought to be also given protection under the CAA.

Empirical Data on Existence of Religious Persecution

Another criticism relates to the lack of authoritative statistics and empirical data on the phenomenon of religious persecution especially in the countries of Pakistan and Bangladesh. It is argued that the CAA does not have a factual backing, especially on the aspect of 'religious persecution'. In this context, the CAA has been argued to be a 'whimsical exercise of power'.

Framework for Discerning Religious Persecution

As per the critics, another questionable sub-element is the absence of proper standards and safeguards on the aspect of determination and cross-verification of a claim of 'religious persecution' which would be made by a potential beneficiary of the CAA. It is apprehended by critics that in the absence of any proper laid out standards for determining 'religious persecution', the end result may be that any migrant from the Classified Communities and Classified Countries will be able to claim benefit of the CAA.[5]

The Cut-Off Date: Absence of Basis

Cut-off dates and baseline(s) relating to migration and citizenship have always been a contentious issue. The CAA has been made applicable only to persons who entered India until 31.12.2014 (i.e. the cut-off date). The critics object to the lack of basis in deciding this date.[6]

It is further argued that, in any event, the CAA does not provide any guidance on the mode and manner of ascertaining this critical requirement. Doubts have been expressed on the manner in which this aspect would be ascertained by the government. Lack of an objective basis on this score may grant to the government an arbitrary handle to decide on its whims and facies.

---

5 As per the author, while the government has, in the Parliamentary Joint Committee Report, broadly explained the mode and manner in which this aspect will be dealt, more guidance needs to be provided in this department. Perhaps the CAA Rules (presently under construction) will throw some light on this aspect.

6 While the Assam Accord also made a classification on the basis of date of entry of migrants into India, critics argue that the CAA has added further elements of faith and source (or region) into the discourse, which makes the cut-off date even more arbitrary.

The opposition to the CAA rues the lack of clarity on the practical nuances on the implementation of the CAA. It is argued that there is absence of a proper framework to regulate or adjudicate claims of potential beneficiaries of the CAA as to 'existence of religious persecution' or 'entry into India by or before the cut-off date'. Normally 'illegal migrants' do not use or would not have used proper or legal travel channels into India, hence the importance of these issues get further heightened or pronounced.

Impact on Existing Citizens

The opposition to the CAA takes a view that the CAA may affect the already existing citizenship of Indian Muslims or may result in persecution of the Indian Muslims. In fact, in various petitions filed in the Supreme Court assailing the CAA, a leading argument is that the CAA and the NRC have been evolved with the principal objective of excluding and prosecuting Muslims who have been in India for decades. It is also contended that a principal purpose of the CAA is to jeopardise the status of 'Indian Muslims' who are actually Indian citizens but may not have the necessary means and documents of establishing the same.

NRC: Dubious Intentions

The proposal of a nationwide NRC has also been questioned on various fronts. Amongst other things, it is argued that the primary purpose behind a nationwide NRC is detection and persecution of Indian Muslims. Another argument is that a nationwide NRC may turn out to be a counter-productive exercise in the sense that there may be various sections of the Indian society (such as tribal communities and marginal sections) who may not possess complete documentation to establish their citizenship and hence may needlessly get labelled as 'illegal migrants' and face prosecution.

Refoulement: CAA Falls Foul

The CAA is also questioned for violating the principle of non-refoulement. The principle of non-refoulement prohibits the expulsion, return or extradition of a person from a state to another state when there exist substantial grounds for believing that the said person would be in danger of being subjected to irreparable harm such as violations of right to life, torture, ill treatment etc. This is an absolute principle and applies with equal force even to illegal migrants. The principle of non-refoulement is enshrined in international human rights law and refugee law. It was formally codified in the Convention on the Status of Refugees of 1951.

On the basis of the above, critics argue that, in keeping with the principle of non-refoulement, migrants to India should not be expelled without an impartial and independent assessment of the risk of irreparable harm to such person. It is contended that an application of the CAA in its present shape and form, would allow for mass-refoulement because, persons who do not qualify under the CAA (for various reasons such as being from an excluded community, an excluded country or coming into India after the cut-off date etc.) but are otherwise susceptible to persecution (including religious persecution) in their home country would be deported or expelled from the country.

Indian Refugee Policy

At this point, it may be useful to digress a little and briefly discuss India's extant refugee policy. India does not have a static domestic policy dealing with stateless persons and refugees.[7]

7 In India, a foreigner seeking asylum is required to apply for and obtain a certificate from the UNHCR. In the absence of a national legislation, UNHCR determines who is refugee on the basis of the Convention Relating to the Status of Refugees 1951. Refugees are registered under the mandate of the United Nations High Commissioner for Refugees (UNHCR) who meets regularly with all refugees and their representatives

India is not a signatory to the 1951 United Nations Convention on the Status of Refugees and the 1967 Protocol thereon (which are the primary international instruments on refugees).[8] There is no national law on refugees at present. At present, India relies on dynamic internal policies for the purpose of dealing with the issue of refugees.

The government in 2011, circulated a Standard Operating Procedure (**SOP**) to all state governments/ union territories for dealing with foreign nationals who claim to be refugees.[9] Some essential features of the SOP are delineated below.

a) Claims for 'refugeeship', which are *prima facie* justified on the grounds of a well-founded fear of persecution on account of race, religion, sex, nationality, ethnic identity, membership of a particular social group or political opinion, can be recommended by the state government/union territory administration to the Ministry of Home Affairs for grant of a Long Term Visa (LTV) after due security verification. The LTV is a renewable document.
b) Economic migrants i.e. foreigners who come to India in search of economic opportunities, without any fear of persecution, are not eligible for grant of LTV.
c) A foreigner considered unfit for grant (or renewal) of LTV is liable to be detained in a detention centre and deported to his home country (through diplomatic channels). The

---

to discuss their concerns and jointly look for solutions to their problems. The UNHCR assists a registrant against forced return, deportation, arbitrary arrest and detention. In exceptional circumstances, the UNHCR provides individual assistance that may include monthly stipends or resettlement to a third country. A certificate of refugee status issued by the UNHCR may be considered as prima facie indication of persecution (or threat of persecution) of the refugee in his home country. *See generally* Dongh Lian Kham v. Union of India, W.P. (Crl.) No. 1884/2015 (21.12.2015, Delhi High Court).

8 *See* https://www.mha.gov.in/MHA1/Par2017/pdfs/par2015-pdfs/ls-050515/6307.pdf

9 This was further revised in the year 2019. *See* https://www.mha.gov.in/MHA1/Par2017/pdfs/par2020-pdfs/rs-05022020/350.pdf

government, in appropriate cases, in consultation with UNHRC, may also consider sending the foreigner to a third country.

d) A foreigner in a detention centre may, as an interim measure, be released in case diplomatic channels do not yield concrete results within a period of 6 (six) months. The release of the foreigner shall be subject to collection of biometric details, a local surety, good behaviour and monthly police reporting, until issue of travel documents and deportation.

Foreigners who are issued LTV get access to various benefits such as ability to take up an employment in the private sector or to undertake studies in an academic institution.[10] It is however, critical to note that the SOP (or other internal policies) of the government do not provide for absorption of such refugees as 'citizens of India'. In other words, while refugees are protected by the SOP, they however, remain refugees and cannot become Indian citizens.

The Principles of Secularism: Overlooked

Critics contend that the CAA, by providing privileges and patronage to a select set of religions, flies in the face of the principles of secularism and its underlying concept of providing equal treatment to all religions.[11] Secularism basically means that the state does not recognise and promote a specific religion.[12]

10 *See* https://pib.gov.in/newsite/PrintRelease.aspx?relid=108152

11 The author would like to point out that the two-nation theory put forward by the Muslim League was based on the principle of religious nationalism and underlined the requirement of separation of India into 2 (two) independent states based on 'religion' i.e. an independent state for Hindus and Muslims. The Partition led to the creation of Pakistan, an Islam-centric state. India on the other hand, set itself up on more secular lines.

12 The word 'secular' was not present originally in the Preamble to the Constitution. It was added thereto by the 42nd Constitutional Amendment in 1976. To put it succinctly, it means that there is no official or state recognised religion in India.

The Citizenship Rules: Questions Raised

The extant Citizenship Rules have also been challenged on various premises, including the following broad aspects:

i) The power to inquire into citizenship status of a person being handed over to administrative officers at the block, taluk and district levels has been brought into question. It is argued that an inquiry into citizenship status is akin to a judicial process and cannot be left at the mercy of such officers.
ii) The provision of the Citizenship Rules which enable 'every person' (or third parties) to contest the inclusion of the name of a person in the local register is also questioned for it is believed that such a provision may allow 'vested interests' to seep into the process.
iii) It is contended that the Citizenship Rules fail to provide the scope and extent of the private information which would be obtained from citizens for the registers. In fact, the Citizenship Rules leave this aspect for the executive which is impermissible.

The NPR: Questions Raised

The efforts of the government to create a national population register (**NPR**) has also been called into question. The preparation of the NPR has been termed as arbitrary for, amongst other things, the following reasons:

i) An absence on regulation on the NPR process and administration makes it susceptible to misuse as well as a threat to national security.
ii) The concept of the NPR (and the instruction manual issued by the government on the NPR) has been questioned for being sans any legal or legislative basis.

THE GOVERNMENT'S POSITION

The central government has defended and sought to justify every facet of the CAA. The underlying premise of the government is that it is not obligated to redress all wrongs in order to redress some wrongs. The CAA is not a panacea for all problems. Simultaneously, India does not have to provide 'refuge to the entire world'. Summarised below are some chief defences and justifications of the government.

CAA: An Amnesty Mechanism

The CAA is argued to be a specifically tailored law and an ameliorative piece of legislation with the solitary objective of alleviating the 'status' of minorities from neighbouring Islamic states who have come to India to escape religious persecution. The beneficiaries of the CAA are declared minorities in otherwise religious centric states. The government further argues as follows in this regard:

a) The CAA is a benign piece of legislation and must be viewed as an amnesty to specific communities from specific countries with a clear cut-off date. The principal basis of the CAA is to tackle the problem of religious persecution in select countries in light of their theocratic constitutional position.
b) The CAA does not create a legislative bar for grant of citizenship to migrants of the excluded faiths. The provisions of the CAA do not imply that persons falling outside of the Classified Communities and the Classified Countries are perpetually ineligible for grant of Indian citizenship. At the same time, it also does not mean that Indian citizens belonging to communities other than the Classified Communities (i.e. muslim community) are at risk of their citizenship being bridled or taken away by the state.

c) The only impact of the CAA is that its beneficiaries will have a faster avenue for obtaining Indian Citizenship. Consequently, the persons falling outside of the CAA (including the Muslim community) will have to obtain Indian citizenship under normal channels (i.e. in the manner prescribed under the unamended provisions of the Citizenship Act).

CAA: No Infraction of Rights

As per the government, the CAA does not impinge upon any existing rights (whether legal, democratic or secular) of the Indian citizens. It is further argued that the existing regime for obtaining citizenship of India available to all foreigners remains untouched by the CAA. It is further argued that the legal migration into India, on the basis of valid documents and visa, continues to be permissible from all countries of the world including from the three specified countries.

Central Government: Plenary Authority

The government also draws on the fact that the question of entitlement and conferment of citizenship and issues related thereto are within the plenary domain of the legislature. The legislature devises its own legislative policy with respect to the issues concerning the citizenship. It is on the basis of such policy that the CAA has been constructed.

Community Classification: Government Discretion & No Discrimination

It is argued that the extent of relaxations which should be given to the (Indian) citizenship and migration law is the sole prerogative of the central government and a matter of policy. CAA is a case of relaxation and not of prohibition. The general Indian law relating to grant of citizenship to all (including muslims) remains the same.

In so far as the refrain of the critics that the 'CAA has been specifically designed to exclude muslims being granted Indian citizenship' is concerned, the government highlights that in the past few years approximately 500 (five hundred) people from the muslim community have been granted Indian citizenship through the normal channel. In fact, the government clearly contends that the general law for grant of citizenship would continue to be applicable to the muslim community, despite the fact that they are not beneficiaries of the CAA.

The Religious Persecution Dimension

There is much said and argued by both sides on the issue of 'religious persecution' which is a cornerstone of the CAA. The government makes the following principal points on the issue.

CAA: Not a Global Panacea

The government disclaims a universal liability on providing shelter to the persecuted. It is the government's position that the CAA does not seek to recognize all or any kind of purported persecution that may be taking place across the world or that may have taken place previously anywhere in the world.

The government takes a position that the CAA is a humanitarian endeavour to grant benefit to refugees belonging to certain faiths and regions, on the premise of 'religious persecution'. What the CAA really does is that it elevates a certain class of 'aliens' belonging to certain regions over and above other classes of 'aliens'. There exists no obligation of the government (based on the Constitution or the citizenship laws) to provide a solution for all forms of 'religious persecution' or 'persecution' occurring across the globe.

Religious Persecution: Existence

It is argued that the empirical data gathered by the Joint

Parliamentary Committee as well as past experiences establishes religious persecution of such Classified Communities in the Classified Countries. This is coupled with presence of 'state religion' in the Classified Countries, which, *per se*, gives rise to apprehension of religious persecution.[13] Further, this *de facto* situation ought to be viewed from another prism i.e. prevalence of military regimes in these countries, civil wars and other destabilising events on various occasions. Such prevailing circumstances in the Classified Countries accentuate the existing religious persecution problem.[14]

In this regard, it is pertinent to point out that the Joint Parliamentary Committee report highlights various examples and instances of discrimination against minorities in neighbouring Islamic states, including forcible religious conversion, forced study and education of the state religion, usage of Urdu language is the only acceptable medium of instruction in various schools and colleges, denial of government job(s) to minorities, denial of cremation ground to minorities, difficulty in owning houses for residents, difficulty in admission processes for higher education et cetera.

Exclusion of other 'Religiously Persecuted' Communities

As regards the issue that the exclusion of Ahamadis, Shias, Bahaiis, Hazras, Jews or Baloch communities from the first tier of classification is arbitrary and discriminatory, the central government explains thus:

---

13 As per the author, there can be no gainsaying that minorities of a nation (which has a state religion) may be subjected to some level or type of operation or discrimination. The fundamental ethos of a state religion (as opposed to the concept of secularism) is that only one religion is promoted and propagated. In fact, even citizen rights are, in many situations, subject to the state religion. An inherent and natural inclination towards one religion may, routinely, result in denial of rights, benefits, entitlements or privileges for persons belonging to the other religions.

14 The recent events in Afghanistan and the resurgence of the Taliban (a military regime) have added to the woes of the minorities and prompted them to seek safer pastures.

> Intra-religious persecutions or sectarian persecution or persecution due to non-recognition of particular sects to be within the fold of majority religion in the said countries, cannot be equated with the persecution of religious minorities admittedly following and practicing a different and completely distinct religion than the majority religion in particular neighbouring countries.
>
> Further, purported persecution arising out of political movement within the recognised border of the particular neighbouring countries cannot be equated with the systematic religious persecution that the CAA seeks to deal with.

Therefore, in response to the above issue, the government has adopted the following stance(s): (i) the issue of Ahmadiyas, Baloch etc. is a sub-religion issue or a sub-sect issue; (ii) these categories are not minorities in Pakistan and the objective of the CAA is focused only on minorities; (iii) insofar as the Baloch is concerned, it is a sub-national issue in Pakistan having political standpoints. In fact the Baloch are seeking a separate state. Hence, as per the government, the CAA has not been formulated to address such internal issues of neighbouring countries.

In other words, it is the stance of the government that the persecutions discussed above arise due to a variety of reasons none of which are similar to the persecution sought to be addressed by the CAA. It is further explained that the Community Classification made under the CAA is not a panacea for all forms of persecutions which are prevalent in various countries in today's times. Additionally, making a classification with mathematical precision is neither practical nor possible.

The further response of the government on this issue appears to be that muslims are not in minority (in Pakistan, Bangladesh and Afghanistan) and hence not in a precarious position of 'religious persecution'. In any event, even if some segment does face any religious persecution, then they would be in a position to seek asylum in other Islamic countries (which may be a non-feasible option for non-muslims).

The Country Selection

Generally speaking, on the aspect of 'selection of countries', the government contends that the choice of countries included within the ambit of the CAA is to be considered reasonable because all the three countries have a 'past connect' with India and are Islamic States.

Specifically, on the issue of selection of only the 3 (three) neighbouring countries (i.e. Pakistan, Bangladesh and Afghanistan) and the exclusion of other neighbouring countries such as Sri Lanka, Myanmar etc., the government offers the following explanation:

a) The selected countries form a class in themselves in as much as they have a specific state religion within the neighbourhood of India i.e. Islam. The intelligible differentia in the 3 (three) countries is on the basis of their respective constitutions, their geographic locations and the systemic functioning of their organs of state. The constitutional provisions of these countries show how the governance of the said countries is centered on religion i.e. Islam.[15]

---

15 *For example* the Constitution of Pakistan contains the following tenets of Islam on aspects of rule-making and governance: (i) Islam is the state religion of Pakistan; (ii) All laws in Pakistan are required to be in conformity with the principles and injunctions of Islam; (iii) Citizen rights (including the freedom of speech and expression) is subject to restrictions of Islam; (iv) Parliamentary participation is subject to Islam. A person cannot be elected to the Parliament unless, *inter alia*, he has adequate knowledge of Islamic teachings and practises obligatory duties prescribed by Islam; (v) Pakistan has a constitutional court called the Federal Shariat Court (FSC) which is a constitutional court consisting only of Muslim Judges. The said FSC has the overriding power to examine whether the laws of Pakistan are compliant with the injunctions of Islam; (vi) An Islam Council is established for advising as to whether a proposed law is or is not repugnant to the Injunctions of Islam.

b) The inclusion of one particular country in the list and the non-inclusion of other countries is in the domain of legislative decision making and legislative wisdom; and hence cannot be subject of judicial review.
c) The CAA is not meant to be an omnibus solution to issues across the world and the government cannot be expected to take note of possible persecutions that may be taking place across various countries in the world.
d) It is further argued that the CAA, in no manner whatsoever, makes religion a basis of determining citizenship of a person.

The government further counters by arguing that the CAA also results in non-grant of any exemptions to other non-muslim communities from the neighbouring countries who also may be facing 'religious persecution' (such as the Tibetan Buddhists from China and Tamil Hindus from Sri Lanka) and therefore, the assertion that the CAA attempts to classify the persons belonging only to the muslim community as 'illegal migrants' has no basis in law or in fact.

The Right to Equality Argument

The design of the CAA has been viewed as antithetical to the fundamental tenets of Article 14 of the Constitution (i.e. equality for all). However, this perception is challenged by the government on the following premise:

a) The well recognised exception engrained under Article 14 is 'reasonable classification made on the basis of intelligible differentia'. In other words, any classification made on the basis of intelligible differentia will not fall foul of Article 14 of the Constitution. The government claims to be within the four corners of this exception.
b) It is argued that the selection of the Classified

Communities (under the CAA) has a reasonable rationale. Each of the Classified Communities is a recognised 'minority' in the 3 (three) religion centric (Islamic) neighbouring countries with a stated history of religion based persecution. Hence, the classification of the beneficiaries of the CAA has a reasonable basis.

c) The CAA has a nexus with intelligible differentia. Only minorities from the 3 (three) Classified Countries are the beneficiaries of the CAA.
d) Courts should not second guess the wisdom of the parliament under Article 14 of the Constitution.
e) Separately, the *Joint Committee Report* records the government's stance that the amendments to the Citizenship Act does not violate Article 14 of the Constitution in as much as it upholds the test of reasonable classification as propounded by the Supreme Court in **State of West Bengal v. Anwar Ali Sarkar**.[16] The Report records thus:

> The Department of Legal Affairs have submitted that differential treatment does not per se constitute violation of Article 14 of the Constitution. It has been very lucidly explained that any legislation may withstand challenge on the ground of discrimination and violation of Article 14 of the Constitution, in case the classification created by it is founded on an intelligible differentia which distinguishes persons or things that are grouped together from others left out of the group, and that differentia has a rational relation to the object sought to be achieved by the statute in question. The Department have further clarified that the positive concept of equality does not postulate equal treatment of all persons

16 AIR 1952 SC 75.

> without distinction but rather stresses on equality of treatment in equal circumstances as to similarly situated persons and the Bill appears to have the object of facilitating all such members of minority communities without any discrimination."

THE CUT-OFF DATE

The government defends the inclusion of a cut-off date in the CAA by stating that India has never had an 'open ended provision' for citizenship. The Parliament has never intended the grant of citizenship or the criterion governing the citizenship to be open ended.

At this juncture, as per the author, it is important to point out that the concept of cut-off date is integral to any immigration legislation. Speaking in the Indian context, the concept of a cut-off date (for determination of citizenship) was introduced for the first time through the Assam Accord (and Section 6A of the Citizenship Act). The subsequent amendments to the Citizenship Act (in the years 1987, 1992 and 2003) had cut-off dates for various purposes of determination of citizenship. It may be an easy task to make a justified basis for every cut-off date introduced in this or other similar context.

Cut off dates and baseline(s) relating to migration and citizenship have always been a contentious issue. Interestingly, during the implementation of the Assam Accord, the cut-off date of 01.01.1966 therein was questioned and challenged by various parties.

In similar fashion, the cut-off date under the CAA is also in the line of fire. As per the author, there may not be an explanation or basis behind the cut-off date. But the real question is, whether is it always possible to have a precise and plausible explanation for deciding baselines in such delicate matters. No matter what baseline or periphery is decided, there will always be people on both sides of the fence either hailing or questioning it.

Treatment of Stateless Persons and Refugees

While the author has not been able to trace any recorded government response on this issue, it is however pertinent to take note of the following on the application of the concept of refoulement to the Indian scenario:

a) India is neither a signatory to nor has ratified the 1951 Refugee Convention or the 1967 Protocol. In fact, India does not have any refugee law in place. Under Indian law, all refugees are to be regarded as 'illegal migrants'.
b) The CAA may not be interpreted in accordance with international conventions or treaties to which India is not a signatory or a participant.

It is also important to point out that recently, the Manipur High Court,[17] while addressing the case of certain refugees from Myanmar (who are seeking provisional protection from deportation) and while passing an interim order, observed that the principle against refoulement i.e. the forcible return of refugees to a country where they are liable to be subjected to persecution can be *prima facie* read into Article 21 of the Constitution (a fundamental right which is available to non-citizens as well). This interim observation was made by the High Court while being mindful and conscious of the fact that India is not a signatory to the Geneva Refugee Convention, 1951 or the New York Protocol, 1967. A somewhat similar view was recently taken by the Delhi High Court which observed that the principle of non-refoulement may be taken as part of the guarantee under Article 21 of the Constitution since it affects/protects the life and liberty of a human being, irrespective of his nationality. The High Court further went on to make a caveat while such

17 Nandita Haksar v. Union of India, W.P. (Crl.) No. 6/2021 (20.04.2021, Manipur High Court).

protection ought to be available to refugees, however, it must not be at the expense of national security of the country.[18]

At the same time, it is also important to highlight a recent order of the Supreme Court of India in **Mohammad Salimullah v. Union of India**[19] wherein the Supreme Court refused to intervene and stall a proposed deportation of Rohingya refugees housed in various detention centres across India. These refugees had left their homeland Myanmar to escape ethnic violence. The refugee community had, *inter alia*, sought to invoke the principles of non-refoulement in an effort to impress upon the court to prevent the government from deporting the refugees. The submissions of the refugees and the government are highly relevant and are summarised below.

Broadly, the refugee community had sought to make the following points before the Supreme Court: (i) the principle of non-refoulement is a part of Article 21 of the Constitution; (ii) India is a signatory of the Universal Declaration of Human Rights, 1948, International Covenant on Civil and Political Rights, 1966 and the Convention on the Rights of Child, 1992 and hence bound by the principles of non-refoulement; (iii) India is a also a signatory to the Protection of All Persons against Enforced Disappearances, Convention against Torture and other Cruel and Inhuman or Degrading Treatment or Punishment; (iv) The International Court of Justice in one of its recent judgements, had taken note of genocide of Rohingyas in Myanmar and there was an imminent danger to their lives in Myanmar.

The government on the other hand, made the following principal responses: (i) the persons sought to be deported were foreigners within the meaning of Section 2 (a) of the Foreigners Act, 1946 and the central government was empowered to regulate, restrict and prohibit movement

18 Dongh Lian Kham v. Union of India, W.P. (Crl.) No. 1884/2015 (21.12.2015, Delhi High Court).

19 I.A No. 38048/2021 in W.P. (C) No. 793/2017 (08.04.2021, Supreme Court of India).

of foreigners in India; (ii) India was not a signatory to the primary instrument relating to refugees *viz.* United Nations Convention on the Status of Refugees 1951 or to its Protocol of 1967 and the principle of non-refoulement applied only to contracting states; (iii) India has porous borders with many countries and hence there existed a continuous threat of influx of illegal migrants; (iv) influx of illegal migrants pose a serious threat to national security; (v) foreigners (or non-citizens) have no right to reside and settle in India which right is available only to Indian citizens by virtue of Article 19 (1) (g) of the Constitution; (vi) intelligence agencies had raised a serious concern about the threat to the internal security of the country on account of illegal migrants.

The Supreme Court in its order, amongst other things, while taking note of the stance of the central government regarding threat to internal security and the proliferation of touts providing entry to illegal migrants into India through porous borders, refused to stay the deportation of the detainees.

Articles 15 & 19 of the Constitution

On the aspect of Article 15 & 19 of the Constitution, the government clarifies that rights under Article 15 are available only to Indian citizens and not to illegal migrants or other foreigners and there is nothing in the CAA which discriminates, or places any disability, liability, restriction or condition on Indian citizens.[20] A similar position is adopted by the government with respect to Article 19 of the Constitution.

Article 21 of the Constitution

On the aspect of Article 21 of the Constitution, the government states that the CAA, by itself, does not result in expulsion/

20 The government has maintained a consistent stance that the CAA does not affect the citizenship status of Indian Muslims.

deportation/refoulement of illegal migrants. All that the CAA does is provide certain relaxations with respect to certain settled principles of citizenship. The government clarifies that the regime concerning the expulsion/deportation/refoulement of persons who may be classified as 'illegal migrants' is governed by other statutes (i.e. the Foreigners Act) with which the CAA has nothing to do.

CAA and Secularism

The CAA has been criticised for being an antithesis to the concept of secularism. The government defends this by contending that under Indian law, any person of any religion from any country in the world can legally travel/migrate to India, satisfy the conditions stipulated in the Citizenship Act and become an Indian citizen. Therefore, there is no question of the CAA doing violence to the principle of secularism.

NRC: The Defence

The legal provisions regarding the National Register of Citizens (i.e. Section 14A of the Citizenship Act) have been in force since December, 2004. The government argues that the preparation of a national register of citizens is a necessary exercise for any sovereign country for identification of citizens from non-citizens.

The government explains that in terms of the extant relevant laws on the subject (i.e. the citizenship law, passport law and foreigners law), there exists a bounden responsibility on it to identify/detect illegal migrants and foreigners, and thereafter, follow the due process of law.[21] In other words, the NRC exercise is only an extension of its primary duty of detecting illegal migrants in India.

---

21 Rights available to a foreigner do not include the right to reside and settle in India. Such a right is only available to Indian citizens. *See* Anand Swaroop Verma v. Union of India, W.P. (Crl.) No. 773/2002 (08.08.2002, Delhi High Court).

On this score, the government further contends that there is a system of maintaining a register of their citizens. In fact, national identification cards are issued based upon the exercise of identification of citizens in these countries. Even in Afghanistan, Bangladesh and Pakistan there is a system of issuance of such cards. In fact the government argues that such system is prevalent in various parts of the globe where identity cards are issued pursuant to a citizenship identification/verification exercise.

CHAPTER 11

The Amendments to the Citizenship Act: Position in Assam

INTRODUCTION

Assam has a special place and status under the Indian citizenship law regime. Historically, special laws have enacted for the purpose of protecting the state from illegal migration (from Bangladesh) and for preserving its indigenous populace.

Assam has witnessed wide protests in the wake of the CAA. However, the protests in Assam highlight certain (additional) issues (which are unique to the north-east region of the country). This chapter attempts to briefly discuss these aspects.

The previous chapter discusses the criticisms and justifications of the CAA in general. This chapter is essentially an extension of the preceding chapter and attempts to highlight the various sides of the controversy concerning the CAA specifically in the context of Assam. It may be said that, in the context of Assam, the protest essentially revolves around 'Assamese versus non-Assamese'. Religion or faith has little importance in this discourse. The challenge to the CAA is *sub-judice* before the Supreme Court of India.

ASSAM: A HOTBED OF ILLEGAL MIGRATION

Assam is a hotbed of illegal migration (especially from Bangladesh). Publicly released data has suggested drastic changes in the population pattern of Assam, as a result of such migration.

The state of affairs in Assam, owing to large scale illegal migration, was recently crystallised by the Guwahati High Court in the case of **Shah Mohammed Anowar Ali v. State of Assam.**[1] The observations of the High Court clearly describe the problematic situation prevailing in Assam owing to 'illegal migration'.

a) Bangladeshi nationals can easily enter into Assam mostly without any valid documents and stay back illegally. The borders are porous and only namesake.
b) Most of the illegal migrants enjoy the rights of Indian citizens, including voting rights. Even the state and central functionaries are helpless on this aspect.
c) Even if the illegal Bangladeshi migrants are identified and determined by the Foreigners Tribunals, they can easily do a vanishing act and the state administration is mostly unable to detect them. In most cases, the illegal migrants are able to successfully elude the authorities. Further, their names are also not deleted from the voter list without direction of the court.
d) Such illegal Bangladeshi migrants can have the luxury of maintaining establishments and family members both in Bangladesh and in Assam with easy passage to and fro.
e) The court lamented the lack of responsiveness on the part of the government authorities in cases where the order(s) of the Foreigners Tribunals were challenged before the court.
f) The court also held that in view of the prevailing situation (as described above) the purpose of establishment of a Foreigners Tribunals would be defeated.
g) In view of the above position, there exists no doubt that the indigenous people of Assam will be reduced to minority in near future, if not already reduced.

1 W.P. No. 7036/2005 (31.01.2014, Guwahati High Court).

It is in this context and background that the Assam NRC was directed by the Supreme Court in the year 2014. The purpose of the Assam NRC was primarily two-fold: (i) To rid the state of illegal migrants who had no locus to settle in India; and (ii) To create and maintain a document or database (i.e. a National Register) containing record/details of all legitimate and genuine Indian citizens residing in Assam.[2]

THE CAA DEBATE: ASSAM CONTEXT

The CAA debate in the context of Assam contains varied dimensions which are unique and peculiar to that region. One primary worry of the indigenous people of Assam is that the CAA will benefit Bengali speaking Hindus who have 'illegally migrated' from Bangladesh and have settled in large numbers across the state. The concern is that such beneficiaries will outnumber the local population of Assam which will result in a Tripura like situation where such Hindus have taken centre stage and pushed the local tribal population to the fringes. The indigenous Assamese appear to be generally against the CAA and unlike the other parts of the country (where the main argument is discrimination of Muslims), in Assam, neither migrant Hindus nor migrant Muslims appear to be welcome by its indigenous populace. Hence, the Assam CAA debate is on an entirely different footing.

In the Assam context, the CAA has been questioned for various reasons, including for having violated the Assam Accord, having defeated the Assam NRC and having violated the Constitution.

A slew of petitions have been filed in the Supreme Court of India questioning and assailing the CAA especially in the context of Assam and Tripura. It is argued that, when it comes

2 This register would serve as an important tool for checking and correcting 'illegal migration' into Assam (both at present and in future).

to the CAA, the situation of the 'Northeast' is different from the rest of the country. In fact, the Supreme Court has, in its wisdom, segregated the petitions pertaining to the Northeast regions from the rest of the petitions concerning the CAA in general.[3]

Amongst others, the following critical issues arise:

a) Whether the CAA directly conflicts with the Assam Accord (and Section 6A of the Citizenship Act) which provides for removal of all illegal migrants (irrespective of their ethnic or religious background) who had come to Assam post 24.03.1971.
b) Whether the CAA discriminates against the illegal migrants belonging to the muslim community who have been excluded from the final list of the Assam NRC since they would never get an opportunity to remove their 'illegal migrant' status, would not get an opportunity to become 'Indian citizens', and consequently would never be able to get their names included in the Assam NRC. In other words, such non-classified communities may not get 'a shot at citizenship', unlike their (similarly placed) peers belonging to the classified communities.

Some of the pertinent questions and challenges to the CAA (specific to the context of Assam) are highlighted below.

Conflict with the Assam Accord

A principal argument against the CAA is that it flies in the face of the Assam Accord (and Section 6A of the Citizenship Act). The CAA has been perceived to be highly inimical to the indigenous people of Assam and the structure/demographic

3 *See* https://www.ndtv.com/india-news/citizenship-act-caa-case-north-east-is-different-say-assam-tripura-protesters-after-top-court-on-caa-2168166

pattern of the state, especially in light of the Assam Accord which provided that all persons (irrespective of religion) entering Assam post 24.03.1971 were to be identified and removed from the state.[4] The influx of illegal migration from Bangladesh is alleged to have been a major reason behind the change in demographic pattern of as well as the perennial state of unrest in the north eastern states of India including Assam, Meghalaya, Tripura etc.

It is contended that, in the context of Assam, the CAA dilutes the previous cut-off date (i.e. 24.03.1971) and introduces a new cut-off date (i.e. 31.12.2014). In other words, illegal migrants (belonging to classified communities) who entered Assam between 25.03 1971 and 31.1.2014 would now be in a position to get the protection of the CAA and get an opportunity to regularise their status in India. Without the CAA, such persons would have, by virtue of Section 6 A of the Citizenship Act and the Assam Accord, been liable to be deported from India.

The Reconciliation Efforts

During the course of discussions of the Citizenship Amendment Bill, it was stressed by various stakeholders that any changes to the Citizenship Act (in the context of Assam) ought to be done in line with the provisions of the Assam Accord and Section 6A of the Citizenship Act so as to protect the indigenous people of Assam and to prevent deprivation of their homeland and linguistic homogeneity. Various proposals (mentioned below) were made in a bid to avoid any perceivable collision with the Assam Accord. However, none of the suggestions seem to have been accepted.

4 It is pertinent to note that the contours of the provisions of Sections 3 and also 6A of the Citizenship Act are pending consideration before the Constitution Bench of the Supreme Court in W.P.(C) No. 562/2012 and W.P.(C) No. 311/2015.

a) Exemption of Assam from the purview of the CAA: The first proposal was to exempt Assam from the purview of the CAA. In effect, this proposal meant that the benefit of the CAA would not be available to illegal migrants who had come to or were residing in Assam. This proposal may have had the effect of resolving many potential controversies on the subject.
b) Removal of Bangladesh from the list of classified countries under the CAA: A second proposal (an alternative to the previous proposal) was to remove Bangladesh as a classified nation from the CAA. This proposal appears to have been made because illegal migration to Assam has been predominantly from Bangladesh and keeping Bangladesh out of the discourse could have been a 'practical solution' to the problem.
c) Removal of the beneficiary communities from the state of Assam: A third concurrent proposal was made which revolved around providing a (disincentive) to the beneficiaries of the CAA for residing in Assam and (incentive) for moving to other parts of the country. This proposal essentially provided that the beneficiaries of the CAA who would be ultimately successful in obtaining Indian citizenship should not be given any state benefits if they decide to (or continue to) reside in Assam.
d) Distribution of CAA Beneficiaries across the Country: A fourth proposal (in line with the third proposal) was that the central government should take an initiative to distribute the beneficiaries of the CAA in the entire country so as to avoid pressure on any specific state/region.

Inclusion of Bangladesh to the CAA: A Fundamental Issue

As discussed previously, the inclusion of Bangladesh to the CAA is argued to 'strike at the root of the Assam Accord'. In fact, a principal objective of the Assam Accord (in the year 1985) was to stem the 'Bangladesh migration problem' and the CAA is argued to have 'undone this'.

In a bid to avoid a conflict with the Assam Accord, a suggestion for removal of Bangladesh (from the list of beneficiary countries) was made during the Parliamentary deliberations (prior to enactment of the CAA). However, this suggestion was rejected by the government for being against the stated purpose and object of the amendment. *The Joint Committee Report* records thus:

> The Government have, therefore, contended that if Bangladesh is kept out of the purview of the proposed Amendment, such migrants from Bangladesh who do not have all or any of the travel documents or whose travel documents have expired, shall continue to remain as 'illegal migrants' under Section 2 of the Principal Act and shall not be eligible to apply for Indian citizenship. As the intent of the Government is to enable the migrants who have come from Bangladesh on or before 31 December, 2014 due to religious persecution or fear of religious persecution and who have entered India with incomplete, expired or no documents, to apply for Indian citizenship, the Committee are of the considered view that keeping Bangladesh out of the purview of the proposed Amendments would negate the very objects and reasons of bringing in the Bill. The Committee, therefore, do not agree with the suggestion received from some quarters that Bangladesh be kept out of the purview of the proposed Amendments and thus the Committee concur with the Government's proposal.

Violation of Provisions of the Constitution

In the Assam context, the CAA is argued to have violated several provisions of the Constitution. The chief criticism in this regard is summarised below.

Article 14 of the Constitution

As noted earlier, the regions/areas kept outside the scope of the CAA include the tribal areas of Assam and the areas falling under the Inner Line notified under the Bengal Eastern Frontier Regulation, 1873 (i.e. Mizoram, Nagaland, Arunachal Pradesh and Manipur). The basis of such exemption/exclusion (as mentioned in the Statement of Objects and Reasons to the CAA) is 'to protect the indigenous population of the northeastern states of India'.

Therefore, while the states of Mizoram, Nagaland, Arunachal Pradesh and Manipur have been excluded from the purview of the CAA (i.e. the Inner Line), however, the entire state of Assam has not been excluded (only the tribal regions of Assam have been excluded). In other words, the 'entire northeastern region of India' which 'geographically includes Assam' has not been excluded. The act of non-exclusion of the entire state of Assam (in contrast to the remaining northeastern region) has been argued to be violative of Article 14 of the Constitution.

Separately, the CAA, in its application, divides Assam into 'tribal' and 'non-tribal' regions. It is argued that the classification of Assam into tribal and non-tribal region (for the purpose of the CAA) has no rational nexus to its stated objective (of protecting the indigenous population of the northeastern states) because the 'indigenous population of the northeast' is spread across the state of Assam and is not only limited to the tribal areas. Also, not exempting the entire state of Assam (which is a historic red zone in the context of illegal influx) as against the other northeastern states (which have been fully excluded) is alleged to be bereft of basis and validity. These aspects, it is contented, further makes the CAA violative of Article 14 of the Constitution.

Article 21 of the Constitution

Another line of argument is that the illegal migration (until 2014) which is sought to be condoned by the CAA affects the 'right to life' of the citizens of Assam since the influx has led to invasion of their 'right to live with human dignity'.

It is contented that the CAA violates Article 21 of the Constitution because the life and personal liberty of the people of Assam shall be adversely affected by regularisation of the large number of illegal migrants who have come to Assam from Bangladesh and have been adversely affecting the demographic nature as well as the socioeconomic condition of the state, apart from risking internal security of the state.

Article 29 of the Constitution

Article 29 (1) of the Constitution provides for, *inter alia*, protection of interests of minorities. It provides rights to minority communities to conserve their language, script and culture.

It is argued that the act of regularisation of a vast number of 'illegal migrants' in Assam through the CAA would result in erosion of the ethnic identity of its indigenous masses.

Article 355 of the Constitution

Article 355 of the Constitution obligates the Union of India to protect every Indian state against external aggression and internal disturbance. In **Sonowal I Judgement**, the Supreme Court of India, *inter alia*, opined that Assam was facing 'external aggression' and 'internal disturbance'. Thereafter, in the Assam NRC Judgement, the Supreme Court held that the Union had failed in its obligation of protection of states enjoined under Article 355 of the Constitution.

It is argued that the CAA (by condoning illegal migration) would result in 'further aggression and disturbance' thereby violating Article 355 of the Constitution. It is further argued that the CAA also conflicts with the **Sonowal I Judgement**.

Increased Migration to Assam

As discussed previously, several northeastern states such as Meghalya, Arunachal Pradesh etc. have been kept outside the scope of the CAA. Put differently, illegal migrants in these states, even if otherwise eligible to take the benefit of the CAA, will be precluded from doing so, on account of the said region being excluded from the scope of the CAA.

Hence, with the exclusion of such (other) northeastern regions from the purview of the CAA, it is contented that Assam (which remains un-excluded) is likely to face the brunt because migrants (from the other northeastern states) will be encouraged to shift/relocate to Assam and seek to project themselves as residents of Assam in order to seek benefit of the CAA.

Jeopardy to the Assam NRC

It is argued that the CAA (with its pro-illegal migration undertones) may jeopardize the ongoing NRC exercise in Assam. It is believed that the CAA will upset the process of the NRC because many persons who have been excluded from the NRC will now seek benefit under the CAA and claim a re-inclusion in the NRC. The entire NRC exercise undertaken till date under the supervision of the Supreme Court may be undone in the process.

It is said that the principal objective of the Assam NRC (i.e. to weed out illegal migrants) runs counter to the ethos of the CAA which, in effect, regularises and legalises illegal migration. It is argued that the CAA has been designed for the benefit of such excluded persons.[5]

On the other side of the spectrum, there exists a counter argument in favour of the CAA on this aspect. It is argued that a large number of Bengali speaking Assamese community have

5 It begs mention that the amendments to the Citizenship Act (which proposed benefit to the Classified Communities) had been first proposed in the year 2016 when the Assam NRC was at its preliminary stages. The final results of the Assam NRC could not be known at that time.

become 'suspect' citizens and have been harassed by the system in various ways over the years. The CAA (which will benefit this community) will put an end to their trials and tribulations; and help normalise their existence in Assam.

The United Nations Declaration on the Rights of Indigenous Peoples

It is contended that the CAA endangers the position of the indigenous populace of Assam and is hence violative of the United Nations Declaration on the Rights of Indigenous Peoples (UNDRIP). The UNDRIP was adopted by the General Assembly on 13.09.2007 and is one of the most comprehensive international instrument on the rights of indigenous peoples. It establishes a universal framework of minimum standards for the survival, dignity and well-being of the indigenous peoples of the world and it elaborates on existing human rights standards and fundamental freedoms as they apply to the specific situation of indigenous peoples. The UNDRIP addresses both individual and collective rights, cultural rights and identity, rights to education, health, employment, language, and others. The text says indigenous peoples have the right to fully enjoy as a collective or as individuals, all human rights and fundamental freedoms as recognized in the Charter of the United Nations, the Universal Declaration of Human Rights and the rest of international human rights law.[6] India is a signatory to the UNDRIP.[7]

Part II of the Constitution of India

Part II of the Indian Constitution relates to the aspect of citizenship (discussed in detail in the preceding chapters). The following 2

6 *See generally* https://www.un.org/development/desa/indigenouspeoples/declaration-on-the-rights-of-indigenous-peoples.html

7 Please note that UN Declarations are generally not legally binding. *See also* Article 50 (c) of the Constitution.

(two) principal arguments are being made by the critics of the CAA to allege a violation on this aspect: (i) The Constitution does not contain any provision which permits or authorises the central government to make laws permitted or condoning 'illegal migration'; and (ii) The Constitution does not contain a 'right to return' mechanism similar to that of Israel which permits Jews to return to Israel from anywhere in the world.[8] Hence, it is argued that a return of 'ethnic Indians' to India with full consequential benefits (in the manner sought to be done by the CAA) falls foul of the provisions of the Constitution.

Violation of the Immigrants (Expulsion from Assam) Act, 1950

As discussed previously, the Immigrants (Expulsion from Assam) Act, 1950 has its genesis in the large scale migration that had commenced from East Pakistan (erstwhile Bangladesh) into Assam as a consequence of the Partition in 1947. Under this law, the central government reserved with itself the right to expel any person who migrated to Assam from outside India and whose stay was detrimental to the interests of the people of Assam and the general public of India. It is thus being argued that the CAA (where it legalises the status of illegal migrants from Bangladesh to Assam) conflicts with the provisions of the Immigrants (Expulsion from Assam) Act, 1950.

Government Clarification on CAA and NRC

Recently, the Press Information Bureau, Government of India, released a questionnaire on the NRC wherein various

8 It needs to be borne in mind that the Indian Constitution only clarified the citizenship status and position on the date of its enforcement (i.e. in 1950). Article 11 of the Constitution ought to be seen in the context of this argument because it fills the gap on issues of citizenship and allows the Parliament to make laws relating to the aspect of citizenship. The Citizenship Act was enacted in 1955 to cover all aspects relating to (present and future) citizenship laws and processes.

clarifications were sought to be made on various aspects of the CAA and the NRC in general as well as in specific to the NRC exercise.[9] Mentioned below is a summary of such clarifications.

Interrelation between the CAA and the NRC

There is no inter relationship between the CAA and the NRC. While the CAA has been implemented, a nation-wide NRC is only under contemplation with no final decision on its implementation. Presently, the NRC is going on in Assam pursuant to the Assam Accord and orders of the Supreme Court.

Potential Impact of the CAA and the NRC on Indian Muslims

Both the CAA and the NRC have no impact on any Indian citizen of any religion.

Relationship between NRC and religion

NRC has nothing to do with religion. NRC is for every citizen of India. It is a citizen register in which the names of every citizen will be recorded. Whenever the NRC will be implemented, it will neither be on the basis of religion nor can it be implemented on the basis of religion. Hence, no one can be excluded from the citizens register merely on the basis of his/her faith.

Difference between the NRC exercise for Assam and the NRC exercise in general

The basis of NRC in Assam is the Assam Accord and the Supreme Court rulings. However, for the rest of the country, the NRC, if carried out, shall be on the basis of the Citizenship (Registration of Citizens and Issue of National Identity Cards) Rules 2003.

9 *See* https://www.hindustantimes.com/india-news/government-releases-q-a-on-national-register-of-citizens-nrc/story-xdrAd6jGcOIXTKs0TqNcDN.html

Proof of Indian Citizenship

Citizenship can be proved by submitting documents relating to date of birth and place of birth. However, a decision is yet to be taken on the acceptable documents. This is likely to include voter card, passport, Aadhar card, license, insurance papers, birth certificate, school leaving certificate, documents relating to land and home or similar documents issued by the government officials.

Whenever the NRC is announced at the national level, then rules and instructions will be made for it in such a way that no one will face any trouble. The government has no intention of harassing its citizens or putting them in trouble.

In case the persons do not have adequate documents to prove citizenship, then in such case the authorities will create alternative verification mechanisms such as bringing in a witness, community verification etc. Needless to state, a proper procedure will be followed.

THE ASSAM NRC AND THE CAA

As discussed previously, the primary objective of the Assam NRC exercise was to identify illegal migrants in the state (coming essentially from Bangladesh) and to take adequate steps for their detention and consequent deportation. The underlying idea was protection of the original inhabitants/population of the state.

Critics of the CAA 'link' the CAA with the Assam NRC and attribute its genesis to the said NRC exercise.

The final list of the Assam NRC published in August 2019 excluded approximately 19 (nineteen) lakh people, which included both Hindus and Muslims. It is argued that the one of the reasons behind introducing the CAA and extending it to Assam was to provide a 'new channel' or 'avenue' for reinstatement of the Hindus, including those who were excluded pursuant to the NRC exercise, by presenting them with an opportunity to get their status in India regularised and legalised. It is further argued that the CAA may have the result of 'undoing' the Assam NRC.

The Assam Context: Interplay between the CAA and the NRC

The government has, time and again, emphasised that the CAA and the NRC are not interrelated.[10] The questionnaire issued by the Press Information Bureau, Government of India (discussed above) completely disclaims any inter-relationship between the CAA and the NRC. However, as per the author, in the context of Assam (a special case situation), one may argue that the paths of CAA and NRC 'appear' to converge, especially in keeping with the fact that the NRC exercise is ongoing in Assam. This may be better explained in a point wise manner.

a) As mentioned previously, Assam has been a hub of illegal migration especially from Bangladesh (one of the Classified Countries under the CAA).
b) The Assam Accord (as also Section 6A of the Citizenship Act) were brought into effect for the purpose of detection, determination and deportation of illegal migrants who had entered post 24.03.1971. Pertinently, the definition of 'illegal migrant' by itself, is not 'community or faith specific'. Further, no distinctions, exceptions or relaxations are made either in the Assam Accord or under Section 6A of the Citizenship Act in this regard. In other words, all illegal migrants, regardless of their religion or region, are to be targeted by the government as per the Assam Accord.
c) The Supreme Court of India has, on various occasions, dealt with the Assam issue and directed steps to stem the

10 The previous chapters discuss the relationship between the CAA and the NRC in general.

problem of illegal migrants into Assam, including fencing of borders, setting up of foreigner tribunals, streamlining deportation etc.

d) Admittedly, the state of Assam is not excluded from the CAA. Data also suggests that a vast majority of illegal migrants in Assam have come from Bangladesh. Also, many such illegal migrants belong to the Classified Communities and have come from Bangladesh fleeing 'religious persecution'. In other words, such persons will be eligible to take the benefit of the CAA.

e) Presently, the population density of Assam is high. The Assam NRC exercise is not yet finally concluded. In such a situation, granting an opportunity to illegal migrants from Bangladesh (who already reside in large numbers in Assam) an option to legitimize their stay in Assam may dilute and defeat the Assam Accord.

f) In sum and substance, evidently, the history of Assam on the issue of illegal migration is slightly different from that of the rest of India. Apparently, it is not about 'religion' or 'religious prosecution'.

g) The effect of applying CAA to the state of Assam may result in the following situation. Illegal migrants belonging to the Classified Communities coming from Bangladesh would be in a position to be regularised. Consequently, they would be in a position to acquire Indian citizenship upon completion of the (reduced) naturalisation term. One can safely assume that many of such beneficiaries would presently be excluded from the final list of the Assam NRC (it is noteworthy that more than 20 lakh persons have been excluded from the final NRC list and many such persons have assailed such exclusion in courts of law). However, on account of the application of the CAA, they would suddenly find themselves eligible for citizenship and consequently for inclusion in the

NRC as well. This will certainly affect the ongoing NRC exercise in Assam as also the ongoing litigation in various forums regarding their exclusion from the final list of the NRC.

It remains to be seen how the obligations of the government towards the people of Assam would be balanced with their 'other objective' of 'protecting the persecuted communities' which is sought to be achieved by the CAA. In case the CAA passes muster in court then in such case, it would be interesting to see its interplay with Section 6A of the Citizenship Act.

CHAPTER 12

CAA & NRC: The Road Ahead

INTRODUCTION

The previous chapters of this book describe the various aspects of the Indian Citizenship and Immigration law regime, including the key features of the Citizenship Amendment Act (CAA), its various criticisms and justifications. As discussed previously, the CAA (as also its accompanying aspects) is subject matter of challenge before the Supreme Court of India and the matter is *sub-judice*. In fact various Indian states (such as Kerala, Punjab etc.) have also questioned and challenged the CAA with some states openly claiming that the CAA would not be implemented by them in their states.[1]

Assuming the CAA and the NRC (and their corresponding aspects) are able to withstand judicial scrutiny of the Supreme Court, the central government will have to contend with and tackle a wide variety of possible issues, situations and challenges in connection thereto, including the modalities of grant of citizenship to the beneficiaries of the CAA, creation of nationwide NRC, detection and deportation of foreigners etc. This chapter attempts to analyse the road ahead for the CAA and NRC.

1 Citizenship is a List I subject and hence under the exclusive domain of the central government.

THE NATIONAL REGISTER OF CITIZENS: A NATIONWIDE EXERCISE

The Assam NRC exercise was the first of its kind and an uphill task for the government. As discussed previously, various hurdles and challenges were faced by the government during the exercise. New issues continue to emerge to this day and are being tackled by the government on an ongoing basis. Numerous lessons have been learnt from the Assam NRC and this experience will benefit the government going forward.

The ruling dispensation appears to indicate the conduct of a NRC on a nationwide basis. Conduct of a NRC on a national platform, if any, will be a monumental exercise, both from an economic as well as a logistical standpoint. The government will have to learn from past experience and create adequate processes and procedures for streamlining the entire activity so as to reduce the pain and trouble for all stakeholders, as also to avoid unwarranted harassment to the citizens. This section attempts to analyse the various 'on the ground' aspects of the NRC.

Nationwide NRC: The Necessity Argument

From a necessity point of view, one cannot argue with the position that India has faced the brunt of large-scale illegal migration since the time of Partition. The state functionaries have been able to do little to stem this (almost) perennial problem. Under such circumstances, the author feels that it may not be wrong for the nation to make an effort to identify the citizens from the non-citizens. Just because a foreigner has illegally resided in India for a long time may not be a justified reason to let them be and look the other way. However, at the same time, the mode and manner in which the identification process is made is critical. A process riddled with arbitrariness and bias would be counter-productive.

Presently, there is no certainty on whether there actually will be a nation-wide NRC exercise.[2] The rumours and speculations around it have already sparked protests and condemnations. Evidently, such protests are being made on an 'anticipation' of persecution by the government along religious lines. According to the author, while a process of identifying the citizens from the non-citizens is desirable, there exists a corresponding obligation of the state to carry it out in a non-arbitrary, unbiased, non-discriminatory and transparent manner. The current dispensation has given various public assurances that all citizens need not fear or worry about the NRC exercise being arbitrary or whimsical. One hopes that the government will stay true to its word.

Costs to Exchequer

The sheer exercise of carrying out an NRC on a PAN India basis will be a time-consuming and costly affair. Add to that the costs and delays on account of consequent litigation by persons who are not included in the final list. Further add the additional burden of maintaining and sustaining the 'detected' illegal migrants in detention centres.

As per the author, before embarking upon such an exercise, an analysis of the costs is an aspect which needs to be factored in along with the (other) clear and present national priorities.

The Statelessness Conundrum

The issue of 'statelessness' of the illegal migrants should be a big concern for the government. The NRC exercise in Assam as well as heightened adjudication of citizenship by the Foreigners Tribunals has resulted in detention for a large number of people.

2 *See* https://pib.gov.in/PressReleseDetail.aspx?PRID=1744502 which indicates that there is no decision of the government yet on this score.

The NRC exercise will inevitably result in detection, detention and deportation of illegal migrants from India to the home state. But it is not always that the home state 'acknowledges and recognises' its own. Take the case of Bangladesh (from where a large number of illegal migrants come into India). It is public knowledge that Bangladesh has, in recent times shown reluctance in accepting persons who India determines to be 'a foreigner from Bangladesh'. These events can result in a situation of 'statelessness' for such persons and perhaps 'indefinite detention' in India without any foreseeable recourse. There will be a further issue of 'statelessness of children or minors'. A child born in India to a couple, one of whom is declared an 'illegal migrant' (in terms of Indian citizenship laws) will not be eligible to be an Indian citizen. This may result in the child being classified as 'stateless'.

India is not a signatory to the United Nations Convention on the Reduction of Statelessness, 1961 or the Convention relating to the Status of Stateless Persons, 1954 (the two primary treaties on the aspect of statelessness and treatment to stateless persons).[3]

The Indian Refugee Policy

India does not have a static domestic policy dealing with stateless persons and refugees.[4] India is not a signatory to the

3 As per the author, any activity which results in 'excessive statelessness' may violate the provisions of the Universal Declaration of Human Rights, 1948 (of which India is a signatory) which provides as follows: (i) every person has the right to seek and enjoy in other countries, asylum from persecution (Article 14 thereof); and (ii) no person should be arbitrarily deprived of his nationality (Article 15 thereof). It may also be violative of the United Nations Convention on the Rights of the Child, 1990 (which India has ratified).

4 In India, a foreigner seeking asylum is required to apply for and obtain a certificate from the UNHCR. In the absence of a national legislation, UNHCR determines who is refugee on the basis of the Convention Relating to the Status of Refugees 1951. Refugees are registered under the mandate of the United Nations High Commissioner for Refugees (UNHCR) who meets regularly with all refugees and their representatives to discuss their concerns and jointly look for solutions to their problems. The UNHCR assists a registrant against forced return, deportation, arbitrary arrest and detention. In exceptional circumstances, the UNHCR provides

1951 United Nations Convention on the Status of Refugees and the 1967 Protocol thereon (which are the primary international instruments on refugees).[5] There is no national law on refugees at present. At present, India relies on dynamic internal policies for the purpose of dealing with the issue of refugees.

The government in 2011 circulated a Standard Operating Procedure (**SOP**) to all state governments/ union territories for dealing with foreign nationals who claim to be refugees.[6] This SOP is updated from time to time in an effort to keep pace with the ever-changing illegal migration landscape. The SOP, amongst other things, provides a mechanism for a long term visa (LTV) for migrants who come into India to escape persecution. While the LTV is a renewable document, however, there exists no mechanism for conversion of the LTV into a citizenship, under any circumstances.[7]

A nationwide NRC (with the CAA in the background) is likely to result in large-scale statelessness, deportation or prolonged detention. It is pertinent that, prior to any such exercise, the government puts in place a suitable policy to deal with stateless people. Large scale and prolonged detention of 'stateless persons' and 'illegal migrants' is something that the government can ill afford.

The Judicial Perspective

While on this issue, it is also important to point out that the judiciary generally appears to avoid situations which result in statelessness. Some instances are discussed below.

---

individual assistance that may include monthly stipends or resettlement to a third country. A certificate of refugee status issued by the UNHCR may be considered as prima facie indication of persecution (or threat of persecution) of the refugee in his home country. *See generally* Dongh Lian Kham v. Union of India, *supra*

5 *See* https://www.mha.gov.in/MHA1/Par2017/pdfs/par2015-pdfs/ls-050515/6307.pdf

6 This was further revised in the year 2019. *See* https://www.mha.gov.in/MHA1/Par2017/pdfs/par2020-pdfs/rs-05022020/350.pdf

7 *See* Chapter No. 10 for a detailed discussion on the SOP of 2011.

The Delhi High Court, in **Prabhleen Kaur v. Union of India,**[8] adopted the 'closest connection rule' for resolving any doubt or uncertainty as to the nationality of a foreigner (or perceived foreigner). In the said matter, the nationality of a person residing in India for almost 50 (fifty) years was questioned by the authorities on, inter alia, the ground that her parents were illegal migrants from Afghanistan. The Delhi High Court, while examining Section 8 of the Foreigners Act, 1946 applied the 'closest connection rule' by observing that the person in question had moorings only in India, she knew of no other place that she could even remotely call her home, she had never visited Afghanistan or accepted the culture of that nation, she was born of parents whose faith was in Sikhism and she was an integral part of our community. The High Court also observed that questioning her nationality in the peculiar facts at this stage may render her stateless, a result which must clearly be avoided insofar as possible.

This shows that courts tend to adopt a liberal approach in such situations and lean in favour of the individual in cases of uncertainty and also seek to avoid a situation where a person could be rendered stateless.

Elaborating on this point further, Indian courts have, in appropriate situations, interfered to protect illegal migrants from neighbouring countries and requested the central government to adopt a pragmatic approach. One case in point is **P. Ulaganathan v. The Government of India**.[9] In the said matter, certain 'illegal migrant' Sri Lankans (whose ancestors and existing blood relations were Indians) petitioned the Madras High Court seeking Indian citizenship on the following grounds:

a) They were descendants of indentured labour who settled down in the tea estates of Sri Lanka during the colonial

8 W.P. (C) No. 7974/2017 (03.10.2018, Delhi High Court).

9 AIR 2019 Mad 246.

times. They were tamil speaking people whose fore fathers hailed from what is the present day Tamil Nadu.

b) They faced discrimination at the hands of the Sri Lankans since 1948. They had come to India to escape the discrimination. They could not go back to Sri Lanka.
c) They have been residing in refugee camps since 1985 and are given monthly cash, ration, essential commodities etc. However, they have not been conferred Indian citizenship.

The High Court examined the pitiable conditions of the migrants and observed that they should not be kept in a state of statelessness for such a long time. The court directed the government authorities to examine their unique situation and to consider favourably their case for citizenship. The above demonstrates that courts have, in exceptional circumstances, stepped in and asked the government to adopt a humanitarian approach towards illegal migrants, stateless persons and refugees.

As per the author, a major rethinking is required by the government on this (potential) issue of statelessness before commencing a nationwide process which will, in most likelihood, result in statelessness for many (detected) 'illegal migrants' (which is an undesirable situation).

Detention Centres: A Major Challenge

Detention centres are set up to house illegal immigrants or foreigners whose deportation process to their home country concerned has not been completed. It is also set up to accommodate foreign convicts in criminal cases who have completed their jail terms and await deportation. According to the Ministry of Home Affairs, these holding camps are also 'to restrict the movement of foreigners staying back illegally and thereby ensure that they are physically available at all times for expeditious repatriation or deportation'.

Detention Centres: A Panacea

As discussed previously, being declared as a foreigner by a court of law entails committal to a detention centre. But really it is these questions which come to mind:

a) Are detention centres a permanent and perpetual solution to the problem?
b) Should the children of foreigners be separated from them (for life) as a result of the detention or in the alternative, be confined to a detention centre on account the detention of their parents?
c) Does the government have adequate infrastructure and resources to ensure proper living conditions for detainees at the detention centres?
d) Is the government in a position of maintaining millions of detainees once the NRC exercise in Assam is complete and in case the nation-wide NRC exercise is implemented?
e) How will the government deal with the problem of statelessness of the detainees?

Recently, in the wake of the Covid-19 outbreak, a spate of petitions have been filed in the Supreme Court of India seeking release of detainees in Assam, including foreigner detainees, who had completed 2 (two) years at the detention centres. The justification for seeking such relief was problem of overcrowding and hygiene at the detention centres. In fact, the Supreme Court passed orders for release of detainees who had been incarcerated for more than 2 (two) years on personal bond and surety. In the said proceedings, the Supreme Court also expressed apprehension that release of 'foreigner' detainees could result in them absconding.[10]

10 *See* https://www.livelaw.in/top-stories/sc-orders-release-of-persons-who-spent-more-than-two-years-in-assam-detention-centres-155165

The Covid-19 situation raises various new challenges and issues for the government in so far as detention centres (and also jails) are concerned. In case of release of 'declared foreigners' and their subsequent disappearance, the entire exercise (of their identification/detection, determination and detention) will be set at naught. The government also needs to contend with the infrastructure and resource issue (at the detention centres) for tackling extraordinary situations such as Covid 19.

Detention Centre: The Model Manual

The Ministry of Home Affairs has prepared a 'Model Detention Centre/Holding Centre/Camp Manual' which was circulated to all States and Union Territories on 09.01.2019 (**Model Manual**). The Model Manual specifies the amenities to be provided in such detention centres/camps. The Manual, amongst other things, provides that such centres should be designed to provide all necessary facilities for the inmates to maintain a standard of living with human dignity. It lays down that amenities like electricity, drinking water, hygine, accommodation with beds, sufficient toilets with running water, communication facilities, provision for kitchen etc. shall be provided. Special attention is to be given to women/nursing mothers, children. Children lodged in detention centres are to be provided educational facilities in nearby local schools.[11] As per the author, it is highly imperative for the government to be able to scrupulously comply with the provisions of the Model Manual. Creation and establishment of properly manned and managed detention

11 Starred Question No. 1773, Lok Sabha (answered on 02.07.2019 by Minister of State, Ministry of Home Affairs, Government of India). The Ministry of Home Affairs in the Parliament revealed that, there are 6 (six) operational detention centres in Assam as on November 28, 2019. 4 (four) others are operational in other states. Over 98% of the detainees in Assam are from Bangladesh, while the rest are from Myanmar. The government has approved construction of 3 (three) three others in Assam, Punjab and Karnataka. *See* https://www.thehindu.com/data/data-where-are-detention-centres-in-india/article30451564.ece

centres are essential prior to commencement of the exercise of detection of illegal migrants.

The Indian Deportation Policy

Another imperative requirement is robust and seamless deportation policy, especially with respect to nations from where illegal migrant traffic is high (such as Bangladesh, Afghanistan et cetera).

The Joint Committee Report records various concerns of stakeholders on the extant deportation policies of the government, especially in the context of Bangladesh. The principal concerns (specific to Bangladesh) are two-fold: (i) The deportation policy is cumbersome; and (ii) There were occasions where Bangladeshi authorities refused to accept migrants who had been determined by Indian authorities/courts to be Bangladeshis. It is noteworthy that even the Supreme Court in the Assam NRC Judgement of 2014 has issued directions to the Government of India to enter into discussions with the Government of Bangladesh for the purpose of streamlining the deportation processes.

In fact, the *Joint Committee Report* had red flagged the issue of deportation in general. The report records that in the last several decades, only a fraction of the illegal migrants have been successfully deported. Deportation of illegal migrants has been a perennial problem of the government causing avoidable burden on the original citizens of India, especially Assam. The report concludes on this aspect by stating that there exists an urgent need for the government to effectively address the deportation issue.

It is therefore essential that the deportation policies are streamlined in concert with the neighbouring countries and the enforcement mechanism be made more robust and effective. All efforts will come to naught if the country eventually fails in successfully deporting migrants to their home states.

The Fate of the Undocumented Citizens

It is a matter of fact that, during the Assam NRC process, thousands of persons (with many from the marginal sections of the society) had difficulty in providing necessary documentation to the authorities (to establish their citizenship) owing to bad record-keeping and ignorance. It is true that while many of these persons may be illegal migrants, however, it is equally true that many of them were indeed Indian citizens but unable to conclusively establish their citizenship by means of adequate documents.

Now imagine this NRC exercise being carried out on a nationwide scale. In the absence of streamlining of the procedures, an NRC exercise on a national scale may be arduous and inefficacious. Before embarking on such an exercise, the government should convey clarity on the procedures and mechanisms for establishing citizenship, including at least on the following aspects: (i) the type of documentary evidence which would be required by Indian citizens for establishing their citizenship; (ii) in case of unavailability or lacuna in documentary evidence, the nature of oral or community evidence which would be required to be adduced by the concerned person for the purpose of establishing his citizenship (such as, who can be probable witnesses, whether the witnesses can be relatives, neighbours, friends, colleagues et cetera, the extent of oral evidence which would be required to be led by such witnesses, whether the witnesses would be cross-examined by the authorities et cetera; and (iii) contours of the investigative processes which would be conducted by the government authorities.

The Role of the State Governments

The Ministry of Home Affairs, Government of India has written to state governments on various occasions urging them to take strict action against foreign nationals found to be illegally residing in India, including arrest of such foreign nationals.[12] If an NRC exercise is to be successfully carried out on a nationwide basis, than the central government will have to engage with all the state governments so as to bring them 'on the same page' as regards this issue. An NRC exercise of such scale and magnitude is not possible without the able support and cooperation of the state governments.

THE CAA: THE CHALLENGES AHEAD

While a challenge to the CAA continues to be pending before the Supreme Court, the benefits of the same have begun to trickle down and courts have commenced relying on the amended citizenship law to afford benefit to the (intended) beneficiaries of the CAA in one way or the other. For instance, in **Archona Purnima Pramanik v. State of Karnataka,**[13] bail was granted by the Karnataka High Court to a Bangladeshi Hindu (married to an Indian Hindu) who had come to India from Bangladesh in the year 2002 to escape harassment. She had been indicted for fabricating documents such as Aadhar, PAN card etc. The High Court, while granting the woman bail, amongst other things, placed reliance on the provisions of the CAA of which she was a direct beneficiary.

For the purpose of effective implementation of the CAA, several gaps and grey areas need to be covered. This section summarises some of these gaps which the government could do well to cover.

Religious Conversion: A Major Challenge

It is an admitted position that the CAA does grant certain amnesties and benefits to persons belonging to certain faiths.

---

12 *See* Letter dated 05.12.2012 issued by the Ministry of Home Affairs (Foreigners Division) to the Principal Secretaries (Home), All State Governments and Union Territories.

13 Crl. Petition No. 279/2020 (27.01.2020, Karnataka High Court).

There is also a cut-off date (for entering India) in the fray (i.e. 31.12.2014). In such a situation, the authorities are bound to come across cases of religious converts (both prior to as well as subsequent to the enactment of the CAA). A crucial question arises as to how cases of religious conversion would be dealt with.

The CAA does not appear to provide the mode and manner of dealing with religious converts. This may be better explained by means of the following illustrations:

a) A Muslim migrant entered India well before the cut-off date and subsequently changed his religious faith to say Christianity or Hinduism before the cut-off date.
b) A Muslim migrant entered India before the cut-off date but changed his religious faith after the cut-off date (but before the enactment of the CAA).
c) A Muslim migrant entered India before the cut-off date but changed his religious faith after the enactment of the CAA.

While some cases of religious conversion may be genuine (i.e. without any extraneous or compelling reasons), some cases may indeed be an attempt to escape deportation and/or to become a beneficiary of the CAA. There are several reports available in public domain which indicate that many muslim refugees have converted to Christianity in an effort to become eligible for Indian citizenship in terms of the CAA.[14] It is critical to point out that, under Indian law, the procedure to change religion is fairly simple. A person who wishes to change his religion is broadly required to do the following: (i) execute a religion change affidavit; (ii) place an advertisement regarding the same

14 *See generally* https://economictimes.indiatimes.com/news/politics-and-nation/muslim-refugees-become-christians-to-take-caa-benefit/articleshow/77117484.cms?from=mdr

in a daily newspaper having wide circulation; (iii) obtain a conversion certificate from the concerned institution of the faith sought to be followed;[15] (iv) publication of the notice for change of religion in the Gazette of India Part IV.[16]

Further, assuming the benefit is given to religious converts, the issue of re-conversion cannot be ruled out (i.e. persons changing their religious faith for the purposes of gaining benefit of the CAA and thereafter, upon grant of Indian citizenship, re-converting to their original faith).

The government, while addressing this issue of religious conversion, will also have to keep in mind the elements of Article 25 of the Constitution of India which provides, as a fundamental right, the freedom of religion, which includes the right to convert to any faith. This right is available even to non-citizens.

Relocation from Northeast

As discussed previously, several northeastern states such as Meghalya, Arunachal Pradesh etc. have been kept outside the scope of the CAA. Put differently, illegal migrants to these states, even if otherwise eligible to take the benefit of the CAA, may be precluded from doing so, on account of the exclusionary nature of the CAA. With the exclusion of (other) northeastern regions from the purview of the CAA, illegal migrants (who are potential

15 A brief process of conversion of religion in India is as follows: (i) For conversion to Christianity, the person is required to approach a church. Post the ceremonial process, the person will be given a new christian name and will be issued a certificate by the church. (ii) Hinduism does not provide any official or prescribed conversion process or religious ceremony. A person who wishes to convert to Hinduism may approach an Arya Samaj temple expressing a willingness to conversion upon which the certificate of conversion will be issued to him. (iii) For conversion to Islam, a person is required to visit a mosque and undergo a religious ceremony in the presence of a Maulvi and 2 (two) witnesses. Post the ceremony, a conversion certificate is issued to the person by the Maulvi and the mosque.

16 *See* https://online2pdf.com/convert-docx-to-pdf, which provides the guidelines for advertisement by individuals in the weekly Gazette of India, part for regarding change of religion.

beneficiaries of the CAA) may relocate to other parts of the country (including Assam) with the intent of securing the benefit of the CAA. It remains to be seen as to how the government will tackle this issue of relocation/attempted relocation.

The Grant of 'New Citizenship': The Process

Presently, there is little guidance on the mode and manner in which the beneficiaries of the CAA would be granted citizenship. The author understands that the CAA rules are presently under construction. These rules should be able to provide the answer to this issue.

Rehabilitation of the 'New Citizens'

Mere grant of citizenship (to the beneficiaries of the CAA) is not sufficient. The central government is required to take steps to fully rehabilitate (the illegal migrants who become Indian citizens) and bring them into the mainstream. As per the author, amongst other things, the following aspects will need to be taken care of in this regard: (i) Provision of basic and essential amenities such as drinking water, electricity, gas connections, hospital, BPL/caste certificates, ration card, Aadhaar card, bank account et cetera. (ii) Assistance in education of the migrant students such as in school and college admission, financial assistance et cetera; and (iii) Assistance in procurement of meaningful employment, loans et cetera. This is not all. A proper rehabilitation also includes bringing about a change in outlook and perceptions regarding such persons in India. The general public will have to be sensitised in this regard.

List of Cases

A

A.K. Mukherji v. Prodip Ranjan, A.F.A.D 51/1985 (19.08.1987, Calcutta High Court)

Abdul Aleem v. State of Andhra Pradesh, AIR 1963 AP 441

Abdul Kuddus v. Union of India, AIR 2019 SC 2834

Abdul Majeed v. The State of Telangana, Criminal Petition No. 5266/2019 (01.04.2021, Telangana High Court)

Abdur Rashid v. Union of India, W.P. (C) No. 7413/2016 (27.09.2018, Guwahati High Court)

Abdus Samad v. State of West Bengal, 1973 CriLJ 1 SC

Abhijit Sen v. Superintendent (Administration) Regional Passport Officer, 2004 (1) CHN 66.

Abid Hussain v. Union of India, AIR 2013 J&K 90

Aboo Chettiyanthodi v. Regional Passport Officer, 2008 (1) KLT 992

Abubacker v. Union of India, 2000 (2) ILR 732 (Ker)

Adishri Saisha Manan v. Union of India, W.P. (C) No. 8682/2005 (31.05.2005, Delhi High Court)

Aditya Khanna v. The Regional Passport Officer, 2009 (156) DLT 172

Ajeit Saksena v. The Deputy Director Directorate of Enforcement, 2018 (2) Crimes 227 (Mad)

Akansksha Amar Naik v. Government of India, Ministry of External Affairs & Others, 2007 Cri LJ 575 (Bom)

Akbar Khan Alam Khan v. Union of India, AIR 1962 SC 70

Akhilesh v. State of Kerala, Crl. Misc. No. 185/2021 (01.03.2021, Kerala High Court)

Alex Varghese v. The Chief Passport Officer and Ors., W.A. No. 1104/2007 (29.05.2007, Kerala High Court)

Al-Haman Exports & Imports v. Union of India, W.P. (C) No. 9053/2008 (08.04.2009, Delhi High Court)

Alibhiya Das v. Union of India, W.P. (C) No. 11865/2018 (11.02.2019, Delhi High Court)

All Assam Ahom Association & Others v. Union of India, W.P. (C) No. 876/2014 (17.12.2014, Supreme Court of India)

Amina Khatun v. Union of India, W.P. (C) No. 7339/2015 (19.04.2018, Guwahati High Court)

Anand Tewari v. Union of India, 2014 (1) JCC 186

Ananda Bhavanani and Ors. v. Union of India, (1991 LW (Crl.) 393 (05.12.1990, Madras High Court)

Ananda Ghosh v. Union of India, 2017 (3) GLR 815

Anil Barman v. Union of India, W.P. (C) No. 266/2019 (10.06.2019, Guwahati High Court)

Anitha R. Radhakrishnan v. The Regional Passport Officer, Passport Office, W.P. (MD) No. 1547/2012 (03.09.2012, Madras High Court)

Annai Jayabharathi v. The Debt Recovery Tribunal, 2005 (1) KLJ 737

Anowar Ali v. State of Assam, W.P. (C) No. 1043/2013 (13.06.2014, Gauhati High Court)

Anwar-ul-Haq v. Union of India, AIR 2008 J&K 35

Archona Purnima Pramanik v. State of Karnataka, Crl. Petition No. 279/2020 (27.01.2020, Karnataka High Court)

Arockia Jeyabalan v. The Regional Passport Officer, W.P. (C) Nos. 18637 & 22205/2014 (15.09.2014, Madras High Court)

Ashim and Brothers v. Union of India, W.P. (C) No. 2695/2012 (11.10.2013, Delhi High Court)

Ashma Khatun v. Union of India, W.P. (C) No. 8592/2018 (30.01.2019, Guwahati High Court)

Ashok Kumar Sharma v. Regional Passport Officer, 2019 (173) DRJ 427

Ashok Muthana v. The Regional Passport Officer, W.P. (C) No. 33546/2013 (24.09.2014, Madras High Court)

Ashutosh Das v. Union of India, 2019 (2) GLT 393

Asit Kumar Rout v. Principal Secretary to Government of Odisha, 2014 (II) OLR 248

Aslam Khan v. Fazal Haque Khan, AIR 1959 All 79

Assam Public Works v. Union of India, W.P. (C) No. 274/2009 (Order dated 13.08.2019, Supreme Court of India)

Assam Sanmilita Mahasangha v. Union of India, W.P. (C) No. 562/2012 (21.07.2015, Supreme Court of India)

Ayesha Khatun v. Union of India, (2017) 3 CLR 820

Azimusshan Haider v. Union of India, W.P. (C) No. 3087/1996 (04.07.2008, Delhi High Court)

B

B.T. Deva Varma v. State of A.P, 2002 (2) ALD (Cri) 371

Bachhittar Singh v. The State of Punjab, AIR 1963 SC 395. *See also* Rajiv Saxena v. Union of India, 276 (2021) DLT 245

Balwinder Singh v. State, Crl. Misc. No. 3630/2006 (09.10.2006, Delhi High Court)

Bangantavida Nazir v. Inspector of Customs, W.P. (C) No. 32496 of 2014 (11.12.2014, Kerala High Court)

Barsa v. State of Rajasthan, 2011 Cri LJ 2503

Basdeo Agarwalla v. Emperor, 1945 (47) Bom LR 392

Bawalkhan v. B.C. Shah AIR 1960 Bom 27

Bela Rani Devi v. Union of India, W.P. (C) No. 5852/2016 (10.05.2018, Guwahati High Court)

Bhagwati Prasad Dixit v. Rajeev Gandhi, AIR 1986 SC 1534

Bhaktiarkhan v. Union of India, AIR 1961 Guj 109

Bhanwaroo Khan v. Union of India, (2002) 4 SCC 346

Bhupinder Singh Cheema v. The State of Haryana, 2012 (5) RCR (C) 286

Bismillah Khan v. Union of India, W.P. No. 928/2020 (24.02.2020, Calcutta High Court)

Biswajit Debnath v. Union of India, W.P. (C) No. 4497/2019 (12.03.2021, Guwahati High Court)

Brijlal Zumbarlal Sarda v. Amrulla Asadulla Irani, W.P. No. 2788/1986 (11.09.1986, Bombay High Court)

Burn & Co, Calcutta v. Their Employees, Civil Appeal No. 325/1955 (11.10.1956, Supreme Court of India)

C

C.T. Abraham v. J.R. James and Ors., C.M.P. No. 11866/1992 in A.S. No. 874/1991 (17.11.1992, Madras High Court)

Chanda Paul v. Union of India, W.P. (C) No. 4634/2017 (12.01.2018, Guwahati High Court)

Christo Thomas Philip v. Union of India, W.P. (C) No. 1775/2018 (08.01.2019, Delhi High Court)

Craig Maxwell Sterry v. Ministry of Home Affairs, Union of India & Ors., W.P. No. 513/2009 (11.09.2009, Bombay High Court at Goa)

D

D.P.Joshi v. State of Madhya Bharat, (1955) 1 SCR 1215

Daivid John Hopkins v. Union of India, W.P. No. 11063/1995 (31.08.1995, Madras High Court)

Daler Singh v. Union of India and Ors., CWP No. 12143 of 2015 (O&M) (01.10.2015, P&H HC)

Dalwinder Singh v. Union of India, 2012 (2) ILR P&H 133.

Deepak Dwarkasingh Chhabria v. Union of India, AIR 1997 Bom 181

Deepak Sadashiv Nikalje v. Union of India, AIR 2003 Bom 255

Devadasan Dayalal v. Collector of Customs, 1986 (9) ECR 558

Devan Parameswaran v. The Union of India, W.P. No. 4617/1997 (19.04.2004, Madras High Court)

Dhiren Baxi v. Regional Passport Officer, AIR 2003 Guj 108

Dongh Lian Kham v. Union of India, WP (Crl.) No. 1884/2015 (21.12.2015, Delhi High Court)

Dr. Madas Venkat Goud v. State of Andhra Pradesh, 2010 KHC 7572

Dr. Pradeep Jain v. Union of India, (1984) II LLJ 481 SC

DTC v. DTC Mazdoor Congress, (1991) I LLJ 395 SC

E

Ebrahim Vazir Mavat v. The State of Bombay, AIR 1954 SC 229

F

Faisal P.A. and Ors. v. Regional Passport Officer and Ors., 2019 (369) ELT 184 (Ker)

Faizal Ibrahim v. Union of India, W.P. (C) No. 2109/2017 (12.09.2017, Delhi High Court)

Falu Das v. Union of India, W.P. (C) No. 1157/2018 (09.04.2018, Guwahati High Court)

Farida Khatun v. Union of India, W.P. (C) No. 1455/2020 (10.06.2020, Guwahati High Court)

Fateh Mohd. v. Delhi Administration, AIR 1963 SC 1035

Firoz Meharuddin v. Sub-Divisional Officer, AIR 1961 MP 110

G

G. Venkatesh v. Bridge Federation of India, W.P. (C) No. 2559/2011 (24.06.2015, Madras High Court)

Ghaurul Hasan v. The State of Rajasthan, W.P. (C) No. 26/1957 (08.04.1958, Rajasthan High Court)

Gilden Jacob v. The Foreigners Regional Registration Officer, W.P. (MD) No. 24591/2018 (11.02.2020, Madrah High Court, Madurai Bench)

Golam Rasul v. Superintendent of Police, AIR 1965 Cal 302

Government of A.P. v. Mohd. Khan, AIR 1962 SC 1778

Gurpreet Singh Bal v. Union of India, 2008 (2) PLR 746

H

Habatullah Haji Fazale Hussain v. The State, AIR 1964 Guj 128

Habsons Jobsup Ltd. v. Union of India, W.P. (C) 5980/2011 (25.08.2011, Delhi High Court)

Haider Ali v. Union of India, W.P. (C) No. 1818/2019 (30.03.2021, Guwahati High Court)

Hajra Iqbal Memon v. Union of India, 1997 (41) DRJ 108

Hans Muller of Nurenburg v. Superintendent, Presidency Jail, Calcutta AIR 1955 SC 367

Harbanslal Sahnia v. Indian Oil Corporation, AIR 2003 SC 212

Hari Shanker Jain v. Sonia Gandhi, AIR 2001 SC 3689.

Harjit Singh v. Union of India, 2008 (2) ILR 188 (P&H)

Hasan Ali v. Union of India, W.P. (Crl.) No. 17/2006 (09.03.2006, Supreme Court of India)

Hasan Khan v. State AIR 1961 Raj 182

Hazram Imam v. Union of India, (1999) 80 DLT 19

Hiral P. Harsora v. Kusum Narottamdas Harsora, Civil Appeal No. 10084/2016 (06.10.2016, Supreme Court of India)

Hitesh Kapoor v. Union of India, 2012 (4) RCR (C) 135.

HRA Choudhury v. Election Commission of India, 2002 (1) GLT 1

I

ICICI Limited v. The Passport Office, AIR 2002 Kar 118

Inder Lall v. Lal Singh, AIR 1961 Raj 122

Indira Newar and Ors. v. Union of India, W.P. (C) Nos. 8490/2018 etc. (29.11.2019, Guwahati High Court)

Institute of Chartered Accountants of India v. L.K. Ratna, (1087) 164 ITR 1 (SC)

International Cargo Services vs. Union of India, 2006 (193) ELT 546 (Del)

Ismail v. State of Rajasthan, 1959 RLW 299

Izhar Ahmed v. Union of India, AIR 1962 SC 1052

J

J.M. International v. Union of India, W.P. (C) 6284/2011 (29.08.2011, Delhi High Court)

J.R. Parikh v. The Director (PV) Chief Passport Officer, 1970 (2) ILR Del 378

Jae Young Chung v. State of A.P., W.P. No. 25639/2020 (05.01.2021, Andhra Pradesh High Court)

Jahir Ali v. Union of India, W.P. (C) No. 3402/2020 (03.03.2021, Guwahati High Court)

Jamuna Singh v. Bhadai Shah, AIR 1964 SC 1541

Jan Balaz v. Anand Munipality, LPA No. 2151/2009 (11.11.2009, Gujarat High Court)

Jayan v. Union of India, 2019 ILR (1) Ker 56; Shashank Gupta v. Union of India, AIR 2018 All 253

Jehirul Islam v. Union of India, W.P. (C) No. 7347/2016 (16.05.2017, Guwahati High Court)

Jeyachandran v. State of Tamil Nadu, H.C.P. No. 2460/2019 (04.06.2020, Madras High Court)

Jose Peter v. C.K. Vijaya Kumar, W.P. (C) No. 8217/2009 (O) (18.06.2009, Kerala High Court)

Junaid Iqbal Mohammed Memon v. Union of India, AIR 2019 Del142

K

K. Mohammed Ahmed v. State of Kerala, 1983 KLT 1009

K. Sowmya v. Regional Passport Officer, Secunderabad and Ors., W.P. No. 4370/2015 (16.08.2016, Hyderabad High Court)

Kaja Mohaideen v. The Senior Intelligence Officer, 2013 (1) LW 114 Madras

Kalavathy v. State of Tamil Nadu 1995 (2) LW (Crl.) 690

Kamalakhya Dey Purkayastha and Others v. Union of India, W.P. (C) No. 1020/2017 (05.12.2017, Supreme Court of India)

Karm Kumar v. Union of India, (2010) 172 DLT 521

Karma Gyaltsen Neyratsang v. Union of India, W.P. (C) No. 6074/2014 (29.08.2017, Delhi High Court)

Karti P. Chidambaram v. Bureau of Immigration, Ministry of Home Affairs, Government of India, W.P. No. 21305 & 20798/2017 (23.07.2018, Madras High Court)

Khair Mohd. Reas Mohd. v. State of Maharashtra, First Appeal No. 541/1978 (27.06.1994, Bombay High Court)

Khatoon Nessa v. Union of India, W.P. (C) No. 2098/2013 (30.08.2013, Guwahati High Court)

Kiran Gupta v. The State Election Commission, 2020 (6) BLJ 539.

Kirandeep Kaur v. Regional Passport Office, AIR 2006 Del 2

Krushnakant Kantilal Pancholi v. State of Gujarat, Crl. Application No. 5047/2008 (05.09.2008, Gujarat High Court)

Kulathil Mammu v. The State of Kerala, AIR 1966 SC 1614

Kulvir Singh v. Union of India, 2015 (147) DRJ 295

L

Lal Babu Hussain v. Electoral Registration Officer, (1995) 3 SCC 100

Lalit Kr. Modi v. Union of India, 2013 (IV) ILR Del 2484

Lawyers Beyond Borders (LBB) India & Others v. Union of India & Others., W.P. (C) 13444/2020 (S) & W.P. (C) 14496/2020 (S), (25.08.2020, Kerala High Court)

Lee Anne Arunoday Singh v. Ministry of Home Affairs, W.P. (L) No. 3443/2020 (27.10.2020, Bombay High Court)

LIC of India v. Ram Pal Singh Bisen, (2010) 4 SCC 491

Ligy Abraham v. Union of India W.P. (C) No. 10499/2016 (11.09.2017, Delhi High Court)

Lijeesh v. State of Kerala, 2012 (3) KLJ 240

Louis De Raedt v. Union of India (1991) 3 SCC 554

Luingam Luithui v. Union of India, W.P. (C) 1546/2014 (23.08.2017, Delhi High Court)

M

M. Natarajan v. The Regional Passport Officer, 2012 (4) CTC 709

M.D.K. Immigration Consultant, Chandigarh v. Union of India, 1999 (4) RCR (C) 535

Madhu Tyagi v. State of Uttar Pradesh, 2019 SCC OnLine All 6909

Maganlal Bagti v. Emperor, Air 1934 Nag 71

Mahammad Nazaharul Haque v. B. Bagchi, A.F.O.O No. 479/2961 (29.11.1972, Calcutta High Court)

Maheswaran v. State of Tamil Nadu, H.P.C. No. 1208/2005, (21.03.2006, Madras High Court)

Malkit Singh Bamrha v. Union of India, W.P. (C) 9263/2016 (05.02.2019, Delhi High Court)

Maneka Gandhi v. Union of India, AIR 1978 SC 597

Manish Kumar Mittal v. Chief Passport Officer, 2013 (202) DLT 317

Mary v. State of Kerala, Crl. Rev. Pet. No. 3265/2005 (25.01.2018, Kerala High Court)

Masud Khan v. State of Uttar Pradesh, (1974) 3 SCC 469

Matbar Khan v. Union of India, W.P. No. 33067 (M/B)/2018 (05.04.2019, Allahabad High Court, Lucknow Bench)

Mathumari China Venkatareddy v. State of Andhra Pradesh, 1994 Cri. LJ 257 (A.P).

Md. Ajijul Hoque v. The Union of India, W.P. (C) No. 1488/2013 (30.08.2013, Guwahati High Court)

Md. Elahi v. State of West Bengal, C.R.R No. 1354/2008 (12.11.2008, Calcutta High Court)

Md. Ishaque v. The Under Secretary to the Government of India, Const. Writ Appellate Side (17.12.1990, Calcutta High Court)

Meharuddin v. Sub-Divisional Officer and Ors., AIR 1961 MP 110

Menaka Gandhi v. Union of India, 1978 (1) SCC 248

Minoo Maneckshaw Khalifa v. Union of India, 1974 (76) Bom LR 788

Mohammad Abdul Moyeed v. Union of India W.P. (C) No.10587/2016 (20.07.2018, Delhi High Court)

Mohammad Hassan Jafari Naeimi v. Union of India, W.P. No. 1316/2012 (06.09.2013, Bombay High Court)

Mohammad Salimullah v. Union of India, I.A No. 38048/2021, W.P. (C) No. 793/2017 (08.04.2021, Supreme Court of India)

Mohammad Sediq v. Union of India, (1998) 47 DRJ 74

Mohammed Hussain Pangadan v. State of Kerala, Crl. Misc. No. 493/2015 (10.06.2015, Kerala High Court)

Mohammed Naseeruddin v. State of Andhra Pradesh, AIR 1960 AP 106

Mohd. Ayub Khan v. Commissioner of Police, AIR 1965 SC 1623

Mohd. Faruq Kureshi v. State of Rajasthan, 2016 (1) RLW 252 (Raj)

Mohd. Ilyas v. Union of India, 1970 (3) SCC 61

Mohd. Irfan Gani v. Union of India, W.P. (C) No. 3605/2011 (30.09.2011, Delhi High Court).

Mohd. Javed and Ors. v. Union of India and Ors., LPA 168/2019 (28.05.2019, Delhi High Court)
Mohd. Khaa v. State of Andhra Pradesh, AIR 1967 AP 1047
Mohd. Nasrullah Khan v. Regional Passport Officer, 2005 (1) ALD 95
Mohd. Umar v. State, AIR 1961 Ori 150
Momin v. State of Tamil Nadu, W.P No. 1141/2019 (28.03.2019, Madras High Court)
Monika Karmakar v. Union of India, W.P. No. 24020(W)/2015 (01.10.2015, Calcutta High Court)
Moosa v. Union of India, 2000 (1) KLJ 417
Mst. Rihena Maryam v. The State, 1969 RLW 322
Muhammed v. Union of India, 2018 (4) KHC 945
Mumtaz Parveen v. State, (Crl.) Revision Petition No. 367/2006 (28.01.2013, Delhi High Court)
Musthafa Nambiamkulam Abdulkader v. Ministry of External Affairs, 2013 (4) KLT 527

N

N. Venkata Ram Babu v. State of Kerala and Ors., Crl. Misc. No. 4252/2015 (18.03.2016, Kerala High Court)
Namgyal Dolkar v. Government of India, Ministry of External Affairs, W.P. (C) No. 12179/2009 (22.12.2010, Delhi High Court)
Nandita Haksar v. Union of India, W.P. (Crl.) No. 6/2021 (20.04.2021, Manipur High Court)
Naresh Lalchand Bhagchandani v. Union of India, 2007 SCC OnLine Bom 376
Nasir Ahmed v. The Chief Commissioner, Delhi, AIR 1959 PH 261
National Human Rights Commission v. State of Arunachal Pradesh, [1996] 1 SCR 278
Navjot Singh Sidhu v. State of Punjab, 2007 (93) DRJ 661 (SC)
Nazir Ahmedkhan v. The Superintendent of Police and Registration Officer 1989 CriLJ 2044
Neera Chandra v. Union of India, 2019 (9) ADJ 791

Nilesh Heda v. Union of India, S.B. W.P. (C) No. 14683/2015 (14.10.2015, Rajasthan High Court)

Niyas v. State of Kerala, 2011 (3) ILR 981 (Ker)

Noor Mohammad v. The State, Civil Misc. Case No. 17/1956 (07.05.1956, Madhya Pradesh High Court)

Norman Swaroop Issac v. State Bank of India, AIR 2007 AP 40

Noufal M.H v. State of Kerala, 2017 (3) KLT 660

P

P. Shibu Kumar v. The Deputy Inspector General of Police, 2010 (5) ALD 732

Padam Prasad Sharma v. Union of India, W.P. (C) 8077/2009 (15.03.2011, Delhi High Court)

Patel Mukeshkumar Karshanbhai v. Regional Passport Officer, 2012 GLH (1) 682

Pawan Kumar v. State of Rajasthan, Crl. Misc. Petition No. 69/2000 (16.02.2000, Rajasthan High Court)

Pedda Veera Reddy v. The State of A.P., AIR 1990 SC 79

Peter Samouel Wallace v. The Regional Passport Officer, 1972 (8) DLT 433

Phuntsok Wangyal v. Ministry of External Affairs, W.P. (C) No. 3539, 4275 & 7983/2016 (22.09.2016, Delhi High Court)

Prabhat Vikram Sah v. The State of Bihar, MANU/BH/0064/2010 (18.01.2010, Patna High Court)

Prabhleen Kaur v. Union of India, W.P. (C) No. 7974/2017 (03.10.2018, Delhi High Court)

Prashant Bhushan v. Union of India, 2016 (154) DRJ 385

Pratap Sakharu v. Union of India W.P (C) No. 6594/2019 (19.02.2020, Gauhati High Court)

Priya Parameswaran Pillai v. Union of India, 2015 (VII) AD Delhi 10

Public Prosecutor, High Court of A.P. v. Gopichetty Rajendran and Ors. 2004 (11) CCR 438

Pushpal Swarnkar v. State of Chhattisgarh (03.12.2008, Chhattisgarh High Court)

R

R. Venkateshwara Rao v. Union of India, W.P. No. 12998/1998 (23.04.1999, Andhra Pradesh High Court)

R.I. Jebaraj v. Union of India, W.P. No. 25613/2008 (19.01.2009, Madras High Court)

Raghuram v. Union of India, W.P. (C) No. 7524/2018 (13.04.2018. Madras High Court)

Rahima Khatun v. Union of India, W.P. (C) No. 8284/2019 (08.04.2021, Guwahati High Court)

Rahmat Ullah v. State, AIR 1969 All 165

Raj Kumari v. State of U.P, Civil Misc. W.P. No. 2098/2017 (17.01.2017, Allahabad High Court)

Rajat Gangwar v. State of U.P., PIL No. 2497/2019 (27.12.2019, Allahabad High Court)

Rajbardhan Singh Rajpoot v. Union of India, W.P. (C) No. 6679/2013 (18.12.2013, Delhi High Court)

Rajesh P. Mankad v. State of Gujarat, Civil Application No. 497 of 2010 (22.04.2011, Gujarat High Court)

Rajinder Kaur and Ors. v. Union of India, AIR 2004 P&H 347

Rajiv Saxena v. Union of India, 276 (2021) DLT 245

Rama Narang v. Ramesh Narang, 1995 (2) SCC 513

Ramesh Chennamaneni v. Union of India, 2019 (5) ALD 118

Ramesh Ganeriwal v. Union of India, W.P (C) No. 3652/2017 (18.08.2017, Delhi High Court)

Ranjit Bajaj v. Regional Passport Authority, AIR 2004 P&H 327

Ranjit Kumar Mazumdar v. The State of Bengal, C.R.M No. 10076/2015 (09.03.2016, Calcutta High Court)

Rashminara Begum v. Union of India, (2017) 4 CLR 282

Rashtriya Mukti Morcha v. Union of India, 137 (2007) DLT 195

Raveendran Pillai G. v. Vice Consulate General of India, 2011 (3) KLT 652)

Ravikant S. Patil v. Sarvabhouma S. Bagali, 2007 (1) SCC 673

Rebecca Ann Malstead v. Union of India, 2017 (4) CTC 167

Regional Passport Officer v. Kokilaben, AIR 2009 Guj 59

Rehana Ali v. Union of India and Ors., S.B. W.P. (C) No. 15/2013 (26.11.2015, Rajasthan High Court)

Resham Singh v. Union of India, (2008) 149 PLR 621

Rev. Mons Sebastiao Fransisco Xavier Dos Remedios Monterio v. State of Goa, AIR 1970 SC 329

Reza Abdullatif Saboonchi v. The State of Maharashtra, CDJ 2012 BHC 1634

Rina Rani Das v. Union of India W.P. (C) No. 2706/2019 (10.03.2021, Guwahati High Court)

Rofikul Islam v. Union of India, W.P. (C) No. 6993/2018 (23.03.2021, Guwahati High Court)

Rohit Goswami v. Ministry of External Affairs, W.P. (C) No. 7706/2016 (18.09.2017, Delhi High Court)

Rupjan Begum v. Union of India, (2018) 1 SCC 579

S

S. Mohsfii Shah v. The Union Govt. of India, W.P. No. 31/1971 (31.10.1973, Jammu & Kashmir High Court)

S. Mosin Shah v. Union Govt. of India, AIR 1974 J&K 48

S. Nalini Srikaran v. Union of India, Writ Appeal No. 1599/2006 (07.03.2007, Madras High Court)

S.J. Overseas v. Union of India, 2019 (174) DRJ 533

S.M. Sobha v. The Joint Secretary, 2016 (3) LW 850 Mad.

Saeeda Mohammad Kayum v. State of Rajasthan, AIR 2006 Raj 284

Sahar Gharachorloo v. Union of India, C.W.P. No. 16577/2014 (30.06.2016, Punjab and Haryana High Court)

Sahib Jaskaran Singh v. Union of India and Ors., C.W.P. No. 19551/2015 (O&M) (13.10.2015, Punjab & Haryana High Court)

Sakeena v. State of Rajasthan, 1968 RLW Raj 143

Salim Khan v. Union of India, O.J.C. No. 17236/1998 (24.06.1999, Orrisa High Court)

Samsul Haqu v. Member, Foreigner's Tribunal, W.P. (C) No. 464/2009 (07.08.2009, Guwahati High Court)

Santha Kumar v. Collector of Customs & Ors., 1990 (29) ECR 46 (Ker)

Santi Ranjan Dey and Others v. State of Assam and Others, 2006(4) GLT 716.
Sarabari Begum v. State of Assam (25.07.2008, Guwahati High Court)
Sarath v. Regional Passport Officer, W.P. (MD) No. 18609/2018 (04.09.2018, Madras High Court, Madurai Bench).
Sarbananda Sonowal v. Union of India, (2007) 1 SCC 174
Sarbananda Sonowal v. Union of India, 2005 (5) SCC 665
Sasikala v. The State of Tamil Nadu, H.C.P. No. 157/2008 (30.04.2008, Madras High Court)
Sasikumar v. State of Tamil Nadu, W.P. (MD) No. 10080/2008 (25.08.2011, Madras High Court, Madurai Bench)
Satish Nambiar v. Union of India, 2007 (5) Bom. C.R. 247
Satwant Singh Sawhney v. D. Ramarathnam, Assistant Passport Officer, New Delhi and Others, AIR 1967 SC 1836
Seana Shanth v. Union of India, AIR 2017 Ker 17
Shabbir Hussain v. The State of Uttar Pradesh, AIR 1952 All 257
Shabu Kottoli Parambil Adimaikutty v. The Regional Passport Officer, 2019 (1) Writ LR 156
Shahid Ali v. Commissioner of Customs, Airport and Administration and Ors., W.P. No. 641/2013 (25.09.2012, Calcutta High Court)
Shaik Abdul Jabbar v. State of A.P., 2019 (1) ALT (Crl.) 130 (AP)
Sham Roj v. Additional Superintendent of Police, AIR 1978 Cal 252
Shamim Bano v. Union of India, 1979 RLW 444
Shanno Devi v. Mangal Sain, AIR 1961 SC 58
Shereef v. State of Kerala, 2019 (1) KHC 702
Shishuwala Pal v. Union of India, Misc. Petition No. 246/1984 (31.10.1988, Madhya Pradesh High Court)
Shrimati Ujjambai v. State of Uttar Pradesh, AIR 1962 SC 1621
Shymesh v. State of Kerala 2014 (3) KLJ 632.
Siddhartha Ashish Dey v. Union Of India W.P.(C) No.7339/2015 (08.12.2015, Delhi High Court)
Siddiqui Suraiya Bano v. The Regional Passport Officer, 2007 (6) ALD 568
Sikandar Khan v. Union of India, W.P. (C) No. 5315/2017 (06.07.2017, Delhi High Court)

Sirajul Haque v. State of Assam 2019 (5) SCC 534
Sorab Singh Gill v. Union of India, C.W.P. No. 18093/2009 (18.03.2010, Punjab and Haryana High Court)
Soumen Paul v. Union of India, W.P. No. 19153 (W)/2001 (06.02.2002, Calcutta High Court)
Sree Latha v. Secretary to Government, Public Department, Government of Tamil Nadu, (2007) 2 MLJ (Crl.) 1320
Stadtmuller Gabriele v. Union of India, 254 (2018) DLT 384
State (Delhi Administration) v. Master Tameej, ILR (1985) II Del
State of A.P. v. Abdulkhader, AIR 1961 SC 1467
State of Assam and Others v. Muslem Mondal and Others, 2013 (1) GLT 809
State of Assam v. Jamait-E-Ulema-E-Hind 2018 (4) GLT 264
State of Assam v. Jamait-E-Ulema-E-Hind 2018 (4) GLT 264
State of Assam v. Jilkadar Ali, 1972 (2) SCC 320
State of Bihar v. Amar Singh, AIR 1955 SC 282
State of Bihar v. Kameshwar Singh, AIR 1952 SC 252
State of Gujarat v. Iliyasbhai Adambhai Vohra and Ors., Criminal Appeal No. 867/2000 (03.08.2016, Gujarat High Court).
State of Gujarat v. Lal Singh Kishan Singh, AIR 1981 SC 368
State of Kerala v. C.K. Kunju, Criminal Appeal No. 602/1987 (13.10.1988, Kerala High Court)
State of Madhya Pradesh v. Mumtaz Ali Faiz Ali, AIR 1959 MP 387
State of Madhya Pradesh v. Peer Mohd., AIR 1963 SC 645
State of Maharashtra v. Gajanan, 2003 (12) SCC 432
State of Orissa v. Binapani Dei, AIR 1967 SC 1269
State of U.P. v. Mohammad Din AIR 1984 SC1714
State of U.P. v. Rehmatullah, 1971 Cri LJ 1103
State of U.P. v. Shah Mohammad (1969) 3 SCR 1006
State of U.P. v. Shamsul Huda, 1971 Crl. LJ 977
State of Uttar Pradesh v. Shah Mohammed, 1969 (1) SCC 771
State of West Bengal v. Union of India, AIR 1963 SC 1241
State Trading Corporation of India Ltd. v. Commercial Tax Officer, AIR 1963 SC 1811

State v. Abdul Hamid, AIR 1957 Punj 86

State v. Anil Grover, Crl.M.C 2087/2010 (06.01.2017, Delhi High Court)

State v. Ghoraishi (Qureshi) Sayed, AIR 1964 Bom 235

State v. Sharifbhai Jamalbhai, AIR 1959 Bom 192

Sterling Agro Industries Ltd v. Union of India, W.P. No. 6570/2010 (01.0.2011, Delhi High Court)

Subhas Chandra Bose Mandava v. Union of India, 2018 (5) ALD 664

Subhash Chandra Roy v. State of Assam, Rev. Petition No. 86/2016 (17.11.2016, Guwahati High Court)

Subramanian Swamy v. Union of India, W.P. (C) No. 7529/2001 (21.04.2005, Delhi High Court)

Suman Sehgal v. Union of India, 2006 (88) DRJ 721

Sumer Singh Salkan v. Assistant Director, 2010 (6) ILR Del 706

Suneer E v. Union of India, 2012 (111) AIC 588

Sunil Jaiswal v. Union of India, 2010 (3) GLT 775

Suresh Nanda v. Central Bureau of Investigation, (2008) 3 SCC 674

Syed Safiullah Qadri v. State of Andhra Pradesh, W.P. No. 11922/1996 (04.09.1996, Andhra Pradesh High Court)

Syeda Afshan Rahman v. Union of India, W.P. (C) No. 12520/2009 (02.07.2010, Delhi High Court)

T

T.A. Mahomed Usman v. State of Madras, AIR 1961 Mad 29

Tasleem Murad v. Government of A.P., 2002 (5) ALD 307

Tenzin Passang v. Union of India, 2017 (164) DRJ 100

Tenzin Tselha v. Union of India, W.P. (C) No. 7035/2016 (23.11.2016, Delhi High Court)

Thamarai v. Union of India and Ors., H.C.P No. 1456/2020 & W.P. No. 11754/2021 (23.06.2021, Madras High Court)

The State v. G. Karunairaj, Writ Appeal No. 651/2012 (26.11.2013, Madras High Court)

Tudor Gunasekhar Jayavardene v. The Government of India, W.P. No. 2538/1981 (10.07.1981, Madras High Court)

Tuta Mia v. Union of India, W.P. (C) No. 6280 & 7088/2016 (14.05.2018, Guwahati High Court)

Twisha Prasad v. Union of India, 2014 (134) AIC 380 (Patna)

U

Ulaganathan v. The Government of India, AIR 2019 Mad 246

Union of India and Others v. Ghaus Mohammad, AIR 1961 SC 1526

Union of India v. Chand Putli, Second Appeal No. 2575/1968 (12.10.1972, Allahabad High Court)

Union of India v. IC Lala, AIR 1973 SC 2204

Union of India v. Roopesh, 2015 (1) KLJ 398

Union of India v. Satnam Singh, AIR 2018 Del 72.

Union of India v. Savitha Kumar, LPA No. 219/2019 (28.08.2019, DHC)

Union of India v. Smt. Chiranjit Kaur, 1987 SCC (1) 671

Union of India v. Sunil Kumar, 2015 (3) KLT 501

V

V.A. Mohammed Rafeek v. Union of India, 2011 (3) KJL 183

Veenita Gupta v. State, 2011 (1) RCR (Crl) 915 (Ker)

Venkatesh Kandasamy v. Government of India, AIR 2015 Mad 3

Vijayan v. State of Kerala, 2009 (4) ILR 864 (Ker)

Vijoy Kumar Chaudhary v. The State Election Commissioner, LPA No. 510 of 2008 (11.04.2008, Patna High Court)

Vikram Sharma v. Union of India, 2010 (171) DLT 671

Vikram Sharma v. Union of India, W.P. (C) No. 10180/2009 (27.07.2010, DHC)

Viraaj Pratap Singh Pannu v. Chandigarh Administration, C.W.P. No. 15667/2012 (29.09.2012, Punjab & Haryana High Court)

W

W. Jaihar William v. State of Tamil Nadu, 2014 (8) MLJ 61

Wahid Mian Haddin v. The State, AIR 1961 All 111

Y

Yogesh Bhardwaj v. State of U.P., (1990) 3 SCC 355

Subject Index

A

B

C

E

F

G

I

P

R

S

Acknowledgements

This is my second endeavour at book writing. My first book *Law of Sexual Harassment at Workplace: Practice and Procedure* which was published in the year 2017 by Niyogi Books set the tone for my 'second calling' as an author.

I am extremely grateful to the Hon'ble Judges for their gracious messages and endorsements.

My special thanks to my friend Mr Harsh Prabhakar, Advocate, for having meticulously examined various chapters of the book and providing valuable feedback. His inputs have helped me improve the overall quality of the content of the book.

I am extremely thankful to Mr Ayush Beotra, Advocate, for lending me his valuable assistance towards the authorship by reviewing several chapters and providing valuable inputs. I thank him for having taken out time for this exercise despite a busy work schedule.

Mr Tejasvi Mahajan, a budding lawyer, deserves a special mention. I thank him for spending long hours assisting me in review of the book.

I thank my parents for their support and encouragement.

I thank my wife Aparna for being my constant sounding board and also for regularly reminding me that I have a 'book to finish writing'.

I acknowledge the efforts put in by the entire team at Niyogi Books towards this endeavour.

All errors and mistakes are mine.

Amish Tandon

About the Author

Amish Tandon is a corporate commercial lawyer practising in New Delhi for almost 13 years with extensive experience in areas of dispute resolution and corporate advisory.

He is the co-founder of a law firm 'Innovatus Law' which specialises in litigation, alternate dispute resolution and general corporate practice.

He is also the author of the best selling book titled *Law of Sexual Harassment at Workplace: Practice and Procedure.*

He can be reached at amishtandon@gmail.com